Nebraska Symposium on Motivation 1977

Nebraska Symposium on Motivation, 1977, is Volume 25 in the series on CURRENT THEORY AND RESEARCH IN MOTIVATION

University of Nebraska Press
Lincoln/London 1977

Nebraska Symposium on Motivation 1977

Social Cognitive Development

Herbert E. Howe, Jr. *Series Editor*

Charles Blake Keasey *Volume Editor*

Marilyn Shatz

*Assistant Professor of Psychology
Human Performance Center,
University of Michigan*

John H. Flavell

*Professor of Psychology
Stanford University*

Elliot Turiel

*Professor of Psychology
University of California, Santa Cruz*

D. B. Bromley

*Professor of Psychology
The University of Liverpool, England*

Martin L. Hoffman

*Professor of Psychology
University of Michigan*

Charles Blake Keasey

*Professor of Psychology
University of Nebraska–Lincoln*

Robert L. Selman

*Lecturer and Senior Research Associate
Laboratory of Human Development,
Graduate School of Education,
Harvard University*

Marcia Guttentag

*Professor of Psychology
Graduate School of Education,
Harvard University*

Preface

*A*s has been true for the last several volumes of the Nebraska Symposium on Motivation, the twenty-fifth focuses on a central theme: social cognitive development. Professor Keasey's work in organizing this symposium is greatly appreciated. Thanks must also go to the University of Nebraska Research Council, which contributed major financial support to this year's symposium.

The editors and everyone else associated with the Nebraska Symposium on Motivation were greatly saddened to learn of the death of Professor Marcia Guttentag, one of this year's contributors, on November 4, 1977. The excellence of her paper and presentation were greatly enhanced by her warmth and sensitivity throughout her stay in Lincoln.

HERBERT E. HOWE, JR.
Series Editor

Contents

Introduction

*I*f an attempt had been made seven or eight years ago to hold this symposium on social cognitive development, the major difficulty would have been the paucity of relevant empirical data in most areas. The supplying of such data in recent years has been accompanied, unfortunately, by a new difficulty, one that is well described by Roger Brown in his book *Social Psychology* (1965). Although he is speaking of research on achievement motivation and the authoritarian personality, the syndrome he describes is one that frequently afflicts areas of burgeoning interest in psychology. At first the infection of interest spreads rapidly. Journals are filled with reports of innovative studies, which invariably conclude that further studies will be needed to establish their findings. But no attempt is made to bring order to the findings, and innovation is not balanced by replication, so that eventually the profession begins to feel queasy because of the large mass of undigested studies. It is hoped that this volume will help to remedy that situation by integrating the current theoretical and empirical research literature, thus providing both perspective and some guidelines for further study.

The one area of social cognitive development to have escaped the more severe symptoms of Brown's Syndrome is that of moral development. It was the subject of pioneering efforts in the field, and is the one area that has been extensively reviewed previously, by Lawrence Kohlberg in 1963, 1964, and 1969, and by Martin Hoffman in 1970 and 1977. It is not, therefore, the focus of any one chapter in this volume, though several of the papers are concerned with aspects of it.

The first two chapters, by Marilyn Shatz and John H. Flavell, deal with two of the methods by which children gather information about their social environment—communication skills, and visual perception. Shatz, drawing heavily on notions from the adult information-processing literature, develops a cognitive process approach to account for children's successes and failures in communication tasks. In this approach, it is assumed that although humans are limited capacity information processors, they develop techniques for effectively deploying their limited resources in order to satisfy the various assessing and integrating demands imposed by complex tasks. For each information-handling technique there is a workload value indicating the amount of resources required for its application. The processor calls up combinations of various workload-weighted techniques to do the work required by any complex cognitive task.

It follows from these assumptions that the degree of skill displayed on any one task is a function of the cognitive workload required by that particular task. Children's performance on complex tasks tends to improve with age because of the gradual acquisition, consolidation (or routinization), and application of additional information-handling techniques; development is seen as gradual and continuous, rather than as a sequence of qualitatively different stages. From this perspective, the regularity with which any single skill is displayed depends on the degree of competence with that skill and other skills, and on the overall cognitive workload. Consequently the presence or absence of a particular skill is best assessed by employing various light workload tasks. Shatz reviews empirical data supporting this generalization and its obverse, the assumption that the presence of particular skills may be masked by heavy workload tasks.

Indicating that the cognitive process approach is not antithetical to Piaget generally, Shatz argues that the egocentrism, or centration, argument is insufficient in explaining variation in performance on complex cognitive tasks like communication. She also discusses various component skills models that attempt to deal with the development of communication skills, observing that the inadequacy of such explanations is indicated when components found lacking in one experimental situation are displayed in another. In conclusion, Shatz outlines the advantages of her approach and advocates more studies in the development of communication skills—studies which might well provide new insights on concepts like learning, consciousness, and metacognitive skills.

Flavell, in his chapter on visual perception, notes two recent developments in the area. First, it has been clearly documented that children can accurately infer another's visual perspective at a considerably younger age than had previously been believed. Secondly, there are now data suggesting the existence of at least two developmentally sequenced levels of knowledge about visual perception.

At the first level, the child knows that other people also see things, but that they do not necessarily see the same things that he or she sees at any given moment. Children at this level may be able to infer *what* things others currently do and do not see, if they are given adequate cues. But children at the second level have the additional knowledge that the same things usually look different to others than they do to the self if their viewing positions are different. A child at this level may be able to infer approximately *how* these things look from another's position if adequate cues are provided. Factors underlying the adequacy of the cues include the simplicity of the visual displays and the clarity with which the task is communicated to the child.

Flavell first briefly speaks of the intuitive plausibility of such a two-level distinction, and then discusses at length the empirical support for it. Within Level 2, he distinguishes between *computation* and *rules*. Computation refers to the actual cognitive processes used and behavioral steps taken by a child to figure out how a visible object appears to a visible other viewing the object from a specific location. Flavell mentions studies that have investigated several possible computational processes. His chief concern at present, however, is with Level 2 *rules*, which consist of the most basic facts about perspectives and perspective-taking, and express knowledge about very general relationships between the observer's position and his or her visual experiences. He describes the current research into such rules being conducted by himself and his colleagues, and specifies extensive future research that might be done on the two levels of knowledge about visual perception and on the distinction between them.

In the following chapter Elliot Turiel, like Flavell, proposes a distinction—in this case, a distinction between social convention and morality. He suggests that they constitute two distinct conceptual domains which develop independently of each other and stem from different aspects of social interaction. Beginning with a discussion of the definitional basis for the distinction, he defines social conventions as behavioral uniformities which serve to coordinate the actions of individuals participating in any particular social system. Social conventions are arbitrary and culture-specific, based on social regulations; moral issues are neither arbitrary nor relative to social context. As Turiel notes, this distinction implies a narrow definition of morality as justice. He contrasts his theory with the "differentiation" model which assumes that at lower levels of development convention and morality are undifferentiated, while at higher levels morality displaces convention.

Examining research into the development of social-conventional concepts, Turiel points out that development oscillates between affirmation and negation of concepts. He distinguishes seven qualitatively different developmental levels which are determined by an individual's response to a series of hypothetical situations involving various social conventions. He then presents data from a number of studies showing that individuals ranging in age from four to nineteen distinguished between morality and social convention in several different contexts, though he notes that the distinction between the two is not always clear-cut.

In order to provide a framework into which the two conceptual domains can be placed, Turiel next sketches out a theory of the development of domains of social cognition, stating his basic assumptions and identifying three fundamental domains—moral, societal, and psychological. Drawing a distinction between methods of information-gathering and conceptual frameworks, he illustrates the distinction with the example of one method, role-taking, demonstrating that methods, in contrast to conceptual frameworks, undergo quantitative rather than qualitative change. His chapter, therefore, consolidates a wealth of empirical data and provides a theory which is supported by that data.

D. B. Bromley, an Englishman and the only non-American contributor to the symposium, represents a totally different approach. Bromley's stated predilection is to compare the way we describe ourselves with the way we describe others; his basic assertion is that children become able to think and to talk about themselves and others through their tacit acceptance of commonsense notions about human nature and of the meaning and use of psychobehavioral terms found in the ordinary language of everyday life. Such an approach has the advantage of recognizing the close interweaving of a child's experiences, actions, and forms of language.

After reviewing the methodological problems of various measurement procedures, Bromley presents the advantages and disadvantages of his own preferred method of research, that of using free-response descriptions of self and others and techniques of content analysis. He then turns to abstract issues, presenting his view on the origins and development of the self, and on continuity, consistency, and change in the self-system. In the following empirical section he reexamines part of an earlier study of his in which descriptions of others, written by children between the ages of seven and fifteen, had been preceded by a self-description. Comparing the self-descriptions with other-descriptions, he finds that the categories used in the content analysis of descriptions of others apply equally well to descriptions of self. Disparities between the proportion of statements in each category for self and others can generally be explained in terms of the privileged access that individuals have to their own inner psychological processes. His discussion of developmental trends is accompanied by some lively samples of self-description.

The pattern of developmental changes that Bromley finds in children's self-descriptions is, not surprisingly, similar to that he had previously found in their descriptions of others. He points out that there is more to a self-concept than a mere list of self-attributes or self-assertions; it is an organized system that produces functional effects and varies over time as a function of factors within the person and external factors from the environment. Self-concept thus serves as a frame of reference for self-understanding, for self/other comparisons, and for the self-regulation of behavior.

The focus then shifts from self-concept to empathy as Martin Hoffman reviews and synthesizes the literature on empathy, examining both methodological and theoretical issues. Although he notes that the affective and cognitive components of empathy interact, his concern is with empathy as a vicarious affective response to others and as an important basis for prosocial motives. In his theoretical section he reviews two provocative arguments for a biological basis for empathy, arguments involving the limbic system and the pressures of natural selection. Next he outlines his own rudimentary model of empathy, which has three components— affective, cognitive, and motivational. Focusing on empathic distress, Hoffman identifies five distinct modes of empathic arousal and four hypothetical levels of empathic response that result from the progressive coalescence of the affective and cognitive components. The emergence of these levels is largely dependent upon the development of a clear self/other distinction; as this distinction becomes clarified, empathic distress is transformed to sympathetic distress—experiencing a feeling of compassion for a victim. Such feelings are commonly assumed to provide a motivational basis for prosocial action, and Hoffman concludes his theoretical section with an attempt to provide a comprehensive explanation for that assumption.

Beginning his review of the empirical literature with a consideration of the advantages and disadvantages of various measures,
Hoffman delineates the qualities that an ideal measure of empathy
should have, discussing research that uses physiological indices and
verbal and behavioral indices. Though none of these are ideal measures, they have produced a small body of research literature which
he examines critically. He presents considerable evidence that
people have a tendency to respond empathically and that such
responding has an involuntary element to it. After reviewing a
substantial body of data from correlational and experimental research documenting the relationship between empathic arousal and
prosocial action, he arranges the findings developmentally. His
lengthy discussion of the findings of sex differences in empathy is
rounded off with a tentative interpretation of the pattern of differences. Hoffman concludes this definitive review of theory and data
on affective empathy with suggestions for further research.

Charles Blake Keasey, like Hoffman and especially Turiel, deals
with a topic related to moral development. He begins his chapter by
distinguishing between the concepts of intentionality and motive.
He suggests that intentionality be used only to refer to the accidental
or purposeful nature of any particular action. Motive would be used
to refer to the purpose or reason behind a particular action. He notes
that although Piaget included both concepts under his broader
concept of subjective responsibility, he nonetheless made the distinction between intentionality and motive.

Keasey suggests that since 1970 the focus of researchers has
shifted from objective and subjective responsibility to intentionality.
Recent investigators have criticized Piaget's original paradigm because it confounded intentionality and consequence information.
By means of various paradigm modifications, investigators have
found evidence that children as young as five and six were aware of
intentionality. Keasey points out that Piaget's original paradigm
was designed to assess children's relative usage of objective and
subjective responsibility and not their awareness of intentionality.
In fact Piaget concluded that children evidenced an awareness of the
accidental/intentional distinction in reference to their own day-to-
day behavior between three and four years of age. However, Piaget
noted that it took three to four years before this awareness manifests
itself in children's verbal responses to hypothetical situations about
other people's behavior.

It is also pointed out by Keasey that the index used to assess
awareness of intentionality makes a considerable difference. He

suggests that Piaget's reliance on reasoning rather than numerical ratings would account for his finding less evidence of intentionality in young children than has been found by investigators using rating rather than reasoning data.

Keasey goes on to suggest that most of the new paradigms suffer from another kind of confounding, that of intentionality and motive. The few studies that have explicitly differentiated between the two have found evidence that they follow different developmental timetables, with the concept of motive generally being mastered before that of intentionality. Lastly, Keasey presents some evidence suggesting that certain features of the domain of moral reasoning may delay the child's use of intentionality. Consequently, he suggests that children's developing awareness of intentionality might best be studied outside the domain of moral reasoning.

The last two chapters deal in part with the presentation of results of studies recently completed by their authors. The first of these chapters is by Robert Selman and Dan Jaquette, both of whom are associated with the Judge Baker Guidance Center. They suggest that a more complete understanding of the development of interpersonal awareness can be gained by integrating developmental psychology with social and clinical psychology. The methods and theoretical approaches of the former can yield information relevant to the practical concerns of the latter, whose naturalistic research can in return shed light on various conceptual and methodological issues generated by developmentalists.

They begin their study of interpersonal development by presenting a model that integrates a cognitive-developmental approach with relevant issues in child clinical and social psychology. Looking specifically at the ways in which children relate to others, they focus on conceptions in three domains—awareness of the individual, awareness of close friendship relations, and awareness of group processes and organizations. A set of issues is specified, and five developmental stages are identified which cut across the three major domains and the seventeen more specific issues. A form of developing awareness termed social perspective-taking is assumed to underlie the individual's interpersonal awareness. One of the issues, leadership, is used for purposes of illustration; the questions presented to the children attempt to capture their view of their day-to-day social world. The section concludes with a clarification of the relationship of this model to the more generally accepted cognitive or stage-developmental approach.

Selman and Jaquette next selectively draw upon research findings to demonstrate how the developmental principles just discussed guided the design and data analysis of their work. Then, after stating their belief that the description of a developmental sequence should be followed by attempts to understand its application, they deal with the work they are currently doing in a clinical intervention setting. Their program is geared toward children between the ages of seven and fifteen with learning and emotional problems; a common referral complaint is disturbed interpersonal relations, especially with peers. The authors describe in some detail their intervention program, which is intended to develop more adequate social skills for the children at the same time as it constitutes a basic research effort in which interpersonal reasoning is assessed and daily social interaction observed. Generally they find that emotionally disturbed children lag behind more normal children, but still follow the same stage sequence. Their chapter demonstrates that the integration of developmental, clinical, and social psychology can be both theoretically and practically productive.

In the concluding chapter, Marcia Guttentag and Cynthia Longfellow focus on social attribution, the process of explaining the behavior of self and others. They note that the study of children's attributional processes occurs at the intersection of two different theoretical positions, cognitive developmental and social psychology, the former emphasizing the similarities in children's constructions of the social and physical worlds, and the latter attending to the dimensions of social stimuli that carry "social meaning" to the observer.

Although past understanding of attribution processes has been based on studies done with adults, a number of studies have been carried out with children, and it is these that Guttentag and Longfellow review. Looking first at causal attributions, and focussing on the choice between possible causes, they conclude that the development of schemes for making such choices is closely paralleled by the development of logical thought and apparently involves the same cognitive operations. Their discussion of the self-other distinction in the attribution literature is followed by a review of research on achievement attributions—the use of causal themes, the effect of setting, attributions of positive and negative outcomes, and actor and perceiver characteristics.

As an illustration of attribution processes in children, Guttentag and Longfellow summarize the results of a recent study conducted by Guttentag and her associates. The first phase involved the examination of developmental differences in sex-role attributions; the second phase was a large-scale intervention program designed to undo children's sex-role stereotypes. Kindergarten, fifth, and ninth grade students were involved in a six-week program in their school environment. Among the interesting findings were these: Although children at all three grade levels had fairly androgynous concepts of themselves, they attributed rather stereotyped beliefs to others; they consistently overstereotyped the opposite sex; and they were most stereotyped about male occupations. The ninth graders were most sensitive to the intervention, with girls reducing their stereotyping but boys increasing theirs. Generally girls' attitudes changed more than boys' during the intervention, perhaps—as Guttentag and Longfellow suggest—as a function of the intervention material, which emphasized a more positive and less powerless role for women in many spheres of action. In general, the study provides further evidence for a social psychological understanding of the development of sex-role attributions.

The authors of these eight papers, representing various points of view and a wide variety of research interests, provide in combination an extensive view of the area of social cognitive development. Their integration of the theoretical and research literature in specific areas, their presentation of their own research, and their suggestions for further study will, it is hoped, be of help to students and scholars, and will stimulate both discussion and research—leading, perhaps, to the eventual cure of Brown's Syndrome.

CHARLES BLAKE KEASEY

REFERENCES

Brown, R. *Social psychology*. New York: Free Press, 1965.

Hoffman, M. L. Moral development. In P. H. Mussen (Ed.), *Carmichael's manual of child psychology* (3rd ed.; Vol. 2). New York: Wiley, 1970.

Hoffman, M. L. Moral internalization: Current theory and research. In L. Berkowitz (Ed.), *Advances in experimental social psychology* (Vol. 10). New York: Academic Press, 1977.

Kohlberg, L. Moral development and identification. In H. W. Stevenson (Ed.), *Child psychology. 62nd Yearbook of the National Society for the Study of Education*. Chicago: University of Chicago Press, 1963.

Kohlberg, L. Development of moral character and moral ideology. In M. L. Hoffman & L. W. Hoffman (Eds.), *Review of child development research* (Vol. 1). New York: Russell Sage, 1964.

Kohlberg, L. Stage and sequence: The cognitive-developmental approach to socialization. In D. A. Goslin (Ed.), *Handbook of socialization theory and research*. Chicago: Rand McNally, 1969.

The Relationship Between Cognitive Processes and the Development of Communication Skills[1]

Marilyn Shatz

University of Michigan

*I*n recent years, research has burgeoned on the development of communication skills as they are evidenced in referential communication tasks and in natural conversational settings. Interest in such research stems largely from two distinct sources. The first is Piaget's theory of cognitive development and subsequent attempts to test it in the communication domain. A second influence is found in the philosophical, linguistic, and sociolinguistic work on pragmatics, the use of language in social settings. Researchers coming from each of these traditions have been motivated, albeit for different reasons, to reveal skills not previously assumed to be within the young child's communicative capacities. Many of their efforts have proven so successful that we now have a newly found respect for young children's communicative skill, particularly with regard to their ability to orient to, adjust to, and respond to others. (See, for example, Garvey & Hogan, 1973; Keenan, 1974; Maratsos, 1973; Mueller, 1972; Shatz & Gelman, 1973.)

Yet, despite such sociocentric skills, children do perform poorly in many communicative situations. For example, they often fail to recognize the lack of informativeness in their own or another's messages (Asher, 1976; Ironsmith & Whitehurst, in press; Robinson

1. Thanks are due to William Labov and Rochel Gelman, who provided the impetus and support for the toy choice studies; to the numerous participants in the developmental psychology program at the Graduate Center of the City University of New York who listened to and commented on my thoughts on communication skills for the better part of a year; and especially to Elissa Newport, whose insightful criticism of earlier drafts of the paper helped bring order to those thoughts. I am grateful to Blake Keasey for his patience as an editor, and to Brigitte Kahan and Clare Raizman for their help with manuscript preparation. Our work was supported in part by NIMH grant #1R01–MH 30996–01. The author's current address is Human Performance Center, 330 Packard Road, Ann Arbor, MI., 48104.

& Robinson, 1976). The task of a sound theoretical approach to children's communicative skills is to account for both the successes and the failures. In this chapter I shall argue that traditional views and explanations of children's abilities are inadequate to that task; they cannot account for the kind of variation we find in children's behavior in a range of situations requiring communicative skill. In their stead, I shall propose a more comprehensive view of the development of children's communicative skills. In order to do so, I offer an account of cognitive processes that draws heavily on notions from the adult information processing literature, particularly notions postulated to account for limited attention and memory capacity. Examples from the recent communication skills literature will be used to argue that such a processing approach is necessary here as well. However, I have not attempted to provide a comprehensive review of the literature. For such reviews, see Glucksberg, Krauss, and Higgins (1975) and Higgins (1976) on the referential literature; and Rees (in press) on the literature on developmental pragmatics.

In the first section, I begin with some remarks on fundamental aspects of good communication and then outline the basic notions behind a cognitive process approach. The second section presents evidence for that approach from research on children's performance in natural conversation, role-taking tasks, and referential communication tasks. This is followed, in Section III, by a review and discussion of the cognitive process approach as it applies to adult research and to the issue of metacognition. In Section IV, I deal with earlier explanations of communicative skill in children, point out the inadequacies of such approaches, and show how these earlier approaches relate to the present one. In the final section I summarize the relative advantages of the cognitive process approach.

I. THE COGNITIVE PROCESS APPROACH TO THE DEVELOPMENT OF COMMUNICATION SKILL

Aspects of Communicative Skill

There are two basic kinds of understanding that are involved in communicative skill: social understanding and understanding of message content. The social knowledge relevant to communicative ability can be viewed as the knowledge of participant relations and responsibilities in social interactions. Basic to such knowledge is an understanding that interaction involves cooperation on the part of both speaker and listener. Both participants share the work of constructing good communicative interactions. The sorts of cooperative obligations that each participant has are determined in part by one's role in the conversation, with listeners making an effort to understand (that is, not being unduly obtuse or recalcitrant), and speakers not intentionally misleading or haranguing their listeners.

More specifically, Grice (1975) has noted that the obligations of the cooperative speaker include avoiding ambiguity, saying only what one knows to be true, being concise, and so on. To be cooperative, then, one must take the listener into account. For example, choosing the appropriate level of conciseness depends on assessing the listener's state of knowledge. Thus, Gricean principles of cooperative conversations entail some role-taking skills for their fulfillment. The principles are behavioral procedures for conducting conversations. Adherence to them allows us to infer the role-taking skill of the conversationalist.

Do young children manifest in their conversations any understanding of these obligations of cooperative interaction? Both anecdotal and experimental evidence indicate that they do. The anecdotal evidence shows that children expect cooperation from their interlocutors and complain when it is not forthcoming. Consider the 5-year-old who consistently initiated conversations with the utterance, "Know what?" In frustration at getting the child to abandon the habit, her mother responded one day with a "Yes," thereby refusing to observe the conversational convention. After several attempts to engage her mother with repetitions of her attention-getting phrase, all of which were met by "yes," the child complained, "You can't do that. You're supposed to say *What*." The more general requirement that it is incumbent upon an addressee to respond is recognized by some children as young as 2. Thus, a 28-month-old girl complained to her unresponsive 2-year-old companion, "Hear what me say?" (Fulani, Note 1). Moreover, preschoolers are in control of some of the more specific and subtle kinds of knowledge underlying cooperative behavior. Gelman and Shatz (1977) found that, when talking to younger children, 4-year-olds quite appropriately confined their conversations to topics that were within the range of a 2-year-old's understanding. They talked about and directed activity, but did not talk about mental state. Nor were they concerned with qualifying the certainty of their statements with hedges like "I think" when they talked to listeners who were hardly in a position to question the validity of their statements. To adults, however, these same children both talked about mental states and hedged their statements. Thus, young children have an idea that conversation requires cooperation, and they have some notions of how to go about effecting cooperation as a function of listener characteristics.

But, knowing the requirements of cooperative communication does not necessarily assure that one will produce good communications. The speaker must also have an adequate understanding of what he or she wants to encode in a message. Even writers like Piaget and Flavell who have stressed the importance of role-taking abilities for communicative skill have recognized the importance of the speaker's own understanding of message content (Piaget, 1926; Flavell, Botkin, Fry, Wright, & Jarvis, 1968). On one level, the claim that role-taking skill is insufficient for communicative skill is obvious. For example, if one recognizes abstractly the need to be specific for a listener but does not notice the relevant disambiguating dimensions of a stimulus set, one cannot communicate unambiguously. Likewise, one cannot adequately describe some referents without reasonable vocabulary skills. But, on another level, the point is subtler and more important: one may be able to make the discrimination of disambiguating features or to find the necessary vocabulary, but it may require considerable effort to do so.

Our concern here is with the degree of work required to do any of the cognitive operations involved in successful communication, be it finding the right words or syntactic forms for describing a referent, or doing the feature analysis to distinguish unambiguously a target referent from field items, or judging the characteristics and knowledge of one's listener, or doing interactional work like organizing the turns in a conversation and focusing a listener's attention. Regardless of which particular set of subskills underlies successful performance on a particular communicative task, it is how hard one has to work in exercising each of those subskills that is crucial for determining whether overall successful performance will in fact occur. From a processing point of view, the two domains of understanding, social and message content, are not independent of one another. The facility with which one functions in one domain has repercussions for the display of knowledge in the other. The postulation of this interaction between knowledge domains is a result of the view of the human information processor presented below.

Making the Most of a Limited Capacity Processor

The above description of good communication makes it clear that communication tasks generally qualify as instances of complex cognitive tasks which require assessing and integrating multiple sources of information from various perceptual, social, or cognitive domains. The position to be outlined here attempts to account for variable success at executing such tasks.

There are four assumptions underlying the model. The first one is that humans are limited capacity information processors. That is, their resources for performing mental work are limited (Kahneman, 1973). Secondly, there are means for effectively deploying those resources to satisfy the various assessing and integrating demands imposed by complex tasks. I call such means "information-handling techniques." These techniques apply various kinds of organization to the multiplicity of variables involved in complex tasks. Any system of rules governing the organization of knowledge into behavioral procedures counts as an information-handling technique. One such system is syntax, where rule-governed organizations of words allow us to lay sequential structure on our thoughts. Another is based on social conventions, where we have standard organizations for the conducting of interactions, e.g., standard conversational openings and closings (Schegloff, 1968; Schegloff & Sacks, 1973). Such techniques, then, are ways of ordering information in standard or expected ways.

The third assumption is that each technique has associated with it a workload value signifying the amount of resources required for its application. Such workload values depend on both the properties of the technique and the degree to which the processor has mastered it. Thus, the weight of a technique is determined in part by how well-learned or well-practiced it is, with less well-learned techniques requiring more effort for execution than better-learned ones. Finally, the processor calls up combinations of weighted techniques to accomplish the work of a complex cognitive task. However, given the limited resources (R) of the processor, the sum total of resources required by a set of techniques cannot exceed R.

The postulation of such information-handling techniques has two important behavioral consequences. First, the possession of a technique, even one not fully mastered, provides a means for tackling some part of a complex task that would otherwise be intractable. Secondly, the more efficient the processor's techniques, the better he or she can accomplish complex tasks by using freed-up resources to do more work. That is, capacity for mental work can be "stretched" by the use of information-handling techniques with low workload values that organize as much information as techniques with higher values.

Still another consequence of this approach is that tradeoffs occur between the best possible performance on part of a task and the best possible overall performance on the whole task. Assume that a complex task can be decomposed into subtasks $S_1 \ldots S_n$. Suppose that the most successful outcome for subtask S_1 involves the use of technique T_a. However, T_a uses more resources than T_b, which will also provide an output for S_1, but not quite as successful a one (where "successful" here can stand for complete, certain, appropriate, elegant, etc.). If substantial resources are required to accomplish the remaining subtasks $S_2 \ldots S_n$, a more successful solution to the overall task is likely if T_b is selected rather than T_a. That is, overall task performance is better when S_1 is degraded by the use of T_b but more resources remain to $S_2 \ldots S_n$ than when S_1 is most successfully executed by T_a but insufficient resources remain for $S_2 \ldots S_n$.

A major hypothesis of this approach, then, is that the set of information-handling techniques selected to accomplish a task is not necessarily the set of those which accomplish individual subtasks most successfully, but rather those which together are most likely to approach successful resolution of the larger task.

Development in the Limited Capacity Processor

The developmental corollary of the approach outlined above is that performance on complex tasks improves over time as capacity is stretched to accomplish more work. The main mechanisms of this development are the gradual acquisition, consolidation (or routinization), and application of information-handling techniques.

In this view, performance on a complex task cannot by itself be taken as evidence that a given technique is absent from a child's repertoire. Recall that mere possession of a technique does not assure its automatic or effortless functioning. If a technique is in the process of being mastered, it may take a great deal of effort to utilize it, resulting in little or no savings from pre-acquisition costs. The costs and benefits of applying a technique are in part dependent upon the degree to which its execution has become routinized or automatic. Moreover, combinations of techniques are selected to maximize the level of success on the whole task. These arguments imply that the display of particular skills varies with overall cognitive workload. Techniques requiring considerable resources (e.g., newly acquired techniques) are not likely to appear in all of the cases where a formal task analysis would predict them, but only in those cases where the processing conditions of the task additionally promote their selection and execution. Such cases include tasks with light workloads, that is, where little other work is required or where all other demands can be met with efficient techniques requiring little effort. In both these cases, sufficient resources can be made available for the costly technique without seriously jeopardizing overall task outcome.

There are two cases where a costly technique appears even though sufficient resources are not readily available to it. First, there are tasks for which the application of the costly technique is essential to anything resembling successful task outcome. The point is that some work is more essential than other work; even minimal degradation here may be more detrimental to overall success than leaving insufficient resources for the remainder of the task. In such cases, we would expect poor performance on the less critical parts of the task regardless of performance levels attained in other situations. Secondly, when best possible performance on the task is not an important behavioral goal, the processor may select a technique which absorbs more than its just share of resources if the practice of it will facilitate its efficient use in the future. As Bruner (1974) has noted, play often provides such nonconsequential opportunities for children to practice new skills.

It is important to note that this approach assumes no processing capacity differences per se between adults and children. (See Section IV for discussion of a theory that does assume such differences.) Human processors of all ages are expected to have workload difficulties in situations where their information-handling techniques fail them. Children are more subject to failure only because they have fewer means (i.e., well-learned techniques) for distributing their limited resources efficiently.

In sum, this approach implies the following kinds of variation in skill display as a function of cognitive workload: A skill is likely to appear sporadically depending on the degree of competence with it and other techniques called for in a given task. A particular skill will be revealed most readily when other cognitive demands are minimized. Conversely, the performance of a skill will be most degraded when the task which requires it makes other heavy processing demands. We turn now to empirical evidence supporting these implications.

II. VARIATIONS IN CHILDREN'S PERFORMANCE AS A FUNCTION OF COGNITIVE WORKLOAD

First Things First: Accomplishing Critical Subtasks

I argued above that a skill may not be fully displayed when resources for it are usurped for purposes more crucial to task success. Our evidence for this comes from observations of children's naturally occurring conversations. We shall see that children often do not maximally display the full range of their linguistic abilities when they have to work hard at the more basic aspects of a task.

The maintenance of interaction is in some regard the bottom line of communicative behavior. In our earlier terminology, it is a critical subtask of any larger communicative endeavor. In recent years evidence has accrued showing that 2-year-olds are sensitive to the need to initiate and maintain contact with another. For example, Merkin (Note 2) studied two girls aged 2½ who produced socially adapted conversational turns on over 75% of their turns, where "socially adapted" is defined as "contingent upon the behavior of the other." Mueller and his associates report a similar finding for three male 2-year-olds: by the end of their third year 60% of their utterances were listener-relevant (Mueller, Bleier, Krakow, Hegedus, & Cournoyer, 1977; see also Wellman & Lempers, 1977). Thus children show their co-participants that they are attentive and responsive. Even children as young as 18 months old seem to know they should respond when spoken to. In fact, the majority of their speech is in response to another's utterances (Bloom, Rocissano, & Hood, 1976). Yet, their responses often bear no relation to the previously introduced topics. Bloom et al. suggest that such young children simply do not have the resources to process the utterances directed to them and to come up with related replies. Rather, they use the language directed to them as an invitation to say anything on their minds.

Two-year-olds also have difficulty producing simultaneously creative and discourse-appropriate replies, but they apparently have a device for easing the work of maintaining discourse: They repeat segments of prior utterances in the conversation. (Bloom, Miller, & Hood, 1975; Keenan, 1974; McTear, in press; Keenan, Note 3). Such repetitions function as signals of joint attention, acknowledgments of statements, and answers to questions. Thus, while repetition may not provide opportunities for displaying the full range of one's linguistic ability, it does, at the very least, satisfy the conversational obligation of responding to one's interlocutor in a topic-relevant way.[2]

The use of repetition as a conversational device is not limited to 2-year-olds. Preschoolers also commonly use repetition to maintain interaction without having to generate discourse-appropriate responses from scratch (Garvey, 1977). The following sequence from Garvey's data illustrates preschoolers substituting lexical items into syntactic frames maintained within and across turns.

Girl: 'Cause it's fishy too; 'cause it has fishes.
Boy: And it's snakey too 'cause it has snakes and it's beary too because it has bears.
Girl: And it's . . . and it's hatty 'cause it has hats.

Garvey argues that these children were playing with language. Additionally, I suggest that repetition may have occurred here as a way of lightening the participants' cognitive workload. What these children were doing in the process of their conversation was taking note of the objects they saw in the playroom. They were, it appears, making a joint inventory, and that required considerable effort: They had to focus on objects, name them, and keep contact with

2. I refer to these borrowings from prior utterances as "repetitions" rather than "imitations" because "imitation" implies more automatic or parrot-like behavior than children actually display. Indeed, the work cited suggests that repeated elements are selected from prior discourse on quite systematic grounds.

their listener. Maintaining the syntactic frame and simply inserting new items in the "catalogue" is an elegant solution for providing continuity to the discourse without doing much generative work on a syntactic level. One finds adults doing similar things when they retrieve words from early in a conversation and repeat them later. Not only do such repetitions help to maintain continuity in the conversation; they also ease the load of generating a turn while keeping up the pace of an interaction.

The critical-subtask argument can also be invoked to explain variation in the complexity of children's utterances. Knapp (Note 4) suggests that new linguistic forms take more effort to produce than more practiced ones. When new forms are obligatory, they force a limitation to the complexity of the additional elements allowable in an utterance. For example, when the negative first appears, its use inhibits the production of other newly acquired syntactic or lexical items in the same utterance (Bloom, 1970). In her early work, Bloom suggested that such variation in constituent complexity is the outcome of a syntactic reduction transformation limiting the production of constituents to a set number. In contrast, Knapp postulates it to be the result of the distribution of limited resources over the most essential elements expressing the child's intention. Thus, Knapp's position attempts to bring the linguistic facts of early language into the domain of a cognitive process approach.[3] Olson (1973) has made similar arguments about the amount of work required to produce linguistic elements that have been learned to varying degrees and the effect which the degree of learning may have on their incorporation into larger units.

In the above examples, the accomplishment of a critical subtask affects the display of linguistic skills. The examples illustrate workload interactions both within and between cognitive, social, and linguistic skill domains. What they share in common is that they all can be handled by a process approach postulating the distribution of limited resources.

3. In a later attempt to explain reduction, Bloom, Miller, and Hood (1975) draw on psychological notions like limited memory and degree of learning as support for their argument that variable rules best represent the child's linguistic competence. While this argument is more in line with a cognitive process approach, it is still basically a linguistic enterprise, not a psychological one. Variable rules describe the probability of occurrence of syntactic combinations; they do not directly treat all the forces responsible for variable occurrence. The constraints governing probability of occurrence are at least in part cognitive. It is these constraints that Knapp appears to be addressing.

Revealing Skills on Light Workload Tasks

In this section I show that children, when they are given an opportunity to perform in light workload situations, can reveal communication skills that they have been assumed not to possess. Such
situations are those in which the levels of vocabulary, physical
knowledge, and social understandings required to do the task are all
within the common experience of the child. That is, children
capitalize on the well-learned techniques they have for dealing with
their everyday world.

One of the traditional ways of testing children's skill at communicating has been to assess the adequacy of their explanations to
a listener. Often their failure to provide clear, concise statements has
been taken as evidence that children are incapable of assessing
another's needs or of attempting to construct explanations adequate
to those needs. The classic example of such work is Piaget's analysis
of children's explanations of the workings of a water tap (Piaget,
1926). In his study, children were provided with an explanation of
the tap and then asked to explain the operation of it to another child.
By and large, the children's descriptions were vague and incomplete. For example, they often neglected to mention that they were
describing a water tap, they did not name the parts of the device
they referred to, nor did they explain in causal terms how the valve
came to be open or shut, or how it controlled the flow of water.
Piaget claimed that the children had indeed heard and understood
all of these items when they had been given their explanations, but
that they merely neglected to realize that their listeners did not
know them and that such information was essential to their understanding.

However, it is unclear, given the complex and unfamiliar nature
of the object to be explained, how well the children understood the
explanations they had received. Moreover, Piaget's instruction to
the children was to tell their listeners "the same thing I told you."
The children may have interpreted such an instruction to mean that
verbatim memory was required, and this could have seriously
changed the nature of the task for them. Trying to remember word-
for-word what had been said to them could have absorbed many of
the resources that might otherwise have gone to constructing a more
informative message for a listener.

When children are asked to explain objects that they are more
familiar with and when the task instructions are clear, they do much

better. In our work with 4-year olds, Gelman and I asked children to explain the workings of a toy (either a dumping station with trucks and balls or an ark with wooden animals) to both 2-year-olds and adults (Shatz & Gelman, 1973). Using a variety of measures, we were able to show that the child speakers adjusted their messages as a function of their listener. For example, they broke up their messages to young children into shorter, more action-directing units than those they directed to adult listeners. Moreover, they were often quite specific in their use of names and directions to their young listeners, as evidenced by the following excerpt from the transcript of a 4-year-old boy addressing a 2-year-old girl:

> Lookit, Patty. Hi, Patty. We got an ark. Looka! Isn't that fun? We can put lots of animals on back. Can't you want animals? (Demonstrating.) See? That's the way. Two hands around it.

In fact, some of the children, when they realized just how incompetent their young listeners were with language, attempted to teach them some vocabulary. Witness the following attempt by a child-teacher:

> Look, Danny. See? That's a desk. Can you say *desk*? That's a chair. Say *chair*. Chair.

Recent research confirms that children do reveal an ability to take account of their listener's capacities and to adjust their messages accordingly, as long as they are talking about familiar toys or activities. Like Shatz and Gelman, Masur (Note 5) used a toy explanation task to find evidence that preschoolers adjusted to the conversational abilities of their young listeners. Menig-Peterson (1975) found that preschoolers did name items and specify referents appropriately for adult listeners when they were describing an experience they had had. Moreover, they were more likely to do so when their listeners were naive with regard to the experience being described than when their listeners observed the event. In a direct test of the effect of referent familiarity on quality of message, Goldstein and Kose (Note 6) found that kindergartners and second-graders were better able to explain to others how to reach toys at the end of a maze the more they themselves had gone through the maze. Similarly, children aged 5 to 9 were better at producing listener-appropriate messages when they had to communicate about building a horse out of blocks than when talking about an unfamiliar object (Hoy, 1975). All of the above studies suggest that the workload demands of a task play an important part in the success with which children reveal their ability to take account of and respond to listeners' needs. In other areas too, such as spatial perspective-taking, classification skills, and causal reasoning, researchers have found that varying task demands often reveals abilities believed to be lacking in the young child (See Gelman, in press, for a review). Children reveal more of a given ability when other task and situational demands are confined to their level of knowledge and are consonant with their presuppositions about the world. I suggest that this is because under such conditions children can handle those other demands with very little effort and are therefore free to devote more of their congitive resources to producing the behavior of interest to the experimenter.

The Other Side of the Coin: Increasing Workload and Decreasing Performance

If the expression of an ability can be enhanced by the use of light workload tasks, we should likewise be able to degrade or eliminate its expression by the use of heavy workload conditions. We have already seen that one's full range of linguistic abilities is often not displayed when required work, such as maintaining conversational interaction, takes much effort. In that case, two demands compete for resources, and the display of a skill is affected by execution of other techniques more central to success on the task. However, there are other cases of heavy workload in which the difficulty is not so much competition among demands as the quality or quantity of information a given technique must handle. There seem to be two aspects to this kind of difficulty, both of which affect the success of using a given technique. One is the degree of preorganization of the information that is to be input for the new technique. Many of the cases of effect of familiarity discussed in the section above would fall into this category. For example, familiarity with toys "preorganizes" the access to lexical items that can be used in describing the stimuli; that is, deciding what to say to a listener about toys is easier than deciding what to say about water taps. The other is the amount of information one has to deal with. Talking about ten toys with ten different names is presumably harder than talking about two, even if each of those names is easily accessed. In the sets of studies reported below, increasing the quantity of information over which a given technique has to range leads to a consequent degradation of performance.

Degrading role-taking performance. The studies to be reported here do not involve a communication task, but they are included for two reasons. First, as noted earlier, the argument that performance varies with cognitive workload is a general one and applies to cognitive domains other than communication. Secondly, role-taking is such an integral part of good performance on most communication tasks that it has particular as well as general relevance as an example.

In order to find evidence that preschoolers know something about 2-year-olds apart from the face-to-face communicative situation explored in Shatz and Gelman (1973) I adapted Flavell's gift selection task (Flavell et al., 1968) to a situation familiar to all preschoolers: the selection of birthday presents for children. (For a complete description of the study, see Shatz, Note 7.) A picture of either a peer or a 2-year-old was shown to 4- and 5-year olds, who were asked to pick a present from a set of four toys for that child. Of the four toys, two, a pull toy and a set of stacking cups, were considered appropriate for the younger child and two, a magnetic board with letters and numbers and a set of sewing cards, were considered appropriate for the preschool peer. Children in both groups were then invited to select a toy from an identical set for themselves. Since there were no significant differences between the 4- and 5-year-olds' choice behavior, the results of both groups are combined in Table 1.[4] It can be seen from Table 1 that toy selection was a function of intended recipient. Children selecting for a 2-year-old and children selecting for a peer both chose appropriate toys significantly more often than chance. Moreover, as Table 2 shows, most children chose for themselves toys that were different from those they had selected for a 2-year-old. Regardless of their own desires, these children were able to take account of another's needs and preferences.

To see how robust this ability was, I complicated the task a bit. I ran two conditions in which all subjects were asked to choose presents for 2-year-olds; however, in both conditions there were

4. I had picked the four toys for the two age groups largely on the basis of a priori notions of appropriateness. However, the coding scheme allowed any toy selected by a given child for himself or herself to be categorized as an appropriate preschool toy for that child only. Hence, a child selecting the pull toy both for himself or herself and for a 2-year-old would not be listed in Table 1 as selecting appropriately for a 2-year-old.

Table 1
Number of preschoolers selecting a given type of toy for either two-year-olds or preschoolers (N = 58), Four-Toy Experiment

Intended Recipient	Toys appropriate for	
	Two-year-olds	Preschoolers
Two-year-old	21	8
Preschooler	2	27

Table 2
Number of subjects picking either the same toy or a different toy for self as that picked for other, Four-Toy Experiment

Intended Recipient	Toy	
	Different	Same as Other
Two-year-old	24	5
Preschooler	17	12

now six toys (rather than four) to choose from. The six toys included the four of the earlier study, plus two others. In the infant condition, the additional toys were a teething ring and rattle, toys appropriate for an infant; in the school-age condition, the two additional toys were an activity-puzzle book and a number game called "Racko," toys appropriate for a school-aged child. In short, the subjects' task was identical to that for subjects choosing for 2-year-olds in the earlier study except that there were more irrelevant toys from which to choose in the later studies. Table 3 shows how many of the 4- and 5-year olds in the school-age condition selected each of the three kinds of toys for a 2-year-old recipient. While the school-age toys were almost never chosen their very presence seemed to create difficulties, especially for the 4-year-olds. In the four-toy-study, only one-third of the 4-year-olds selected pre-school toys for a two-year-old; in the school-age condition, two-thirds did so. In the infant condition reported in Table 4, the selection behavior was even worse, with little apparent differentiation among any of the three groups of toys. Thus, the very same sorts of subjects who in the previous study succeeded quite well at choosing toys appropriate to a 2-year-old from among two categories of toys showed much less ability to do so when confronted with a six-toy, three-category array.

Table 3
Number of subjects in each age group choosing various types of toys for a two-year-old. School-age condition, Six-Toy Experiment

	Toys Appropriate For		
Age of Subjects	Two-year-old	Preschooler	School-age
Four-year-olds	3	8	1
Five-year-olds	8	4	0

Table 4
Number of subjects in each age group choosing various types of toys for a two-year-old. Infant condition, Six-Toy Experiment

	Toys Appropriate For		
Age of Subjects	Two-year-old	Preschooler	Infant
Four-year-olds	3	5	4
Five-year-olds	6	3	3

Moreover, an examination of the data on selecting toys for self from six-toy arrays confirms the view that the six-toy tasks were more difficult, especially for the 4-year-olds. Table 5 shows that more than one-third of the 4-year-olds picked the same toy for a 2-year-old as for themselves, a much larger proportion than did so in the earlier study. The 5-year-olds, while they did not differentiate infant from 2-year-old toys very well, still did not very often select the same toy for themselves as they did for a 2-year old. Apparently when faced with analyzing a six-toy array as well as keeping the features of the intended recipient in mind, 5-year-olds were more able to maintain the distinction between themselves and another than were 4-year-olds. But under such circumstances even 5-year-olds lost the more specific information of just what a 2-year-old is like, and they too selected infant toys for them.

We did not run a study with only four toys, two infant and two 2-year-old, to assure that 5-year-olds could make appropriate selections under such conditions; however, there is evidence from other sources to suggest that children of this age can make some distinctions between 2-year-olds and infants. For example, Sachs & Devin (Note 8) found that when preschoolers were told to talk "like a baby

Table 5
Number of subjects picking either same toy or a different toy for self as that picked for other, Six-Toy Experiment

| | Toy | |
Age of Subjects	Different	Same as other
Four-year-olds	15	9
Five-year-olds	22	2

just learning how to talk," they babbled; but when told to "be a little bit older," they produced short, simple utterances. It does seem reasonable, though, to assume that such fine distinctions are learned later than those between self and other. If behavior is degraded by cognitive overload, it should break down first on less well-learned distinctions. The 5-year-olds lost specific knowledge of the 2-year-old, but maintained the distinction relatively well between self and younger child. For the 4-year-olds, even the distincton between self and other presented problems.

One might argue that the inability to maintain such distinctions while carrying out an analysis of six toys is an example of the lack of operative behavior, that is, an inability to perform recursively the comparative analysis for each toy and then, on the basis of six subanalyses, make the best selection. Given such an argument, one might explain the success at four-toy arrays by claiming that such recursive operations are not available in that situation either. Rather, some figurative process allows the child to "see" or recall the intended recipient playing with one of the objects. One problem with such an interpretation of our findings is that it is unclear why figurative processes should be adequate with four stimuli but not six. It would appear that some notion of processing limitation would be necessary in addition to an operative-figurative distinction in any case.

Even more to the point, the children's justifications for their choices give little support to the distinction. Very few of the children in the four-toy study gave justifications like "My brother has a pull-toy and he's two", which could be interpreted as based on a figurative representation. Rather, many of them gave some indication that they were engaging in toy-by-toy comparative analyses. For example, one boy defended his choice of a pull-toy by saying, "Sewing cards are too hard for little hands."

Of course, operative behavior can be seen as one kind of information-handling technique that organizes the input for multiple analyses and arranges the comparison of those analytic outcomes. My point is that young children may indeed have such a technique, but that the successful execution of it depends on the quality and quantity of the informaton it must handle. As we shall see in Section III, even adults perform certain ordering and recursive operations more easily in some circumstances than in others.[5]

Degrading performance on referential communication tasks. In the area of referential communication skills too, previous explanations of children's performance cannot account for all the results of recent studies. Here again the evidence for degraded performance as a function of increasing processing demands supports the cognitive process approach. For example, we shall see that the technique of distinctive feature analysis is available to but not always utilized by children.

The typical paradigm for referential communication tasks is some variant of the Krauss and Glucksberg (1969) test in which children are asked to tell a listener who cannot see the speaker's stimulus set to select a target object from a set of field items. Preschool children typically do well on stimulus sets for which they can assign conventional name labels to the items, but when stimuli such as abstract figures preclude labeling, their performance is inadequate. In these latter cases children often fail to describe distinctive features; rather they remain the labeling strategy, assigning idiosyncratic names to the targets. The claim has been made that such labeling is indicative of the child's egocentrism, his or her inability to see that idiosyncratic description will be of no value to a listener who has a different history of experience with the world from the speaker.

However, research with a somewhat different task suggests that children who produce idiosyncratic messages for listeners later find them inadequate even for themselves. Using a task that required children to give listeners clue words to help identify a target word, Asher and Oden (1976) found that speakers who had produced inadequate clues for listeners did as well selecting the target words

5. Similarly, the linguistic literature provides examples of sentences that are hard to comprehend for seemingly nonstructural reasons. Indeed, to keep linguistics "free" from such problems, the performance-competence distinction has often been invoked. The experimental scientist is then faced with the difficult task of determining what data, if any, are evidence for the competence theory, given that data are contaminated by unknown performance variables.

without any clues as they did using the clues they themselves had generated for listeners two weeks earlier. Thus, their own clues did not seem to be a product of some private process appropriate to their own concerns without regard to the listener, but rather they seemed to be the output of analyses incomplete even for themselves.

Subscribing to Rosenberg and Cohen's (1966) two-stage model of referential processes, Asher and Oden argue that their subjects selected clue words by forming associations to target words but then neglected to compare the strength of the association to nontarget words as well to assure that the clue was sufficiently different in associative value for target and nontarget words. But other work suggests that children are at least sensitive to the need to keep both target and nontarget items in mind when creating a referential message. Children produce more feature descriptions when told to describe abstract objects so a listener can pick them out of a set than they do when they are asked just to describe the objects (Higgins & Akst, Note 9). Also, they use color names when required to communicate about referents in a set of objects varying in color, but when asked just to describe the same objects, they are more likely to do so with nondiscriminating object labels (Harris, Macrae, & Bassett, in press).

The comparison of target to nontargets is of course crucial if a successful distinctive feature analysis is to be carried out. The work of Whitehurst and his colleagues investigates the information conditions under which preschoolers do engage in the comparison process. The basic paradigm for the Whitehurst studies is one in which children must specify in their messages an item which differs from nontarget items along one to three two-valued dimensions, for example, spottedness, size, and/or color. Messages are then categorized as either incomplete, contrastive, or redundant, depending on whether insufficient, sufficient, or more than sufficient information is given in the message. In an early study children had to describe the cup under which a marble had been hidden, given a set of two or three cups. On some trials one attribute was sufficient; on others two were required (Whitehurst, 1976). The kindergarten children were most likely to give only one-attribute descriptions (75% of the time), and these turned out to be contrastive just about as often as predicted by chance. Children in first grade and beyond were contrastive more often than predicted by chance, but their tendency was to be redundant. Whitehurst proposed that the kindergartners had the strategy of picking an attribute, any attribute, just to produce a message, while the older children had a strategy of stringing together attributes in a more fully descriptive but similarly uncritical fashion. He suggested that while older children, at least, can produce contrastive messages, "talk is cheap" for them; being redundant is equally effective and easier than doing a critical feature analysis. In that line, it is important to note that the listener selected the cup with the marble on each trial regardless of quality of message, thus reinforcing the older children for redundancy and the younger children for their incomplete messages. Extending White-hurst's least effort principle, one could argue that the children had no reason to do a critical attribute analysis, given that any message produced apparent success on the task.

Indeed, Whitehurst's later work shows that children as young as five can be contrastive. Moreover, his results can be interpreted as support for the position that cognitive overload, in addition to lack of incentive, may have caused poor performance on the earlier task. Whitehurst and Sonnenschein (in press) asked 5-year-olds to describe one of two triangles for a listener. In one condition, only the correct value of the relevant dimension, but not the relevant dimension itself, changed over trials. In the other condition, the relevant dimension was one of three varying dimensions that changed from trial to trial. In the one-dimension condition, the 5-year-olds produced messages that were contrastive more often than expected by chance; that is, they talked only about distinctive features. In the three-dimension condition, they were less able to isolate the relevant dimension on each trial, and they produced many more uninformative messages. In a second experiment, the children's ability to produce contrastive messages was lowered, even when relevant dimensions were held constant and only irrelevant changes occurred from trial to trial. Several other studies using tasks calling for critical feature analyses have recently shown similar decrements in contrastive performance as a function of varying the number of features over trials (Ford & Olson, 1975; Garmiza & Anisfeld, 1976).[6] In Whitehurst's 1976 study, the number of cups and relevant dimensions changed from trial to trial, making the task similar in terms of processing demands to the three-dimension condition of the later

6. All the studies cited show difficulties in processing over trials. Garmiza and Anisfeld argue that the child has trouble changing perspectives from trial to trial. But one could argue equally well that the child's coding of the world around him is a continuous process. For the child, one trial may be the context for the next; it may be only the experimenter who makes the trials discrete. Thus, the results of the studies should not be surprising.

study. It is not surprising, then, that contrastive messages were rare in the earlier study.

All of this work suggests that children's difficulty in producing contrastive messages stems not from their failure to recognize the need to include distinctive featues in their messages, but from their difficulty in isolating critical from uncritical dimensions in a multidimensional stimulus set. In all of the Whitehurst and Sonnenschein conditions, kindergartners produced a high proportion of redundant messages (approximately 30 to 50 %, depending on condition). From the point of view of the processor, the more efficient or least effortful way of producing an adequate message about multidimensional stimuli may be to run off a list of attributes without isolating critical dimensions. The messages based on this notion of efficiency are potentially redundant in information, whereas the experimenter's criterion of efficient messages has typically been those with the least possible number of descriptors bearing sufficient information (cf. Ford & Olson, 1975; D. Olson, 1970). What experimenters seem to have forgotten is that, despite the extra mileage, a trip around a mountain is often cheaper in time and energy consumption than one transversing it. Redundant rather than contrastive messages may be cheaper in situations where there are several dimensions or dimensional changes to consider when comparing target to nontarget items. Rather than being labeled as "inefficient," redundancy might more profitably be considered the result of an acceptable alternative technique which leads to a high probability of success on referential tasks.[7]

The basis of incomplete messages is uncertain, but they could be abortive attempts at attribute listing. In any case, even incomplete messages cannot be taken as indexing insensitivity to the quality of one's messages. Children from 5 to 8 were asked by Robinson and Robinson (1976) to tell who was at fault when an incomplete message failed to result in successful referential choice behavior on the part of a listener. The youngest children almost always picked the listener as being at fault. However, in a later study, it was found that children as young as 5 did blame the speaker for inappropriate

7. It should be noted that Whitehurst and Sonnenschein do not subscribe to a cognitive overload hypothesis but propose instead a perceptual saliency argument. The difficulty with their explanation is that it does not account for the high proportion of redundant responses. Nor does it provide a clear definition of what is considered perceptually salient. Moreover, it seems reasonable that, whatever it is, perceptual salience may be a determiner of what happens *after* overload occurs. That is, it can be considered a possible result of overload and not an alternative explanation.

children as young as 5 did blame the speaker for inappropriate messages but not for insufficiently informative ones, thereby demonstrating at least some sensitivity to message quality (Robinson & Robinson, Note 10). In difficult situations, children may view messages more as clues to meaning than as unambiguous sources of information. Given their experience with adult listeners who do their best to make sense of young children's speech, it would not be surprising to find children expecting a great deal of help from their listeners. Robinson and Robinson suggest that the ease with which children can judge a message to be insufficient may determine to whom they assign blame for failure. It may be that on stimuli as uncomplicated as those used in Whitehurst's one-dimension condition, children would assign the blame for insufficient messages to the speaker.

Summary

In this section I have presented evidence from various research domains showing that new skills first occur in uncomplicated familiar settings, that performance of skills can be degraded by the overloading of information-handling capacities, and that when requisite skills are not well learned, those which go the farthest toward producing success on a task will be allocated the most resources at the expense of others. Not only phenomena of early language and early conversational behavior but also variation in the performance of role-taking and referential communication tasks have been handled within the framework of a cognitive process approach. We turn now to a brief review of the origins of that approach as it is found in the adult literature.

III. FROM BIG OAKS LITTLE ACORNS FALL: THE ADULT BASIS OF A DEVELOPMENTAL COGNITIVE PROCESS THEORY

Delimiting Limited Capacity in Attention and Memory

That humans are limited capacity processors, that they have ways of making the most of their capacities, and that the routinization of these ways is itself a device for increasing system capacity are hardly controversial assumptions. We all can relate personal instances of "overload," be they the childhood occupation of trying to pat one's head while rubbing one's stomach or the experience of trying to follow rapid speech in a foreign language. And most of us have delighted in our improved performance following increased practice time at sequential motor activities like swinging a golf club or tennis racquet. Since William James's time, psychologists have speculated on our limitations and our means for coping with them. For example, back in the 1890s, Bryan and Harter studied the role of practice in improving the performance of telegraph operators. The contribution of modern-day cognitive psychologists has been to elaborate the nature and scope of the limits to our capacities that we all recognize intuitively.

One such elaboration concerns the notion of limited capacity. Much early work in information theory defined limited capacity in terms of a passive channel along which a set amount of information could pass in a given time. The influence of such work was felt in the psychology of the late 1950s, for example, in Broadbent's 1958 theory of selective attention based on the idea that sensory input was filtered through a single information channel of limited load capacity. Subseqent research on the parameters of a limited attention system suggested a system in which the processor plays a more active role. Instead of a passive limited-capacity channel, the performance of the system depends in part on the relationship between the characteristics of the input and the characteristics (including knowledge and expectations) of the perceiver (e.g., Broadbent & Gregory, 1964; Treisman, 1960). Similarly, in the area of memory, Miller (1956) proposed a limitation on short-term memory of seven plus or minus two items, but noted that items in short-term memory are not equivalent to "bits" of information as defined in information theory. Bits represent the amounts of information required at binary decision points in a communication system; items in memory can be composed of any number of such bits. They are "chunks" of information, psychological units determined by the characteristics and learning history of the processor as well as the characteristics of the input. Supporting this view is a large body of literature on the use of semantic and syntactic principles as chunking devices on a variety of memory tasks (for reviews see Fodor, Bever, & Garrett, 1974; N. Johnson, 1970; Kintsch, 1970). The procedures for utilizing such principles to alter memory capacity are just what we have called information-handling techniques. Whether one calls such techniques recoding, chunking, or integrating procedures, they accomplish one end: the efficient packaging of information into psychologically manipulable units, incorporable into higher-order tasks such as communication. In both attention and memory research, then, evidence has been found for a limited capacity processor whose organizations of knowledge interact with the organization of stimulus materials to determine the success (in terms of both quality and quantity) of processing (cf. Moray, 1967).

Just how chunking procedures work is still unclear. Organizational systems based on the accessing of associative networks and on formal properties of hierarchical semantic and/or syntactic systems have both been proposed (see, for example, Anderson & Bower, 1974). In either case they can be seen as devices constraining the way information will be encoded and utilized. That is, organizational procedures reduce the degrees of freedom in the information-handling system by narrowing the options for relating information in various ways. The predetermination of relations reduces the possibility of unsystematic error at just those places where relational decisions no longer need be made. Concatenations of information can then be handled as single units, resulting in savings from the amount of mental effort required to process each bit separately.

The effects of practice and familiarity on performance have also received the attention of cognitive psychologists in recent years. Several have argued that the level at which processing is carried on, conscious or automatic, affects the amount of resources consumed by the processing and hence the overall ability of the processor to handle multifaceted tasks (Bruner, 1974; Mandler, 1975; Posner & Warren, 1972). Conscious processes require more resources for the monitoring activities of the processor. Automatic processing, on the other hand, depends on internal feedback systems which require little attention for their operation. The effect of practice is to allow for the information-handling procedures to be routinely applied without much cost in the allocation or monitoring process. Thus, managerial chores previously handled by conscious processes can be handled automatically. Moreover, routinization lowers the probability of variable performance over time due to differences in resource allocation or interference from competing demands on a conscious processor. (See Posner & Boies, 1971; Posner & Klein, 1973; and Posner & Snyder, 1975, for work on interference in attentive processes.)

The notion of an automatic level of processing is justified on both intuitive and experimental grounds. Experienced drivers often report they travel customary routes without any subsequent memory of anything more than getting themselves into the car. More controlled evidence comes from LaBerge's experiments in perceptual learning. He found that under conditions of distraction, the identification of well-practiced figures was better than the identification of less practiced figures even though the two sets of stimuli produced equivalent results under nondistraction conditions (LaBerge, 1975). Such evidence suggests that well-learned processes are not merely organized differently from less well-learned ones, but that the control mechanisms involved in their utilization may be qualitatively different. If this is so, then our earlier argument that the possession and use of an information-handling technique does not guarantee a saving of effort is justified, for the way techniques are accessed and controlled will affect their workload values.

In sum, adults, like children, cannot utilize at once everything they know. Well-learned information-handling techniques allow for limited resources to be spread more thinly to cover a wider range of task demands. Hence, as more well-learned techniques are available to processors, they can accomplish increasingly complex tasks.

Freeing Capacity for Metacognitive Activity

A two-level model of processing invites some interesting speculation about the nature of another cognitive skill in which children appear deficient: metacognitive ability. If consciousness functions mainly as a control process for the organization and deployment of cognitive effort, then the more cognitive operations are handled automatically, the more consciousness itself is freed up for other activities. If consciousness is not involved in carrying out cognitive operations, it can be engaged in watching them. Then the automatized processes become the objects of a more detached or uninvolved consciousness. Thus, metacognitive ability depends on an objectivization of process resulting from the release of consciousness from the major chores of selecting and controlling processing operations. [8]

8. This is not to suggest that metacognitive introspection gives us a true picture of our cognitive processes; in fact, our unique windows on our minds appear to be rather clouded. This may be the result of an inevitable paradox. As we turn our attention to the automatic process, we necessarily disturb it to the point where

Flavell and his colleagues have pointed out the importance of objectivity for high level performance on complex tasks like explicit memory and communication tasks. Only when one disengages sufficiently to view one's memory or message objectively can specific mnemonic or perspective-taking strategies be invoked to make the fine adjustments needed to produce quality performance (Flavell & Wellman, 1977; Kreutzer, Leonard, & Flavell, 1975; Flavell, Note 11). While the Flavell group has focused primarily on the kinds of knowledge (e.g., means-end relations) revealed in metacognitive activity, they have said little about the necessary and sufficient conditions for the manifestation of metacognitive skills generally. Viewing metacognitive behavior as a function of amount of processing resources implies that any meta-ability will be displayed best when one is engaged in a task involving well-learned techniques. Some of those techniques may be relevant to the logical structure of the task, but they need not be. Even those that are not will influence the display of metacognitive ability. Hence, since older people have more well-learned techniques of all sorts than do younger ones, they can engage more readily in metacognitive activity and perform better on tasks requiring objectivity. This fact is not necessarily a result of their "stage" of cognitive development.[9] Rather it is a consequence of the resources of the conscious executive regularly being freed from more mundane chores to view and tune the operation of mainly automated techniques.

Markman's recent work on children's ability to assess their own level of understanding can be interpreted in this framework. Markman (1977) found that first graders who received incomplete game instructions did not question their adequacy unless they could observe the instructions being acted out or they themselves acted them out. She suggests that the action conditions forced a deep enough level of processing to make the relationship between goal and instruction manifest to the child. However, it is unclear what is meant by a "deeper" level of processing, how actions could force

conscious control again exerts some influence. Thus, our observations of process are always partially confounded by the ongoing exertion of some degree of conscious control.

9. Stage theories typically define levels of development in terms of a set of logical operations supposedly organizing behavior at that level. Since it is often the case that children perform variably on tasks which are logically isomorphic but which differ in content, décalage factors are incorporated to account for the mismatch between theory and data. See Section IV for further discussion of such factors.

processing to such a level, or why awareness of means-end relationships occurs on one level versus another. Placing the problem explicitly in the framework of the limited capacity model that takes account of familiarity effects on resource allocation clarifies Markman's processing explanation. In her task, decoding and remembering the instructions are prerequisites for considering the instruction-goal relationship. In the condition where children received only verbal instructions, the decoding and memory operations may have consumed all the conscious resources of the children, leaving no capacity for evaluating the instruction-goal relationship. If, on the other hand, processing actions is a more familiar and less taxing activity for young children, then in the action conditions, more resources may have been available for the evaluation procedure. [10] Thus, action conditions facilitate performance because they allow for a different distribution of resources under which the ability to assess the instruction-goal relationship can be evinced and utilized by the children to ask questions.

If degree of learning affects the amount of resources available for metacognitive activity, it should also be the case that children should be better able to talk about the reasons for their behavior when the operations involved in producing that behavior are well-learned. We have some evidence for this from the toy selection studies presented earlier. Recall that 5-year-olds appeared to have firmer notions than 4-year-olds of the nature of the 2-year-old "other." Even in the six-toy conditions, 5-year-olds' toy selections indicated that they maintained the distinction between self and other. Given this, they should also have been better able to defend their toy choices for younger children in those conditions. When the children were asked to justify their choices, 5-year-olds were indeed more able to provide appropriate reasons for their selections than

10. At first glance, it may appear as though accessing both action representations and verbal ones as required in the action condition would take more effort than working only in the verbal domain. But this need not be so. The action condition may provide an instance of how traveling around the mountain can be "shorter" than going over it. If accessing action representations is a much easier process than initially accessing a verbal representation, the added work required to evaluate that action representation against a presumably verbally represented goal may still result in total savings. Indeed, differences between action and language may be only in the access paths. The ultimate representations on which evaluation procedures operate may be made of the same "stuff" regardless of whether the paths are through action or language.

were 4-year-olds. Thus, one 5-year-old defended her refusal to select a spelling board for a 2-year-old by saying, "I think he doesn't know letters"; 4-year-olds were more likely to say simply, "He won't like it." It is also not surprising to find that preschoolers can predict others' motor skills better than they can their memorial skills (Markman, Note 12). Surely they have more opportunity to become familiar with physical rather than mental prowess.

Making Adults Look like Children: Varying Performance as a Function of Cognitive Workload II

The above discussion suggests that there may be certain procedures or information-handling techniques that do not become automatic but remain subject to a conscious limited capacity system. An example is the standard referential communication task, in which a target item must be distinguished from field items. The task involves analysis of the features of the target as well as the field items before some comparison process like a critical feature analysis can be accomplished. While the analysis of individual items may become automatic, the comparison process is much less likely to do so. How often, after all, does one describe an item as a function of the *same* set of field items? Thus, the critical feature comparison process is typically confined to the conscious level.[11] When the initial analyses of individual items are sufficiently simple, either because they are well-learned or because the stimulus field is relatively uncomplicated, then resources remain for conducting the comparison process on this level. However, when the initial processes take too much effort, even a fairly common comparison technique like critical feature analysis should lack sufficient resources for its application.

If our reasoning is correct, it should be possible to make adults behave like children in cases where the complications of a stimulus set do not allow lower order processes to operate economically enough to provide sufficient resources for higher order processes to be carried out. A study of adult behavior on referential communication tasks allows us to test this prediction.

11. It should be the case that repeated presentations of target items in an unchanging set of field items eventually induce automatic processing. The consequent savings could be measured using an interference task.

Recall that in Whitehurst's studies, children were found to behave in ways that did not correspond with the psychologist's definition of efficiency: They were often redundant in their featural descriptions of target referents instead of being contrastive. Freedle and Kingsley have shown that adults as well do not always observe a minimum redundancy principle (Freedle, 1972). Using a referential communication task, they found that the number of attributes or values on a dimension, or the number of irrelevant correlated dimensions subjects had to check, affected their degree of redundancy, as did factors like familiarity with and codability of the stimuli. That is, adults, although certainly capable of critical feature analysis under some conditions, found it easier (or possibly necessary) to do something else, i.e., be redundant, when the situation got complicated. Freedle's explanation is that subjects did not filter out irrelevant aspects of the stimuli, an argument similar to Whitehurst's explantion of second-graders' behavior. In contrast, my argument is that critical feature analyses tend to be conscious operations that take considerable resources, which are available only when the lower level operations of stimulus feature descriptions are made available from routine processes. When conscious effort is required to keep track of the output of the lower level processes because the stimuli are so complicated, then the additional effort of critical feature analysis is no longer feasible. An obvious alternative to critical feature comparison is simply to run off an unedited list of the output of the lower level process, namely, an uncritical listing of features. Both adults and children appear to adopt this alternative. The more sophisticated procedure of stimulus description as a function of field is not a basic cognitive operation but one that depends on sufficient resources being available to a conscious executive.

Adults, then, can be made to look like children, given a sufficiently complicated stimulus field. Of course, because of children's other deficits in comparison to adults (for example, their greater difficulty in identifying and naming features), deficiencies in their performance on referential tasks should be and are found more frequently. But it would be surprising if adults and children did not show similar effects; they are after all, both "fallible human information processors" (Freedle, 1972).

To summarize this section, we have seen that research and theory in adult cognition support the basic assumptions of our approach. We have found an explanation for when those rather mysterious metacognitive abilities occur. Perhaps most important, we have seen that there is a continuity in the behavior of adults and children that can be obscured in the absence of an interactive, process-oriented approach to behavior.

IV. OTHER APPROACHES TO THE DEVELOPMENT OF COMMUNICATION SKILLS

Piaget: Egocentrism Revisited

Piaget was, of course, one of the first to investigate children's abilities to use language in appropriate communicative ways (Piaget, 1926). His findings produced a picture of children as less adequate than adults at a variety of descriptive and instructional tasks, such as the water tap task discussed earlier. Piaget argued that children were unable to perform adequately because they lacked the operational abilities underlying adaptation of their own perspective to that of their listeners. Subsequent research revealing inadequacies on communication tasks was then taken as evidence in support of Piaget: Young children were "egocentric." On the other hand, success on communication tasks was taken as evidence that Piaget was wrong: Children were not "egocentric." The ensuing Talmudic discussions over what really counted as evidence for or against Piaget have done little to integrate these seemingly diverse findings. Nor, it seems to me, are such discussions likely to do so, for they ignore two facets of Piaget's theory that are at the heart of its difficulty in addressing adequately the variation in performance issue.

First, on the basis of the theory dividing children into distinct, qualitatively different stages, within-subject behaviors are characterized dichotomously. For example, a given child's communications are either listener-adapted or not listener-adapted, but not both. Variation in performance is not a central concern, and is generally accounted for by a series of ad hoc "décalage" arguments that hedge or soften the prediction of invariant behavior entailed by the theory. Such arguments become progressively less convincing the more variation is found. I have already cited many of the studies showing variable performance in the communication domain. One can argue that such variation is simply indicative of a transition from one stage to another. Communication tasks draw on social experiences which are thought to be frequent and salient even for young children. Hence, communication tasks are likeliest to reveal emergent perspective-taking ability. But in other domains as well, slight changes in test procedures have often produced improved perspective-taking performance. For example, children perform better on Piaget's standard three-mountain task of visual perspective-taking (Piaget & Inhelder, 1956) when they are exposed to the other's view before their own (Garner & Plant, 1972). Using a person rather than a doll as the "other" also enhances performance (Cox, 1975). (Also see Flavell, this volume.) Results like these suggest that a more satisfying theory may be one which grants perspective-taking ability to the young child but handles in a more systematic fashion the question of why that ability is variably displayed.

A second difficulty with the Piagetian framework is that it provides a solitary explanation for failure on tasks involving perspective-taking: Children fail because they centrate on only one perspective. To test this claim, several researchers have taken within-subject performance measures on multiple tasks involving perspective-taking. Generally, correlations among them are poor (D.W. Johnson, 1975; Piché, Michlin, & Rubin, 1975; Rubin, 1974; Sullivan & Hunt, 1967). Moreover, using factor analytic techniques to compare performance across tasks, other researchers have found centration to be only one—and not necessarily the most important one—of multiple factors implicated in poor performance (McCaffrey, Note 13; O'Connor, Note 14). These findings are consonant with a cognitive process interpretation. Centrating is a focusing of all one's efforts in only one area; it is one possible strategy for allocating limited resources. As we have seen, there are others. For example, speakers who give redundant messages, such as those in Whitehurst's and Freedle's studies, are not centrating. Rather they appear to be resorting to the best technique available to get as good a job of describing done as possible. Sometimes subjects do centrate because, given task demands and the level of their information-handling abilities, centrating is the best they can do. But this does not mean that they necessarily cannot do otherwise in other circumstances.

Finally, it is worth noting that "egocentrism" was in Piaget's early writing a description of a functional condition, the one during which processes of assimilation and accommodation were out of balance. It was not intended to be taken as the exclusive misfortune of early childhood. At least in the early work, functional and structural aspects of the theory were kept separate, where structural aspects were just those organizational descriptions of thought that provided a link between functional elements and behavior (Piaget, 1952). While egocentrism was not originally intended as a structural term, it was misconstrued by others, in its natural language sense, to be a basic property of children's thinking. It is not surprising, then, that in later writings Piaget deplored the confusion over the term and dropped it in favor of "centration." Regardless of the terminology, however, the above objections still stand.[12] The egocentrism, or centration, argument is inadequate to the task of explaining variation in performance on complex cognitive tasks like communication.

However, the cognitive process approach is not antithetical to Piaget generally. "Structures d'ensemble" are, after all, a way of talking about integrated organizations of information that allow for the accomplishment of increasingly complicated tasks. The virtue in the process approach is that it incorporates logically based operations into a broader framework that can better accommodate the vagaries of behavior.

Component Skills Models: Cutting the Pie into Smaller Pieces

The various component skills models, exemplified by the role-taking model of Flavell et al. and the referential skills model of Rosenberg and Cohen, represent other attempts to deal with the development of communication skills. Such models typically analyze particular tasks into the subskills required to do the tasks successfully. Thus, instead of an apparently unitary ability like decentering, Flavell proposes five kinds of knowledge a successful communicator has to have: A speaker must know that perspective exists, that in a particular situation perspective-taking is needed, how to carry out the role-analysis, how to maintain the results of that analysis, and how to translate them into an effective message. Similarly, researchers using referential tasks have broken down these sorts of communication problems into component processes

12. While Piaget's use of the word "egocentrism" has undoubtedly exacerbated the tendency to misinterpret him, the basic confusion does seem to lie in a lack of precision about the structural properties of preoperational thought. It is not surprising that many later efforts of the Piaget school have been directed to filling this gap (e.g. Inhelder, Sinclair & Bovet, 1974).

like association and comparison (See Section II). Such models commonly assume that at least some of these component skills can be acquired and utilized independently of one another. Deficits in performance are then described in terms of deficits on a given component.

The difficulty with these sorts of explanations is that components found lacking in one experimental situation are often displayed in another. Yet component skills models have little to say about the conditions under which competence in the various components will be displayed. What these models do is to cut the explanatory pie into smaller pieces than does the Piagetian approach, but possible interactions among those pieces still receive no systematic treatment. The end result is that behaviors are again classified in mainly all-or-none terms. Performance is assessed in terms of success or failure, and a subskill as present or absent. However, performances might better be considered as falling on a continuum from some ideal of success to complete failure. The principles of "graceful degradation" then become a proper topic of investigation. (See Norman & Bobrow, 1975, for an argument that human processing systems are best conceptualized in this way.)

While it deals with other complex cognitive tasks and not communication skills per se, there is a version of the component skills approach somewhat more compatible with the notion of a performance continuum. It is exemplified by Case's work, based on the functional theory of Pascual-Leone (Case, 1974). Tasks are again analyzed into subskills (schemes) with each subskill utilizing a set amount of processing space or mental effort (M-power) for its execution. Thus, any task can be assigned an M-value based on the total units of processing space required to accomplish it. Young children have less mental resources, or M-power, at their disposal than more mature processors; hence they do less well on tasks with high M-values. With the growth of M-power (due mainly to maturation) comes success on increasingly complex tasks.

The parallel between this approach and ours is obvious. M-power is analogous to R, the total resources available to the processor. However, there is a crucial difference between the two approaches. M-power describes the number of "overlearned" schemes a processor can activate without external support. No attention is given to the use of less well-learned schemes and how they relate to the distribution of M-power. In contrast, my approach uses the notion of partial learning as a central explanatory device for developmental differences. In doing so, I am able to avoid postulating as a mechanism for development the expansion of M-power as a function of some mysterious maturational process. That construct seems to have little to recommend it other than its importance for that particular theory.

In a recent revision of the theory, Case (Note 15) attempts to counteract such criticism by proposing that M-power, or attentional capacity as it is now called, is fixed early in development. As operations become more automatic, that fixed capacity can be utilized to perform more work. While this change brings Case's approach more into line with mine, there are still important points of difference. For example, Case claims that general experience and maturation are more likely to foster automatization than specific experience. This claim is based on the view that investigations in different task domains yield similar results on the number of items children at given stages can handle. However, what constitutes an item is no longer clear. If all children have equal amounts of M-power, and yet some children can handle only one item while others can handle four, an item can no longer be equivalent to a unit, which was defined as that requiring a set amount of M-power. Without a way of defining and equating items, the claim for general, linear development across tasks as a function of the automatization of abstract operations is unsupported.

In summary, the primary concern of other approaches to performance on complex cognitive tasks has been to explain between-group differences. The explanations offered have emphasized mainly deficiency in the immature organism: the *absence* of logical structures, of particular skills, or of adequate processing space. Consideration as well of variation in performance on complex tasks casts doubt on the adequacy of such explanations. It suggests that the real issue is: How at times can subjects from different groups be so much alike and at other times so different?

V. CONCLUSIONS

A satisfactory explanation of the development of communication skills must account for both success and failure on a variety of communication tasks. I have argued that a theoretical approach including the basic characteristics of the human information processing system offers the best hope for such an explanation. Thus, my

theory uses notions like limited mental resources, weighted information-handling techniques, the allocation of resources among
those techniques, and the importance of practice for the stretching
of resources to explain variation in performance.

One of the distinct advantages of my approach is that it is not a
theory of relations among tasks. Analyzing tasks into their structural components is something that psychologists, and not necessarily subjects, do. Instead, the segmentation by subjects of the
work they have to do rests both on the techniques they possess and
the resources available for applying them. Workload values depend
in part on the individual's level of facilitation with techniques.
Values are attached to techniques, not tasks. Tasks can be characterized as easy or hard only with regard to the resources the processor has at hand to accomplish them. Thus, our formulation puts the
problem of task difficulty right where it belongs: in the head of the
processor.

The approach also explains why we for so long underestimated
preschoolers' abilities. A technique will not always be displayed in
circumstances logically requiring it. Whether a given technique is
selected depends on its relevance for the best route to overall task
success, *given limited resources*. Thus, when complex tasks are en-
listed to index an ability that accomplishes a subtask, competence
can easily be underestimated because the technique of interest may
go unselected so as to fulfill better the overall task demands. In
short, the approach emphasizes the need for caution when making
claims of competence deficiencies.

Still another advantage is that the approach highlights the similarity between child and adult by providing processing arguments
that are appropriate for adult and child alike. The primary
mechanism of development is the acquisition and routinizaton of
new techniques that make efficient use of limited processing capacity. Hence, one can best characterize developmental progress as
mainly gradual and continuous, rather than in terms of discrete
steps or stages. Yet, because progress is not necessarily linear,
behavioral manifestations of development do not always clearly
reflect that continuity. Indeed, what may at first glance appear to be
a discontinuous leap may be an exponential increase, perhaps due
to incidentally simultaneous routinizations of several techniques.
Nor does one need to postulate a cyclic process, as Bower (1974) did,
to account for the appearance and reappearance of skill. Competence may at times be masked or unused, but it does not disappear.

Of course, the question of when to grant competence or knowledge of a technique on the basis of its variable display is a difficult one. Is the skill that a 5-year-old displays in restricted circumstances isomorphic to the one the college sophomore displays whenever necessary? This issue is a conundrum for any theory (cf. Bower, 1974; Flavell & Wohlwill, 1969). Bower has suggested that training studies can help to reveal the genuine relationships among seemingly similar behaviors. However, that line of research would provide only one part of the story. The communication work that we have reviewed suggests that varying the conditons for eliciting skill provides important information about the flexible organizations or "multiple rationalities" (Glick, Note 16) of the human mind. Such organizations are based on more than just logical structure; they are content and context-sensitive. We take the development and display of multiple rationalities to depend on the need to select different sets of information-handling techniques in accord with the constraints of a limited capacity system.

It may appear as though we have done much handwaving over notions like "degree of learning" and "well-learned techniques". However, the emphasis on situation offers a promising means of explicating such notions. Suppose a skill counts as well-learned when there is little uncertainty associated with its application. One source of uncertainty is the determination of which conditions or situations call for the technique. If all the conditions for the application of a skill are known, and those conditions are readily identifiable, the decision to call up the skill is an easy one, requiring little effort. Then, ceteris paribus, the speed with which a technique becomes well-learned should be a function of the quantity and identifiability of its contexts of application. We have already noted that the diversity of contexts for critical feature analysis is a detriment to automatization. The converse situation appears to obtain with sequences of ritual behavior, where the allowable context for their occurrence is often very limited and particular.

Nevertheless, it is true that we have little systematic knowledge about contextual constraints on learning or the degree of learning. Obviously, such knowledge is crucial to the developmental aspects of a cognitive process theory. In fact, both the developmental theory and theories of adult cognition could benefit from deeper understandings of many of the concepts we have borrowed from research with adults. I would like to see the debt paid to cognitive psychology by studies in the development of communication skills which would provide new insights on concepts like learning, consciousness, and metacognitive skills. It is the perfect arena for studying those concepts: Communication tasks are sufficiently complex and they can be set in a wide variety of contexts. Investigating concepts whose essence have long eluded psychologists may seem like a heavy bill to pay, but given what we have already discovered, it is likely there is still much more behind communication skills than meets the ear.

REFERENCE NOTES

1. Fulani, L. *The function of speech in two young children.* Unpublished manuscript, The Graduate Center, City University of New York, 1976.
2. Merkin, S. *Small talk: A causal analysis of conversations between 2½-year-olds.* Unpublished manuscript, University of Pennsylvania, 1975.
3. Keenan, E. O. *Again and again: The pragmatics of imitation in child language.* Paper presented at the meeting of the American Anthropological Association, Mexico City, November 1974.
4. Knapp, D. *Automatization and the child's acquisition of language.* Dissertation proposal, Department of Psychology, University of California at San Diego, 1977.
5. Masur, E. *Four-year-olds' speech modifications as a function of linguistic level of listener.* Paper presented at the meeting of the Society for Research in Child Development, New Orleans, March 1977.
6. Goldstein, D., & Kose, G. *Differential exposure to the referent as a determinant of communication effectiveness of young children.* Paper presented at the Southeastern Conference on Research in Child Development, Nashville, April 1976.
7. Shatz, M. *Preschoolers' ability to take account of others in a toy selection task.* Unpublished master's thesis, University of Pennsylvania, 1973.
8. Sachs, J., & Devin, J. *Young children's knowledge of age-appropriate speech styles.* Paper presented at the meeting of the Linguistic Society of America, San Diego, December 1973.
9. Higgins, E. T., & Akst, L. *Comparison processes in the communication of kindergartners.* Paper presented at the meeting of the Society for Research in Child Development, Denver, April 1975.
10. Robinson, E. J., & Robinson, W. P. *Development in the understanding of causes of success and failure in verbal communication.* Unpublished manuscript, Macquarie University, 1976.
11. Flavell, J. H. *The development of metacommunication.* Paper presented at the Symposium on Language and Cognition, International Congress of Psychology, Paris, July 1976.
12. Markman, E. *Factors affecting the young child's ability to monitor his memory.* Unpublished doctoral dissertation, University of Pennsylvania, 1973.

13. McCaffrey, A. *Communicative competence: How it can be measured and how it can be fostered in young children.* Paper presented at the Third International Symposium on Child Language, London, September 1975.
14. O'Connor, M. *Decentration revisited: A two-factor model for role-taking development in young children.* Paper presented at the meeting of the Society for Research in Child Development, Denver, March 1975.
15. Case, R. *Intellectual development from birth to adulthood: A neo-Piagetian interpretation.* Paper presented at the Thirteenth Annual Carnegie Symposium on Cognition, May, 1977.
16. Glick, J. *Functional and structural aspects of rationality.* Paper presented at the meeting of the Jean Piaget Society, Philadelphia, May 1977.

REFERENCES

Anderson, J. R., & Bower, G. H. *Human associative memory.* New York: Wiley, 1974.

Asher, S. Children's ability to appraise their own and another person's communication performance. *Developmental Psychology,* 1976, **12**, 24–32.

Asher, S., & Oden, S. Children's failure to communicate: An assessment of comparison and egocentrism explanations. *Developmental Psychology,* 1976, **12**, 132–139.

Bloom, L. *Language development: Form and function in emerging grammars.* Cambridge, Mass.: MIT Press, 1970.

Bloom, L., Miller, P., & Hood, L. Variation and reduction as aspects of competence in language development. In A. D. Pick (Ed.), *Minnesota symposia on child psychology* (Vol. 9). Minneapolis: University of Minnesota Press, 1975.

Bloom, L., Rocissano, L., & Hood, L. Adult-child discourse: Developmental interaction between information processing and linguistic knowledge. *Cognitive Psychology,* 1976, **8**, 521–552.

Bower, T. G. R. Repetition in human development. *Merrill-Palmer Quarterly,* 1974, **20**, 303–318.

Broadbent, D. *Perception and communication.* London: Pergamon, 1958.

Broadbent, D., & Gregory, M. Stimulus set and response set: The alternation of attention. *Quarterly Journal of Experimental Psychology,* 1964, **16**, 309–318.

Bruner, J. S. The organization of early skilled action. In M. P. M. Richards (Ed.), *The integration of a child into a social world.* London: Cambridge University Press, 1974.

Case, R. Structures and strictures: Some functional limitations on the course of cognitive growth. *Cognitive Psychology,* 1974, **6**, 544–573.

Cox, M. V. The other observer in a perspective task. *British Journal of Educational Psychology,* 1975, **45**, 83–85.

Flavell, J. H., Botkin, P. I., Fry, C. L., Jr., Wright, J. W., & Jarvis, P. E. *The development of role-taking and communication skills in children.* New York: Wiley, 1968. Reprinted by Krieger, 1975.

Flavell, J. H., & Wellman, H. Metamemory. In R. Kail & J. Hagen (Eds.), *Perspectives on the development of memory and cognition.* Hillsdale, N.J.: Lawrence Erlbaum Associates, 1977.

Flavell, J. H., & Wohlwill, J. F. Formal and functional aspects of cognitive development. In D. Elkind & J. H. Flavell (Eds.), *Studies in cognitive development: Essays in honor of Jean Piaget.* New York: Oxford University Press, 1969.

Fodor, J. A., Bever, T. G., & Garrett, M. F. *The psychology of language: An introduction to psycholinguistics and generative grammar.* New York: McGraw-Hill, 1974.

Ford, W., & Olson, D. The elaboration of the noun phrase in children's description of objects. *Journal of Experimental Child Psychology,* 1975, **19**, 371–382.

Freedle, R. Language users as fallible information processors. In R. Freedle and J. Carroll (Eds.), *Language comprehension and the acquisition of knowledge.* Washington: V. H. Winston & Sons, 1972.

Garmiza, C., & Anisfeld, M. Factors reducing the efficiency of referent-communication in children. *Merrill-Palmer Quarterly,* 1976, **22**, 125–136.

Garner, J., & Plant, E. L. On the measurement of egocentrism: A replication and extension of Aebli's findings. *British Journal of Educational Psychology,* 1972, **42**, 79–83.

Garvey, C., Play with language. In B. Tizard & D. Harvey (Eds.), *The biology of play.* London: Spastics International Medical Publications, 1977.

Garvey, C., & Hogan, R. Social speech and social interaction: Egocentrism revisited. *Child Development,* 1973, **44**, 562–568.

Gelman, R. Cognitive development. *Annual review of psychology,* 1978, **28**, in press.

Gelman, R., & Shatz, M. Appropriate speech adjustments: The operation of conversational constraints on talk to two-year-olds. In M. Lewis & L. Rosenblum (Eds.), *Interaction, conversation, and the development of language.* New York: Wiley, 1977.

Glucksberg, S., Krauss, R., & Higgins, E. T. The development of referential communication skills. In F. D. Horowitz (Ed.), *Review of child development research* (Vol. 4). Chicago: University of Chicago Press, 1975.

Grice, H. P. Logic and conversation. In P. Cole & J. Morgan (Eds.), *Speech acts: Syntax and semantics* (Vol. 3). New York: Academic Press, 1975.

Harris, P. L., Macrae, A., & Bassett, E. Disambiguation by young children. *Journal of Child Language,* in press.

Higgins, E. T. Social class differences in verbal communicative accuracy: A question of "Which question?" *Psychological Bulletin,* 1976, **83**, 695–714.

Hoy, E. A. Measurement of egocentrism in children's communication. *Developmental Psychology,* 1975, **11**, 393.

Inhelder, B., Sinclair, H., & Bovet, M. *Learning and the development of cognition* (S. Wedgwood, trans.). Cambridge, Mass.: Harvard University Press, 1974.

Ironsmith, M., & Whitehurst, G. The development of listener abilities in communication: How children deal with ambiguous information. *Child Development*, in press.

Johnson, D. W. Cooperativeness and social perspective taking. *Journal of Personality and Social Psychology*, 1975, **31**, 241–244.

Johnson, N. The role of chunking and organization in the process of recall. In G. Bower (Ed.), *The psychology of learning and motivation* (Vol. 4). New York: Academic Press, 1970.

Kahneman, D. *Attention and effort.* Englewood Cliffs, New Jersey: Prentice Hall, 1973.

Keenan, E. O. Conversational competence in children. *Journal of Child Language*, 1974, **1**, 163–183.

Kintsch, W. *Learning, memory and conceptual processes.* New York: Wiley, 1970.

Krauss, R. M., & Glucksberg, S. The development of communication: Competence as a function of age. *Child Development*, 1969, **40**, 255–266.

Kreutzer, M., Leonard, C., & Flavell, J. An interview study of children's knowledge about memory. *Monographs of the Society for Research in Child Development*, 1975, **40** (1, Serial No. 159).

LaBerge, D. Acquisition of automatic processing in perceptual and associative learning. In P. Rabbit & S. Dornic (Eds.), *Attention and performance V.* New York: Academic Press, 1975.

Mandler, G. Consciousness: Respectable, useful, and probably necessary. In R. Solso (Ed.), *Information processing and cognition.* Hillsdale, N. J.: Lawrence Erlbaum Associates, 1975.

Maratsos, M. Nonegocentric communication abilities in preschool children. *Child Development*, 1973, **44**, 697–700.

Markman, E. Realizing that you don't understand: A preliminary investigation. *Child Development*, 1977, **48**, 986–992.

McTear, M. Repetition in child language: Imitation or creation? In R. Campbell & P. T. Smith (Eds.), *The Stirling Psychology of Language Conference.* New York: Plenum, in press.

Menig-Peterson, C. The modification of communicative behavior in preschool-aged children as a function of the listener's perspective. *Child Development*, 1975, **46**, 1015–1018.

Miller, G. A. The magical number seven, plus or minus two: Some limits on our capacity for processing information. *Psychological Review*, 1956, **63**, 81–97.

Moray, N. Where is capacity limited? A survey and a model. In A. Sanders (Ed.), *Attention and performance.* Amsterdam: North-Holland Publishing Co., 1967.

Mueller, E. The maintenance of verbal exchanges between young children.

Child Development, 1972, **43**, 930–938.

Mueller, E., Bleier, M., Krakow, J., Hegedus, K., & Cournoyer, P. The development of peer verbal interaction among two-year-old boys. *Child Development*, 1977, **48**, 284–287.

Norman, D. A., & Bobrow, D. G. On data-limited and resource-limited processes. *Cognitive Psychology*, 1975, 7, 44–64.

Olson, D. Language and thought: Aspects of a cognitive theory of semantics. *Psychological Review*, 1970, **77**, 257-273.

Olson, G. Developmental changes in memory and the acquisition of language. In T. E. Moore (Ed.), *Cognitive development and the acquisition of language*. New York: Academic Press, 1973.

Piaget, J. *The language and thought of the child*. New York: Harcourt, Brace, 1926.

Piaget, J. *The origins of intelligence in children*. New York: International Universities Press, 1952.

Piaget, J., & Inhelder, B. *The child's conception of space*. London: Routledge & Kegan Paul, 1956.

Piché, G., Michlin, M., & Rubin, D. Relationships between fourth graders' performances on selected role-taking tasks and referential communication accuracy tasks. *Child Development*, 1975, **46**, 965–969.

Posner, M. I., & Boies, S. W. Components of attention. *Psychological Review*, 1971, **78**, 391–408.

Posner, M. I. & Klein, R. M. On the functions of consciousness. In S. Kornblum (Ed.) *Attention and performance IV*. New York: Academic Press, 1973.

Posner, M. I., & Snyder, C. R. R. Facilitation and inhibition in the processing of signals. In P. M. A. Rabbit & S. Dornic (Eds.), *Attention and performance V*. London: Academic Press, 1975.

Posner, M. I., & Warren, R. E. Traces, concepts and conscious constructions. In A. W. Melton & E. Martin (Eds.), *Coding processes in human memory*. Washington, D.C.: V. H. Winston & Sons, 1972.

Rees, N. Pragmatics of language: Applications to normal and disordered language development. In R. L. Schiefelbusch (Ed.), *Bases of language interaction*. Baltimore: University Park Press, in press.

Robinson, E., & Robinson, W. The young child's understanding of communication. *Developmental Psychology*, 1976, **12**, 328–333.

Rosenberg, S., & Cohen, B. Referential processes of speakers and listeners. *Psychological Review*, 1966, **73**, 208–231.

Rubin, K. The relationship between spatial and communicative egocentrism in children and young and old adults. *Journal of Genetic Psychology*, 1974, **125**, 295–301.

Schegloff, E. A. Sequencing in conversational openings. *American Anthropologist*, 1968, **70**, 1075–1095.

Schegloff, E. A., & Sacks, H. Opening up closings. *Semiotica*, 1973, **8**, 289–327.

Shatz, M., & Gelman, R. The development of communication skills: Modifications in the speech of young children as a function of listener. *Monographs of the Society for Research in Child Development*, 1973, **38** (5, Serial No. 152).

Sullivan, E., & Hunt, D. Interpersonal and objective decentering. *Journal of Genetic Psychology*, 1967, **110**, 199–210.

Treisman, A. Contextual cues in selective listening. *Quarterly Journal of Experimental Psychology*, 1960, **12**, 242–248.

Wellman, H., & Lempers, J. The naturalistic communicative abilities of two-year-olds. *Child Development*, 1977, **48**, 3.

Whitehurst, G. The development of communication: Changes with age and modeling. *Child Development*, 1976, **47**, 473–482.

Whitehurst, G., & Sonnenschein, S. The development of communication: Attribute variation leads to contrast failure. *Journal of Experimental Child Psychology*, in press.

The Development of Knowledge About Visual Perception

John H. Flavell
Stanford University

Social cognition can be defined as any sort of cognition that takes human psychological and social phenomena as its object. It therefore includes our conceptions ("naive theories"), knowledge, inferences, and observations concerning our own and other people's feelings, perceptions, motives, intentions, thoughts, personality traits, social interactions, moral and other norms (social, legal), and numerous other contents of our social world. A recent chapter by Shantz (1975) contains what is probably the best available review of research on the development of social cognition. Other useful surveys of this or closely related developmental topics include: Chandler (1976); Flavell (1974, 1977); Flavell, Botkin, Fry, Wright, and Jarvis (1968); Glucksberg, Krauss, and Higgins (1975); Lickona (1976); and Livesley and Bromley (1973). The definition given above also covers certain forms of thought and knowledge that are not ordinarily conceptualized as instances of social cognition, and hence are not included in these literature reviews. One example would be *metamemory*, i.e., cognitions about memory (Flavell & Wellman, 1977); other examples are cited in Flavell (Note 1).

Shantz (1975) reviewed research in five content areas, namely, the child's growing "understanding of what another person *sees, feels, thinks, intends,* and what the other person *is like*" (p. 259, italics added). The present chapter deals only with selected aspects of the first of these five. Research in this area is sometimes categorized under the headings of "spatial perspective-taking" and "perceptual role-taking," but "visual percept cognition," or simply, "knowledge about visual perception" are more general and more accurate descriptors. Shantz correctly points out (p. 277) that almost all of the existing research here deals with cognitions about *visual* perception. The development of knowledge about nonvisual types of perception seems equally researchable and worth investigating, however. She also argues that this form of social cognition differs from other forms in an interesting way:

An inference about another's perspective is the least social of all the various types of inferences to be reviewed here. It is least social in the sense that anyone and everyone at a particular location viewing a particular object or array has an identical viewpoint on it, and, indeed, a camera would capture the same viewpoint. Thus, the child is predicting the visual experience of a "generalized other" which has no variability between people. The *only* thing he has to consider about the other person is his spatial location, whereas in other types of social inference he must often take into account several aspects of the situation in order to infer the other's psychological experience, be it feelings, thoughts, or other subjective experiences. (p. 269)

This difference may not always be as clear-cut as Shantz suggests. First, we often do assume that others not only see, but also feel or think, much the same thing we would if we were in their position. We may do so simply because we lack the necessary evidence to assume otherwise. Moreover, we may often arrive at an approximately correct inference by following this straightforward, "assumed similarity" or "generalized other" strategy. Second, the eye is not like a camera and others may not in fact see exactly what you would see if you were in their spatial position. Differences in perceptual learning histories, cognitive interests, and other factors may lead, say, a young child, an adolescent, a partially blind adult, and an artist to have very different perceptual experiences when viewing the same visual display from the same spatial position. Finally, let us assume with Shantz that others do see essentially what you would see if you were in their spatial location and were looking in the same direction they are. Even in these circumstances a careful monitoring of their looking behavior over time may reflect a fairly sophisticated, decidedly "social" kind of social cognition. Others' looking patterns may give you clues as to the sort of person they are, or how they feel about you, or how interested they are in what you are saying. You note that they are shifty-eyed, or continually avoid your gaze, or are constantly looking all around the room, as if in search of someone more interesting to talk to. More generally, looking patterns provide clues as to what others find interesting or important to attend to in their visual environment.

Shantz is nonetheless quite right in characterizing the typical spatial perspective-taking task as tapping cognitive activity that is not clearly and completely socially oriented. It is true that such tasks may tell us "more about the child's emerging spatial representation than role taking per se" (Shantz, 1975, p. 273). The main point of this commentary on her argument is only to suggest that there might be much more to the development of visual percept cognition than is ordinarily assessed in conventional spatial perspective-taking tasks. The latter were the tasks that got us started, however, and they continue to be the most widely used assessment devices in this area. As is well known, the developmental study of percept cognition essentially began with Piaget and Inhelder's (1956) work on children's spatial perspective-taking ability, as assessed by their famous Three Mountains task. In tasks of this type, the child subject (S) has to infer how an array of several small objects (X) looks to another person (O) who views the array from a different station point than S's own, e.g., from the opposite side. Piaget and Inhelder (1956) and subsequent investigators (e.g., Flavell et al., 1968; Laurendeau & Pinard, 1970) have found that Ss have considerable difficulty in determining how X looks to O prior to late middle childhood or older. Moreover, they have also found that children are subject to "egocentric" task interpretations and responses; that is, they often respond with their own perspective when asked for O's. Except for details about what spatial features and relations are more and less difficult for children to get right when figuring out O's view and other matters of little relevance to present concerns, that was essentially our picture of development in this area until recently.

Recent work has changed this picture in two related ways. First, it has now become abundantly clear (e.g., Fishbein, Lewis, & Keiffer, 1972; Masangkay, McCluskey, McIntyre, Sims-Knight, Vaughn, & Flavell, 1974; see Shantz, 1975) that children can accurately infer O's view of a visual display at a considerably younger age than had previously been believed, provided that the display is sufficiently simple (e.g., composed of one object rather than three) and the child's task is communicated to him very clearly.[1] Like many other Piagetian tasks (Flavell, 1977; Gelman, 1972), the Three Mountains one appears in hindsight to be a rather "noisy," insensitive measure of the basic knowledge and ability it was designed to assess. The evidence suggests that it will fail to detect low but nonetheless genuine levels of such knowledge and ability. It is obvious, once one thinks about it, that a child could know perfectly well that O's visual

1. In this chapter the individual child or S will be arbitrarily treated as masculine ("he," "him," etc.) and the other individuals (experimenters, Os, etc.) as feminine.

experience of X is different from his own, and yet be quite unable to infer that *particular* visual experience accurately and in full detail (see Section III). The same could, of couse, be true of an adult, if X were made sufficiently complex and multifeatured (Flavell et al., 1968). If the task is greatly simplified and its demands fully clarified, on the other hand, children as young as 4–5 years of age may show evidence of some genuine competence here (Masangkay et al., 1974). As in other areas of cognitive development, one must try to strip the task situation of irrelevant or unessential "performance" demands in hopes of revealing a beginning, often quite rudimentary "competence."

The second change came in the wake of the first, and is perhaps more interesting. There is now reason to suspect that there may exist at least two developmentally-sequenced levels of knowledge about visual perception (Flavell, 1974; Masangkay et al., 1974; Lempers, Flavell, & Flavell, 1977; also cf. Hughes, 1975). The arguments and evidence for this two-level view have so far pertained only to visual percepts; whether the same conceptualization would prove applicable to cognition of perception in other modalities remains to be shown.

I. TWO DEVELOPMENTAL LEVELS OF KNOWLEDGE ABOUT VISUAL PERCEPTION

At later-developing Level 2, according to the theory, the child basically understands the idea of having different perspectives or views of the same display. Thus, he can represent the fact that although both he and O see the same X (e.g., a single complex object) from different station points, O nonetheless sees it differently, or has a different visual experience of it, than he does. Such a child knows that X does not look the same to O as it does to him, although, qua object, it is equally visible to both. Level 2 thinking is essentially the kind of percept cognition all of us had assumed we were studying, beginning with Piaget and Inhelder (1956).

At earlier-developing Level 1, according to our theory, the child understands that O need not presently see X just because he himself does. He can also recognize that O may see an object that he himself

The Level 1 child knows *that* other people also see things, and that they need not see the same things he sees at any given moment. He may also be able to infer *what* things they currently do and do not see, given adequate cues (more on these cues below). The Level 2 child possesses this knowledge too, of course, but is also aware that the *same* things ordinarily look *different* to *O* than they do to him if *O*'s viewing position is different. The Level 2 child may also be able to infer approximately *how* these things look from *O*'s position, again given adequate cues. If shown a variety of photographs depicting different views of the selfsame *X*, a Level 1 child should find them all equally acceptable as representations of *O*'s visual experience of *X*. The reason is that they all equally well show "what *O* sees" in the literal, nonperspectival sense (namely, the object *X* per se), and the Level 1 child codes nothing further about *O*'s visual act or experience. The Level 2 child, in contrast, should understand that only a single photograph can be correct, since he understands the distinction between seeing an object and seeing a particular view of an object. For further elaboration of the Level 1–Level 2 distinction, see Flavell (1974) and Masangkay et al. (1974). Hughes (1975) has independently proposed the same distinction.

There are two reasons for supposing that something like a Level 1–Level 2 distinction might really exist, and that Level 1 representations of visual percepts might be attained earlier in ontogenesis than those of Level 2. First, these suppositions are intuitively plausible, and second, there is some empirical support for them.

As to plausibility, what object is seen by *S* and *O* is normally a much more important, ecologically significant fact to be determined than how that object appears from this versus that viewing position. This is probably as true for us as for the child. Level 1 percept inference abilities seem far more useful in everyday living than do Level 2 abilities. We would accordingly expect the child to acquire knowledge and skills concerning the former earlier than the latter. Further, Level 2 knowledge includes but adds to or goes beyond Level 1 knowledge. For one thing, it embeds an *S–O difference* (different views . . .) within an *S–O identity* (. . . of the same perceived object). Alternatively, it could be said to add a feature to the child's representation: (how what is seen looks) versus simply (what is seen). Cognitive development often proceeds in this "B includes but goes beyond A" fashion (Flavell, 1972). It is in any case plain that, if Level 1 and Level 2 develop at all, they would have to develop either concurrently or in 1–2 order; the opposite, 2–1 order is logically impossible, given the above definitions of the two. Finally, Level 2 thinking seems more clearly and unambiguously to require genuine inference about another's internal visual experience than does Level 1 thinking. Looking at and seeing an object may be tacitly interpreted by the Level 1 child as just another overt act or behavior, much like touching it or picking it up—a kind of aphenomenological, Watsonian-like representation. The Level 2 child, on the other hand, seemingly would have to represent O's view of the object as something akin to a visual experience or impression—more like an internal image than like an external action. Again, there is a great deal of evidence suggesting that social-cognitive development generally proceeds from the outside in—from initial repesentations of people's appearance and overt behavior only to representations of their inner states, dispositions, and processes as well (Flavell, 1977; Shantz, 1975). The hypothesized Level 1–Level 2 sequence would thus be consistent with this general trend.

As to empirical evidence, young children sometimes do act as if they believe that any depicted view of X can adequately represent O's visual experience in tasks of the Three-Mountains type (Flavell, 1974, pp. 101–105). In addition, Coie, Costanzo, and Farnill (1973), using a three-object landscape as their X, found that children tend to discriminate *what* objects in the array are visible from a specific viewing position (e.g., where one object blocks O's view of another) earlier than *how* the objects which are seen appear in the perspectival sense. The most direct evidence, however, was obtained by Masangkay et al. (1974). They attempted to construct pairs of tasks such that pair members were similar in structure and roughly comparable in information-processing demands, but with one member of each pair demanding only Level 1 ability and the other Level 2 ability. The most successful of these attempts produced the following pair:

Picture task (Level 1). The experimenter sat facing the child, holding vertically between them a card with a picture of a dog on one side and a picture of a cat on the other. On each of a series of trials the child (S) was asked which animal the experimenter (O) saw. On some trials the child was first asked which animal the child saw. On some of the latter trials the experimenter turned the card around between the S-sees question and the O-sees question, so that the experimenter now saw the same animal the child had just seen rather than (as on all other trials) a different one.

Turtle task (Level 2). The experimenter held horizontally between the child and herself a side-view, in-profile picture of a turtle, so that both could see it simultaneously. The trials were the same as those just described, with the crucial difference that the child was asked whether the experimenter (and on some trials, the child) saw the turtle "upside down" (i.e., on its back) or "right side up." The meanings of these terms were of course made very clear to the children and, in the event, no child ever used them erroneously in describing how the turtle looked to him.

Of 24 3-year-olds, 24 performed perfectly or almost perfectly on the Picture task but only 9 did so on the Turtle task. The corresponding figures for 24 4-year-olds were 24 and 23. These data, together with other evidence presented by Hughes (1975) and cited in Masangkay et al. (1974), can be taken as at least preliminary and tentative support for the hypothesized Level 1–Level 2 distinction and developmental sequence.

II. RECENT RESEARCH ON LEVEL 1 KNOWLEDGE

As will become apparent in Section IV, many questions remain concerning the meaning and validity of the above distinction and sequence. Before considering these, however, let us turn to some recent developmental research, first on Level 1 phenomena (this section), and then on Level 2 phenomena (Section III). Lempers, Flavell, and Flavell (1977) have described a possible taxonomy of Level 1 knowledge, and have also reported a developmental study of how infants and very young children perform on a variety of tasks designed to assess these hypothesized acquisitions.

In this taxonomy, S, O, and X stand as defined earlier, and A refers to any object interposed between O and X such as to prevent O from seeing X; A is thus any kind of vision-blocking obstacle. Lempers et al. (1977) suggested that a child with full Level 1 competence might know implicitly that the following four elementary conditions must hold if O is to see X: (1) At least one of O's eyes must be open and otherwise unemcumbered by "proximal As"—no vision-obstructing eyelids, blindfolds, hands over eyes, etc. (2) O's eyes must be aimed in the general direction of X. (3) Similar to (1), there must not be any other, more distal As on the line of sight between O and X. There must be no opaque screens directly in front of X, for instance, and a picture of X must present its face (X side) rather than its back to O (recall the Masangkay et al. Picture task in this regard).

(4) What S sees and does not see with regard to O, X, or A has absolutely no effect or bearing on what O sees: that is, the child's percept cognition is assumed to be fundamentally nonegocentric, at least when dealing with Level 1 type problems.

Tacit knowledge of these four facts should permit the child to know, or know how to do, three categories of things apropos of O's seeing of an X in the presence of an actual or potential A. Lempers et al. labeled the three *percept production, percept deprivation, and percept diagnosis.* The child S could *produce* a visual percept in O by variously repositioning X, A, O, and/or S himself (if S should constitute an X or an A with respect to O's visual act) so that O is permitted or induced to see X. For example, S could point to X, physically or verbally turn O around so that she faces X, move or reorient X so that it is in O's line of sight, and reposition either A or X so that A no longer blocks O's seeing of X. Conversely, the child could *deprive* O of a percept by moving X behind an A, by moving an A in front of X, or by causing O to turn away from X. Finally, he could *diagnose* the object of O's current visual attention by noting the orientation, in relation to X, of O's eyes or pointed finger (the latter a measure of "pointing comprehension" versus the aforementioned "pointing production").

The subjects in the Lempers et al. study were 12-, 18-, 24-, 30-, and 36-month-olds, six males and six females at each of these five age levels. The assessment procedures consisted of 24 Level 1 percept production, deprivation, and diagnosis tasks, all solvable by nonverbal responding. The testing was done in the home, often with a parent's help. Each child was seen by two experimenters an average of two times (range of 1 to 4 visits), each visit lasting ½–1 hour. The following summary of the most interesting results will also communicate the nature of the tasks.

Most of the 12-month-old subjects produced pointing gestures. About half of them also correctly interpreted or "diagnosed" O's pointing, even though no gestural movement cues were provided (O's arm was already outstretched in fixed pointing position when S's attention was engaged). About half also showed a toy to O by simply holding it up, i.e., with no attempt to orient it in any particular way with respect to O. Infants of this age were essentially incapable of solving any of our other Level 1 tasks.

A number of the 18-month-olds could show pictures of objects as well as real objects. However, they tended to show them in a characteristic way. Their favored procedure was to hold the picture horizontally rather than vertically, often after coming up and standing next to O. This procedure made it possible for them to maintain visual contact with the depicted object while at the same time showing it to O. In one picture-showing task, for instance, 10 of the 12 18-month-olds were successful in getting O to see the picture, and 8 of these 10 used the horizontal showing method. As can be imagined, the task of showing a small picture glued to the inside bottom of a cup posed problems for them. Some tried to solve it by holding the cup low between self and O, and then trying to make the picture visible to both by tilting the cup back and forth. Horizontal showing has an egocentric flavor to it but is obviously not purely egocentric, since X is made visible to O as well as to S. An instance of purely egocentric showing would be holding the picture vertically, but with the picture facing S rather than O. Interestingly, virtually no behavior of this kind was observed at any of the five age levels. Finally, our hiding tasks generally elicited no response from the 18-month-olds.

In marked contrast to the 18-month-olds, the 24-month-olds almost always showed in the typical adult manner, i.e., by turning the depicted X toward O, so that O now sees it and S himself no longer does. Our data suggest that children of this age have a "generative" knowledge of this form of percept production, often solving showing problems that are presumably novel for them. One example was showing O the cup picture by pointing the cup at her like a gun. Another was showing a picture attached to one end of a vertical stick while holding on to the other end (something like a picketer's sign); children of 24 months and older "invented" the procedure of manually rotating the stick until the picture faced O. A number of the 24-month-olds could also produce percepts by reorienting O rather than X, i.e., manually or verbally getting O to turn around so that she could see a large, immobile object. However, they generally could or would not show things to an O they could not see. If asked to show only their hand or a picture to an O located just out of sight behind a dressing screen, for instance, they would almost always peek or walk around before showing. Also, like the 18-month-olds, they had little success with hiding tasks. On the other hand, they seemed to understand the role of the eyes in seeing, as did some 18-month-olds. If asked to show something to an O whose eyes were covered with her hands, for example, they would usually brush aside those offending "proximal As" before trying to show it to her. Also possibly indicative of some such understanding was their observed tendency to show things more closely to a person or a doll whose eyes were closed. About half of the 24-month-olds could also tell what O was staring at, even when her head and eyes were not oriented in the same direction. That is, they would look to the right when they saw that O's eyes were aimed in that direction, even though O's head was oriented straight ahead, directly facing the child.

The 30-month-olds' performance on most of the above-mentioned tasks was either roughly equivalent to that of the 24-month-olds or somewhat better. The most striking difference between the two age groups occurred on hiding tasks. More than half of the 30-month-olds managed to hide an X from O by moving it behind an obstacle (a "distal A") so that only S could see it, and about half were also able to hide X from O by moving an obstacle in front of X. Likewise, 8 of the 12 successfully hid themselves from O. In one of the most difficult of our percept deprivation problems, S's task was to prevent O from seeing a large, immovable object O was currently looking at. Six of the 30-month-old S's either turned O away from the object or tried (usually unsuccessfully) to interpose a vision-blocking obstacle between her and the object. Level 1 knowledge is obviously quite advanced at this age level. One 30-month-old girl who kept failing to respond to the task request was finally asked by O, "What could I do if I don't want to see the sink?" She responded by shutting her own eyes, covering them with her hands, and turning away from the sink. Unlike the case with showing, we did see some egocentric hiding, e.g., interposing an A between S and X rather than between S and O. It was relatively infrequent, however. Research currently in progress also indicates that 2½- and 3-year-olds have good hiding skills.

The 36-month-old subjects performed at or near ceiling on almost all of the 24 tasks. The task of showing a seen X (S's hand) to an unseen (behind the screen) O was one that continued to be somewhat difficult, with only 7 of the 12 36-month-olds managing to show without also peeking.

The data of the Lempers et al. investigation therefore suggest that by 36 months of age, if not earlier, the child is likely to have acquired the four items of Level 1 tacit knowledge described in the above taxonomy. Specifically:

(1) The child knows that people see with their eyes, and hence must have them open and uncovered if they are to see things.

(2) The child knows that those open, unobstructed eyes must also

be aimed in the general direction of the visual target, if the target is to be seen. Accordingly, he brings portable Xs into O's line of sight, causes O to turn her eyes toward nonportable Xs (or away from them, if the goal is percept deprivation rather than percept production), and correctly diagnoses what O sees by observing her line of regard.

(3) The child also knows that open eyes which look toward X may yet not see it if there is a vision-blocking object A interposed between the eyes and X. He shows this working knowledge when producing a percept for O by moving A out from in front of X or moving X out from behind A, and he also shows it when depriving O of a percept by doing the opposite.

(4) Finally, the child usually acts as if he implicitly assumes that O's seeing or nonseeing of Xs is independent of his own, at least in the task situations used by Lempers et al. He virtually never shows things only to himself when he is supposed to show them to others (egocentric showing), and he does not usually hide things only from himself when he is supposed to hide them from others. This does not mean that young children (or any of us, for that matter) never make egocentric errors when making inferences about another's visual acts or experiences. As a matter of fact, exactly when, where, and why egocentrically-determined responses tend to occur in quantity is a very interesting problem about which we still know practically nothing (see Section IV). The results of Lempers et al. do seem to say, however, that the Piagetian notion of profound and everpresent perceptual egocentrism in early childhood cannot be accurate, at least with respect to level 1 visual percept cognition (cf. Hughes, 1975).

The Lempers et al. project thus appears to have yielded some very useful information about the early development of this type of social cognition. First, it seems to leave little doubt about the psychological reality of an early-appearing Level 1–like knowledge about visual activity, whatever the ultimate fate of the Level 1–Level 2 distinction itself. We had initially been surprised to find that children as young as 3 years of age could so easily solve percept-inference problems like the Picture task (Masangkay et al., 1974). We fully expected, for example, that many of them would egocentrically indicate the object they saw when asked to identify the one O saw. By the time the Lempers et al. data had been collected, however, that ability began to look like but one part of a rather extensive Level 1 repertoire. It became apparent that 3-year-olds have a good functional command of virtually all the varieties of purely Level 1 knowledge we were able to imagine and classify. It began to look, in other words, as though 3 years of age was much closer to the end than the beginning of Level 1 development. Research currently in progress also supports this conclusion.

Moreover, these varieties of knowledge looked interesting in themselves, apart from their implications for any developmental theory of percept cognition. Pointing, showing, hiding, and reading O's attention as indexed by O's pointing gestures and direction of gaze—all these impressed us as ethologically significant communicative and social-interactive abilities in their own right. As will shortly be explained, a number of psychologists in Great Britain have recently—and wholly independently—come to the same conclusion. In addition, as Lempers et al. show, previous evidence in the literature about the initial emergence of these abilities and their subsequent developmental course varied from skimpy (production of pointing, object showing, percept diagnosis) to almost nonexistent (picture showing, percept deprivation).

These latter considerations led Lempers (1976) to do a follow-up study of the development of pointing production, pointing comprehension, and direction-of-gaze (visual attending) comprehension in 9-, 12-, and 14-month-old infants. In Lempers et al. (1977), all of the O pointing and looking was unnaturally nondynamic or "frozen." That is, O's eyes, eyes and face, or pointing finger were already oriented motionlessly toward X when S's attention to O was first engaged. Lempers (1976) found that infants generally comprehended these deictic communications at an earlier age if, as would normally occur in everyday life, they saw the movements that produced them, e.g., saw O move her head and eyes toward X. He also found that S will locate and stare at a pointed-to X several months earlier if O's fingertip and X are fairly close to one another (about .5 meter) than if they are far apart (2.5 meters or more). Finally, it appears that by age 12 months the majority of children can both produce and comprehend pointing, even when X is distal rather than proximal, and can also read O's visual-attentional behavior if the cues are sufficiently salient and redundant (as when S sees O turn both head and eyes toward X.)

Some recent research done in Great Britain is highly relevant to our own for two reasons. First, these studies provide additional empirical evidence on the genesis of certain interesting phenomena related to Level 1. Second, they serve to place the acquisitions we have been studying in a broader social-developmental context by showing how they can be interpreted as more than just developing knowledge about visual perception.

On the empirical side, perhaps the two most pertinent studies are those of Scaife and Bruner (1975) on the infant's visual following of *O*'s looking gestures, and of Murphy and Messer (1977) on the infant's visual following of pointing gestures. In the Scaife and Bruner procedure, *O* and *S* (2 to 14 month-olds) faced each other at eye level at a distance of 1.5 m. After establishing eye contact with *S*, *O* silently turned her head 90° to the right or left and stared at a concealed light for seven seconds. The baby's behavior during this period was videorecorded and later judged for evidence that the baby looked in the same general direction that *O* had looked. All subjects of 11–14 months followed *O*'s gaze, many of 8–10 months did, and some younger infants may also have done so (see Collis's, 1977, interpretation of the Scaife and Bruner data). These developmental findings are very similar to those obtained by Lempers (1976) using an almost identical procedure. Scaife and Bruner also believe, as we do, that "insofar as mutual orientation implies a degree of knowledge in some form about another person's perspective then the child in his first year may be considered as less than completely egocentric" (p. 266).

Murphy and Messer's (1977) subjects were 24 mother-infant pairs, 12 in which the infant was 9 months of age and 12 in which he was 14 months of age. The baby sat in a high chair and the mother sat next to him. Both faced a one-way window, in front of which were suspended one toy to their right, one to their left, and one directly in front of them. The mother was asked to direct her child's attention to the toys in any way she wished, provided that both remained seated. Mothers of both younger and older infants spontaneously used manual pointing as their principal attention-directing device, but also added other cues, such as tapping the baby's arm to get his attention. However, mothers of younger infants found they needed to use more vigorous cues, and also use them more frequently, than did mothers of older infants. The authors add that when mothers of 4–6-month-old infants are tested in this situation they resort to even more heroic attention-directing methods, e.g., physically turning the baby's head toward the target object. These mothers seemed aware that pointing did not mean much to babies that young, and so would ordinarily try to get them to look at objects by touching the objects or bringing them to the child. (Lempers has made similar informal observations.) In the same vein, the 9-month-olds but not the 14-month-olds tended to be successful in following their mothers' point only when pointing finger and object were in approximately the same visual field; this physical situation obtained when the object pointed to was on the mother's rather than the baby's side of center (see Murphy and Messer, 1977, Figure 1). This, too, accords well with Lempers' (1976) findings. The data from both studies are consistent with the conclusion that the infant first manages what might be called quasi- or pseudo-pointing problems, where pointing finger and object are simultaneously visible or even in physical contact, and only later manages genuine ones, where he must actually look away from the finger in a direction specified by its spatial orientation.

As the writings of Bruner, Schaffer, and their co-workers make clear, it would be a mistake to interpret these various acquisitions solely as indices of the infant's developing knowledge about visual perception (Bruner, 1974–1975; Collis, 1977; Collis & Schaffer, 1975; Murphy & Messer, 1977; Scaife & Bruner, 1975; Schaffer, 1977; see also Hughes, 1975). These acquisitions also reflect the baby's growing skill in social exchange and communication. More generally, they reflect the growth of complex cognitive and behavioral coordinations between infant and mother or other significant adult, with the two individuals being conceptualized as a single, dyadic unit of interaction. As we have seen, the infant gradually develops the ability to direct the mother's attention to the object of his attention by various nonsocial (pointing, showing) as well as vocal gestures. He also acquires the ability to interpret the mother's pointing and looking behavior. But the mother, of course, often engages in such behaviors for the express purpose of directing the baby's attention to the object of her own attention. Moreover, the mother diagnoses percepts as well as produces them. How often infants actually monitor their mothers' spontaneous looking behavior in everyday life is not known. It undoubtedly depends upon the age of the infant, the perceptual salience of the mother's looking behavior, and other factors. That mothers do a lot of spontaneous monitoring of their infant's visual attention, on the other hand, is a matter of common observation and has also been verified experimentally (Collis, 1977; Collis & Schaffer, 1975).

The important result of either party engaging in percept production, diagnosis, and probably even deprivation (as in peek-a-boo games) has been variously described as "synchronization of visual attention" (Collis & Schaffer, 1975), "co-orientation" (Collis, 1977), "joint visual attention" (Scaife & Bruner, 1975), or even more generally, "joint action" (Bruner, 1974–1975). As Collis puts it:

> The very essence of co-orientation is that it is a dyadic state defined by the orientation of *both* partners, and it is important that it should be conceptualized as such. Nonetheless, in the mother-infant case it is understandable that there should be particular interest in the developing capacities of the infant as a limiting factor and a source of change. There are two aspects of each partner's role to be considered, the emission of cues reflecting an interest in the environment and the responsiveness to such cues from the other individual. In the very youngest baby the main indication of localised interest is looking—cues from head and eye movements in fixation and tracking. These probably remain important sources of information throughout life but will be augmented by other cues. Firstly, swiping, reaching and grasping directed toward objects in the environment will develop. Later still comes the ability to point toward a distal object in the conventional manner and eventually the ability to label it verbally. Similarly, with responsiveness to potential maternal cues: from very early on the mother can best attract the infant's attention to objects by handling them. Later, responsiveness to the direction of mother's gaze (Masangkay et al., 1974; Scaife and Bruner, 1975) and the pointing gesture (Murphy and Messer, Chapter 13) will develop, and eventually the ability to comprehend the verbal representation of an object also appears . . . . (Collis, 1977, pp. 356–357).

See Bruner (1974–1975) for some intriguing speculations about how the prelinguistic development of various forms of joint action between mother and child might constitute an important foundation for the child's subsequent language development.

III. RECENT RESEARCH ON LEVEL 2 KNOWLEDGE

We have also recently begun some work on an essentially unresearched aspect of Level 2 competence. The point was made in the opening section that it is obviously possible for an *S* to know that object array X looks different to O than it does to S because their viewing positions are different, and yet not be able to figure out exactly how X does look from O's position. Such an S obviously possesses some Level 2 knowledge about visual perception, even though he cannot solve this particular Level 2 problem. A similar distinction was made with respect to Level 1 problems in Section I.

We have recently tried to explicate this distinction in the domain of Level 2 problems and have also done some developmental research based on it. The distinction is currently formulated as one between Level 2 *rules* and Level 2 *computation*. Computation refers to the actual cognitive processes used and behavioral steps taken by S to figure out ("compute") how a visible X appears to a visible O who views it from a specific, visible location in relation to X. S perceives X, O, and the spatial relation between them, and *from these data* constructs a representation (accurate or inaccurate) of how X looks to O. How might S obtain such a reading, i.e., through the use of what cognitive operations or processes? Several possible computational processes have recently been investigated (Huttenlocher & Presson, 1973; Marmor, 1975; Shantz, 1975). S might look at X and try to rotate it mentally so that the side facing O is now visualized as facing S; alternatively, he might try to mentally rotate himself into O's viewing position. S might also or instead try to build up a representation of O's visual experience by noting, say, that one object in the X array is closer to O than others are and located to O's left, presents its narrowest side to O, and partly obscures O's view of another object. It is not known at present exactly what cognitive operations and processes are used with what success in what sorts of Level 2 tasks by subjects of what levels and profiles of ability. There are, in fact, a number of fascinating questions to ask about the nature and development of Level 2 (and also Level 1) computation procedures.

Our current research is not directly concerned with Level 2 computational operations and processes, however. It is more concerned with the developmental attainment and use of Level 2 *rules*. These rules are somewhat reminiscent of the taxonomy of Level 1 knowledge given in Section II, in that they describe some very general things a Level 2 individual knows about Level 2 phenomena. They consist of the most basic facts about perspectives and perspective-taking, and express knowledge about very general relationships among O positions and O visual experiences. These relationships, with trivial exceptions, are invariant across X's. That is, the rules hold true regardless of the specific physical properties of X, and this fact illustrates a fundamental difference between rules and computation: To figure out how X looks to O by mental rotation of X or other methods of direct computation, S must be able to see X (or obtain equivalent iconic information about it by some other means). He obviously cannot mentally rotate an image of X, for example, if he cannot see X. In contrast, consider the completely general rule that S would see whatever view of X O sees, if S were to look at it from the same viewing position as O (Fishbein, et al., 1972). Just as obviously, the validity of this rule does not depend at all upon the specific nature of X, and S need never even see the X that O sees in a particular concrete problem to know that the rule would hold true for that problem. Like computational processes, however, rules can play a role in the solution of actual Level 2 problems. That is, they need not exist solely as abstract and unused knowledge about viewers and views. For example, it is hard to see why a child would ever use the computational strategy of mentally rotating himself into O's viewing position to solve a concrete perspective-taking problem if he did not "possess," in some sense, the general rule just mentioned. Just as rules can play a role in solving Level 2 problems, so also could computational processes achieve a general, rule-like status for the individual. He could come to know explicitly that mental rotation is a good general "rule" (i.e., rule of procedure, or solution rule) to use in perspective-taking problems, just as he could come to know explicitly that he would see X as O sees X if he were to view it from O's position (i.e., a "rule" in the sense used in this discussion).

It can be argued that Piaget and Inhelder (1956) and all of us who followed in their footsteps have largely failed to distinguish sufficiently between: (1) the child's knowledge of and ability to use general Level 2 rules; and (2) his knowledge of and ability to use spatial information-processing strategies which can generate or compute a specific view representation on the basis of concrete, here-and-now perceptual data about X's physical properties and O's location with respect to X. This distinction has not been made either frequently or very explicitly at the conceptual level (Flavell, 1974). It seems not to have been made at all at the experimental level, prior to a recent study by Salatas and Flavell (1976). The subjects in their study were 32 kindergartners (6-year-olds) and 32 second graders (8-year-olds). These children were tested for their command of two Level 2 rules: (1) *one O position implies only one view*—an O has one and only one view of X from any single viewing position; (2) *different O positions imply different views*—a particular view cannot normally[2] be seen from more than one viewing position around X, and hence different positions usually imply different views. The X in this study consisted of three girl dolls seated diagonally on a square board. There were four "observers," one on each side of the board: S, the child subject (0°); a small Donald Duck doll (90° to S's right); Goofy (180°); Micky Mouse (270°). S was first taken to each of these four viewing positions in turn and asked to select that picture (color photograph), from the set of four spread before him, which showed exactly how X appeared from that position. If the child selected the wrong picture, he was so informed and asked to choose again. Almost all subjects were identifying the correct picture on the first attempt by the time they reached the third or fourth viewing position.

Understanding of rule 1 was then tested by asking S to evaluate, one at a time, each picture from a larger set by answering the question, "Does this picture show how the dolls look to Observer A (S, or Mickey, etc.)?" This serial-choice procedure allowed the child to end up having chosen more than one picture as representing A's view. If he did select more than one, he was first asked if the ones chosen were all exactly the same (all children said they were not) and then asked if he still thought they all showed exactly how the dolls looked to A. The child was then tested for understanding of rule 2 by being asked if the selected picture(s) could also show exactly how the dolls looked to B (then to C, then to D). This whole two-part procedure was then repeated for Observer B, then for C, and then for D. The child was assumed to possess rule 1 to the extent that he consistently, over the series of four display positions, either chose only one picture initially, or else spontaneously reduced his selected set down to one when asked the second question. He was assumed to possess rule 2 to the extent that he consistently said that the picture(s) selected to show one observer's view would not show how the dolls looked to the other three observers.

The results suggested that rule 1 may be acquired earlier in childhood than rule 2. Of the 32 subjects at each grade level, 22 kindergartners and 28 second-graders consistently recognized that no more than one depicted view should be attributed to any one ob-

---

2. While rule 1 has no exceptions, rule 2 does. If X were a sphere uniformly illuminated from all sides, for example, one's visual experience of it would be the same from all station points.

server. On the other hand, only 7 kindergartners and 19 second graders consistently denied that one observer's depicted view could be seen by another observer at a different station point. This developmental ordering of these two rules seems plausible (Salatas & Flavell, 1976, p. 108). In addition, command of rule 2 does not appear to be as general and context-independent as we had thought, at least at this age level. A subject could initially (a) correctly identify a doll's depicted view, (b) make a nonegocentric error (selecting neither that doll's view nor his own), or (c) make an egocentric error (select his own). Which of these he did seemed to have some effect on adherence/nonadherence to rule 2 immediately after. That is, the child was likeliest to go on to say that the other observers could also see that same view, contra rule 2, if that view was egocentric (c), less likely if it was nonegocentric but incorrect (b), and least likely if it was correct (a). At the same time, it should be emphasized that the distinction between rules and computation was very much present in the data. For example, although 50 of the 64 subjects ended up selecting (computing) only one view per observer on all four trials of the test for rule 1, that single view was incorrect on at least one trial for all but 14 subjects. In the case of rule 2, similarly, 32 of the 148 correct view selections made were followed by at least one attribution of that same view to another observer, and 45 of the 108 incorrect view selections were followed by no such violations of rule 2. At some later age and/or under different task conditions, it is probable that one could further separate knowledge/use of rules from ability to compute views successfully. Under these circumstances, subjects "should always feel sure that the view from one location will not be exactly the same as the view from another . . . regardless of whether they are able to compute the exact appearance of either" (Salatas & Flavell, 1976, p. 108).

A sharp distinction of this sort was artificially created in a recently completed study by Flavell, Omanson, and Latham (Note 2). Its aim was to follow up and extend Salatas and Flavell's (1976) investigation. The perspectival rule studied was Salatas and Flavell's rule 2 (different positions implies different views) together with the corollary rule that two observers will have the same view of an array if they look at it from the same position (same position implies same view). Flavell et al. (Note 2) were interested not only in the development of knowledge of these rules but also in the possible development of the ability and disposition to use them in solving actual perspective-taking problems.

Each subject was given three types of problems, C, R, and RC. A total of eight problems of each type was presented in an alternating, cyclic sequence, e.g., R, C, RC, R, C, RC, R, etc. In C (computation only) problems, the child saw before him the Salatas and Flavell three-doll object array, a Donald Duck doll observer located 90° to his left and also facing the array, and two view pictures. On every problem (trial), one of these two pictures showed Donald's view of the array and the other showed the view from the opposite side of the array, that is, from a position 90° to the child's right. The array rested on a turntable so that it could be rotated into any of the four cardinal orientations on a given trial. C trials were conventional perspective-taking problems, in that the subject's task was to observe how the array was oriented in relation to Donald on that particular trial, and to select the picture that he thought showed Donald's view of it. At the outset of each C trial, the array was covered with a box and the two pictures were covered with a lid. After a ready signal, box and lid were removed simultaneously, and the subject made his picture selection by pressing the response button next to the chosen picture. Subjects were urged to press the appropriate button just as soon as they were sure which picture showed Donald's view. Removal of the lid started a timer and pressing either button stopped it. Response latencies were recorded in this fashion on every trial.

In R (rule only) problems, the array remained covered by the box throughout each trial. Although the subject could not see the array, Donald could see it through an opening on his side of the box, and there was a similar opening on the opposite side of the box. A second doll observer, Mickey Mouse, was also seen looking at the array on R trials, either standing right next to Donald (on R_s problems) or standing on the opposite side of the array (on R_d problems). A tag with Mickey's picture on it protruded from under the lid that covered the two view pictures; it was positioned directly to the right of the concealed picture that showed *Mickey's* view of the array on that particular trial. This tagged picture would of course also necessarily be the correct, Donald's-view picture on R_s trials, since the two dolls stand side by side on those trials, whereas the other, untagged picture would by elimination necessarily show Donald's view on R_d trials, during which they stood on opposite sides of the array. The subject was naturally not told the foregoing, but he was given ample opportunity to infer it, as the following instructions illustrate:

This tag tells you that this picture is how the dolls look to Mickey . . . . This tag is a hint. If you know how the dolls look to

Mickey, that can help you figure out how they look to Donald. Sometimes Donald will see the same thing as Mickey, so . . . this (shakes tag) will be the right answer. But sometimes Donald won't see the same thing as Mickey, so . . . this (indicates other concealed picture) will be the right answer.

The subject's task on each R trial was then to press the correct, Donald's-view button as quickly as possible after the lid was removed. Despite the impossiblility of ordinary computation in either case, since the array is never visible to the subject, it is apparent that R_d problems can be solved by applying rule 2 and R_s problems by using its corollary.

RC_s and RC_d (rule or computation) problems were identical to R_s and R_d problems, respectively, with the important exception that, as in C problems, the box was removed simultaneously with the lid. It was therefore possible to solve RC problems either by rule, by computation, or by some combination of the two. Since the location of the tag was visible on both R and RC trials before the timer was activated by removal of the lid, a subject who solves these problems by rule would achieve zero-order response latencies. That is, he could note the position of the tag, use rule or corollary to decide which picture must show Donald's view, and press the appropriate button the instant the experimenter lifts the lid. On the other hand, it took more than a second—usually several seconds—to solve an RC or C problem by computation, since subjects have to look at at least one picture and the array orientation before they can know which button to press, and the timer starts running the instant the pictures and array are exposed.

In each of two experiments carried out by Flavell et al. (Note 2), subjects were first familiarized with the three types of problems, then given the series of 24 test trials (8 C trials, and 4 each of subtypes R_s, R_d, RC_s, and RC_d), and finally given an inquiry concerning their methods of solution. Some procedural changes were made in Experiment 2, however, for the purpose of increasing diagnostic sensitivity, i.e., to reduce the gap between what subjects really knew and could do concerning these rules, and what they would actually demonstrate that they knew and could do. Probably the most important of these changes was the introduction of a 5-second "think period" between the initial setting up of each trial (description of what kind of trial it is to be, placement of the tag if it is to be an R or RC trial, etc.) and lid removal, i.e., the signal to respond. The child was told to "think about what you're going to do" at the beginning of each of these periods. The subjects in Experiment 1 were 24 children from each of grades 1, 3, and 5; in Experiment 2, 24 from each of grades 1 and 3. The changes introduced in Experiment 2 seem to have achieved their purpose: on most performance measures, as will be seen, Experiment 2 first and third graders tended to resemble Experiment 1 third and fifth graders, respectively, and age trends were not as clear-cut in Experiment 2 as in Experiment 1. Otherwise, the results of the two experiments were quite consistent.

As indicated above, Salatas and Flavell's (1976) data suggested that knowledge of rule 1 may be acquired earlier than knowledge of rule 2. In contrast, Flavell et al. (Note 2) found no evidence for any developmental ordering of rule 2 and its corollary. R_d problems did not seem to be systematically easier to solve than R_s problems, or the reverse. The data suggested, in fact, that most rule-using subjects probably conceived of them as two closely related parts of the same general fact about perspective. In all data analyses, therefore, R_s and R_d trials and RC_s and RC_d were collapsed into R and RC trials, respectively, and "rule 2" will henceforth refer to rule 2 plus its corollary.

Three response criteria were used to assess children's knowledge and use of rule 2. The first was selection of the correct view picture on seven of the eight R trials. The second was a response latency of less than one second on at least two R trials. As indicated earlier, latencies that short virtually never occurred on C trials. This fact, together with other evidence in the study, strongly suggests that fast responding usually reflected rule use. The third was verbalization of the rule in the posttest inquiry, e.g., "If Donald and Mickey are on the same side, how can Mickey and Donald see something different?"

Table 1 shows the percentage of children in each group who met the first criterion, the second, the third, none of the three, and all three (percentages are reported because the first few subjects tested in Experiment 1 were not given the inquiry). Since consistently correct responding to R problems could only be achieved by using rule 2, it is apparent from the Correct column of Table 1 that consistent use of the rule: (1) tended to become more frequent with age in both experiments; and (2), was relatively infrequent among first graders tested under Experiment 1 task conditions (which had no think period, etc.). There was also, in Experiment 1 only, an age increase in correct solutions to C problems (not shown in Table 1).

Table 1
Percentage of Subjects in Each Grade Meeting Criteria of Rule 2 Knowledge

		Criteria			
Grade	Correct	Latency	Inquiry	None	All
		Experiment 1			
1	17	29	24	67	9
3	54	42	68	32	37
5	71	67	96	4	58
		Experiment 2			
1	50	42	62	33	38
3	75	71	75	21	63

However, the ability to solve R and C problems was largely uncorrelated within each age group. It was interesting to note, in this regard, that some children who were perfectly consistent rule-users on R problems computed incorrectly on a number of C problems, and that a number of subjects who showed no evidence of rule knowledge or use anywhere in the testing session performed perfectly on C problems.

As Table 1 shows, the latency data closely paralleled the response correctness data. That is, there was an increase with age in fast responding to R problems in both experiments and there were relatively few fast responders among the Experiment 1 first graders. Frequency of fast-latency R trials in the test records tended to be either highly skewed or bimodally distributed, with approximately half to three-quarters of the subjects in each group responding in less than one second on either no trials or all eight. The latency measures were also useful in making inferences about how the RC problems were solved. We had expected that a number of subjects would understand and "trust" rule 2 enough so that they would elect to use it on RC problems as well as on R problems. We had also expected, however, that many subjects who used the rule on R problems might, perhaps understanding or trusting it less, shift to a computation strategy on RC problems; they might, in other words, use the rule when they had to (R problems) but compute when they could (RC and C problems). We were surprised to find that very few children did the latter. The product-moment correlations between the number of fast-latency R and RC trials were .86, .91, .95, .95, and

.89 for grades 1, 3, and 5 of Experiment 1 and grades 1 and 3 of Experiment 2, respectively. Moreover, subjects who met the 7/8 correctness criterion on R trials tended in inquiry to report solving RC problems by rule rather than computation. Some children did begin applying the rule to RC problems later in the series of 24 test trials than they applied it to R problems, but most children who used the rule on R problems sooner or later also used it on RC problems. For example, only one subject with no short-latency RC trials had more than three short-latency R trials, and only two subjects with eight short-latency R trials had fewer than six short-latency RC trials.

In Experiment 1 but not Experiment 2, there was also a marked increase with age in the percentage of subjects verbalizing rule knowledge and use during inquiry (Table 1). Table 1 also shows pronounced age trends in the percentage showing none and all three of the criteria of rule knowledge. The three criteria were highly correlated with one another, as might be expected, and there were some interesting relationships among them. For instance, if a child met either the response correctness or the latency criterion, he almost always went on to articulate the rule in the inquiry (a few even verbalized it spontaneously during the test trials). This suggests that those rapid, correct responses to R problems were in fact mediated by rule 2 knowledge—and often by consciously represented rule 2 knowledge, in all likelihood. The data also suggest that awareness of the possiblity of rule use came later rather than sooner for a number of subjects—not until the last few R and RC trials, or even not until the inquiry. Of the 13 subjects who met only one of the three criteria, that one was the inquiry criterion in 10 cases.

These data from Flavell et al. (Note 2) support several conclusions about both the psychological nature and the childhood development of this important Level 2 rule.

As to psychological nature, there was a variety of evidence for its psychological reality and salience in the thought and behavior of many subjects. Many of the older ones, particularly, appear to have (1) deliberately used it, (2) consciously represented it, and (3) strongly believed in it. Deliberate use and conscious representation of the rule are attested to by their many correct, short-latency R responses and inquiry reports of rule use on R problems. Salatas and Flavell (1976) showed that many children of elementary school age have some knowledge of rule 2. Flavell et al. (Note 2) appear to have shown that many will also deliberately and consciously use that knowledge to solve concrete perspective-taking problems. Strong belief in the rule is suggested by their marked tendency to solve RC problems by rule rather than computation. Recall that within-grade correlations between fast R and fast RC trials varied from .86 to .95, and that rule use on RC problems was often verbalized in inquiry.

The data also suggest that some cognitive development occurs with respect to rule 2 during middle childhood, although the evidence for this is stronger in Experiment 1 than in Experiment 2. Some subjects showed no sign whatever of knowing the rule, even under the seemingly very facilitative and "hospitable" testing conditions of Experiment 2. Others seemed to have a very high level, adult-like command of it. The rule knowledge of still other children appears to have been less well developed than that of this second group—perhaps less readily thought of as a solution procedure, less quickly and fluently applied to problems, or less easily formulated in thought or verbal expression.

IV. PROBLEMS FOR FUTURE RESEARCH

An account has now been given of a proposed distinction between two developmental levels of knowledge about visual perception (Section I), of recent research on the acquisition of Level 1 knowledge (Section II), and of recent developmental studies of Level 2 knowledge (Section III). Much scientific work remains to be done in each of these three categories. This final section will briefly describe some of the research possiblities.

Level 2 Research

Flavell et al. (Note 2) have suggested additional research that might be done regarding rule 2 (different positions implies different views) and its corollary rule (same position implies same view). Recall that Flavell et al. did not find evidence indicating that either of these rules was acquired earlier than the other, or even that subjects thought of them as two separate and distinct rules. It is possible, however, that a young child might use rule 2 less confidently and consistently than its corollary if: (1) one of the two observers were the child himself; or (2), the two different observer positions were less markedly different than they were in the Flavell et al. (Note 2) study. In the case of (1), egocentric tendencies or other factors might make a young child feel less certain that another person in a different position sees the object array differently than he himself does, than that two other persons in different positions see the array differently from one another. In contrast, egocentric tendencies should actually reinforce a child's belief in the corollary, when he is one of the two observers who view the array from the same station point. In the case of (2), rule 2 may seem less trustworthy when "different positions" means an angular separation of only 45°, say, rather than the extreme, 180° separation used by Flavell et al. (Note 2). In other words, we do not yet know how much generality children of different ages attribute to rule 2—in the instances just mentioned, generality across observers and across magnitude of difference in their viewing positions. Research techniques of the type designed by Flavell et al. (Note 2) might be used to find out.

There is at least one other Level 2 rule that people could acquire, namely, that right-left and front-back relations among array objects are reversed for two observers who view the array from directly opposite sides. For example, if object 1 appears to S to be leftward and rearward of object 2, it will necessarily appear rightward and forward of object 2 to an O who views the two objects from the opposite side. Once again, Flavell et al. (Note 2) type methods might be used to find out if and when the developing individual learns that this rule is valid for every possible object array, provided that O is located directly opposite S.

The core meaning of Level 2 seems to be that one goes beyond the mere representation that O sees X (Level 1) to a representation of the particular nature or content of O's visual experience of X. We had been assuming that this Level 2 representation could only include a narrowly defined spatial-perspective kind of experience, i.e., what view of X is experienced from a particular station point. Omanson and the writer now believe that there may be other possibilities, however. O might not only see the left-rear vs. the right-front side of X—the conventional, perspective-taking meaning of Level 2. She might also see X partly vs. fully, unclearly vs. clearly, with ease vs. with difficulty, or distortedly vs. undistortedly. These too are descriptions or qualifications concerning how O sees X; like descriptions of O's perspective, they too are "comments" on the "topic"

O-sees-*X*. As such, they appear to conform to the core meaning of Level 2 representations of people's seeing experiences. At the same time, they seem somewhat different from the perspective-taking form of Level 2. For one thing, they are more clearly dimensional than the latter. We can say that *O* sees a tiny *X* "better" (more clearly and completely, etc.) when he gets close to it and "worse" when he moves away from it, but we cannot so consistently differentiate one view of *X* from another along any single, ordered dimension of this sort. Moreover, the dimensions are usually evaluative, referring to more vs. less adequate or "good" visual processing of *X*. This evaluative quality makes these forms of Level 2 knowledge seem more ecologically significant than the perspectival ones—and hence seem more similar in this respect to Level 1 knowledge. That is, while it often may not matter much to a perceiver exactly what view of an object she sees (Level 2 perspective-taking), it does often matter to her how well she sees it (these newly identified forms of Level 2 knowledge), just as it matters whether or not it is seen at all (Level 1 knowledge). It would be interesting to find out if these newly identified forms develop earlier than the perspectival ones, precisely because of their putatively greater ecological importance; recall the suggestion made in Section I that this may be one reason why Level 1 knowledge develops earlier than Level 2 knowledge. When, for example, do young children become aware that an *O* can see a small object better (more clearly, in finer detail) when it is one foot away from her eyes than when it is, say, ten feet away? When do they begin to infer that an *O* cannot see objects as adequately in poor light as in good, with other objects partially blocking *O*'s view as with none, through a dirty window as through a clean one? Are there distinguishable developmental steps in the acquisition of these cognitive achievements? These are some of the questions for developmental research suggested by this broadened conception of Level 2 knowledge about visual perception.

Level 1 Research

There is obviously a great deal more to learn about the ontogenesis of Level 1 knowledge about percept production, deprivation, and diagnosis, as well as about the functional connections between these developments and concomitant developments in the young child's social relationships.

On the percept production side, our knowledge of the developmental course of both pointing and showing is still very fragmentary, but there are hypoyheses that could be tested. For example, observations by Lempers et al. (1977) suggest that there could exist a three-step developmental sequence in showing ability. According to this hypothesis, S develops the ability to show: (1) first, a visible X to a visible O; (2) then, an invisible X to a visible O; (3) finally, either a visible or an invisible X to an invisible O. An example of (1) would be holding up a real object so that O (and also S) can see it, or holding an object picture flat between S and O so that both can see the depicted object. Recall that Lempers et al.'s 12-month-olds did the former and their 18-month-olds did the latter. Thrusting a picture vertically towards O, so that O sees the depicted object while S does not, illustrates (2); this was the favored method of showing of Lempers et al.'s 24-month-olds. The following is an instance of (3): S is on one side of an open door or a screen and O is on the other, with neither person visible to the other; S shows his hand to still-unseen O by holding it out beyond the door frame or the edge of the screen. As mentioned in Section III, only about half of Lempers et al.'s 36-month-olds succeeded on that showing task. It should not be overly difficult to test this developmental hypothesis experimentally.

Further work on percept deprivation abilities is also needed. Flavell, Shipstead, and Croft are currently assessing the ability of young children (29–48 months of age) to: (1) hide a small object from O by putting it behind a small, upright wooden stand (mobile X, immobile A); (2) hide the same object by putting the stand between object and O (immobile X, mobile A); (3) recognize that O still sees the object when only a part of it is concealed from her view by a board interposed between her and the object. Most of the subjects tested perform perfectly on (1), while only a minority do so on (2) and (3).

There are also research opportunities in the area of percept diagnosis. One would be to make more rigorous tests of the suggestion about early pointing comprehension mentioned in Section II. The suggestion was that infants progress from solving only quasi- or pseudo-pointing problems, where both O's pointing finger and the pointed-at object are simultaneously visible to the infant, to solving genuine pointing problems, where the direction of O's point must be followed beyond the present visual field. A careful, psychophysical type experiment would be needed here. It would systematically vary such factors as the visual-angle distance (in S's visual field) of X from the pointing finger, the presence/absence of intervening (non-pointed-at) objects along the child's point-following visual trajectory, and the direction of the point in three-dimensional space relative to the child's viewing position. The research objective would be to find out how successful babies of different ages are at visually locating the target object under these various conditions, and then to make up a plausible scientific story about the development of pointing comprehension based upon these results.

Research on the Level 1–Level 2 Distinction

Are there really two qualitatively different and ontogenetically sequenced "levels" of knowledge about visual perception? It could be argued that most of the past and proposed research described in this chapter would still seem worthwhile even if our Level 1–Level 2 distinction finally proved completely untenable, because the developing knowledge and abilities researched seem basic and important in their own right. At the same time, the Level 1–Level 2 distinction seems theoretically significant, if empirically valid, and one would consequently like to know if it is, in fact, empirically valid.

The presently existing evidence for its validity cited in Section I is uncomfortably meager. Moreover, some recent developmental data obtained by Liben (Note 3) might be interpreted as at least raising questions about the distinction. The subjects in her study were 100 children, 20 each at ages 3, 4, 5, 6, and 7. In her task, the experimenter showed the child a white card and asked first, "What color does this card look like to you?", and then, "What color do you think this card looks like to me?" The latter obviously qualifies as a Level 2 rather than a Level 1 type question. These same questions were repeated, in varied order, under these three conditions: (1) with the child wearing yellow sunglasses and the experimenter none; (2) with the experimenter wearing green ones and the child none; (3) with the child wearing yellow ones and the experimenter wearing green ones.

Condition (1) seems the best test of the three, since the child could not get the right answer to the second question by simply naming the color of the experimenter's sunglasses, as would obviously be possible in conditions (2) and (3). The responses of Liben's (1975) 20 3-year-olds to this task condition are of greatest interest, since children this young would not be expected to be able to solve Level 2 problems, on the basis of Masangkay et al.'s (1974) findings. Of the 20, 3 said the card looked white to *them*, yellow glasses notwithstanding. Of the remaining 17 who said it looked yellow to them, 7 said it looked white to the experimenter (correct response), 6 said it looked yellow to the experimenter (egocentric response, presumably), 1 said it looked green to her, and 3 said they did not know. The correct responses of those 7 subjects are open to at least two interpretations. One possiblity is that, like the three children who said the card looked white to them, they may simply be telling the experimenter what color the card really is, rather than what color it appears to be when seen through the glasses. Like describing the color of the experimenter's sunglasses rather than her visual experience in conditions (2) and (3), merely describing the actual color of the card would obviously not reflect any sort of percept inference, Level 1 or Level 2. Another possiblity is that these 7 subjects were in fact demonstrating a nonperspectival form of Level 2 knowledge. Perhaps this form develops earlier than the conventional perspectival one, as we earlier suggested could be the case with other nonperspectival forms. Which of these possibilities is true, if either, will have to await further studies using Liben's (Note 3) or related task procedures.

Additional evidence on the Level 1–Level 2 distinction is currently being gathered by Flavell and Abrahams. They are continuing the research strategy initiated by Masangkay et al. (1974): (1) devise and administer pairs of tasks that differ as little as possible, except for the level of knowledge about visual perception demanded for their solution; (2) predict that the Level 1 member of each pair will be significantly easier for young children than the Level 2 member of that same pair. One step in this strategy is simply to try to replicate Masangkay et al.'s findings with their Picture (Level 1) and Turtle (Level 2) tasks. Another is to create pairs of tasks that appear to differ less than the Picture and Turtle tasks do in aspects other than the crucial one. This is accomplished by constructing Level 1 and Level 2 versions of essentially the same task, thereby keeping the task materials and procedures more constant within each task pair. The Level 2 Turtle task has already been described (Section I). In a Level 1 version of it currently being used, the experimenter holds a large card vertically over the horizontal turtle picture and touching it. The card is positioned in such a way that it simultaneously blocks the experimenter's view of the turtle's back and the child's view of the turtle's legs. The critical question to the child is then whether the experimenter sees one part-object of the total turtle object (its back) or another part-object (its legs). The task thus becomes a Level 1 problem of *what* object *O* sees, like the Picture task, rather than a Level 2 problem of *how* an object that both *S* and *O* see *looks* to *O* (e.g., "upside down"), as in the original Turtle task. Unlike the Picture tasks, however, the content and spatial orientation of the picture used is of course identical to that used in the Level 2 Turtle task. A second two-version task has also been devised in the same manner. Results to date indicate that all Level 1 tasks used are in fact much easier for 3-year-olds than all Level 2 tasks used.

The possession of a whole battery of such two-version tasks would do more than permit a number of independent tests of the Level 1–Level 2 distinction. It would also make it possible for us to find out how easy or hard it is to get Level 1 children to think in a Level 2 fashion. This might be an important question to answer for the following reason. There are two possible interpretations of the Level 1–Level 2 distinction. One is that it reflects a rather profound difference in how the child basically represents visual perception: people simply see things (Level 1) versus people also see particular views or appearances of the things they see (Level 2). The other interpretation is that the distinction only reflects a difference in what or how many features of the visual input are attended to or coded in the child's representation of others' visual experience. If this latter interpretation is the correct one, it might be reasonable to suppose that a child who currently solves only Level 1 problems could fairly quickly and easily be trained to solve Level 2 problems. If the former interpretation is correct, successful training should be harder to implement, since the change involved is presumed to be more deep-lying, more in the nature of a "world view." While these are certainly not necessary implications from the two positions, they seem plausible. With a number of tasks at our disposal, good training studies could be carried out. We could use some tasks as pretests and posttests, others as training vehicles, and still others to test for near and far transfer of training. As has been shown in the area of Piagetian acquisitions, training studies tend to produce data that are somewhat ambiguous and inconclusive in interpretation, and this will probably also prove true in the present case. Nonetheless, they should give us a clearer idea than we now have of just what the Level 1–Level 2 distinction amounts to, psychologically and developmentally.

VI. SUMMARY

This chapter describes recent theory and research in one limited area of social-cognitive development, namely, the childhood acquisition of knowledge about visual perception. The author and his co-workers have hypothesized that there are two developmental levels of such knowledge. At earlier-developing Level 1, the child understands that others as well as the self see objects, and is also able to infer correctly what objects they do or do not currently see if provided with adequate cues. At later-developing Level 2, the child understands not only that people can see objects, but also that they can have differing visual experiences while seeing the same object; most notably, they can have different spatial-perspectival views of it when looking at it from different positions. Arguments and evidence for the developmental distinction between Level 1 and Level 2 knowledge are briefly presented in Section I. A more detailed model of Level 1 knowledge is presented in Section II, together with an account of several studies of its development during the first four years of life. During these early years, children appear to learn a great deal about how to produce visual percepts in others (showing and pointing to things), how to deprive others of percepts (hide objects), and how to diagnose the percepts they currently have (follow others' direction of gaze and pointing gestures). Section III similarly reviews recent theory and research on the development of Level 2 perspective-taking knowledge in older children. This work is focused mainly on the acquisition and use of very general perspective-taking rules, such as the rule that two observers who look at an object array from the same spatial position must on that account necessarily have identical perspectival views of the array. Section IV describes further developmental research that could be or is being done on Level 2 knowledge, Level 1 knowledge, and on the Level 1–Level 2 distinction.

REFERENCE NOTES

1. Flavell, J. H. *The development of metacommunication.* Paper presented at the Symposium on Language and Cognition, International Congress of Psychology, Paris, 1976.

2. Flavell, J. H., Omanson, R. C., & Latham, C. *Solving spatial perspective-taking problems by rule vs. computation: A developmental study*. Unpublished manuscript, Stanford University, 1976.
3. Liben, L. S. *Young children's performance on traditional and modified perspective-taking tasks*. Paper presented at the meeting of the Society for Research in Child Development, Denver, April 1975.

REFERENCES

Bruner, J. S. From communication to language—a psychological perspective. *Cognition*, 1974–1975, **3(3)**, 255–287.

Chandler, M. J., Social cognition: A selective review of current research. In H. Furth, W. Overton, & J. Gallagher (Eds.), *The yearbook of developmental epistemology* (Vol. 1). New York: Plenum, 1976.

Coie, J. D., Costanzo, P. R. & Farnill, D. Specific transitions in the development of spatial perspective-taking ability. *Developmental Psychology*, 1973, **9**, 167–177.

Collis, G. M. Visual co-orientation and maternal speech. In H. R. Schaffer (Ed.), *Studies in mother-infant interaction*. London: Academic Press, 1977.

Collis, G. M., & Schaffer, H. R. Synchronization of visual attention in mother-infant pairs. *Journal of Child Psychology and Psychiatry*, 1975, **16**, 315–320.

Fishbein, H. D., Lewis, S., & Keiffer, K. Children's understanding of spatial relations: Coordination of perspectives. *Developmental Psychology*, 1972, **7**, 21–33.

Flavell, J. H. An analysis of cognitive-developmental sequences. *Genetic Psychology Monographs*, 1972, **86**, 279–350.

Flavell, J. H. The development of inferences about others. In T. Mischel (Ed.), *Understanding other persons*. Oxford: Blackwell, Basil & Mott, 1974.

Flavell, J. H. *Cognitive development*. Englewood Cliffs, N.J.: Prentice-Hall, 1977

Flavell J. H., Botkin, P. T., Fry, C. L., Wright, J. W., & Jarvis, P. E. *The development of role-taking and communication skills in children*. New York: Wiley, 1968.

Flavell, J. H., & Wellman, H. M. Metamemory. In R. V. Kail & J. W. Hagen (Eds.), *Perspectives on the development of memory and cognition*. Hillsdale, N.J.: Lawrence Erlbaum Associates, 1977.

Gelman, R. Logical capacity of very young children: Number invariance rules. *Child Development*, 1972, **43**, 75–90.

Glucksberg, S., Krauss, R. M., & Higgins, T. The development of communication skills in children. In F. Horowitz (Ed.), *Review of child development research* (Vol. 4). Chicago: University of Chicago Press, 1975.

Hughes, M. *Egocentrism in preschool children.* Unpublished doctoral dissertation, University of Edinburgh, 1975.

Huttenlocher, J., & Presson, C. L. Mental rotation and the perspective problem. *Cognitive Psychology*, 1973, **4**, 277–299.

Laurendeau, M., & Pinard, A. *Development of the concept of space in the child.* New York: International Universities Press, 1970.

Lempers, J. D. *Production of pointing, comprehension of pointing and understanding of looking behavior in young children.* Unpublished doctoral dissertation, University of Minnesota, 1976.

Lempers, J. D., Flavell, E. R., & Flavell, J. H. The development in very young children of tacit knowledge concerning visual perception. *Genetic Psychology Monographs*, 1977, **95**, 3–53.

Lickona, T. (Ed.). *Moral development and behavior: Theory, research and social issues.* New York: Holt, Rinehart & Winston, 1976.

Livesley, W. J., & Bromley, D. B. *Person perception in childhood and adolescence.* London: Wiley, 1973.

Marmor, G. S. Development of kinetic images: When does the child first represent movement in mental images? *Cognitive Psychology*, 1975, **7**, 548–559.

Masangkay, Z. S., McCluskey, K. A., McIntyre, C. W., Sims-Knight, J., Vaughn, B. E., & Flavell, J. H. The early development of inferences about the visual percepts of others. *Child Development*, 1974, **45**, 357–366.

Murphy, C. M., & Messer, D. J. Mothers, infants and pointing: A study of a gesture. In H. R. Schaffer (Ed.), *Studies in mother-infant interaction.* London: Academic Press, 1977.

Piaget, J., & Inhelder, B. *The child's conception of space.* London: Routledge & Kegan Paul, 1956.

Salatas, H., & Flavell, J. H. Perspective taking: The development of two components of knowledge. *Child Development*, 1976, **47**, 103–109.

Scaife, M., & Bruner, J. S. The capacity for joint visual attention in the infant. *Nature*, 1975, **253**, 265–266.

Schaffer, H. R. Early interactive development. In H. R. Schaffer (Ed.), *Studies in mother-child interaction.* London: Academic Press, 1977.

Shantz, C. U. The development of social cognition. In E. M. Hetherington (Ed.), *Review of child development research* (Vol. 5). Chicago: University of Chicago Press, 1975.

Distinct Conceptual and Developmental Domains: Social Convention and Morality

Elliot Turiel

University of California, Santa Cruz
and Institute of Human Development
University of California, Berkeley

*C*onventions are part of all systems of social organization, including those at the level of society. As behavioral uniformities which coordinate the interactions of individuals within a social system, social conventions constitute an integral aspect of social systems. It has been proposed by this author (Turiel, 1975, in press; Note 1) that the understanding of social conventions is related to the individual's conceptualization of social organization. It has also been proposed that moral prescriptions play a different role in the social sphere from that of social convention and that individuals' moral judgments are distinct from their concepts of social convention. Moral judgments are based, not on concepts of social organization, but on concepts of justice. Accordingly, the thesis to be presented in this article is that social convention and morality (a) constitute two distinct conceptual domains, which (b) develop independently of each other and (c) stem from different aspects of the individual's social interactions.

The proposed distinction between social convention and morality is part of a broader theory of development and social cognition. Thus, this chapter has two aims: to present theory and research on social convention, as distinguished from morality, and to present the broader theoretical framework. The chapter begins with a discussion of the definitional basis for distinguishing social convention from morality and then reviews research findings on the developmental course of social-conventional concepts. This review is followed by a consideration of the implications of the distinction between social convention and morality for the individual's understanding of an aspect of the social environment: rules and regulations. Finally, the developmental model of domains of social cognition is presented.

I. SOCIAL CONVENTION AS DISTINGUISHED FROM MORALITY

In contrast to the theory of social convention presented here, there has been a tendency in analyses of social development to relegate convention to underdeveloped states of social systems or to undeveloped states of the individual. For instance, the moral evolution of social systems has been described as a process of differentiating principles of justice from conformity to conventions (Hobhouse, 1906). Such a view of societal evolution assumes that (a) less developed *moral* systems are based on conformity to conventionally defined social rules and values and (b) more advanced moral systems are based on principles, which are distinguished from conventional social rules and values. The implication of this viewpoint is that individuals in "primitive" societies merely conform, without reasoning, to the rules and conventions of their social system. (This perspective on "primitive" peoples, however, has been criticized by Levi-Strauss, 1966; Malinowski, 1926; Shweder, 1977.)

Such an approach to the evolution of social systems has its parallel in psychological explanations of the development of the individual's moral judgments. It has been proposed that moral development entails a process in which principles of justice are progressively differentiated from conventions (Kohlberg, 1969, 1971, 1976; Loevinger, 1976; McDougall, 1908; Piaget, 1932). The scheme generally proposed is one in which the individual's moral development progresses from a state of conformity to the conventions of the social system, to a state of self-accepted autonomous and principled moral reasoning. A dichotomy is thereby drawn between the nonreasoning or conformist states of individuals at earlier developmental levels and the reasoning or principled states of individuals at advanced developmental levels.

In the explanations of individual development, conventional regulation and moral regulation are treated as part of the same conceptual and developmental package—i.e., as one domain. This theoretical perspective can be referred to as a "differentiation" model in that moral reasoning emerges through its differentiation from nonmoral processes: At lower developmental levels convention and morality are presumed to be undifferentiated, while at higher levels the two are differentiated in such a way that morality displaces convention. The basis for viewing such a differentiation process as a developmental sequence seems to be that societal rules and conventions are deemed as "simpler" than more "complex" moral ideals.

Related to the "differentiation" model of reasoning is the assumption that individuals conform to social conventions rather than comprehending their functions in social interactions and social organization. This assumption also needs to be questioned as it is not consistent with research findings to be discussed later in this chapter. If we focus on the phenomena of culture and social organization in themselves (i.e., independent of moral issues), it becomes apparent that they are not simple to comprehend. Indeed, anthropologists and sociologists provide complex and abstract theories in efforts to explain cultural systems and social organizations. Nor should it be assumed that social scientists are the only ones who seek to understand and explain social organizations and their conventional regularities; the developing child, too, forms concepts regarding the social units in which he participates.

An alternative view, therefore, is that social convention and morality should not be treated as part of the same conceptual and developmental package, but as distinct domains (Turiel, in press). In this regard, two separate questions require investigation: (a) How does the individual think about culture and social organization, and (b) How does the individual make moral judgments? In turn, these two questions require separate developmental analyses; if moral and conventional concepts are organized into distinct domains, it must be assumed that their course of development is also distinct.

This distinction can be clarified by considering the definition of social convention (Turiel, Note 1). Social conventions are behavioral uniformities which coordinate the actions of individuals participating in a social system. As such, conventions constitute shared knowledge of uniformities in social interactions. Examples of social-conventional acts include uniformities in modes of dress, usages of forms of address (e.g., first name or titles plus last name), and modes of greeting. Research has shown that these conventional uniformities are based on accepted usage and regulated by social organization. For instance, it has been found (Brown & Gilman, 1960; Slobin, Miller, & Porter, 1968) that usage of forms of address reflects the relative social status of individuals within a social organization (e.g., a business firm). Similarly, modes of greeting serve to maintain social distance, thereby reflecting accepted status distinctions within the social structure (Foster, 1964; Goody, 1972).

Social-conventional acts, in themselves, are arbitrary in that they do not have an intrinsically prescriptive basis. Therefore, alternative courses of action can serve identical functions. That is, a conventional uniformity within one social unit may serve the same function as a different conventional uniformity in another social unit. Consider, for example, conventional uniformities regarding modes of dress. Typically for males, formal attire (e.g., suit and tie) is worn in certain social contexts (e.g., a business firm or place of religious worship) and the content of this conventional uniformity is arbitrarily designated. For instance, uniform modes of dress other than suit and tie could just as well be designated as appropriate for the business office or church.

In the case of conventions, therefore, the specific content of the regularity can be varied without altering the functions served; conventional uniformities are defined relative to the social situational context. Accordingly, within the conventional domain, it is only violations of implicit or explicit regulations that can be considered transgressions. For an individual to regard a particular act as a transgression, he or she would have to possess culture-specific information about the act's status as a socially determined regularity. This is not the case in the moral domain, where the existence of a social regulation is not necessary for an individual to view an event as a transgression. If, for example, one hits another, thereby causing physical harm, an individual's perception of that event as a transgression stems from features intrinsic to the event (e.g., from a perception of the consequences to the victim). Moral issues are neither arbitrary nor relative to the social context.

The distinction between convention and morality implies a narrow definition of morality as justice. It is proposed that children develop concepts of justice which apply to a relatively limited range of issues, including the value of life, physical and psychological harm to others, trust, responsibility, etc. In contrast to convention, moral considerations stem from factors intrinsic to actions: consequences such as harm inflicted upon others, violation of rights, effects on the general welfare. It is on this basis that a distinction is made (Turiel, in press) between (a) convention, which is part of social systems and is structured by underlying concepts of social organization, and (b) morality, which is structured by underlying concepts of justice. (For analyses of the development of justice concepts see Damon, 1975; Kohlberg, 1969; Piaget, 1932; Turiel, 1974.)

The distinction between social convention and morality can also be illustrated by comparing two experimental paradigms that have been used in the study of social behaviors: the Milgram (1963) "obedience" experiments and the so-called "forbidden toy" paradigm. In this regard, it is important to keep in mind that experiments—particularly those measuring social behaviors—are social situations. Consequently, social expectations and conventions constitute an aspect of experimental situations (Turiel, in press). In the Milgram obedience experiments, under the guise of a learning experiment subjects were instructed to administer electric shocks to another person. In the forbidden toy paradigm (Aronfreed & Reber, 1965; Cheyne, 1971; Parke, 1967; Parke & Walters, 1967) subjects were restricted from playing with some toys that were available in the experimental room. In one variant of the paradigm, for instance, the subject was prohibited from playing with the more attractive of a pair of toys.

The Milgram and the forbidden toy experimental situations share a common feature: The experimenter provides the subject with instructions as to how to behave. However, the two experimental situations are fundamentally different in regard to the nature of the action required of the subject. In one case the subject is required to inflict pain upon another person, while in the other case the subject is restricted from playing with a specified toy. The action involved in the obedience experiments is not an arbitrary one and falls within the definition of the moral domain. Subjects can perceive the intrinsic consequences involved in administering painful electric shocks to an unwilling person. This experimental situation essentially poses subjects with a conflict between (a) their moral evaluation of the event (hurting another person), and (b) their perception of the rules and conventions established by the experimental instructions (Turiel, in press). In contrast, the restriction in the forbidden toy paradigm is an arbitrary one established by the experimenter and solely related to the purposes of the experiment. In these situations the experimenter could just as well establish an opposite prohibition and restrict the subject from playing with the less attractive of the pair of toys; any number of such "arbitrary" restrictions could be established. Given the arbitrary nature of the restriction imposed, it is likely that subjects would view it as a convention specific to the interactions within the experimental situation (see Turiel, in press, for elaboration and documentation of this point[1]).

1. Classifying the restrictions in the forbidden toy experiments as conventional represents a reinterpretation of an experimental paradigm that has generally been

Having introduced the theoretical distinction between social convention and morality, the next step is to summarize the results of an investigation of the development of social-conventional concepts. The study discussed in the next section deals with social convention as an aspect of concepts of social systems.

II. A DEVELOPMENTAL ANALYSIS OF CONCEPTS OF SOCIAL CONVENTION

Anthropologists and sociologists have theorized extensively about the structure of social systems and their customs and conventions. As stated earlier, it is plausible to suppose that the members of the social system, like social scientists, engage in efforts to explain its structure. Moreover, if individuals form concepts about social systems, it follows that they would form concepts about the function of conventions within the social system. It is also plausible to suppose that at least by early childhood, when the individual is engaging in group activities, concepts of social convention and social structure would begin to develop.

The study of the development of the individual's concepts of social conventions has been based on these premises. In one study (Turiel, in press) 110 subjects ranging from 6 to 25 years of age were administered an interview that revolved around a series of hypothetical stories. Each of these stories dealt with a form of conventional usage, about which subjects were extensively probed. The stories dealt with (a) forms of address (a boy who wants to call teachers in school by their first names), (b) modes of dress (dressing casually in a business office), (c) sex-associated occupations (a boy who wants to become a nurse caring for infants when he grows up), (d) patterns of family living arrangements in different cultures (fathers living apart from the rest of the family), and (e) modes of eating (with hands or knife and fork). A concrete example of the type of story used in the interview is the following, which deals with forms of address: The story concerns a boy, brought up by his

used for the purpose of studying moral behavior. However, I have maintained (Turiel, in press) that the imposed restriction is arbitrary and that, therefore, subjects are most likely to view the restriction as a convention specific to the social interactions of the experimental situation. In that light, I have also maintained that the results of the forbidden toy experiments can be best interpreted as demonstrating that subjects behave in accordance with the perceived conventions of the experimental situation.

Table 1
Major Changes in Social-Conventional Concepts

Approximate
Ages

1. *Convention as descriptive of social uniformity.* 6–7
Convention viewed as descriptive of uniformities in behavior. Convention is not conceived as part of structure
or function of social interaction. Conventional uniformities are descriptive of what is assumed to exist. Convention maintained to avoid violation of empirical uniformities.

2. *Negation of convention as descriptive social uniformity.* 8–9
Empirical uniformity not a sufficient basis for maintaining
conventions. Conventional acts regarded as arbitrary.
Convention is not conceived as part of structure or function of social interaction.

3. *Convention as affirmation of rule system; early concrete
conception of social system.* 10–11
Convention seen as arbitrary and changeable. Adherence
to convention based on concrete rules and authoritative
expectations. Conception of conventional acts not coordinated with conception of rule.

4. *Negation of convention as part of rule system.* 12–13
Convention now seen as arbitrary and changeable regardless of rule. Evaluation of rule pertaining to conventional act is coordinated with evaluation of the act. Conventions are "nothing but" social expectations.

5. *Convention as mediated by social system.* 14–16
The emergence of systematic concepts of social structure.
Convention as normative regualtion in system with un-
iformity, fixed roles, and static hierarchical organization.

6. *Negation of convention as societal standards.* 17–18
Convention regarded as codified societal standards.
Uniformity in convention is not considered to serve the
function of maintaining social system. Conventions are
"nothing but" societal standards that exist through
habitual use.

7. *Convention as coordination of social interactions.* 18–25
Conventions as uniformities that are functional in coordinating social interactions. Shared knowledge, in the
form of conventions, among members of social groups
facilitate interaction and operation of the system.

parents to call people by their first names, who is expected to address teachers in his new school by their formal titles. He comes into conflict with the teachers and principal who insist that he use titles and last names rather than first names.

The analyses of responses to the interview showed that there is a progression of social-conventional concepts from childhood to early adulthood (Turiel, in press), a progression which is summarized by the seven levels presented in Table 1. The levels represent age-related changes (the correlation of the levels with age was found to be .90) in social-conventional concepts that can be reliably classified (Turiel, Note 1). These findings are supplemented by another study (Damon, 1977) of children from 4 to 9 years of age. Damon interviewed his subjects, using hypothetical stories dealing with sex-typed behaviors (a boy who likes to play with dolls) and modes of eating. In Damon's research, the levels found (levels 1, 2 and 3) within the age range studied directly replicated the ones identified in Table 1.

The levels described in Table 1 show that judgments made about conventions are related to underlying concepts of social organization. Thus, the development of social-conventional concepts progresses toward (a) viewing conventions as shared knowledge of uniformities in interactions within social systems, and (b) viewing such uniformities as functional to the coordination of social interactions. At all levels, however, conventions are understood to be social constructions. Throughout the sequence, two factors are salient. One is the conceived arbitrariness of social-conventional acts, and the other is the conceptual connections made between such acts and the societal context. Each level, then, reflects a change in the conceptualization of social systems on the one hand, and in the understanding of the connections between convention and social structure, on the other.

In addition, it should be noted that the development of social-conventional concepts does not follow a simple linear course. Development involves a pattern of oscillation between the affirmation and negation of concepts of convention and social structure. This pattern of oscillation reflects the process of development within the social-conventional domain. In each affirmation phase there is a construction of concepts of convention and social structure. Each phase of affirmation is followed by a negation of the validity of that construction. The negation phases entail a reevaluation of the social structure conception of the previous level and thereby provide the basis for the construction of concepts at the next level. Consequently, each phase of negation leads to a new construction of concepts of convention and social structure. These observed patterns of affirmation and negation are consistent with the proposition that conceptual development is a self-constructive process (Langer, 1969; Piaget, 1970b; Turiel, 1974). It is the individual's own reevaluation of existing concepts that prepares the way for the construction of new concepts.

In what follows each of the seven levels are briefly described. More detailed descriptions can be found elsewhere (Turiel, in press).

Level 1. The first level represents an affirmation phase. Thinking about social conventions at this level is distinguished by assumptions made regarding social uniformities. Insofar as social convention has relevance to these children's thinking it is related to the meaning attributed to what are perceived to be uniformities in behavior. Uniformities in social behavior are not understood to be means for coordinating social interactions or as part of a social system; rather, they are descriptive of behaviors and are, on that basis, interpreted as requiring conservation. As examples, for children at this level titles are viewed as associated with classes of people (e.g., child, adult), or certain occupations (e.g., nurse, doctor) are viewed as associated with the class of male or female.

The following responses from a 6-year-old subject provide an illustrative example. This story deals with a young boy who wants to become a nurse caring for infants when he grows up, but his father thinks that he should not do so.

SHOULD HE BECOME A NURSE?
Well, no, because he could easily be a doctor and he could take care of babies in the hospital.

WHY SHOULDN'T HE BE A NURSE?
Well, because a nurse is a lady and the boys, the other men would just laugh at them.

WHY SHOULDN'T A MAN BE A NURSE?
Well, because it would be sort of silly because ladies wear those kind of dresses and those kind of shoes and hats.

WHAT IS THE DIFFERENCE BETWEEN DOCTORS AND NURSES?

Doctors take care of them most and nurses just hand them things.

DO YOU THINK HIS FATHER WAS RIGHT?
Yes. Because well, a nurse, she typewrites and stuff and all that.

THE MAN SHOULD NOT DO THAT?
No. Because he would look silly in a dress.

These subjects interpret observed behaviors or physical traits of classes of persons as essential to the classification. This notion was clearly apparent in subjects' consideration of whether or not a male could become a nurse. It was maintained that two types of (nondesirable) violations of empirical uniformity would result if a male became a nurse: type of activity and type of dress. Activities and physical characteristics (e.g., dress) serve to classify roles and persons for these subjects. The role of a nurse is defined by (a) activities like taking care of babies, giving injections, typewriting, etc., and (b) wearing a particular kind of dress. In turn, females are defined by similar activities and types of dress. According to subjects at this level, if a male were to become a nurse the necessary associations of activities or dress to the classes male and female would be violated because a male would be engaging in female activities and wearing female dress. Insofar as there is a conception of social structure at this level, it is based on the perceived status distinctions that stem from empirical uniformities.

Level 2. At the second level there is negation of the basis by which social convention was affirmed at the first level. It is asserted that empirical uniformity is not a sufficient basis for judging behaviors as necessary, fixed, or requiring conservation. It is understood that there may exist (or at one time there may have existed) uniformities in these behaviors; however, uniformity does not imply necessity. The empirical associations of activities, roles, or labels (e.g., titles) with classes of person are no longer seen as necessary associations. An 8-year-old subject stated it as follows:

Right, because it doesn't matter. There are men nurses in the hospitals.

WHAT IF THERE WERE NOT ANY IN JOE'S TIME, DO YOU STILL THINK HE SHOULD HAVE DONE IT?
Yes. It doesn't matter if it is a man or woman it is just your job taking care of little children.

WHY DO YOU THINK HIS PARENTS THINK HE SHOULD NOT TAKE CARE OF LITTLE KIDS?
Because his father might be old-fashioned and he would think that men could not take care of babies.

WHY DO YOU THINK HE THINKS THAT?
Because it is a lady's job, because ladies know what babies are because they have them.

YOU DON'T THINK THAT IS TRUE?
No. Because ladies are the same and men might know a lot about babies too.

The most salient feature of the social-conventional thinking at this level is that the acts are regarded as arbitrary. It is assumed that there is no intrinsic basis for acting one way or the other. On the basis of the assertion of the arbitrariness of these actions, subjects at the second level negate the necessity for convention. However, children at this level have yet to construct an understanding of convention as a means for coordinating social interactions.

Level 3. Subjects at the third level still regard social-conventional acts as arbitrary—in the sense that it is assumed that there is no intrinsic basis for the action. At this level, however, there is a concrete conception of social structure: social-conventional acts are evaluated in relation to the rules and authoritive expectations which are part of a social system. Social relationships are now seen as governed by a system in which individuals hold positions of authority, such as principals or teachers in a school or employers in a business firm. The authority is seen to come primarily from the power of individuals in such positions. Rules pertaining to conventions (i.e., acts otherwise regarded as arbitrary) are viewed as requiring adherence. Additionally, it is assumed that maintenance of an existing social order is based on conformity to rules and authoritative expectations.

At this level, therefore, conventions are contingent upon the social context: rules and authoritative expectations require adherence to the conventions. The demands of authority or existing rules may vary from one context to the next—as from one school to another. However, in each context conventions should be maintained if there are authoritative expectations or rules pertaining to them. The following response from an 11-year-old subject provides an illustrative example:

DO YOU THINK PETER WAS RIGHT OR WRONG TO CON-
TINUE CALLING HIS TEACHERS BY THEIR FIRST NAMES?
Wrong, because the principal told him not to. Because it was a
rule. It was one of the rules of the school.

AND WHY DOES THAT MAKE IT WRONG TO CALL A
TEACHER BY HIS FIRST NAME?
Because you should follow the rules.

DO YOU THINK IF THERE WEREN'T A RULE, THAT IT
WOULD BE WRONG—OR WOULD IT BE RIGHT TO CALL
TEACHERS BY THEIR FIRST NAMES?
Right. Because if there wasn't a rule, it wouldn't matter. . . . It
wouldn't matter what they called her if there wasn't a rule.

Subjects at the third level regard social-conventional acts as arbitrary, in the sense that it is assumed there is no intrinsic basis for the
action. Apart from concrete rules or specific demands for compliance from authorities, conventional acts are not seen as necessary. In the absence of rules or authoritative expectations, conventions like forms of address, modes of dress, or manner of eating "do
not matter." However, rules pertaining to conventions (i.e., acts
otherwise regarded as arbitrary) are viewed as requiring adherence.
Additionally, rudimentary notions of social order emerge at this
level. It is assumed that maintenance of an existing social order is
based on conformity to rules and authoritative expectations. For
subjects at this level, therefore, the evaluation of what are regarded
as arbitrary conventional acts is dependent upon whether or not a
rule exists. This means that the subject's conception of convention is
not coordinated with his conception of rules or social context. That
is, the rule is treated as obligatory and invariable even though it
pertains to an act which is otherwise treated as variable.

Level 4. At the fourth level, rules and action are coordinated and
there is a concomitant negation of convention. At this level the
conception of conventional acts as arbitrary is maintained, as was
the case with subjects at the previous two levels. Unlike subjects at
the third level, however, subjects at the fourth level coordinate their
evaluation of an act with the evaluation of the rule or expectation to
which the act pertains. Given that conventional acts are viewed as
arbitrary, it is maintained by these subjects that rules or expectations
about such acts are not valid. For instance, the use of titles or mode
of dress are regarded as arbitrary. It is the ability to communicate

with others that these subjects regard as important; names are seen as ways of identifying people, and they assume that communication can be achieved via the use of first names or titles. Similarly, modes of dress have little meaning to these subjects. It is believed that these kinds of decisions are up to individual choice: Individuals have the right to make their own choice of how to address teachers or how to dress.

The change from the third to the fourth level in the conception of rules pertaining to conventional acts results in the view that conventions are *nothing but* the expectations of others. This orientation stems from an awareness that expectations do indeed exist regarding what appear to these subjects as arbitrary acts. Consequently, social expectations are rejected as an insufficient basis for prescriptions of behavior.

Level 5. The third and fourth levels can be viewed as forming the foundations for concepts of convention as mediated by social structure; at the third level conventions formed part of uncoordinated concepts about concrete rules and authoritative expectations. The fourth level, which constitutes a negation of convention through the coordination of conventional acts and prescriptions (rules and expectations), leaves the adolescent without a systematic understanding of the organization of social interactions. At the fifth level, there is the formation of systematic concepts of social organization. Subjects at the fifth level have formed notions about the role of individuals within social units or collective systems. Social units are defined as systems of individuals interconnected in an organization with a hierarchical order.

At this level, convention is defined as shared behavior mediated by common concepts of society. Normative characteristics are viewed as central to social units. Conventionally shared behavior is necessary because of the function served by uniformity in the social system. At this level, therefore, convention is viewed as normative regulation in a system with uniformity, fixed roles, and hierarchical organization.

There are two distinguishable phases in the fifth level. During the first phase uniformity is a defining characteristic of a collectivity, and adherence to conventional uniformities is necessary for participation in the social system. In the second phase, uniformity represents a general consensus that is codified and that functions to maintain the social order.

During the first phase social acts are judged in relation to a group or social system in which the individual is subordinate. For these subjects, the individual's adherence to uniformities is a necessary accommodation to the group in order to be a participant. Participation in group or collective life is not considered an obligation for the individual; however, if an individual is part of the group, then adherence to its uniformities is necessary. Deviance from the prescribed behavior is a violation of the legitimate expectations of others who are part of the group. In the following example from a 17-year-old we can see how uniformity is related to the social system:

DO YOU THINK PETER WAS RIGHT OR WRONG TO CONTINUE CALLING HIS TEACHERS BY THEIR FIRST NAMES?
I think he was wrong, because you have to realize that you should have respect for your elders and that respect is shown by addressing them by their last names.

WHY DO YOU THINK THAT SHOWS RESPECT?
Informally, you just call any of your friends by their first names, but you really don't have that relation with a teacher. Whereas with parents too, you call them Mom and Dad and it's a different relation than the other two.

WHAT IF PETER THOUGHT IT DIDN'T MAKE ANY DIFFERENCE WHAT YOU CALLED PEOPLE, THAT YOU COULD STILL RESPECT THEM NO MATTER WHAT YOU CALLED THEM?
I think he'd have to realize that you have to go along with the ways of other people in your society.

In the second phase of this level the conception of social systems is extended. While in the first phase uniformity in conventions is related to group participation, in the second phase it is also assumed that conventional uniformities in social groups, particularly at the societal level, are also necessary for its maintenance. Convention represents common or shared knowledge on the part of the members of a social system. Conventions are determined by general acceptance and are thereby binding on all members. Furthermore, the nature of relations between members of a social group are determined by social organization. For instance, the relation between student and teacher is determined by the social context of the school. Within the school context, the use of titles represents a uniform means for signifying the student-teacher relation.

Having formed systematic concepts of social organization, subjects at the fifth level now define society as hierarchically ordered. Individuals are thereby classified on the basis of their role and status within the system. Conventions symbolize roles, status, and competence. Status distinctions place constraints upon relationships, such that interactions between individuals of unequal status require conventional usages (e.g., forms of address). In this sense, conventions are seen to regulate those relations between individuals which are determined by the social context and relative to the status of the actors.

Level 6. The formation of concepts of the social system in which conventions are interpreted as societal standards providing uniformity leads to the view, at the sixth level, that conventions are "nothing but" societal expectations. The negation of convention at the sixth level represents a rejection of the reasoning of the previous level. Conventions are still regarded as part of the social system in that they are defined as codified societal standards that serve the purpose of providing uniformity of behavior within the group; at the sixth level, however, uniformity, per se, is no longer regarded as a necessary condition for the adequate functioning of social systems. Diversity or variation in the behavior of individuals is seen as compatible with the organization of a social system. Without the uniformity requirement, conventions are regarded as arbitrary dictates. Furthermore, it is assumed that conventions exist not to serve societal functions but because they have become habitual. Convention is perpetuated by tradition. At this level tradition means the existence of conventions that have become unquestioned standard procedures.

Level 7. The seventh level is marked by the conceptualization of conventions as integral elements of the interactions of groups of people in stable relationships (e.g., school, business firm, society) forming an organizational system. The basic function of convention is to coordinate interactions between individuals and to integrate different parts of the social system. Conventional acts are regarded as arbitrary in that alternative courses of action may be equally valid. However, uniform or specified courses of action on the part of members of the social system are agreed-upon and shared modes of behavior. The purpose of these uniformities is to coordinate interactions and thereby facilitate the operation of a social system. As one 19-year-old subject put it:

WHAT WOULD YOU PREFER TO BE CALLED OR TO CALL A TEACHER?

I don't really care, it is not what you call them, but what you think calling them a certain thing means. I would just address the teacher by what I thought was conventional and be thinking all the time or have established in my mind what my relationship with the teacher is. The name doesn't really matter.

WHY WOULD YOU DO WHAT WAS CONVENTIONAL?
Because it is the easiest thing to do. If I did something unconventional than I would have to stop and explain to the teacher why I am doing things that are unconventional and it is really trivial, the reason for it.

WHAT ARE THE REASONS FOR CONVENTIONS?
Well, conventions make things move along smoothly and also—are most consistently understandable communication. If something involved in the communication of two people involves a certain way, if you communicate with somebody about something, you probably have some conventional way of talking about the thing you want to communicate and the person you are trying to communicate to is also familiar with the general way of communicating this convention. Therefore he is able to follow you more quickly because he automatically is familiar with the way you start to do something, if it is the conventional way of doing something. So he doesn't have to stop and think how is that working, how is this thing said, because he has already been familiar with it. It shortens the process in many cases.

DO YOU THINK IT IS EVER WRONG TO GO AGAINST CONVENTIONS?
It is wrong if quickness of communication is of great importance. Then obviously doing things that are unconventional or communicating things in an unconventional manner slows up the thing which is communicated. Or whatever you are doing, if you are not communicating, if you are going about a way of building up a building or you have a conventional way of doing it you might think of another way which is no quicker, but is just a different way to do it. And if everyone was unfamiliar with it, the building might be built in just as quick a time because you have to spend time communicating to everybody else just everything about it. You have to explain it to them and if they haven't been exposed to it, it slows up the time of the thing that you are trying to accomplish.

For subjects at this seventh level, therefore, convention is based on common or shared knowledge and its primary function is to facilitate social interactions. Violations of conventions produce the "inconveniencies" stemming from the failure to coordinate interactions or to maintain a social organization. It is assumed that individuals adhere to convention on the bases of (a) the expectation that others do so, and (b) the view that conventional acts are arbitrary (i.e., there are no intrinsic consequences to the act).

III. THE INDIVIDUAL'S UNDERSTANDING OF SOCIAL REGULATIONS

A natural outgrowth of our studies of social convention has been a concern with a major form that conventions take, that of explicit rules or regulations. Before considering a series of studies on children's concepts of social rules, it is necessary to clarify how this term is being used. It is not limited, by any means, to regulations within social domains; it may be used in several different ways (Black, 1962), including the nonsocial "instructional" sense (as in rules about how to shift gears in an automobile) and the prudential or pragmatic sense (such as "do not touch the hot stove"). Other nonsocial uses of the term include "rules" pertaining to the physical and mathematical realms.[2]

Of greater relevance to the present purposes is how individuals distinguish among social rules. It is the proposed distinction

2. In a recently completed study (in collaboration with D. Weston) we found that children discriminate between social and nonsocial forms of regularity. In that study, 5-, 6-, and 7-year-old subjects were presented with two stories depicting children who had engaged in social transgressions and one about a child who had made an arithmetical error: In one story a child took something belonging to another child; in a second story a child violated a prohibition against eating in designated areas of the home; in the third story a child maintained that one plus one equals three. In each of these stories a parent observed the child's actions. Subjects were asked whether or not the parent should and would punish the child for the depicted act. While many subjects stated that punishment should and would be administered for the social transgressions, virtually all subjects stated that the child making the arithmetical error should not be given any form of punishment. If we take as an indicator the judgment that parental punishment should be administered, these findings show that young children, at some level, understand the social nature of certain regulations and discriminate them from nonsocial uniformities.

between rules in the conventional domain and rules in the moral domain that was the subject of the series of studies to be reviewed in this section. The findings of these studies clarify the differences between these two types of regulations and provide evidence for the more general thesis that social convention and morality constitute distinct conceptual domains.

Recognizing the salience of rules and regulations in the child's social environment, social scientists have given a fair amount of attention to the study of behavioral reactions to prohibitions and conceptions of regulations (Aronfreed, 1968; Durkheim, 1925/1961; Hogan, 1973; Piaget, 1932; Sears, Maccoby, & Levin, 1957; Tapp & Kohlberg, 1971). Failing to recognize that rules can have different meanings, however, they have generally assumed that regulations are of one kind and that individuals possess a unitary concept of rules. However, a rule always pertains to an action (or class of actions) and, as has been maintained throughout, actions can be classified according to domain. Therefore, from this perspective, it is hypothesized that individuals would not possess a unitary conception of rules; rather, the meaning and functions attributed to a rule would vary on the basis of the domain of the action to which the rule pertains. If it is the case that moral concepts are distinct from social-conventional concepts, then the meaning attributed to rules pertaining to moral acts (e.g., stealing) would be different from the meaning attributed to rules pertaining to social-conventional acts (e.g., use of titles in forms of address). That is, judgments made about the origins, changeability, relativity, enforcement, and functions of any given rule will, in part, depend upon the domain to which the rule pertains.

Let us first consider examples of children's interview responses which illustrate the basis for the distinction between rules pertaining to moral acts and rules pertaining to social-conventional acts. It will be recalled that it was stated that social-conventional acts, in themselves, are arbitrary, and that such acts have no intrinsically prescriptive basis independent of social organization; this orientation to convention is reflected in each of the seven levels described in Section II. It was also stated that moral acts are not defined by their social context, but by factors intrinsic to actions. Consequently, subjects would not be expected to evaluate the validity of moral acts on the basis of social regulations. In the course of the social-conventional interview (as discussed in section II), subjects 10 years of age and above were asked to respond to a hypothetical situation about a social context in which stealing from others was not considered wrong and in which no rules or laws prohibited stealing. The responses of a 10-year-old boy whose social-conventional concepts were at level 3 (see Table 1) illustrate how he distinguished between the two types of rules. Specifically, he was questioned about a story in which an adolescent boy had cheated an old man out of money. The subject was asked whether or not cheating would be wrong if no rule or law prohibited such cheating and if everyone agreed it was acceptable. The interview proceeded as follows:

I still think that would be wrong.

WHY?
Because you're still cheating the old man. It doesn't matter whether he's stupid enough or not, and it's not really fair to take the money.

WHAT DO YOU MEAN, IT'S NOT FAIR TO STEAL?
It's not nice to do it, because maybe he needs it too.

WHAT IF THE RULE WERE CHANGED ABOUT CALLING PEOPLE BY THEIR FIRST NAMES SO THAT EVERYBODY COULD CALL THEIR TEACHERS BY THEIR FIRST NAMES? DO YOU THINK IT WOULD BE RIGHT OR WRONG IN THAT CASE TO DO IT?
I think it would be all right then because the rule is changed. Right? And everybody else would probably be doing it too.

HOW COME THE TWO THINGS ARE DIFFERENT?
Because it's sort of a different story. Cheating an old man, you should never do that, even if everybody says you can. You should still never cheat off an old man.

Another subject, who was 13 years old and at level 4, responded as follows to similar questions:

SUPPOSE THAT IN PETER'S FAMILY THEY DON'T CARE ABOUT CHEATING FROM AN OLD MAN. THEY CONSIDER IT ACCEPTABLE TO CHEAT SOMEONE OUT OF MONEY IF THE PERSON WAS STUPID ENOUGH TO ALLOW HIMSELF TO GET SWINDLED. WOULD IT BE RIGHT OR WRONG IN THAT CASE TO CHEAT SOMEONE OUT OF $500?
Wrong.

WHY IS THAT?
They are still taking something away and they said they would
help someone, so it doesn't really matter what they think, it is
what they do. And what they say.

WHAT DO YOU MEAN?
Well, what difference does it make that they think it was right or
they think it is wrong, because it is still not right, it is still the
same thing, what they think.

WHAT IF THE RULE WAS CHANGED FOR EVERYONE AND
THERE WAS NO LAW AGAINST CHEATING OR BAD FEEL-
ING ABOUT CHEATING. EVERYONE THOUGHT IF THEY
WERE STUPID ENOUGH TO GET CHEATED, IT WAS
WORTH IT. DO YOU THINK IT WOULD STILL BE WRONG
TO DO IT?
Yes.

WHY?
No matter what the law is or the rule, it doesn't change it being
right or wrong.

From these subjects' responses it can be seen that the relationship
between a moral act and a rule is conceptualized differently from the
relationship between a conventional act and a rule. This is not
specific to the age group of the subjects cited; like these two subjects,
the majority of subjects in all the age groups maintained that stealing
would be wrong regardless of the existence or nonexistence of rules
or laws.

Although moral and social-conventional concepts undergo developmental changes, the conceived relation of act and rule in each
domain has a basic component that is constant across development.
First consider the relation between a moral act and a corresponding
rule. In these cases, the regulations are explicit formulations of
moral prescriptions. *The rule stems from the act to which it pertains.* An
example might be a rule prohibiting theft. In this example, the rule
stems from the judgment that it is wrong to steal someone else's
possessions. The rule, therefore, is an explicit formulation of a
prescription regarding the justice or injustice of an action (or class of
actions); there is a necessary relation between act and rule. Thus, the
rule is justified on the basis of factors intrinsic to the act. Judgments
and evaluations about a given rule would correspond to judgments
and evaluations of the act to which it pertains. If an act is intrinsically

valued, then a rule pertaining to the act would be viewed as unchangeable and universally desirable. Furthermore, the aims served by the rule would not be regarded as specific to a given social context.

In regard to the social-conventional domain, the premise is that *the rule does not stem from the act* to which it pertains. As already stated, since social-conventional acts are arbitrary, such uniformities serve to coordinate interactions within a social system. A rule is an explicit formulation of the uniformity. Thus, the uniformity leads to the rule, which guides the action. Since this aim can be served by a variety of actions, such rules would be viewed as changeable and relative to their social context. It can be seen, therefore, that in the conventional domain the act-rule relation is different from that in the moral domain: i.e., in the conventional domain there is no necessary relation between act and rule.

A series of studies have been done with subjects of various ages to determine if the relation between acts and rules is conceived in the way just outlined. In one study (Nucci and Turiel, in press), preschool children were questioned about spontaneously occurring moral and social-conventional events (as classified by our criteria) that they had observed. The children were asked: "What if there were no rule in the school about (the observed event), would it be right to do it then?" When questioned about social-conventional events, in 81% of the cases the children stated that the act would be right if no rule existed in the school. When questioned about moral events, in 86% of the cases the children stated that the act would *not* be right even if no rule existed.

Using a somewhat different method, Nucci (1977) has extended this type of investigation to include subjects ranging in age from 7 to 19 years. In the Nucci study subjects were presented with a series of statements describing transgressions of rules pertaining to moral and social-conventional acts; they were then requested to select those statements which described acts that they considered "wrong regardless of the absence of a rule." At each of the five age groups (grades 2, 5, 7, 11, and college sophomores) subjects selected almost all the statements depicting moral transgressions and very few of the statements depicting social-conventional transgressions.

The findings from the Nucci and Turiel and the Nucci studies support the hypothesis that judgments about acts within the moral domain are not based upon social regulation, while judgments about social-conventional acts depend on their status as regulations within a social context. There were no age-related differences in this regard; the same responses were made by 4-year-olds and 19-year-olds.

Additional aspects of judgments about the relation of rules to social contexts were examined in a study conducted by D. Weston and this author. The purposes of that study can best be explained by first describing the procedures. Two hypothetical situations, in story form, were presented to subjects (ages 5, 7, 9, and 11 years). One story, which deals with an act in the moral domain, describes a school in which children are allowed to hit (and hurt) each other. A second story, dealing with a social-conventional act, describes a school in which children are allowed to be without any clothes. In each case subjects were asked (a) whether or not it was all right for the school to allow the act, and (b) to evaluate the act of a child who engaged in the action (i.e., hitting another child or removing one's clothing). Thus these procedures were designed to examine how children think about the presence or absence of rules within certain social contexts.

Our expectation was that within the moral domain evaluations would be based on the act and not on the social context (i.e., whether a rule exists). Accordingly, it was predicted that subjects would negatively evaluate a social context that allows hitting. In contrast, within the conventional domain our expectation was that evaluations of the act would be based on what is designated in the social context, since alternative acts (dress or undress) can be legitimately prescribed.

The findings were in accord with these expectations:

(1) The majority of subjects in each age group stated that it was not all right for the school to permit hitting, because such a policy would result in harm to persons. Correspondingly, the majority of subjects stated that it would be wrong for a child to adhere to that policy.

(2) The majority of subjects in each age group stated that it was all right for a school to permit children to remove their clothes, because it is up to the school authorities to determine the presence or absence of such rules. The majority of subjects also stated that it would be all right for a child to adhere to that policy.

One last study (Turiel, Note 1) in this series speaks to the issue of the relativity of rules. The subjects in this study ranged in age from 6 to 17 years. They were interviewed about a variety of moral and social-conventional rules, some of which they had generated (e.g., rules in their homes and schools) and some of which were presented by the experimenter. As part of a moral general inquiry, subjects were questioned about their view of the relativity of these rules (e.g., Suppose there is another country in which the rule does not exist?). As expected, it was found that subjects discriminated between the two types of rules on the dimension of relativism and universality. Most subjects at all ages, on the one hand, regarded the conventional rules as legitimately changeable from one setting to another, and, on the other hand, did not regard the moral rules as legitimately changeable from setting to setting.

In sum, the pattern of results presented supports the hypotheses regarding social regulations. These hypotheses have implications for some of the research that has been done on social cognition and behavior. First, they have a bearing upon experimental studies of children's reactions to prohibitions and restrictions (Aronfreed & Reber, 1965; Cheyne, 1971; Parke, 1967; Parke & Walters, 1967). In those experiments, no domain distinctions have been made among the acts being prohibited; it is assumed that the effects of prohibitions are the same regardless of the type of action involved. For example, in experiments using the "forbidden toy" paradigm discussed earlier (Section I), it has been assumed that the restriction upon playing with designated toys can be used to study the learning of moral prohibitions. The findings summarized here, however, suggest that children are not likely to react to all types of prohibitions in similar ways, and it is likely that they would not regard a restriction on playing with a toy as a moral one.

In addition, the findings clearly demonstrate that in the study of conceptions of social rules, inquiries should not be made of subjects about "rules" as a general category (as in Tapp & Kohlberg, 1971); given that various meanings are attributed to rules, responses to such questions would be ambiguous. Moreover, the findings indicate that it is inappropriate to generalize from the study of one type of rule, such as game rules (Piaget, 1932), to other types of rules. (For a more detailed discussion of this issue see Turiel, in press.)

In summary, the studies reviewed show that the meaning and functions attributed to rules vary according to domain. Furthermore, the results of this series of studies support the proposition that social-convention and morality constitute two distinct conceptual systems. We have seen that subjects ranging from 4 to 19 years of age distinguished the two domains. Nevertheless, important questions remain regarding what may appear to the reader as less clear-cut instances of a separation between social convention and morality. For example, there are situations that contain both moral and conventional issues, either in conflict or in synchrony with each other. Additionally, there are instances, such as with sex-typed uniformities, in which conventions may result in injustices to groups of people. However, these examples do not contradict the position presented; rather, they raise questions that can best be answered by explaining how the two conceptual systems are coordinated and/or confused with each other.

As a heuristic device, I have chosen to postpone investigation of possible coordinations and confusions between the two systems until the domains are better understood. In this view, explanations of how domains are coordinated first requires explanations of the conceptual domains involved. Moreover, a fuller understanding of the domains we have discussed here can be achieved by placing them into a broader theoretical framework. Toward this end, the chapter will be concluded by sketching out the parameters of a theory of the development of domains of social cognition.

IV. SOCIAL COGNITION: A DOMAIN ANALYSIS

Three assumptions about social cognition and development form the starting point for this analysis. The first is that individuals develop conceptual frameworks or "theories" which serve to *structure* social phenomena. The second assumption is that these social conceptual frameworks are *constructed* out of the individual's interactions with the environment. The third assumption is that individuals utilize *methods* for gathering information or data from the social environment.

These assumptions constitute the basis for the model of domains of social cognition presented here. In order to understand social cognition it is necessary to distinguish between (a) the individual's knowledge of extrinsic information, as obtained through the methods, and (b) the individual's concepts about relations among social phenomena. The individual extracts and reproduces information about people, about interactions between people, and about systems of social organization. Under the general category of social information we may include knowledge about: the behaviors and existing psychological states (thoughts and feelings) of specific persons; the composition of individuals within social groups; the rules, laws, and regulations of social systems; the institutions existing within specific societies, etc. These forms of social information are extracted and reproduced through the use of what may be referred to as methods, which include such activities as *observation, communication, imitation,* and *symbolically taking the perspective of another* (commonly labeled role-taking). As methods of information gathering, these activities serve as means for representing social information, without directly producing conceptual transformations. Thus, through the use of methods the individual attempts to accurately reproduce what is given in the external environment. This does not mean, of course, that information is necessarily reproduced accurately. Inaccuracies in the reproduction of data, however, needs to be distinguished from conceptual constructions (however adequate or inadequate), through which meaning is formed and inferences made.

It is being proposed, therefore, that the methods do not form organized systems but rather unitary skills. Since the methods are means for extracting and reproducing data, they are not transformational systems. In turn, methods do not undergo structural changes in ontogenesis. Insofar as there are age-related changes in the methods, they are *quantitative* rather than qualitative ones. With age, methods may increase in accuracy and scope.

As already indicated, cognitive activities are not limited to information gathering. Individuals also develop conceptual frameworks, which are ways of structuring or organizing the social environment. It is the conceptual frameworks that undergo qualitative changes (reorganizations) in ontogenesis. Thus the development of conceptual frameworks entails step-wise changes in the structure of thought. And, in turn, the level of conceptual development will influence the type of information or level of information complexity sought through the methods discussed above.

Three fundamental domains of social concepts can be identified: the *moral, societal,* and *psychological.* The moral and societal domains have already been discussed. The presentation of the sequence of changes in social-conventional concepts represents a developmental analysis of a conceptual domain (i.e., the societal). The third domain, the psychological, refers to concepts of the person. Analogous to the interpretation of social-conventional concepts as demonstrating that individuals attempt to explain cultural and social systems, it can be maintained that individuals attempt to explain the person as a psychological "system" (Heider, 1958; Jones & Davis, 1965; Kelly, 1967; Ross, 1977).

Within the psychological domain, attribution theorists working with adult subjects have researched and theorized about judgments regarding the causes of behavior, inferences about attributes of persons, predictions of behavior, and biases in attributions (see Ross, 1977). It is only recently that the developmental study of psychological concepts has begun to receive some attention. Research has been reported on the development of concepts of personal identity (Lemke, 1973; Wolfson, 1972), of personality dispositions (Pratt, 1975), and of cognitive processes (Flavell & Wellman, 1977; Gordon & Flavell, 1977). In addition, Josephson (1977) has examined children's predictions of others' behaviors, and N. Gordon (1976) has studied the development of concepts of others' emotional states. Nucci's (1977) summary of some of this research suggests that children do not form stable concepts of the person until approximately 6 to 8 years of age. It appears that in the absence of such concepts, younger children rely primarily upon situational factors to explain behavior.

In summary, the broader theory proposes (a) that the methods serve different cognitive functions from conceptual frameworks, and (b) that conceptual domains are analytically as well as ontogenetically distinct from each other. It would take us too far afield to consider questions regarding relations between methods and conceptual frameworks or between the different conceptual domains. However, some hypotheses have already been mentioned. In regard to the methods, it has been hypothesized that conceptual development may influence and set limits to the type of methods used; this issue is briefly considered below. With respect to the conceptual domains, it has been hypothesized that the relationship between them is that of informational exchange rather than of structural interdependence. That is, at any given point in development different conceptual domains may be coordinated with each other.

In the remainder of this section aspects of the model will be elaborated. First, as a means of explaining what is meant by methods of information gathering, and how such methods differ from conceptual frameworks, one example is considered: the activity of taking another's perspective (role-taking). Role-taking is being used as an illustrative example because it has often been assumed (in my view incorrectly) to be a structural-developmental dimension, and because it has been the object of much research and thus a good deal of data is available which can be used to illustrate what is meant by a method. The developmental basis for distinguishing between conceptual domains is then considered.

A. An Example of a Method: Role-Taking

Consider the following hypothetical situation. Person A, for whatever reason, wants to know what person B is thinking or feeling during a particular interaction between the two of them. Were person B to communicate verbally what he is thinking or feeling (assuming he would do so honestly), then person A would have the sought-after information. In the absence of such a communication, person A can observe B's behavior and/or symbolically place himself in B's position (role-taking) and thereby attempt to obtain the information. In this case, the use of role-taking would constitute a more indirect way of obtaining the information than through verbal communication; however, in some situations role-taking may be the only means available.

As illustrated by this example, role-taking (a) represents the attempt to symbolically put oneself in the place of another, and (b) serves the (limited) function of obtaining information about the other. Alternative activities, such as communication or observation, can serve the same function. Information about the other, once obtained, may then be put to varied conceptual uses (such as to make a medical diagnosis, or to swindle the person, or for a moral end). However, the role-taking activities or the information derived through such acts do not in themselves constitute concepts about the person, although they are influenced by existing conceptual structures. Moreover, given that role-taking is a symbolic activity, the development of representational thought would be a prerequisite for its emergence.

The proposition that role-taking serves information-gathering functions is not in accord with most of the theoretical explanations of role-taking put forth, but is consistent with the research findings. Discussions of role-taking and perspectivism go back to Piaget's (1926, 1928, 1932) early work on communication, spatial perspectives, and moral judgment. Piaget proposed that children's cognitive development progresses from an egocentric orientation in which there is a failure to differentiate between subject and object (self and other), and thus an inability to take the perspective of another, to a nonegocentric orientation, in which the self is differentiated from the other and there is the ability to take another's perspective. At the time, Piaget viewed this progression as reflecting a general dimension of qualitative transformation in the child's cognitive functioning. (Since that time Piaget's theory has undergone major revision [1970b], as have his views on egocentricism [1962, 1970a]).

As Flavell (1974, and this volume) points out, contemporary research on role-taking (e.g., Byrne, 1973; Chandler & Greenspan, 1972; Feffer & Gourevitch, 1960; Flavell, Botkin, Fry, Wright, & Jarvis, 1968; Looft, 1972; Selman, 1976) was stimulated by some of the Piaget and Inhelder (1956) research on spatial perspective-taking ability. In one task (the Three Mountain task) Piaget and Inhelder presented subjects with a model landscape of three different-sized mountains and tested their ability to identify the appearance of the mountains to observers in various positions other than their own (see Flavell's chapter in this volume for a detailed description). The finding that children below the ages of 8 or 9 years attributed their own perspective to others in different locations has been taken as an affirmation of Piaget's original proposition that in cognitive development there is a general and qualitative change from egocentricism to perspectivism. Subsequently, attempts were made to characterize sequentially ordered stages of role-taking development (Feffer & Gourevitch, 1960; Selman, 1976; Selman & Byrne, 1974; Shantz, 1975).

However, the view that development progresses from a general egocentric orientation to a perspectivistic orientation is not supported by the available evidence. That is, the findings of a variety of studies on role-taking have not shown anything like the expected patterns of consistent change from egocentricism to role-taking. Instead, it has been found that the presence or absence of similar types of role-taking responses, in subjects as young as 3 or 4 years and as old as 12 to 13 years, vary according to the type of task and experimental method used. For instance, Flavell et al. (1968) administered a battery of tasks and found wide variability on the average ages at which subjects displayed role-taking responses. On some visual perception tasks children as young as 3 or 4 years engaged in role-taking, while on other visual perception tasks role-taking was not displayed until 12 or 13 years of age. Correspondingly, on some communication tasks children showed role-taking responses by the age of 6 or 7 years, while on other tasks requiring the subject to guess another's strategies in a game context, role-taking was not displayed until 10 or 12 years of age. In addition, the method used by Flavell et al. to present a form of the Three Mountain task resulted in non-role-taking responses for subjects as old as 16 years; in the original Piaget and Inhelder version of this task the average age is 8 or 9 years. (In a form used by Laurendeau and Pinard [1970], role-taking was not manifested until 12 or 13 years of age.)

Further documentation of the variability of age norms in role-taking can be found in extensive reviews by Flavell (1974) and Shantz (1975). It is also important to note that there have been studies in which systematic attempts were made to determine the youngest ages at which children can produce role-taking responses. In studies of visual perception (as summarized by Flavell in this volume; also see Fishbein, Lewis, & Keiffer, 1972; Shantz & Watson, 1970), role-taking responses have been made by children as young as 3 and 4 years of age. Similarly, 3- and 4-year-olds are able to take the perspective of another in the context of communication tasks (Mossler, Marvin, & Greenberg, 1976; Shatz & Gelman, 1973).

These observed wide-ranging age discrepancies in performance can be explained through the distinction that has been drawn between conceptual frameworks and role-taking as a method of information gathering. On any given role-taking task it is necessary to make a distinction between the activity of putting oneself in another's perspective and the concepts (e.g., spatial, psychological, moral) inherent in the problem posed. In actuality, the so-called role-taking tasks entail *both* role-taking activities and conceptual activities on the part of the subject. Subjects having the competence to engage in role-taking will be unable to perform role-taking activities on a task that calls for a level of conceptualization they have not yet developed, but on a different task requiring a conceptual level already attained by them, they will display their role-taking competence. For instance, it has been found that most 3- to 5-year-old subjects do not display role-taking when presented with a task (e.g., the Three Mountain task) requiring a level of spatial conceptualization normally not attained at that age (Laurendeau & Pinard, 1970; Piaget & Inhelder, 1956), while most 3- to 5-year-old subjects do display role-taking (Flavell, this volume; Fishbein et al., 1972) when presented with a task (e.g., a spatial configuration with one object) requiring a level of spatial conceptualization normally attained by that age.

106

The necessity for separating role-taking activities from concepts does not apply solely to spatial tasks. At least as frequently, role-taking has been confounded with the domain of psychological concepts. In many of the tasks that have been used the subject is required to take the perspective of the other's feelings, thoughts, or intentions (Shantz, 1975). As stated earlier, one way (interchangeable with other ways) of obtaining knowledge about what another person is feeling or thinking is to attempt to place oneself in the other's position. To reiterate what was stated earlier, this is the information-gathering function of role-taking. However, in order to accomplish this the child must first have concepts about internal psychological states (self or other). That is, for children to take the perspective of another's thoughts or feelings they must first have stable concepts of thinking and emotion (part of the psychological domain). In the absence of such concepts on the part of the subject, it becomes trivial to say that the subject does not take the perspective of the other: It is as if there were no person (in the psychological sense) there.

Furthermore, a subject who has not yet formed stable concepts of internal psychological states and who is asked to identify the thoughts or feelings of another will rely on what is available: either one's own perspective or situational factors. Indeed, it has been found that children under 5 or 6 years of age make judgments about others either on the basis of the external situation (Burns & Cavey, 1957; Flapan, 1968; N. Gordon, 1976; Josephson, 1977) or on the basis of their own states. Thus it is not accurate to say that the subject is egocentric and cannot differentiate self from other; rather, given that the child does not have a stable concept of the person, he relies on the only information available to him:— i.e., self or situation. From this point of view, therefore, it would be expected that qualitative changes in psychological concepts allow for quantitative increments in (a) the accuracy of assessments of others' psychological states, and (b) the complexity of situations in which assessments of the states of others occur (e.g., successively or simultaneously taking the perspectives of more than one person, including the self).

In conclusion, the proposition that role-taking is a method is consistent with the widespread finding that its manifestation is dependent on the type of task and complexity of its presentation. As a method, role-taking can be used across conceptual domains; unlike development within conceptual domains, age-related changes in methods are quantitative rather than qualitative.

B. Conceptual Domains and Individual-Environment Interactions

In contrast with the methods, conceptual frameworks are proposed to be systems of organization that undergo structural reorganizations in ontogenesis. It is also proposed that individuals develop distinct conceptual domains, within which there is a unity of organization. Focusing on moral and social-conventional concepts, the developmental basis for the distinct-domain hypothesis is now considered and contrasted with the differentiation models mentioned earlier, in which morality and convention are treated as part of one domain.

The characterization of thought as forming systems of organization has been put forth most convincingly by Piaget (1950, 1970b, 1970c). A central idea underlying Piaget's approach to cognitive development is that thought forms an organized whole, in which the elements or parts are subordinated to the laws of the whole (Piaget, 1970c). Developmental changes are reflected in progressive restructuring of systems of organization. However, the idea of structure requires specification regarding the aspects of thought to which it applies. It is necessary to consider the boundaries of structural systems: Are their boundaries so fluid that the various conceptual systems are best analyzed as a unitary structure on the level of the mind as a whole, or are their boundaries rigid enough to demand a separate analysis of each system?

It should already be apparent that within the model presented here structure does not refer to the unity of all cognitive functioning. First, the structural notion does not apply to methods of information gathering in that they do not form organized systems. Furthermore, structure does not refer to a unity of all aspects of conceptualization.[3] In distinguishing conceptual domains, it is implied that all concepts are not subsumed under the same system of organization. Thinking is organized within domains, so that, for instance,

3. The structural notion has been interpreted to mean that all forms of thought are interrelated. However, the interrelations between domains, such as logical, physical, and moral concepts, has been subjected to empirical examination solely through correlational studies. Such studies, which entail assessments of correlational levels between different measures, are inadequate ways of testing proposed structural relations between different aspects of cognitive development. As discussed elsewhere (Turiel, in press), correlations provide measures of relations in rates of development, but they do not provide evidence for, or information about, structural interrelations between the domains measured.

the sequentially ordered systems of organization of social-conventional concepts are empirically distinguishable from those of moral concepts.

This proposition has its basis in a constructivistic and interactional explanation of development. That is, the child's conceptual knowledge is formed out of his actions upon the environment: To form concepts about objects and events the child must act upon them. Thus conceptual development is a constructive process stemming from individual-environment interactions. As an example, the affirmations and negations that characterize the levels of social-conventional concepts were interpreted as reflecting the constructive nature of development.

The hypothesis that the child's concepts are constructed through interactions with the environment is a basis for the proposition that distinct domains are formed. Since conceptual knowledge is constructed through an interactive process, it is not determined by the environment. By the same token, since such constructions originate from the individual's interactions, they are influenced by the environment. In turn, it follows that interactions with fundamentally different types of objects and events should result in the formation of distinct conceptual frameworks (Turiel, in press). That is, the interactive process results in the construction of distinct conceptual frameworks, given fundamentally different properties in the environment.

Consequently, to understand the conceptual products of the child's interactions, it is necessary to distinguish between different types of events. The environment with which the child interacts includes objects in the physical world, social objects, and social systems. With regard to social-conventional and moral concepts, the hypothesis is that experiences stimulating development within one domain are different from those stimulating development in the other domain. If we consider one of the more visible types of event experienced by the child, that of social transgressions (by self or others), it becomes clear that there are two rather different aspects of such experiences. In the case of events that would stimulate moral concepts it is not necessary that there be a violation of social regulation or deviation from uniformity for the child to respond to those events as transgressions or to begin formulating prescriptions about them. Take the example mentioned earlier of one child hitting another and inflicting pain upon him. Children do view this sort of event as a transgression (Nucci & Turiel, in press) and formulate moral prescriptions regarding this class of activity. Such a response on the part of a child is likely to originate from the event itself (e.g., from a perception of the intrinsic consequences of the act), independently of social regulations or authoritative expectations. In contrast, for a child to respond to a social-conventional event as a transgression there must be a violation of social regulations, authoritative commands, or general expectations which have been communicated to the child prior to the event. It is regulations (or their violations) and behavioral uniformities forming part of social organization that stimulate concepts of social convention and their function.

There is some indication that the experiential origins of social convention are as early as infancy. Bruner (1974–1975) has maintained that through interactions with the mother, infants begin to use conventions in their communications and to assume conventionalized roles in games. Furthermore, some interesting speculations regarding conventionalized communication during infancy have recently been put forth by Bower (1977), who proposed that the now well-known phenomena of mother-infant attachment and infant anxiety at their separation can be explained as a function of idiosyncratic forms of communication between the mother and infant:

> Over a period of time each baby and mother develop a particular, individualistic communication style, a style of interaction specific to that mother and that baby. . . . Indeed, by seven months or so, the age at which separation anxiety starts to appear, mother and baby have established quite well worked out routines for communicating with each other. . . .
>
> Now, what happens when the mother leaves the baby with someone else? The baby's only partner in communication is gone and the baby is left with a stranger, someone who doesn't "speak the same language," who doesn't respond to the baby's social gestures, social invitations, social ploys, or other forms of interaction. The baby is, in effect, left alone. He is isolated from other adults by the very development of the communication routines he shares with his mother. (pp. 55–56)

If Bower's interpretation is correct, it would mean that an infant, in close interaction with the mother, develops conventional —or consistently organized—ways of coordinating interactions within that specific "social system." Since these particular conventions do not exist in other "social systems," the infant is unable to communicate with others.

In research with 3- and 4-year-old children (Nucci & Turiel, in press) it has been observed that the types of social interactions they experience differ according to whether the interactions occurred in the context of social-conventional or moral events. In the Nucci and Turiel study, child and adult reactions to moral and social-conventional transgressions were observed in a number of preschool settings. The feedback in the context of moral transgressions generally focused on the effects of actions upon others and on emotional reactions. In contrast, the feedback in the context of social-conventional transgressions focused on aspects of social order, such as rules, sanctions, and norm violations. This study, therefore, shows that children's interactions revolving around social-conventional events differ from those revolving around moral events.

The hypothesis that different social events stimulate the development of children's social-conventional and moral concepts was supported by the Nucci and Turiel study in that the different types of social interactions were associated with the preschool children's concepts. As discussed in the previous section, it was also found that the children made a conceptual discrimination between social-conventional and moral transgressions. The fact that this discrimination is made at an early age, and is maintained across a wide age span (see Section III), demonstrates its nondevelopmental nature.

The analyses presented regarding the relation between conceptual constructions and individual-environment interactions form the basis for the hypothesis with which this chapter was begun— namely, that the developmental course of social-conventional concepts is distinct from that of moral concepts. It was on this basis that, at the outset, the distinct domain approach was contrasted with the "differentiation" models. It will be recalled that in the differentiation models it is presumed that morality emerges out of its differentiation from convention. Furthermore, it is maintained that earlier developmental levels (of moral judgment) are characterized by conformity to convention, while the most advanced levels are characterized by autonomous principles of moral reasoning.[4]

That approach to social development as the increasing differentiation of different domains does not accord with the theoretical model presented here. In addition to obscuring the distinction between morality and convention, in those models the origins of moral reasoning are left unspecified, since they are explained through a different domain (i.e., convention) while giving the illusion that they are explained within their own domain. That is, the "moral judgments" of younger children are, in actuality, being explained through other forms of judgment that they make. Consequently, the precursors and the interactional basis for developmentally advanced moral judgments remain unspecified. In fact, the evidence does show that even young children form distinctively moral concepts (Damon, 1975, 1977) as well as the distinctively social-conventional concepts discussed here.

4. Both Piaget (1932) and Kohlberg (1971, 1976) have relied on models of differetiation between domains to explain the development of moral judgments. In Piaget's theory moral development is described as progressing through two stages: At the first (the "heteronomous" level) convention and morality are undifferentiated, while at the second (the "autonomous" level) morality is differentiated from, and displaces, convention. Kohlberg has modified Piaget's stage scheme, proposing a more extensive version of the differentiation model. As reflected in the following passage, moral development is viewed as stemming from a cognitive state in which several domains are undifferentiated:

> Moral judgments, unlike judgments of prudence or aesthetics, tend to be universal, inclusive, consistent, and grounded on objective, impersonal, or ideal grounds. Statements like "Martinis should be made five-to-one, that's the right way" involved "good" and "right," but lack the characteristics of moral judgments. We are not prepared to say that we want everyone to make them that way, that they are good in terms of some impersonal ideal standard shared by others, or that we and others should make five-to-one Martinis whether we wish to or not. In similar fashion, when a ten-year-old at Stage 1 answers a moral question . . . he does not answer with a moral judgment that is universal or that has any impersonal or ideal grounds . . . . The individual whose judgments are at Stage 6 asks "Is it morally right?" and means by morally right something different from punishment (Stage 1), prudence (Stage 2), conformity to authority (Stages 3 and 4), etc. Thus, the responses of lower-stage subjects are not moral for the same reasons that responses of higher-stage subjects to aesthetic or other morally neutral matters fail to be moral . . . .

> This is what we had in mind earlier when we spoke of our stages as representing an increased differentiation of moral values and judgments from other types of values and judgments. (Kohlberg, 1971, pp. 215–216)

The model that has been proposed is based on the premise that it is necessary to identify (a) the different cognitive functions (i.e., information gathering and conceptual structuring), (b) the distinct conceptual domains, and (c) their origins in individual-environment interactions. The body of data presented supports this domain analysis of social cognition.

REFERENCE NOTE

1. Turiel, E. Social-convention and the development of societal concepts. Unpublished manuscript. University of California, Santa Cruz, 1977.

REFERENCES

Aronfreed, J. Conduct and conscience: The socialization of internalized control over behavior. New York: Academic Press, 1968.
Aronfreed, J., & Reber, A. Internalized behavioral suppression and the timing of social punishment. Journal of Personality and Social Psychology, 1965, 1, 3–16.
Black, M. Models and metaphors: Studies in language and philosophy. Ithaca, N.Y.: Cornell University Press, 1962.
Bower, T. G. R. A primer of infant development. San Francisco: W. H. Freeman, 1977.
Brown, R., & Gilman, A. The pronouns of power and solidarity. In T. A. Sebeok (Ed.), Style in language. New York: Wiley, 1960.
Bruner, J. S. From communication to language—a psychological perspective. Cognition, 1974–1975, 3, 255–287.
Burns, N., & Cavey, L. Age differences in empathic ability among children. Canadian Journal of Psychology, 1957, 11, 227–230.
Byrne, D. F. The development of role-taking in adolescence. Unpublished doctoral dissertation, Harvard University, 1973.
Chandler, M. J., & Greenspan, S. Ersatz egocentrism: A reply to H. Borke. Developmental Psychology, 1972, 7, 104–106.
Cheyne, J. A. Some parameters of punishment affecting resistance to deviation and generalization of a prohibition. Child Development, 1971, 42, 1249–1261.
Damon, W. Early conceptions of positive justice as related to the development of logical operations. Child Development, 1975, 46, 301–312.

Damon, W. *The social world of the child*. San Francisco: Jossey-Bass, 1977.

Durkheim, E. *Moral education*. Glencoe, Ill.: Free Press, 1961. (Originally published, 1925.)

Feffer, M. H., & Gourevitch, V. Cognitive aspects of role-taking in children. *Journal of Personality*, 1960, **28**, 383–396.

Fishbein, H. D., Lewis, S., & Keiffer, K. Children's understanding of spatial relations: Coordination of perspectives. *Developmental Psychology*, 1972, **7**, 21–33.

Flapan, D. *Children's understanding of social interaction*. New York: Teachers College Press, 1968.

Flavell, J. H. The development of inferences about others. In T. Mischel (Ed.), *Understanding other persons*. Oxford: Basil Blackwell, 1974.

Flavell, J. H., Botkin, P., Fry, C., Wright, J., & Jarvis, P. *The development of role-taking and communication skills in children*. New York: Wiley, 1968.

Flavell, J. H., & Wellman, H. M. Metamemory. In R. V. Kail and J. W. Hagen (Eds.), *Perspectives on the development of memory and cognition*. Hillsdale, N.J.: Laurence Erlbaum Associates, 1977.

Foster, G. M. Speech forms and perceptions of social distance in a Spanish-speaking Mexican village. *Southwestern Journal of Anthropology*, 1964, **20**, 107–122.

Goody, E. "Greeting," "begging," and the presentation of respect. In J. S. La Fontaine (Ed.), *The interpretation of ritual*. London: Tavistock Publications, 1972.

Gordon, N. *Children's recognition and conceptualizations of emotions in videotape presentations*. Unpublished doctoral dissertation, Harvard University, 1976.

Gordon, R. F., & Flavell, J. The development of intuitions about cognitive cueing. *Child Development*, 1977, **48**, 1027–1033.

Heider, F. *The Psychology of Interpersonal Relations*. New York: Wiley, 1958.

Hobhouse, L. T. *Morals in Evolution*. London: Chapman and Hall, 1906.

Hogan, R. Moral conduct and moral character: A psychological perspective. *Psychological Bulletin*, 1973, **79**, 217–232.

Jones, E. E., & Davis, K. E. From acts to dispositions. In L. Berkowitz (Ed.), *Advances in experimental social psychology* (Vol. 2). New York: Academic Press, 1965.

Josephson, J. *The child's use of situational and personal information in predicting the behavior of another*. Unpublished doctoral dissertation, Stanford University, 1977.

Kelley H. H. Attribution theory in social psychology. In D. Levine (Ed.), *Nebraska Symposium on Motivation, 1967* (Vol. 15). Lincoln: University of Nebraska Press, 1967.

Kohlberg, L. Stage and sequence: The cognitive-developmental approach to socialization. In D. A. Goslin (Ed.), *Handbook of socialization theory and research*. Chicago: Rand McNally, 1969.

Kohlberg, L. From is to ought: How to commit the naturalistic fallacy and get away with it in the study of moral development. In T. Mischel (Ed.), *Psychology and genetic epistemology*. New York: Academic Press, 1971.

Kohlberg, L. Moral stages and moralization: The cognitive-developmental approach. In T. Lickona (Ed.), *Moral development and behavior: Theory, research and social issues*. New York: Holt, Rinehart & Winston, 1976.

Langer, J. Disequilibrium as a source of development. In P. H. Mussen, J. Langer, & M. Covington (Eds.), *Trends and issues in developmental psychology*. New York: Holt, Rinehart & Winston, 1969.

Laurendeau, M., & Pinard, A. *The development of the concept of space in the child*. New York: International Universities Press, 1970.

Lemke, S. *Identity and conservation: The child's developing conceptions of social and physical transformations*. Unpublished doctoral dissertation, University of California, Berkeley, 1973.

Levi-Strauss, C. *The savage mind*. Chicago: University of Chicago Press, 1966.

Loevinger, J. *Ego development: Conceptions and theories*. San Francisco: Jossey-Bass, 1976.

Looft, W.R. Egocentrism and social interaction across the life span. *Psychological Bulletin*, 1972, **78**, 73–92.

Malinowski, B. *Crime and custom in savage society*. London: Routlege & Kegan Paul, 1926.

McDougall, W. *An introduction to social psychology*. London: Methuen, 1908.

Milgram, S. Behavioral study of obedience. *Journal of Abnormal and Social Psychology*, 1963, **67**, 371–378.

Mossler, D. E., Marvin, R. S., & Greenberg, M. T. Conceptual perspective taking in 2- to 6-year-old children. *Developmental Psychology*, 1976, **12**, 85–86.

Nucci, L. *Social development: Personal, conventional, and moral concepts*. Unpublished doctoral dissertation, University of California, Santa Cruz, 1977.

Nucci, L., & Turiel, E. Social interactions and the development of social concepts in pre-school children. *Child Development*, in press.

Parke, R. Nurturance, nurturance withdrawal and resistance to deviation. *Child Development*, 1967, **38**, 1101–1110.

Parke, R., & Walters, R. Some factors influencing the efficacy of punishment training for inducing response inhibition. *Monographs of the Society for Research in Child Development*, 1967, **32**, 1.

Piaget, J. *The language and thought of the child*. New York: Harcourt, Brace, 1926.

Piaget, J. *Judgment and reasoning in the child*. New York: Harcourt, Brace, 1928.

Piaget, J. *The moral judgment of the child*. Glencoe, Ill.: Free Press, 1932.

Piaget, J. *The psychology of intelligence.* London: Lowe & Brydone, 1950.

Piaget, J. *Comments on Vygotsky's critical remarks.* Cambridge, Mass.: MIT Press, 1962.

Piaget, J. Introduction to M. Laurendeau and A. Pinard, *The development of the concept of space in the child.* New York: International Universities Press, 1970. (a)

Piaget, J. Piaget's theory. In P. H. Mussen (Ed.), *Carmichael's manual of child psychology.* New York: Wiley, 1970. (b)

Piaget, J. *Structuralism.* New York: Basic Books, 1970. (c)

Piaget, J., & Inhelder, B. *The child's conception of space.* London: Routledge & Kegan Paul, 1956.

Pratt, M. *A developmental study of person perception and attributions of social causality: Learning the what and why of others.* Unpublished doctoral dissertation, Harvard University, 1975.

Ross, L. The intuitive psychologist and his shortcomings: Distortions in the attribution process. In L. Berkowitz (Ed.), *Advances in experimental social psychology* (Vol. 10). New York: Academic Press, 1977.

Sears, R. R., Maccoby, E. E., & Levin, H. *Patterns of child rearing.* Evanston, Ill.: Row, Peterson, 1957.

Selman, R. L. Social cognitive understanding: A guide to educational and clinical practice. In T. Lickona (Ed.), *Moral development and behavior: Theory, research and social issues.* New York: Holt, Rinehart & Winston, 1976.

Selman, R. L., & Byrne, D. F. A structural-developmental analysis of levels of role-taking in middle childhood. *Child Development,* 1974, **45,** 803–806.

Shantz, C. V. The development of social cognition. In E. M. Hetherington (Ed.), *Review of child development research* (Vol. 5). Chicago: University of Chicago Press, 1975.

Shantz, C.V., & Watson, J. S. Assessment of spatial egocentrism through expectancy violation. *Psychonomic Science,* 1970, **18,** 93–94.

Shatz, M., & Gelman, R. The development of communication skills: Modifications in the speech of young children as a function of listener. *Monographs of the Society for Research in Child Development,* 1973, **38**(5).

Shweder, R. Culture and thought. In B. Wolman (Ed.), *International encyclopaedia of psychiatry, psychoanalysis, psychology, and neurology.* New York: Van Nostrand Rhinehold, 1977.

Slobin, D., Miller, S., & Porter, L. Forms of address and social organization in a business organization. *Journal of Personality and Social Psychology,* 1968, **8,** 289–293.

Tapp, J., & Kohlberg, L. Developing senses of law and legal justice. *Journal of Social Issues,* 1971, **27,** 65–92.

Turiel, E. Conflict and transition in adolescent moral development. *Child Development,* 1974, **45,** 14–29.

Turiel, E. The development of social concepts: Mores, customs and conventions. In D. J. DePalma & J. M. Foley (Eds.), *Moral development: Current theory and research*. Hillsdale, N. J.: Laurence Erlbaum Associates, 1975.

Turiel, E. The development of concepts of social structure: Social convention. In J. Glick & A. Clarke-Stewart (Eds.), *Studies in social and cognitive development* (Vol. 1). New York: Gardner Press, in press.

Wolfson, A. *Aspects of the development of identity concepts*. Unpublished doctoral dissertation, University of California, Berkeley, 1972.

Natural Language and the Development of the Self

D. B. Bromley

The University of Liverpool

*A*mong the best-known names in the history of the psychology of the self are those of Baldwin (1897/1968), James (1910), Cooley (1902), Mead (1934), and Allport (1955). More recently, Gordon and Gergen (1968) have provided an array of classical and contemporary perspectives, Gergen (1971) has summarized the problems and approaches to self-understanding, and Lewis and Cherry (1977) have described some interesting laboratory studies. Although these sources will not be reviewed, they provide the general framework of ideas within which the particular topic of natural language and the development of the self can be discussed.

The traditional view of the self combines the clinical insights of psychodynamics with the perspectives of social and developmental psychology; more recently it has incorporated psychometric concepts and methods (see Wylie, 1961, 1974). The self has been regarded as a sort of reflective, constructive, and defensive impression that individuals form of themselves in response to their own behavior and experience in the context of their biological and cultural circumstances. The concept of self has been used to help explain such diverse phenomena as autonomy, adjustment, and creativity on the one hand, and conformity, neurosis, alienation, and failure on the other.

The reflexive or recursive nature of the self has been an important and intriguing but difficult problem to deal with. It enables people to represent themselves (as known) to themselves (as knower), to represent others to themselves (in the form of personality impressions), and to represent themselves in relation to others (through role rehearsal). In this way they can plan their actions, revise their plans, form expectations about themselves and others, revise their expectations, and speculate about possible situations and different courses of action. These various symbolic representations, in the form of words and plans, are not necessarily rational and based on empirical fact, but may be highly speculative, defensive, and distorted. Moreover, normal individuals are aware that other people are capable of reflexive and defensive psychological reactions, and they may try to take those reactions into account in their dealings with others. The result is that the analysis of the self in social interaction is exceedingly complicated, at least if the social situation is one that calls for some kind of adjustment other than routine role enactment.

The self is a complex issue which can be raised in various psychological, sociological, or philosophical contexts. My predilection is to look at the way we describe ourselves in comparison with the way we describe others, and to ask whether we understand ourselves in the same way that we understand others. Also, I regard the study of personality-description and self-description *in ordinary language* as the royal road to understanding oneself and others. These issues will be dealt with in detail by comparing the contents and organization of self-descriptions with descriptions of others as expressed in ordinary (written) language by children at different ages.

I. PRESUPPOSITIONS AND RESEARCH METHODOLOGIES

A. Presuppositions

In her most recent book, Wylie (1974) has reviewed many of the methodological considerations and psychometric procedures relevant to research into the self-concept (see also Wylie, 1961, 1968). She argues that, on the whole, the concepts, methods, and findings produced over more than two decades of investigation are not at all impressive, and concludes that either the whole enterprise should be abandoned or substantial and long-term improvements should be made in theorizing and methodology. Her view is that the second of these alternatives should be chosen, whereas my own view is that we need to examine the *presuppositions* underlying our notions about the self on which our research concepts, methods, and findings rest. This is not to abandon existing approaches, but rather to reconsider the nature of the enterprise.

One such presupposition is that the main problem is with observation and measurement, rather than with theory and conceptual
analysis. It seems likely, however, that theory construction in respect of the self (or self-concept) has not been satisfactory hitherto,
since theory construction in many, perhaps most, areas of psychology and sociology (both of which have an interest in the self) is a
particularly difficult matter (see Bromley, 1970, 1973, 1977). The
difficulty, briefly, is that of formulating a reasonably concise argument in which suitably qualified, context-dependent conclusions
can be related to relevant empirical evidence by means of inference
warrants (of various kinds, including definitions) and backed by
appropriate methodological and conceptual justifications.

The initial problem of theory construction in an area like the
psychology of the self is not that of formulating neat axiomatic
systems, complete with theorems and corollaries (after the fashion
of geometry—see Section VII), but rather that of putting together, in
an orderly fashion, what we already seem to know from commonsense and established research findings, and to do so in ordinary
language. If this is done thoroughly, then the main theoretical
concepts and substantive arguments can be made explicit; omissions, contradictions, and distortions can be discerned; reserva-
tions, qualifications, implications, distinctions, and primitive (irreducible) terms can also be worked out. If necessary, the whole
system or network of arguments can be laid out systematically in a
quasi-formal manner. I have carried out such a systematic analysis
for the theory of disengagement in social gerontology (Bromley,
1970), but I have not so far attempted to do it for any of the so-called
"theories" of the self. My guess would be that such theories would
be incomplete and fragmented, would lack both adequate empirical
evidence and well-defined concepts.

A systematic quasi-formal reorganization of our basic ideas about
the self would not *necessarily* provide us with a satisfactory foundation for a fresh scientific endeavor in this area, but the apparent
failure of technical concepts and psychometric methods, adequately
documented by Wylie (1961, 1974), suggests that it is *possible*. There
is much to be learned about the way even our professional and
scientific thinking is constrained by ordinary language (see Bromley, 1977). For example, the problem of nonphenomenal aspects of
the self—"unconscious self-concept variables"—to which Wylie
(1974) refers, is one that has not been solved by psychometric research, but it is not difficult to find phrases in commonsense lan-

guage which express such variables, e.g., "He is not aware of his dependency"; "She won't admit that she is jealous." This should make us wary of rejecting so-called "unconscious" thoughts, feelings, and desires as determinants of individual behavior and self-awareness, in spite of the difficulties associated with psychometric validation.

It seems likely that formal testing methods, even of the free-response variety, will not penetrate far into the self-concept; and if it is the deeper, more private, components of the self that determine a person's adjustment, then clinical and indirect (or anonymous) methods of eliciting personal disclosures are the methods most likely to reveal them. It does not follow, however, that the deeper, more private, aspects of self are necessarily more important to individuals; on the contrary, people are often willing to subordinate these private inclinations to their public interests. Reputation is more important than self! Reputation is an important but surprisingly neglected issue in social psychology (see Bromley, 1966).

It may be that much of the information that people "keep to themselves" is not all that important in determining their adjustment; it may consist of acknowledged (but controlled) deviant and infantile tendencies, and of spontaneous but unreal fantasies and fears, which function as a kind of play in imagination. It is possible that we overestimate the psychodynamic importance of some of these private aspects of the self; and if the individual does disclose them, or expresses them safely, for example in fantasy or vicariously, then they may not be important as major determinants of personal adjustment. It is now taken for granted, however, that failure to acknowledge and deal with primitive feelings and desires *can* lead to serious maladjustment; but the question is whether we need the whole paraphernalia of psychopathology to study the *normal* person's adjustment and self-concept. It does not follow that the concepts and methods that have proved useful in analyzing maladjustment are equally appropriate in analyzing normal adjustment. Some psychometric measures of personality and the self are based on psychodynamic theory, but psychometric methods based on self-reports seem not to have been very successful in advancing our understanding of normal behavior, according to Mischel (1968) and Wylie (1974).

Another common presupposition in the study of the self is that psychometric methods are essential. In connection with the question of whether, or to what extent, we can investigate the psychology of the self without recourse to measurement, I have argued (in Bromley, 1977) that psychometric assessment rests absolutely on an infra-structure of commonsense and ordinary language, and that, although quantitative data can enter into the appraisal of self or personality, they are by no means essential. Numbers without meanings are unsatisfactory in comparison with meanings without numbers! If one adopts an individual-differences approach emphasizing descriptive dimensions, then one is likely to use psychometric methods; if one adopts an individual-case approach emphasizing situational and adaptive patterns of adjustment, then one is likely to use quasi-judicial (case-study) methods. The latter should incorporate suitable procedures for making comparisons and contrasts between cases for the purpose of identifying types of case and establishing a kind of psychological case-law; unfortunately, psychological case-law is a very neglected area. Stein and Neulinger (Note 1) and Stein (Note 2) have tried to combine the two approaches by examining profiles on a self-description questionnaire, based on Murray's needs system.

B. Research Methodologies

We have seen that the weaknesses of psychometric studies of the self have been examined by Wylie (1961, 1974). She mentions the basic problems associated with validity and reliability, and further problems associated with response set, item selection, operational definition, scales of measurement, statistical analysis, and experimental artifacts. Furthermore, Mischel (1968) and others have argued that psychometric tests of personality do not measure stable traits within individuals. It seems fair to say that there is a close relationship between our presuppositions about an aspect of human nature and the research methodologies we employ to study it. The study of individual differences in the self has tended to concentrate on those features that can be investigated by means of psychometric methods—such as self-esteem, real versus ideal self—and on the relationship of these "self-variables" to behavior, such as academic success or the effects of psychotherapy. Such research has been reviewed at length by Wylie. I shall not attempt to examine this area, although some of my own work is concerned with normal adult age differences in the use of ordinary language in self-descriptions.

An individual differences approach to the self-concept seems to assume that measureable self-variables—those assessed by self-ratings, Q-sorts, and so on—can be treated as personality variables, like introversion, dominance, or achievement motivation. Thus, as we shall see in Sections IV and VI, measures of "self" and measures of "personality" using self-reports are sometimes scarcely if at all distinguishable. Consider also, for example, the way in which items in the Minnesota-Ford pool of phenotypic personality items (see Meehl, Note 3) can be phrased as "personality" or "self" statements.

Wylie (1974) makes it clear that, in her opinion, one should begin by giving a literary definition of the terms one wishes to use in describing the self. Each construct or term of reference should be distinguished, as far as possible, from other constructs; the boundaries between concepts should be as well defined as it is possible to make them. Moreover, one needs to go beyond mere formal definition to a fuller explication of a term, giving representative examples so that independent observers can agree on its meaning and use. This is broadly the procedure I have used (in Bromley, 1977) to identify 30 categories of information in the description of personality in ordinary language; it will be seen that these same categories apply, with very minor modifications, to the description of the self. I have not attempted to operationalize these 30 conceptual categories, since part of my argument is that the boundaries between some of them are fuzzy and vary from one context to another. The basic problem is not that of operational definition but that of conceptual clarification. Furthermore, I do not regard them as scalar dimensions of personality (or self), although they might give rise to scales of one sort or another suitable for measuring differences between individuals. My interest has been directed more to the problem of how we map our experience of ourselves and others onto the forms of natural language, and vice versa. I have been concerned, one might say, with that basic framework of commonsense ideas that forms our social construction of personality and the self, and underpins our psychological research work.

One of the basic problems in research on the self, then, is to explore the nature and scope of the problem, and to establish some *prima facie* arguments about it based on commonsense and ordinary language. Wylie, however, seems to presuppose that we are already well beyond this level of understanding and need only concern ourselves with improving the psychological concepts and methods appropriate to this area. Thus she puts considerable emphasis on the need to distinguish one self-concept variable from another (discriminant validity) and to develop diverse methods of measuring each variable (convergent validity).

A particularly important source of variability between subjects may arise as a consequence of differences between them in the way they interpret the meaning of adjectives in a checklist or of items in a self-report inventory, or the instructions and scales in a rating scale. There seems to be no way of defining the population from which items for checklists, Q-sorts, rating scales, and so on are drawn; this makes it difficult to justify measures of personality or self (but see Section V below). It seems unlikely that the application of elaborate multivariate statistical techniques to the results obtained from unsatisfactory psychometric tests will do more than compound the confusion.

There are good reasons for keeping the techniques of observation simple; hence my preference for free-response data and techniques of content analysis rather than structured psychometric tests. This is not to say that free-response data are *necessarily* to be preferred. Such a preference is as much a matter of the personal inclination, interest, and ability of the investigator as a matter of clear methodological superiority. Content-analysis, as a method for dealing with free-response data, mirrors some of the defects of the psychometric method listed by Wylie. Subjects may interpret the instructions to a free-response exercise in different ways, so that their responses do not reflect common determinants. Furthermore, there is no guarantee that free-response surveys will disclose the population from which such responses are drawn, although this is a more reasonable expectation in the free-response approach than in the psychometric test approach, and one can even estimate relative frequencies of occurrence for certain kinds of statement in self-descriptions, for different populations of subjects (see Livesley & Bromley, 1973).

Wylie (1974) has very little to say about ordinary language descriptions of the self, except in connection with the WAY (Who Are You?) and TST (Twenty Sentences Test) test. She does say, however, that responses by means of open-ended essays cannot always be coded in the same way that responses by means of other methods can be coded, and that subjects may fail to mention, in a self-description, characteristics which seem to be important when assessed by other methods. Open-ended self-reports are limited by the willingness of subjects to disclose information about themselves. Moreover, unless the test instructions specify very closely what areas of the self are to be described, subjects may well give quite diverse accounts. This may be useful in the early stages of an inquiry when one is interested in exploring the nature and scope of self-statements; but it is a disadvantage when one wishes to make careful comparisons between subjects on specified facets of the self. However, it appears that even when subjects are rating themselves (or others) on reasonably clear categories, e.g., an adjective checklist, the ratings may vary as a function of the context of the item and its order of appearance in a series.

According to Wylie we do not know to what extent free-description self-reports are affected by the frequency of occurrence of words and phrases in ordinary language. My own work and my work with my colleagues has confirmed that ordinary language self-descriptions (and descriptions of others) are regulated by the rules of common usage—e.g., word collocations, phraseology, idiom—but frequency as such has not been considered except (a) in relation to developmental age differences (see Livesley & Bromley, 1973), and (b) in relation to category of statement (see Section V below).

A method which seems to fill the gap between the relatively unstructured self-description method that we have used and the highly structured psychometric tests of self and personality is the above-mentioned method discussed by Wylie—the WAY (or WAI) test or the TST (see Bugenthal & Zelen, 1950); Kuhn & McPartland, 1954; and Gordon, 1968, 1969). I shall not examine the history of research with this method (for that, see Wylie, 1974), but I shall make some comments in due course on Gordon's article. Wylie points out that, like some other tests, the WAY/TST is influenced by the "specific interaction context"—for example, the setting and instructions of the test—and that we cannot be sure that the subject's responses reflect a general disposition which is consistent across situations. It is obvious that the way a question is phrased greatly influences the sorts of answer given, simply because ordinary language restricts us in this way. For example, the question "Who am I?" can be expected to generate different answers from questions like "What am I?", "Who do I think I am?", "What do I feel about myself?", "What do I want of myself?"

Gordon (1968) mentions one sort of restriction that some check-lists and other psychometric methods impose, namely the exclusion of noun forms of description (roles, activities, relationships, etc.) as contrasted with attribute (adjectival, adverbal) forms of description (traits, states, abilities, etc.). It is a distinct advantage of the unstructured free-response method that such restrictions can be avoided by means of the test instructions. It is a further advantage that the results give a better indication of the range and nature of self-descriptions (and descriptions of others) and so help to integrate the psychological and sociological approaches to personality. Wylie, however, says that most subjects do not feel that a relatively unstructured free-response test such as the TST enables them to give a more accurate account of themselves than do some other, more structured, tests like an adjective checklist or a semantic differential scale.

We must remember that difficulties arise when we try to study the accuracy and validity of personality impressions that do not arise when we simply try to study the processes at work. For example, Wylie cites inflences such as acquiescence and extreme-response sets, carelessness, faking, the limitations of forced-choice or free-response items, misinterpretation of instructions and items, ignorance, and bias. Thus, although we can identify these as potential sources of error in our attempts to study the *process* of self-understanding and understanding others, we may be unable to remedy them in studies which investigate or depend upon the *accuracy* and *validity* of such impressions.

The self can be studied on the basis of a person's behavior in natural or contrived (experimental) situations, or on the basis of self-disclosures and responses to self-report tests. The scientific study of the self is fraught with conceptual and methodological difficulties. It is advisable to approach the topic in a variety of ways in the hope that in the end we shall reach convergent conclusions.

We have considered some of the presuppositions and research methodologies in the study of the self. Without prejudice to the psychometric approach we need to reexamine the foundations of our understanding of the self (and others) in the language of commonsense. We look next, therefore, at the developmental origins of self-understanding and understanding others.

II. THE ORIGINS AND DEVELOPMENT OF SELF-UNDERSTANDING AND UNDERSTANDING OTHERS

The origins of the self seem to lie in the infant's earliest encounters with other persons. Then, throughout infancy and childhood, a series of further experiences, associated with diverse kinds of social interaction, normally gives rise to a relatively stable self-concept.

Persons are persistent, important, and salient features in the world of the infant and young child (see Schaffer, 1971, and Rheingold, 1961). It is hardly surprising, therefore, that infants come to view the world in which they live as peopled with agents which are active, powerful, and sometimes capricious or even magical. In one sense, infants are conditioned to react animistically and anthropomorphically, so that they have to learn that some aspects of nature—e.g., objects, physical events—do not have human attributes (such as intention, life, awareness, feeling). Piaget (1929) used the word "animism" to refer to children's tendency not to distinguish the physical and psychological aspects of their world, or themselves from their environment. It is not until about the age of 11 years that the average child becomes able to distinguish between persons and things and is able to shed animistic and magical ways of thinking; and this depends, of course, on the attitudes and beliefs which prevail in the community to which he or she belongs.

The animism of infancy and early childhood is not a logical construction; it is, rather, an unwitting (tacit or implicit) animism in which children presuppose that some aspects of their world behave autonomously and are reactive in the sense that the children can sometimes influence them in ways that they cannot influence other aspects of their environment and in ways that they do not fully understand. The young child's animism is prelogical.

During the first few years of life, children rapidly acquire notions about their own behavior (and the behavior of other people) that are familiar to common sense and spoken about in the ordinary language of everyday life. By the age of 5 or 6 years, the average child can give a competent running commentary on the human activities of daily living, including the associated mental states (see Livesley & Bromley, 1973). This facility with the language of actions and mental states, however, is not adequate for dealing with complex and extended forms of behavior or with the underlying dispositions (traits, abilities, motives, and so on). In other words, the average child aged 5 or 6 years has little or no facility with the language of *personality* description. Similarly, although children can describe their own actions and mental states (wanting, being frightened or happy, for example), they cannot describe their own "personality," that is, they cannot attribute stable psychological characteristics to themselves. They do not have the necessary cognitive abilities or language forms.

The developmental psychology of self perception, like the developmental psychology of person perception, is the process which takes the child from a concrete level of understanding simple actions and mental states to a more abstract and general level of understanding personality and adjustment.

An empirical study of developmental age differences in self-understanding is described in Section V. Relevant research in the development of social cognition is reported in Flapan (1968), Livesley and Bromley (1973), and Shantz (1975).

It is not possible to deal here with the various ways in which ordinary language affects our description and analysis of personality and adjustment; that problem is dealt with in detail in Bromley, 1977. We can, however, touch on one aspect, namely, the way ordinary language and common sense provide children with a frame of reference for describing and analyzing actions, mental states, personality attributes, and patterns of adjustment both for themselves and for others. This framework exists as a social construction of human nature in the language and culture of the community to which children belong. In the normal course of social learning they come to share a common language and a common set of assumptions, beliefs, and practices. Through a succession of inter- and intra-personal comparisons, involving reference to both overt behavior and covert psychological processes, most children tacitly accept the ordinary language of personality and adjustment and so acquire a kind of understanding of themselves and other people. By means of what Vygotsky (1962) refers to as "inner speech," children are able to think with socially derived meanings and concepts. The development of "outer speech" enables them to communicate their thoughts to others. The concepts of "self" and "other" are thus very closely related in the developmental psychology of language. The internalization of speech makes reflective thought possible and provides a psycholinguistic link between overt actions and covert states of mind. In addition, the internalization of the associated forms of language gives rise to powerful self-regulating functions, such as self-aspirations, self-criticisms, self/other comparisons, self-consistency.

Young children's egocentrism restricts their awareness of other people as individuals , and so restricts their awareness of how they compare and contrast with them. As they grow older, they become more aware of themselves in relation to other people, and more aware of the extent to which they can account for, and regulate, their own behavior. By the age of about 6 years they become aware that another child may think differently from they way they think. By the age of about 9 years they become aware that another child can wonder about *their* thoughts and feelings. A little later, they can speculate about another child's thoughts, feelings, and desires, and compare them with their own. This last achievement is a meta-perspective—regarding oneself from the point of view of another. It is presumably different from what G. H. Mead (1934) had in mind with his notion of "taking the role of the other," in that it is a relatively late development in self-awareness (and not merely a tacit acceptance of social expectations). Recursive perspectives—"He thinks I think he thinks, etc."—are difficult to sustain and to extend beyond three cycles; the major achievement is the reciprocal first cycle perspective (see Feffer, 1970; Flapan, 1968; Flavell, 1968; Selman, 1971; and Shantz, 1975).

Children grow up and adapt to a semantic environment; their actions and states of mind, and the actions and states of mind of other people, children and adults alike, are constantly being mapped onto the forms of language provided for the child by others, such as narrative descriptions, interpretations and value judgments. Children become able to think and to talk about themselves and other people in virtue of their *tacit acceptance* of commonsense notions about human nature and of the meaning and use of psychobehavioral terms in ordinary language. Young children's accounts of themselves are egocentric; they do not and cannot view themselves as other people view them (even though paradoxically, their view of themselves has its origins in the views that other people have had of them). They usually tend to view themselves positively, as entirely good—so much so that they deny their "bad" aspects or exclude them from awareness. It is some years before they can accept that other people can have both good and bad components in their makeup, and that they themselves have good and bad features.

Gradually they extend their lexicon of psychobehavioral terms;

for example, they acquire dispositional terms for describing personality, mentalistic terms for describing various states of mind, and behavioral terms for describing complex and extended actions. Their command of language improves so that they can generate more intricate syntactical structures, and so reach more advanced forms of thought and finer shades of meaning. Consider, for example, what is required before a person can fully appreciate a statement like, "He is jealous because he does not understand that his father is trying to comfort his sister who has been made to feel inferior because her table manners were not quite correct." The ability to understand and use complex grammatical statements is an important index of psychological development, not only in self-understanding and self-control but also in understanding others and influencing others.

We have seen that the reason why we seem to be able to understand other people (to know what is in their mind; to know what they are able and inclined to do) is that we tacitly assume they are like us (and we are like them) because the same language is equally applicable to both them and us. We assume that other people can understand our actions and states of mind; otherwise why should we bother to explain ourselves to them? Difficulties arise only when the evidence or explanation needed to account for our behavior (or that of others) is not available, as in temporary misunderstandings, or in cases involving complex psychological factors.

Thus, from the beginning, children's experiences, actions, and forms of language are closely interwoven. It is not surprising that the verbal labels and selective interests that they acquire are derived from the social environment in which they grow up. G. H. Mead (1934) in particular has described how individuals' behaviors and states of mind are modeled on the behavior and states of mind of those around them. In due course, however, given a degree of autonomy and social mobility (and given perhaps conflicting viewpoints or weak social constraints) individuals become more able to think and act for themselves, although there are wide differences between them in this regard.

Young children's selective adaptations to various other people are thus not entirely passive acts of conformity, nor can they be achieved without their taking thought and learning from experience. Vygotsky (1962) explains that the child's thoughts become socialized through language, and Baldwin (1897/1968) explains how children copy and learn from certain sorts of people and then exercise and practice what they have learned on others. But the inward grasp of language and thought, and the inherent variability of children's behavior (see Fiske & Maddi, 1961), make it possible for them to achieve some degree of detachment from and independence of the social influences which surround them. Indeed, children seem to exert considerable personal influence on their social world (see Richards, 1974). Work in behavior modification has examined the relationships between social learning and self-control (e.g., Aronfreed, 1968).

Children's ability to see differences and similarities between themselves and other people gives rise eventually to what we might call "self-identity," when they are able to reflect upon, and to control, their own individuality. The child develops a reflective self-awareness and capacity for self-regulation from what was initially a kind of nonreflective awareness and unthinking social responsiveness (adaptation and compliance); this development is possible only with the help of cognitive and linguistic functions.

It is not likely that self-awareness and self-control develop in clear-cut stages; it seems rather that different facets of the child's adjustment come into systematic relationship with each other at various ages depending upon a variety of constitutional and environmental factors (see Feldman & Toulmin, 1976).

In the normal adult, the self can be regarded in at least as many ways as the other person can be regarded. Thus, for example, we can distinguish our usual self from our temporary or situational self, just as we can distinguish Jones's characteristic behavior from his momentary actions. Similarly, we can compare the person we used to be (former self) with the person we are now (present self) and with the person we expect or hope to be (future or possible self), just as we can compare the past, present, and future of (or possibilities for) another person.

In one sense our "self" is our conception of ourselves as a person (or personality); William James (1910) would call this the "objective me" as known by the "subjective I." Our self-concept, however, becomes part of our own nature (in a reflexive sense), so that someone who knows us, especially someone who knows us better than we know ourselves, may form an impression of us, i.e., of our "personality," that incorporates ideas about our self-concept, our "objective me." Hence personality descriptions of other people frequently include statements about what those people think and feel about themselves as well as statements about their traits abilities, social relationships, and so on. The individual's self-concept, similarly, can range over all aspects of his or her own personality. A person writing a self-description sometimes adopts a reflective mood, and says things like "I think of myself as friendly and helpful" or "I regard myself as less hardworking than I should be." These reflective pronouncements say no more than "I am friendly and helpful" or "I am less hardworking than I should be," which is psychologically similar to saying "Jones is friendly and helpful" or "Jones is less hardworking than he should be," except that the former are subjective pronouncements while the latter are objective (in the sense of being independent of the person making them). Thus, if we examine common sense and ordinary language, much of the mystery of the self disappears (only to reappear perhaps as a mystery in developmental psycholinguistics!).

There are several reasons for assuming that the various ways in which people can experience *themselves* are different from the ways in which they can experience others. First, they have direct and privileged access to many of their own thoughts, feelings, desires, and sensations, and much more intimate, direct and frequent awareness of their own behavior. Second, these diverse and changing experiences can develop into a stable and coherent self-image only if they can be coordinated and regulated by central organizing processes such as beliefs, values, and dispositions. The existence of such internal regulators of individual behavior is perhaps a convenient fiction; but it does enable us to describe and explain our own behavior in the same terms as we explain the behavior of other people. Third, these descriptive and explanatory terms are associated with the acquisition of commonsense notions about human behavior, expressed in the ordinary language of everyday life; this provides us with a framework of ideas for relating our own experiences with our own actions, and for comparing our experiences and actions with those of other people. Psychologically speaking, our relationships with other people, in social interaction and communication, are governed largely by our tacit acceptance of commonsense notions, normal conduct, and ordinary language.

III. CONTINUITY, CONSISTENCY, AND CHANGE

We have not so far distinguished carefully between the strategic aspects of the self and its tactical aspects. During the course of their lives, people evolve a life-style or strategy of adjustment which reflects the way in which they have come to terms with the constraints and opportunities of their environment on the one hand and the limitations and potentialities of their own makeup on the other. Their self-concept comes to play a strategic role in their personal adjustment because it provides a frame of reference and a mechanism for the self-regulation of normal and long-term behavior—that is, it provides the desires which instigate, direct, and sustain their actions, it provides the beliefs and values which lead the individual to take up certain attitudes and lines of conduct, it tends to adjust itself to the consequences of the individual's actions, for example, by modifying its beliefs and desires. This self-regulatory system, of course, is by no means perfect.

The dispositional features of the self-system—e.g., certain beliefs, traits, abilities, aspirations, and values—are relatively stable in the sense that they are thought to give rise to consistent and regular patterns, or strategies, of adjustment. Situations arise, however, which call for tactical variations in behavior, such as discretion rather than valor, reliance on others rather than on self. Such tactics may simply be ways of coping with the immediate situation but they may also provide variations which lead eventually to changes in long-term strategies of adjustment. Behavior is modifiable; self-regulated behavior is modifiable; reflective awareness and recursive thinking provide one means whereby individuals can change the rules by which they regulate (or try to regulate) their own behavior.

The notion of self-consistency is scarcely distinguishable from the notion of the consistency of personality. Psychological consistency as an empirical issue must be separated from consistency as a conceptual issue. The empirical issue is whether one can define patterns of behavior as consistent or inconsistent and then observe whether the behavior patterns so defined are or are not, in fact, mutually compatible—for example, Republican (or Conservative) voting behavior and adherence to Democratic (or Labour) opinions. The conceptual issue is whether one can be sure that apprently inconsistent patterns of behavior are *logically* contradictory. The problem is that consistency in human behavior has to be assumed rather than empirically established. (Otherwise, how could we make sense of behavior?) This philosophical assumption is different from the psychological assumption that a person's makeup tends towards consistency. Behavior (and the central organizing processes thought to lie behind it, such as beliefs, values, traits, and so on) need not be *psychologically* coherent even though it can be explained. However, it must be *logically* coherent, even though we may not understand the logic behind it.

The problem for individuals is to account for themselves in such a way as to achieve a subjective impression of compatibility between the different aspects of their personality and behavior. The nature and extent of this psychological compatibility (or consistency) in conduct varies from one person to another. The effort after consistency may be simply another aspect of the effort after meaning whereby we try to make sense of our own behavior and that of other people. Apparent inconsistencies in behavior generate puzzlement and questioning which may lead to the discovery of additional evidence and arguments by means of which an apparent inconsistency can be eliminated; for example, one may be puzzled as to why one's wife, who is normally good-tempered, is in a bad temper, or as to how an individual's academic competitiveness can exist alongside his relaxed social relationships.

The attempt to find consistency in our own behavior or in that of other people must take situational factors into account, in the sense that there need not be much actual behavioral consistency from one occasion to another if the demands of the situation are different. The "consistency" refers to the central organizing processes in personality (see Bromley, 1977).

Our self-conceptions can be thought of as momentary and partial, and as adaptive (in the widest sense of this term). There is no essential contradiction in people's adopting a tactical adaptive impression of themselves in a particular situation at a particular time and their sustaining a longer-term strategic impression of themselves which is different. For example, I can think of myself as "Someone whose instructions must be obeyed" in a situation which calls for the assertion of authority, although as a matter of general policy I think of myself as "Someone who is prepared to have his authority questioned."

Just as people's orientation towards the outside world may be selective or erroneous, so may their orientation to (awareness of) themselves. Indeed, we may be able to explain their behavior in part by reference to their lack of self-understanding or to their misunderstanding of themselves, e.g., "He doesn't realize how strong he is"; "He does not seem to realize the extent of his self-centeredness." The classical problems of neurosis have been described in terms of inadequacies in the way people come to terms with the realities of their personal tendencies and characteristics, which in turn underlie their attempts to come to terms with the realities of the world outside. For example, we are not always successful in labeling or describing ourselves correctly—for example, as aggressive, ambitious, or cold—and this may lead to unsatisfactory social relationships.

The process of personality development and the development of individuals' understanding of themselves are not necessarily smooth and progressive. They can be small and gradual, or substantial, or even kaleidoscopic. Maturational changes (within the person) and environmental conditions interact to produce a particular life-style and self-concept. Successive images of the self have a kind of evolutionary history, in the sense that out of the fortuitous events that give rise to particular notions about the self, some will survive and stabilize, others will thrive and differentiate, and others will wither away.

Persons are not only *active* agents like other sentient creatures, they are to some extent *self-regulating* agents; they are self-regulating not simply in the organismic sense, but also in the psychological sense. The capacity for symbolic representation and recursive thinking enables normal adults to think ahead, to rehearse, to consider consequences and alternatives, and so on. If they are to be effective as active agents in relation to their own well-being, they need to arrive at a realistic assessment of their own best interests and capabilities. Looked at in this way, the self-concept (as self-awareness and self-regulation) is an adaptive characteristic with evolutionary significance insofar as it helps individuals to survive, thrive, and reproduce their kind.

In the broadest sense, then, the psychological study of the self is concerned with elucidating the conditions which are most relevant to understanding the evolution of systems of ideas and feelings about selves in general; it is also concerned with the evolution of systems of ideas and feelings about selves in particular (as seen in life histories, biographies and autobiographies, and in fictional accounts of characters in novels). Indeed, much of what is presented as the psychology of the self is an attempt to identify these ontogenetic developments and to account for the differences between individuals in their self-images.

Our main concern, however, is not with these broad and abstract issues, and we must return to the basic problem of self-description in ordinary language.

IV. THE LANGUAGE OF SELF-DESCRIPTIONS

Self-descriptions

The term "self-description" refers to any set of statements which purports to offer a sensible answer to questions like "What sort of person am I? What do I think of myself? How would I describe myself as a person?" Self-descriptions are simply spoken or written accounts of the impression people have formed (or wish to give) of themselves.

I have argued that self-impressions and impressions of others are normally formed within a framework of commonsense notions about human nature and expressed in the ordinary language of everyday life. Thus the language of overt behavior and the language of psychological processes *is one and the same language*: behavioral and psychological terms are coordinated at all levels—lexical, syntactical, and semantic. Similarly, the language of self-description and the language of descriptions of others is one and the same kind of psychobehavioral discourse. They differ only in their relative emphasis on certain categories of statement.

Self-descriptions (and descriptions of others) can be analyzed in terms of their *contents* (the words and phrases used) and in terms of their *organization* (the way the words and phrases are put together to form meanings and to produce effects). As we have seen, the *contents* of a self-description range widely from characteristics like physical appearance, name, and social role, to those like motives, beliefs, and relationship with others; see Bromley, 1977, for a detailed account of the content categories in personality descriptions. The *organization* of a self-description is a function of syntax, style, and phraseology which seem to develop greatly after the age of about 13 years. This makes it possible for children to integrate and qualify their ideas, to introduce explanatory and comparative terms, to distinguish real from apparent characteristics, to use tenses and suppositions. In this way, the self-description (like descriptions of others) becomes more than a simple, syncretic string or aggregation of words and phrases; it becomes a coherent and rational system of ideas.

The account of the contents of self-concepts in Gordon (1968) proposes that we should study the organization of "a structure of available meanings" (p. 116); these ideas or "meanings" tend to become consistent with one another and to go through a series of transformations during development. Gordon points out that when people make assertions about themselves, they can say a lot of different things: they can assign themselves to a category: "I am an American"; they can assign themselves an attribute: "I am intelligent." They can also exclude themselves from a category—"I am not a communist"—and deny that they have a certain attribute: "I am not well-liked."

My own research work shows that although people do use relatively simple phraseology of the category and attribute kind, they also use more complex phraseology. Consider, for example, the differences between "I teach," "I am a teacher," "I suppose I am a sort of teacher," "I think I am the sort of person who can teach retarded children well." The range of words and phrases and syntactical structures is very wide, and although it has been possible to categorize the different kinds of statement that people make about themselves (in terms of their content), and although it has been possible to describe the syntactical forms commonly used, it has not, so far, been possible to reduce the language of self-description to a simple formula. In this respect, therefore, any psychometric test which employs a restricted and greatly simplified set of terms and an artificial format, such as an adjective checklist, a Q-sort, or a rating scale, may fail to reveal the richness and variety of self-impressions and may give a seriously distorted result.

Gordon's original answer to the problem of how to operationalize the self-concept was to use a relatively unstructured free-response method, viz. the "Who Am I?" (WAI) test. Grammatically speaking, the question permits only answers of a certain kind—answers appropriate to a "Who?" question. In practice, subjects are not restricted to answers of that grammatical type (although they may feel constrained initially to give such answers), but may say anything about themselves that can complete the sentence stem "I am . . .": "nearly 27," "expecting to emigrate."

We need not go into the details of Gordon's findings, except to notice that he was able to differentiate what he called "tenses of the self"—that is, references to past, present and future selves—into which he incorporated what I would call "modal" (i.e., possible) selves. He also emphasized the fact that evaluative terms, reflecting degrees of self-esteem or self-derogation, were commonly found in responses to the WAI test. My own research findings, based on the content analysis of free descriptions of self, confirm the existence of tenses of the self, possible selves, evaluations of self, and a range of other aspects of the self (see Livesley & Bromley, 1973, and Bromley, 1977).

I have not so far examined the order of appearance of items of information in self-descriptions. That order may reflect the degree of openness or disclosure associated with each item, such that the more widely known, more public aspects of the self are reported early in the series, and the less widely known, more private aspects are reported later. Such a tendency, however, is subject to all kinds of influences associated with the situation in which the data are collected.

Gordon (1968, 1976) lists 30 general categories of information found not only in responses to the WAI test but in any description of any person by any person. He refers to McLaughlin (1966) and Gordon (Note 4) in connection with a self-concept dictionary developed for the General Inquirer system. It is an interesting reflection on the nature of scientific investigation that psychologists using the same general approach (the content analysis of ordinary language) to basically the same problem (personality description and self-description) should nevertheless reach such different conceptualizations of personality and the self as those reported by Richardson, Dornbusch, and Hastorf (Note 5), Gordon (1968, 1976), Ossorio and Davis (1968), and Bromley (1977).

Gordon's (1968) content categories are as follows: sex; age; name; race or nationality; religion; kinship role; occupation; student role; political affiliation; social status; residence; group membership; existentiality; abstract category; ideological beliefs; likes; intellectual concerns; artistic activities; other activities; possessions; physical health and appearance; moral worth; self-determination; sense of unity; competence; interpersonal style; mood and feelings; other people's reactions; circumstances; uncodable responses.

The content categories (for statements in self-descriptions) listed above can be compared and contrasted with those described in Section V, Table 1, below; (see also Bromley, 1977). It could be argued that these two taxonomies of self-description are really not so different, and that with some minor modifications they could be brought into line with one another. Nevertheless, the differences do demonstrate that the self can be conceptualized—described and analyzed—in various ways depending upon one's assumptions, concepts, methods, and purposes.

The Other Person's Self

When people make appraisals of another person, their references to that person's self-concept are usually rather few. Moreover, the statements usually take the form of value judgments referring to the other person's selfishness, self-preoccupation, or inflated opinion of himself or herself. Some statements, however, do identify specific characteristics of the self relatively free from evaluative overtones: "likes to feel that she is important," "thinks of herself as always up to date in matters of fashion in clothes." Statements like these, of course, can easily be transformed into "personality" statements—"likes to feel important," "thinks she is up to date in clothing fashion"—which are basically the same as the earlier statements. Hence my doubts about the value of using "self" and "personality" as concepts which are distinguishable in an empirical sense (as opposed to a grammatical sense).

Thus, an observer's assessment of another person's "self" may contribute very little to a personality description. This is partly because self-conceptions are very private aspects of personality, protected by a variety of social strategies and psychological defenses not easily penetrated except by confidants and therapists.

By contrast, a self-description—a description of one's own personality—should be much more revealing and could contain statements spread across 30 different categories of information, more or less identical with those found in descriptions of other people's personalities. As we shall see, self-descriptions, as compared with descriptions of others, place more emphasis on inner psychological processes, such as motives and attitudes and less emphasis on adverse value judgments. Self/other comparisons and contrasts in self-descriptions seem to be implicit, and available on request as it were, without being salient in self-awareness. Such comparative judgments are fairly easy to make and sometimes more appropriate than absolute judgments, especially in relation to psychological characteristics; they are made use of, for example, in the Repertory Grid technique (see Bannister, 1970).

Personal Identity

Some statements in personality descriptions and self-descriptions serve to identify the person referred to. In a previous study (Bromley, 1977), I have relegated the notion of personal identity to a relatively minor functional role in personality description and self-description. This is compatible with the part played by identification statements in such descriptions. I realize, of course, that the notion of personal identity can be of the utmost importance if it is associated with psychological crises, as in loss of identity, alienation, and disorientation. However, I think these abnormal conditions are very different from each other and require further investigation. I would argue that personal identity is, at base, fairly simple and psychologically robust; its function is simply to identify us as individual persons, to distinguish us from other people with whom we might be confused, and to place us in a network of relationships with other identifiable individuals. Personal identity and individuality is a feature of human societies (if not of insect or other communities), but it sometimes shrinks to within very narrow limits, as in military or industrial identifications. Some complex role relationships can work effectively (perhaps *more* effectively) when "personality" and "individuality" are reduced to a minimum in the interests of collective survival and well-being.

The notion of identity can be expressed in absolute and definite terms—name, address, parentage—and in convenient or relativistic terms, such as social role or self/other comparisons. The choice of the characteristics in terms of which people compare and contrast themselves with others perhaps reveals something of the frame of reference they use to stabilize their own identity and the identities of other people.

If we take a wider view of personal identity, however, and regard it as equivalent to self-understanding, then we are reminded that self-impressions and impressions of others influence each other through self/other comparisons. Our awareness of our own behavior and psychological characteristics sensitizes us to similar behavior and psychological characteristics in other people, and vice versa. In the end, the range of our awareness—in terms of the kinds of ideas we use to conceptualize ourselves and others—is similar, whether we are dealing with ourselves or other people. Thus, although in one sense our personal identity coincides with our complete account of ourselves (our extended self-description), there is little to gain by using the term in this sense. It might be better to regard it as simply (a) the irreducible minimum characteristics necessary for identification and (b) the characteristics we use to define ourselves in relation to others, i.e., those we use in routine self/other comparisons. These characteristics can be expected to vary with time and circumstances and to be associated with the way we label and identify ourselves in everyday life.

V. AN EMPIRICAL STUDY OF THE DEVELOPMENT OF SELF-DESCRIPTIONS

Method and Results

A study by Livesley and Bromley (1973) examined changes in self-understanding and understanding others through the years of childhood and adolescence. A form of content analysis was carried out on one self-description and descriptions of eight other stimulus persons written by each of 320 normal subjects ranging in age from 7 to 15 years. The children wrote the descriptions under standard conditions, including carefully phrased instructions intended to encourage the children to avoid describing obvious, surface characteristics, such as physical appearance and clothing, without suggesting what characteristics should be described in response to the general questions: "What sort of person is he or she?" and "What is he or she like?" The intention was to investigate the children's commonsense notions as expressed in ordinary language.

The self-description was written first and used as a "buffer item" to ease the subjects into the main part of the exercise, which required them to write descriptions of eight people they knew reasonably well. These eight descriptions were for specific kinds of people, such as "A boy I like," or "A woman I dislike." The data derived from an analysis of the contents of these descriptions were studied by means of a repeated-measures analysis of variance. The data from the self-description buffer item were studied separately (see Livesley & Bromley, 1973, pp. 229–241). The results were presented there mainly in terms of empirical observations and tests of statistical significance, without much regard for their theoretical implications or practical applications. It is interesting and convenient, therefore, to reexamine this part of the investigation in order to see what implications, if any, it has for a psychology of the self.

The 33 descriptive categories used in the content analysis of the children's descriptions of others were developed during the course of the main investigation, but were not very different from those developed by other investigators working independently (see Livesley & Bromley, 1973, pp. 1–71). We came to feel that we had developed a comprehensive and exclusive system of categories for analyzing the contents of personality descriptions.

The 33 categories used in the content analysis of the children's descriptions of other people are listed in Table 1.

Table 1
Types of Statement in Descriptions of the Self (and Others)

1. Appearance
2. General information and identity
3. Routine habits and activities
4. Actual incidents
5. Possessions
6. Life history
7. Contemporary social circumstances
8. Physical condition
9. General personality attributes
10. Specific behavioral consistencies
11. Motivation and arousal
12. Orientation
13. Expressive behavior
14. Intellectual aptitudes and abilities
15. Achievements and skills
16. Preferences and aversions
17. Interests and hobbies
18. Beliefs, attitudes, and values
19. Attitudes towards self
20. Evaluations
21. Social roles
22. Reputation
23. Friendships and playmates
24. Effect upon, and relations with, others
25. Other people's behavior towards the self
26. Relations with opposite sex
(27. Mutual interactions)
(28. Subject's opinion of, and behavior towards, stimulus person)
(29. Comparison with self)
30. Comparison with others
31. Family and kinship
32. Collateral facts and ideas
33. Irrelevant and unclassifiable facts and ideas

The first question is whether the system of conceptual categories used to analyze children's descriptions of others can also be used to analyze their *self*-descriptions. It can be shown that one can make statements about *oneself* (as the stimulus person) that would fit into one or another of the categories, including No. 19, attitudes towards self; statements in this category, however, are confusable with statements in several of the other categories. The essential feature of the self-statements in category 19 is that they describe the subjects' attitudes to themselves rather than describe their appearance, possessions, life-history, interests, and so on, as in other categories.

Some categories of statement that are found in descriptions of others are not found in self-descriptions. This is not so much a matter of empirical fact as a matter of logic: for example, category No. 27, mutual interactions between the subject and the stimulus person he or she is describing, cannot *logically* apply to self-descriptions; category No. 28, subject's opinion of, and behavior towards, the stimulus person he or she is describing, is identical with category No. 19 in a self-description; category No. 29, comparisons between the subject and the stimulus person he or she is describing, also cannot *logically* apply to self-descriptions.

One answer to the first question, therefore, is that *some* statements describing the self can be categorized in the same way as statements describing others. This leaves open the question of whether *all* statements describing the self can be so categorized. The results of the investigation by Livesley and Bromley (1973), however, seem to show that *all* statements describing the self can in fact be classified by means of the same system of content categories that is used for classifying statements describing other people. This possibility is given further consideration below.

In the Livesley and Bromley (1973) study, the units of analysis were not individual words or sentences but rather "statements," defined as any fact, idea, or item of information referring directly or indirectly to the stimulus person or to the self. The children wrote an average of 12 statements (words or phrases) per description for their self-description compared with 9 statements for their descriptions of other stimulus persons. It is not clear why the self-descriptions were longer than descriptions of other persons—possibly because the self-descriptions were written first in a series of nine personality descriptions.

The average length of the self-descriptions decreased from 14.2 statements at age 7:10 (7 years 10 months) to 10.9 statements at age

10:10, then decreased from 13.0 at age 12:4 to 10.7 at 15:3. The reason for this irregular age trend is not clear, but sampling errors cannot be ruled out. The average length of the descriptions of another person increased from 7.4 statements at age 7:10 to a maximum of 9.7 at 14:3, but then fell back to 8.9 at age 15:3. Part of the fall-off can be attributed to lessened interest in the exercise on the part of school-leavers in that age group. Other sampling errors cannot be ruled out. The results are summarized in Table 2.

Table 2
Age Differences in the Number of Statements per Description for "Self" and "Other"

Age group	7:10	8:10	9:10	10:10	12:4	13:2	14:3	15:3	All
Self	14.2	12.1	11.8	10.9	13.0	11.4	11.1	10.7	11.9
Other	7.4	9.1	9.1	8.7	9.4	9.6	9.7	8.9	9.0

Note: The values are calculated on the basis of one "self" description and 8 "other" descriptions for 40 subjects in each of 8 age groups.

Perhaps the simplest and most obvious explanation for the results in Table 2, particularly if we look at the ratio of the number "self" statement to the number of "other" statements, is that very young children are very much better at describing themselves than describing other people, perhaps on account of their egocentric outlook; the changes that occur at puberty also increase the child's self-centeredness, and this diminishes only slightly, at least up to the age of 15:3.

The next question is whether the statements in the self-descriptions are distributed over the 30 content categories in the same way as they are for descriptions of others. This question can be answered by examining the results summarized in Table 3.

It can be seen that whereas there is fairly good overall agreement between the frequency (or proportion) of statements in each category for the two types of description (self and other), there are a few large disparities. The rank correlation between the two distributions is +0.70. The large disparities are for the following seven types of statement: No. 11, motivation and arousal; No. 12, orientation; No. 17, interests and hobbies; No. 18, beliefs, attitudes, and values; No. 19, attitudes towards self; No. 21, social roles; No. 33, irrelevant and unclassifiable facts and ideas.

Table 3

*The Frequency and Proportion of Statements about "Self" and "Other" in
30 Content Categories, Each Ranked from Highest to Lowest Value*

Category	Self f	%	Rank	Other f/8	%	Rank
1	164	4.30	7	188	6.53	5
2	211	5.54	5	240	8.34	3
3	51	1.34	19	18	0.63	24
4	132	3.46	9.5	122	4.24	7
5	91	2.39	13	61	2.12	10
6	22	0.58	24.5	9	0.31	30
7	5	0.13	30	13	0.45	27
8	22	0.58	24.5	15	0.52	26
9	400	10.50	2	373	12.96	2
10	358	9.40	3	432	15.01	1
11	103	2.70	11	11	0.38	28
12	52	1.36	18	10	0.35	29
13	56	1.47	15.5	66	2.29	9
14	140	3.67	8	54	1.88	12
15	132	3.46	9.5	57	1.98	11
16	912	23.94	1	113	3.93	8
17	290	7.61	4	40	1.39	15
18	76	1.99	14	15	0.52	25
19	14	0.37	27	27	0.94	17.5
20	203	5.33	6	220	7.64	4
21	29	0.76	22	51	1.77	13
22	19	0.50	26	26	0.90	19
23	54	1.42	17	27	0.94	17.5
24	13	0.34	28	23	0.80	20
25	41	1.08	20	18	0.63	23
26	33	0.87	21	20	0.69	21.5
27	N/A	N/A	N/A	193	6.71	
28	N/A	N/A	N/A	174	6.05	
29	N/A	N/A	N/A	19	0.66	
30	25	0.66	23	20	0.69	21.5
31	94	2.47	12	141	4.90	6
32	56	1.47	15.5	48	1.67	14
33	12	0.31	29	36	1.25	16
	3,810	100.00		2,878	100.07	

Table 3 shows that, as might be expected, some aspects of the self
and some aspects of our impressions of another person are more

salient than others (as judged by the number of statements referring to those aspects as compared with others).

The most frequently occurring type of self-statement was category No. 16, preferences and aversions (likes and dislikes), which accounted for 24% of all self-statements. This same category accounted for only 4% of other-statements.

The second most frequent type of self-statement was category No. 9, general personality attributes (traits), which accounted for 10½ % of self-statements. For this aspect of personality description, however, the corresponding value for other-statements was 13%, although here too it ranked second in frequency of occurrence (saliency).

It seems reasonable to suppose that the privileged access people have to their own thoughts, feelings, and desires provides them with a source of information about themselves which is direct (as contrasted with the indirectness of information about another person's thoughts, feelings, and desires). Statements describing personality traits, on the other hand, are abstract and general statements about the consistencies and regularities in a person's behavior and experience; they seem to reflect certain central organizing processes associated with the growth of stable strategies of adjustment.

Our assessment of our own personality traits and the personality traits of others, however, is not given wholly, or perhaps even largely, by privileged access to our private thoughts, feelings, and desires; it arises in part from a series of reflective assessments of our conduct and achievements in comparison with the conduct and achievements of other people. Common sense and ordinary language provide us with terms and phraseology, and with the sorts of evidence and modes of reasoning we need to attribute personality traits to ourselves and to other people. This process of attribution may be complicated (see Jones, Kanouse, Kelley, Nisbett, Valins, & Weiner, 1972), and may be different in self-attribution as compared with other-attribution. Nevertheless, my assumption is that the underlying process is much the same in both cases; I would not go as far as Bem (1972) seems to go in basing self-attributions on people's perceptions of their own *behavior*. There is more to personality appraisal than the attribution of traits, and more to self-appraisal than the assessment of one's own conduct.

The third most frequent type of statement in self-descriptions is category No. 10, specific behavioral consistencies. These can be thought of as habits, or as narrowly defined personality traits relevant to specific sorts of situation, e.g., "careless of my/his or her appearance" (see Bromley, 1977). This category accounts for over 9% of statements in self-descriptions, and for 15% of statements in other-descriptions. In fact, it is the most frequently occuring type of statement in other-descriptions. It would seem to follow that the cognitive processes and opportunities for learning that govern the attribution of *general* personality traits to oneself and others also govern the attribution of *specific* personality traits. It is not that we are better able to attribute habits to others than to ourselves (as the disparity in percentage frequency of occurrence might lead one to believe), but rather that some characteristics, like preferences and aversions (No. 16) and interests and hobbies (No. 17) to which we have privileged access, tend to be relatively more prominent in self-descriptions and so decrease the prominence of other characteristics like habits (No. 10) and identity (No. 2).

The fourth most frequent type of statement in self-descriptions was category No. 17, interests and hobbies. This category accounted for nearly 8% of statements in self-descriptions as compared with less than 1½% in other-descriptions, where it ranked 15th in order of frequency. This finding also fits in with the idea that privileged access is a factor which helps to account for differences in the way we understand ourselves and other people. In this case, it could be argued that some interests and hobbies are relatively private and therefore less accessible to outside observers than to ourselves. Both the external (behavioral, material) and the internal (psychological) evidence would be much more readily available to ourselves than to another.

The fifth most frequent type of statement in self-descriptions is category No. 2, general information and identity, with a frequency of 5½%. This same category ranks third in descriptions of others with a frequency of over 8%. Thus, in comparison with most other features, identity is a relatively prominent feature of both self- and other-descriptions. Its slightly greater saliency for descriptions of others probably arises because of the subjects' need to clearly "identify" the other person they are writing about, whereas in a self-description such information is taken for granted.

The sixth most frequent type of statement in self-descriptions is category No. 20, evaluations, with a frequency of over 5%. In other-descriptions, this category ranks fourth, with a frequency of nearly 8%. This finding suggests that, like personality traits, the mechanisms and terminology governing evaluations of the self are similar to those governing evaluation of others, i.e., those of common sense and ordinary language. Self-evaluations by young children were often quite egotistically favorable, whereas older children often viewed themselves unfavorably.

The remaining 24 categories of statement in self-descriptions each have a frequency of occurrence of less than 5%, the smallest being 0.13% for statements about contemporary social circumstances (category No. 7). This very low frequency is surprising in some ways, considering the easy access to this sort of information about oneself. This category is also relatively infrequent in descriptions of others and ranks 27th with a frequency of .45%.

The least frequent type of statement in descriptions of others is category No. 6, life history, with a frequency of .31%. The low frequency of life-history statements illustrates how little we really know about other people. However, this same category ranks low at 24.5 with a frequency of just over half of one percent in self-descriptions; it shares this rank with category No. 8, physical health and fitness, which also ranks low at 26th with a frequency of half of one percent in descriptions of others. The "life-history" and "body-image" aspects of the self are constant and familiar features to which we are normally well adapted, and they tend to fall into the background (although some situations will bring them to the fore). Such aspects of another's personality, however, are relatively inaccessible to an outside observer.

A major conclusion, therefore, seems to be that whereas privileged access to inner psychological processes (thoughts, feelings, desires) tends to bias self-description in the direction of information of this kind, our easier, more direct, and fuller access to public or semiprivate information about our own behavior, achievements, and circumstances seems not to make much difference—perhaps because we forget that our information is not so easily available to others and so simply assume that it is understood. Thus some of the observed differences in the contents of self-descriptions as compared with descriptions of others arise because of differences in the perspective from which they are written: the former are written from the inside, as it were, the latter from the outside. Much significant information about personality (or self) refers to the central organizing aspects of behavior—abilities, motives, attitudes, beliefs, and values—which have an experiential (covert or private) aspect as well as a behavioral (overt or public) aspect.

We saw that category No. 16, preferences and aversions, likes and dislikes, was by far the most frequently used type of statement in self-descriptions but not in descriptions of others. This suggests that subjective and affective factors are more salient in self-assessment, whereas objective and behavioral factors are more salient in other-assessment. Self-descriptions incorporated semiprivate and ego-involving activities as in statements about interests and hobbies (No. 17). Self-descriptions tended to incorporate those characteristics emphasized in the child's social milieu, as in statements about intellectual aptitudes and abilities (No. 14), since competence and scholastic attainments are an important feature of self/other comparisons during childhood and adolescence. We can expect analogous areas of emphasis to exist at other stages throughout the life cycle.

Some types of statement used more frequently in self-desciptions than in other-descriptions were also used more frequently to describe children (rather than adults) and persons liked (rather than persons disliked). These were No. 16, preferences and aversions; No. 14, intellectual aptitudes and abilities; and No. 17, interests and hobbies. The self-descriptions and descriptions of other "liked" children are similar in content. Livesley and Bromley (1973, p. 237) suggest that self-understanding develops mainly through comparisons with children and adults who are similar to the child and with whom the child interacts more (because he or she likes them). Self-understanding and understanding others are two aspects of a single, if complex, process.

In a previous work (Bromley, 1977), I emphasize the importance of self/other comparisons (category Nos. 29 and 30) in the development of self-understanding, and say that such comparisons take place via concepts and procedures familiar to common sense and are mediated by ordinary language. Nevertheless, only 0.7% of statements in descriptions of others (No. 29) are explicit comparisons between the subject and a stimulus person; similarly, 0.7% of statements about others (No. 30) are comparisons between the stimulus person and another person, and 0.7% are explicit comparisons with others (No. 30) when the subject is describing himself or herself. Comparisons with the self in descriptions of others remain fairly constant in frequency from one age group to the next, whereas comparisons with others in self-descriptions increase in frequency with age (and are absent altogether in the age group 7:10). This finding suggests that, given privileged access to their own thoughts, feelings, and desires, and easier and fuller access to their own behavior and circumstances, young children have little or no need to define themselves relative to others. However, they seem to learn the necessary concepts and terminology for self-description partly in terms of such comparisons made explicit by other people in the form of comments on a child's own behavior and on the behavior of other children. In the same way, children seem to learn the concepts and terminology necessary to coordinate their own subjective (psychological) states with their own overt behavior, and to relate their dispositional states (traits, values, abilities, beliefs) to stable strategies of adjustment: "I am clever because I always get my sums right," "I am annoyed because I can't have my own way." Hence, one would have expected that explicit self/other comparisons would have been more prominent, even taking into account children's egocentric orientation.

So far, we have compared the *contents* of self-descriptions with the contents of descriptions of others. We have not compared the *organization* of these two kinds of description, but our general impression is that their syntax, style, and coordinating phraseology are similar. We now need to look at the changes that take place in the contents and organization of self-descriptions as the child grows up (in the present study we look at age differences in the years between 7 and 15).

Several problems were encountered: First, with only 40 subjects in each age group, the observed age trends were not consistent and could not be regarded as highly reliable; second, it is possible that the meaning of statements classified into the same category may be different for groups differing widely in age—e.g., "I like reading"; third, with regard to Table 3, it is possible that the effect of averaging values for groups differing in age, sex, and intelligence has been to obscure the relationships between self-description and other-description, and that the similarity would be closer if subjects' self-descriptions were compared with their descriptions of people *like themselves*.

Some large differences were observed between groups of children separated by only one year. We had no theoretical expectations relevant to such differences; so that only post hoc interpretations are possible, and these are of no great help unless followed up by specific empirical tests. For example, there is a sharp drop in the frequency of statements about appearance and identity from age 7:10 to 8:10, and a corresponding increase from 14:3 to 15:3. There is a sharp increase in statements about general and specific traits from age 9:10 to 10:10.

The fluctuations in the distribution of self-statements among the different categories from one age group to another are, perhaps, less impressive than the overall framework within which all age groups can be compared. The same applies to comparisons between males and females; the disparities are small and unimportant in comparison with the overall agreement as regards terms of reference and modes of reasoning (see Livesley & Bromley, 1973, and Bromley, 1977).

Among the more interesting age trends are the following. First, a shift from egocentric to more detached and dispassionate self-appraisals is suggested by the observed age differences in category No. 19, attitudes to self, No. 30, comparisons with others, and No. 32, collateral facts and ideas. The percentage frequency of occurrence for each of these categories is very small, but the age trends are consistent. Naturally, the older children tended to make more reference to their relationships with members of the opposite sex. Second, category No. 13, expressive behavior, showed an unusual age trend, from near zero at age 7:10 rising abruptly to 6% at age 15:3. This suggests, but does not of course confirm, that different aspects of human nature tend to come into sharper focus at different stages of development. The mapping of such developmental patterns for self-understanding and understanding others would be laborious, and we need some sort of developmental theory of social cognition in order to investigate the gradual and kaleidoscopic changes that seem to take place. The developmental patterns can be expected to vary with the intelligence, sex, social class, personality, and other characteristics of the subjects.

Conclusions and Examples

In general, the developmental changes in self-description during childhood and adolescence are similar to those that take place in descriptions of others. There is an increase in vocabulary and in the types of statement children are able to make; they learn to use words and phrases more precisely and with greater flexibility; their descriptions become more coherent, more complex, better organized, and more selectively focused; they learn to use subtle syntactic structures to qualify and connect the descriptive terms they are using; their first-hand experience of human behavior is increased and they may benefit from vicarious experience through literature and other arts, and may receive formal instruction about human nature; they become increasingly aware of the need to form impressions about themselves and about others which are effective in interpersonal relationships.

They learn to map the words and phrases of ordinary language onto their own experiential states ("angry," "afraid," "jealous") and onto their own behavior ("being rude," "wasting time," "playing fair"). This, in conjunction with similar sorts of mapping in relation to the behavior and mental states of other people, enables children to coordinate their own thoughts and actions with the intersubjective (objective) concepts and terminology of common sense and ordinary language. Individual differences apart, we understand ourselves and other people by virtue of the common sense and ordinary language we acquire in the process of social learning.

The following examples of actual self-descriptions are taken from Livesley and Bromley (1973). They illustrate some of the features to which we have just referred, and the gradual change from brief, concrete, fragmented, self-centered strings of statements in younger children's descriptions to the longer, more abstract, more coherent, more objective systems of statements in the descriptions of older children.

A boy aged 7:0
"I am 7 and I have hazel brown hair and my hobby is stamp collecting. I am good at football and I am quite good at sums and my favourite game is football and I love school and I like reading books and my favourite car is an Austin."

A girl aged 7:0
"I am 7 years old. I have one sister. Next year I will be 8. I like colouring. The game I like is hide the thimble. I go riding every Wednesday. I have lots of toys. My flowers is a rose, and a buttercup and a daisy. I like milk to drink and lemon. I like meat to eat and potatoes as well as meat. Sometimes I like jelly[gelatine dessert] and soup as well."

A boy aged 9:0
"I am quite good tempered when I get going. I like other children. I like to play practical jokes on people and I am in the habit of forgetting things. I like rough games especially rugby. I am hurt easily and my brother always picks on me. I am a scouser [a person from Liverpool, England]. I always try to

make friends with other children. I dislike jokes that are meant to be funny but aren't."

A boy aged 9:0

"I have dark brown hair, brown eyes and a fair face. I am a quick worker but am often lazy. I am good but often cheeky and naughty. My character is sometimes funny and sometimes serious. My behavior is sometimes silly and stupid and often good it is often funny my daddy thinks."

A girl aged 12:10

"I have a fairly quick temper and it doesn't take much to rouse me. I can be a little bit sympathetic to the people I like, but to the poor people I dislike my temper can be shown quite easily. I'm not thoroughly honest, I can tell a white lie here and there when it's necessary, but I am trying my hardest to redeem myself, as after experience I have found it's not worth it. If I cannot get my way with various people I walk away and most likely never talk to that person again. I take an interest in other people and I like to hear about their problems as more than likely they can help me solve my own. My friends are used to me now and I don't really worry them. I worry a bit after I have just yelled somebody out and more than likely I am the first to apologise."

A girl aged 14:2

"I am a very temperamental person, sometimes, well most of the time, I am happy. Then now and again I just go moody for no reason at all. I enjoy being different from everybody else, and like to think of myself as being fairly modern. Up till I was about 11, I was a pretty regular churchgoer (R.C.), but since then I have been thinking about religion and sometimes I do not believe in God. When I am nervous I talk a lot, and this gives some important new acquaintances a bad impression when I am trying to make a good one. I worry a lot about getting married and having a family, because I am frightened that I will make a mess of it."

It seemed to us that the self (as revealed in unstructured self-descriptions at least) develops not only by systematic differentiation and integration but also by unsystematic separation and coalescence. The unsystematic changes are perhaps more characteristic of the early stages of social and cognitive development, up to the age of about 9 years, when children have less choice and less control over the environment and the experiences it engenders, and when their thinking is to a large extent self-centered and not wholly subject to the constraints of logic, consistency, and social conformity.

The social awareness of adolescents, as revealed by their self-descriptions, incorporates a concern with what other people think and feel about them, and a concern with the effect that they as individuals have on other people. The inhibiting effects on behavior of the internalized phrase "What will people think?" or "What will this, that, or the other person say?" are fairly well understood at a commonsense level. The phrase is used extensively during social development, although its effects at different age levels are not easy to determine. By adolescence, however, for normal children, the phrase is explicit, reflected upon, and helps to constrain the individual's personal identity even in the absence of actual reactions from others. By contrast, earlier in childhood, individuals are likely to express their natural inclinations overtly if they do not anticipate adverse consequences. One could say that the transition from childhood to adulthood (via adolescence) is a transition which seeks to minimize the discrepancy between personal identity and social identity; at the same time, those adolescents whose personal identity deviates from the prescribed forms of social identity in the community to which they belong will tend to seek more congenial social surroundings elsewhere. So variations in personal identity at adolescence or in early adult life provide a mechanism for the diversification of forms of social behavior which are then subject to the selective pressures of cultural evolution. The analysis is complicated by the complex physiological and anatomical changes that accompany adolescence, and by the existence of cultural differences and wide individual differences in adolescent behavior. Nevertheless, it would be unwise to neglect the possibility that there are deep biological roots for the identity crises of adolescence (and for those at other stages of life).

The contrast between personal identity and social identity is expressed in adolescents' ambivalence. They want to "belong" with other people (or some other people), but they also want to assert their individuality, at least in the sense of extracting from others some recognition of their own personal existence. This may take the form of adopting or accepting some simple identification characteristics, such as a nickname, a social role, stable habits with regard to appearance, expressive behavior, social relationships, interests, and so on. By contrast, many adolescents, particularly girls, dislike differences, arguments, and disagreements within the groups to which they belong and try to resolve such interpersonal differences.

In adult life we usually try to understand other people at the level required to interact with them effectively. The impressions we form naturally center on those aspects of the other person which are salient and relevant to our interest. These aspects, however, are first and foremost external and social attributes (appearance, behavior, social position) which have to be interpreted as expressions of internal psychological attributes (dispositions, abilities, beliefs; see Bromley, 1977). The central organizing processes of personality are covert, and individuals themselves may not be fully aware of how their conduct is regulated. Normally, however, they have easier and fuller access to relevant internal states and a better appreciation of the central organizing processes which regulate and explain their own behavior than to those that explain the behavior of others.

Perhaps the most intractable aspect of the self is not what we *know* of our behavior and circumstances (since much of this information is available to others) but rather what we *feel* about ourselves and what we *want* of ourselves. This sort of experience does not alway obtain clear expression in spoken or written accounts of the self. Insofar as it is not made explicit in words, it tends to remain autistic (in Vygotsky's sense) and cannot be communicated effectively, in which case it remains part of the nonphenomenal self (in Wylie's sense), i.e., unconscious or unrealized. Personal maladjustment often reflects a failure to coordinate self-tendencies with socially prescribed forms of conduct, as expressed in common sense and ordinary language.

In the next section, we show one example of how our knowledge about self-description in ordinary language might be used systematically in the study of the self. It should be noted that the categories listed in the semistructured self-appraisal questionnaire in the next section are slightly different from those listed above. The former are based on Livesley and Bromley's (1973) research with children; the latter are based on my research with adults (1977).

VI. A SYSTEMATIC SEMISTRUCTURED SELF-APPRAISAL QUESTIONNAIRE

There is an almost inexhaustible set of statements that one could make about oneself. Hence the value of semistructured tests such as the WAY test, which gives individuals no guidance as to what sorts of statement they should make, but gives them the opportunity to say what they think is worth saying and to qualify and individualize the statements they make.

The systematic semistructured self-interview schedule described below shows how one might obtain certain kinds of basic information on identity, and then obtain further information on a comprehensive range, but limited number, of well-defined aspects of the self. Self-interview schedules could be designed for special purposes, such as student selection, marriage guidance, psychiatric screening. The method could be used to provide a basis for a case-study or for individual counseling. Table 4 shows a selection of "probe" questions that can be incorporated in a systematic semi-structured self appraisal schedule. It will be seen that the questions are much less specific than their counterparts in personality questionnaires; they may have to be modified to suit specific practical applications.

Table 4
A Draft for a Systematic Semistructured Self-appraisal Questionnaire

Identity and Appearance: What is my name and address? Who am I? How can I be recognized and identified? Have I any special distinguishing characteristics?

Life-history: What is the story of my life so far? How did I come to be the person I am now? What formative experiences have I undergone?

Present Circumstances: What are the main circumstances currently facing me? How have these circumstances arisen?

Future Prospects: What does my immediate future hold? What opportunities and constraints are there in my circumstances? What possibilities are open to me? What will be the likely long-term consequences of my current actions and circumstances? What is to become of me?

Routine Habits and Activities: How do I live my life? How do I spend my time, my money, and my energies?

Material Circumstances and Possessions: What financial and material resources do I have at my disposal?

Actual Incidents: What actual incidents reveal my psychological characteristics or the circumstances in which I have been involved?

Physical and Mental Health: What is the state of my physical health? Is there anything unusual in my thoughts, feelings, desires, or actions?

General Personality Traits: How am I inclined, in general, to behave? What regularities and consistencies are there that characterize my behavior in different situations?

Specific Personality Traits: How do I behave in these particular (specified) situations?

Expressive Behavior: How do I express my feelings? What is my usual manner or demeanor?

Motivation and Arousal: What do I want? What am I trying to do? What are my hopes and fears? What do I like and dislike?

Abilities and Attainments: What am I able to do? What am I *not* able to do? How competent am I to cope with this particular (specified) situation?

Orientation and Feelings: How do I see my situation? What do I expect to happen? What options do I think are open or closed to me? How do I think and feel things are going for me?

Principles, Character and Moral Rules: What are my basic beliefs, values, and rules of conduct?

Self-concept: What is my attitude to myself? What do I think and feel about myself? What do I want of myself? How would I describe myself? To what extent am I the sort of person I ought to be ?

Objects of Interest: What things are important to me? How do I relate to them? How do they affect me?

Social Position: What is my position in society? What do other people expect of me?

Family and Kin: Who are my closest relatives? What is my family like? What are my relationships with them?

Friendships and Loyalties: Who are my friends (or enemies)? To whom am I friendly and loyal (or unfriendly and disloyal)?

Self's Response to Others: What is my attitude to people in general (and in particular)? What do I think of other people? What do I expect of them? What do I want of them? How do I react to them?

Others' Response to Self: How do other people in general (and in particular) react to me? What do other people think of me? What do they expect of me? What do they want of me?

Self's Interaction with Others: What activities and interests do I share with other (named) people?

Similarities and Differences Between Self and Others: How do I compare with others? In what ways am I similar to and different from other people?

It is easy to see that by rephrasing the questions slightly—"What is *your* name and address?" "What does *your* immediate future hold?"—one could transform the list of self-appraisal questions into an open-ended self-report method of personality appraisal. The method is based on one approach to the problem of assessing personality (and the self) by means of the content analysis of personality-descriptions and self-descriptions in ordinary language. Relevant issues in content analysis are discussed in Livesley and Bromley (1973), Bromley (1977), and Bilsbury (Note 6).

The questions listed in Table 4 are adapted from a detailed analysis of the case-study method in Bromley (1977); they are derived from a set of thirty categories of information found in adult personality descriptions in ordinary language. A different set of probe questions has been used by Bilsbury (Note 6) to study self-understanding and understanding others in educationally subnormal children. The list is illustrative rather than exhaustive, since different sorts of self-appraisal may be required for different sorts of people and for different purposes, such as marriage guidance or occupational guidance. Taken individually, the items show the kinds of questions any normal reflective individual asks himself from time to time (or indicate the kinds of information he has readily available).

Self-appraisal methods must, by definition, be self-reports. Personality appraisal methods can be, but need not necessarily be, self-reports; For example, they can be objective or projective. The question of the extent to which self-report methods provide valid and useful personality appraisals is one that would take us into the controversy that Mischel (1968) had dealt with, namely, whether the traditional personality questionnaires measure stable and general dispositions.

My view is that it is better to study "persons in situations" than "personality"; and that a sensible approach is to study them as individual cases by means of a quasi-judicial method. This method is problem oriented and provides an account of individuals with as much (or as little) relevant information as is needed to understand whatever it is that we wish to understand about them. This account not only covers the kinds of descriptive information to which we have already referred, but also includes an explanatory framework which attempts to show why people act in the way they do. The quasi-judicial case-study method forms part of a "general theory" of personality (see Bromley, 1977).

The concept of self has no special place in this general theory of personal adjustment because the distinction I make is simply that between an outside (objective) view of the person and an inside (subjective) view. Knowledge of the insider's view (via self-reports) makes an important contribution to the objective appraisal (the description agreed to by others); knowledge of the outsiders' view makes an important contribution to the subjective appraisal (the self-concept).

When all is said and done, there is only *one* thing to study—the person, in the context that of person's life and circumstances. The fact that a person's self-concept may be variable, multiple, confused, nonexistent, or erroneous must be reconciled somehow with the facts of his or her personal adjustment.

VII. SOME THEORETICAL ISSUES IN THE PSYCHOLOGY OF THE SELF

The abstract concept of "self" must be distinguished from a particular person's self-concept or self-image. The abstract concept consists of a general framework of ideas in terms of which the self-concept or self-image of individual people can be described and analyzed. Thus, whereas the abstract concept of self comprises the sorts of general ideas put forward by James (1910), Mead (1934), Allport (1955), Rogers (1961), Goffman (1959), Erikson (1959), and so on, the "self" or "self-concept" of this or that individual person comprises whatever characteristics the person attributes to himself or herself either explicitly or tacitly, taking account of life-history changes and variations associated with changes in circumstances.

There is obviously more to a self-concept than a list of attributes or assertions by people about themselves. To begin with, the self-concept is a *system* of ideas, feelings, and inclinations—that is, it not only has these sorts of features, it also has them *organized* in relation to each other so that certain kinds of functional effect are produced. The functional effect is adaptation to life's circumstances; but adaptation exhibits at least three tendencies: the fulfillment of psychological capacities through the exploitation of environmental opportunities; resistance to frustration through the mastery of environmental constraints and psychobiological limitations; and psychological coherence through the elimination of inconsistencies in the organization of behavior. Notions similar to these are discussed at length by Maddi (1972) in relation to his comparative analysis of personality theories.

The organizational aspect of the self-concept can be explained in terms of the relationships between its constituent thoughts, feelings, and inclinations. Thus, if normal people are asked to describe themselves (to say what sort of people they are), they can usually give an account, in words, of these constituents, which is organized in terms of syntactical structures and semantic patterns. Their account, however, is necessarily brief and partial and therefore incomplete and distorted, so that one cannot necessarily accept it as a reliable, valid, or useful self-appraisal. The nearest we can come to a complete account of an individual's self-concept is one that gives the fullest account possible after exhaustive inquiries—for example, by means of a semistructured self-appraisal questionnaire. In a similar way, a full account of an individual's "personality" is one that is based on exhaustive inquiries, as in an intensive case-study. This does not mean that there is only *one* true and complete account (whether of the self or personality); accounts are always relative to the occasion and the purpose, so that investigators may need to study only those aspects of the person's self that are relevant to their practical purposes as in marriage guidance or student counseling.

I have argued that our "self-concept" is our "personality impression" of ourselves and therefore analyzable in the same terms as a personality impression of another person, that is, it has similar contents and a similar organization. But does it have similar functions? Livesley and Bromley (1973, pp. 184–227) offer a cognitive theory of impression formation and change that would appear to account equally well for personality-impressions and self-impressions. This theory, briefly, would regard the self-concept as a complex schema (map or guide) by means of which people orientate themselves in the world (and especially in relation to other people). They need only become aware of their self-characteristics insofar as they have to be taken into account in organizing their behavior, as in handling conflicting desires or learning from experience. Reflective self-awareness enables individuals to place themselves more securely in the world by helping them to adapt themselves to the world (and the world to themselves).

People are selective in the way they perceive and remember their own behavior and states of mind. Their attention is selectively focused according to their interests and circumstances, and they seek to impose a convenient pattern of meaning onto their experience. Thus a person's self-descriptions can be expected to vary from one occasion to another because they tend to be functionally adapted to the demands of the situation: we give a different "account" of ourselves to a prospective employer, counselor, research worker, spouse, or parent. The self-description, as we have seen, is normally composed of words and phrases (the lexicon) referring to a variety of personal characteristics—such as physical appearance, traits, values, abilities, social relationships—suitably qualified and organized into complex syntactical structures capable of conveying meaning (and influencing behavior). Certain kinds of behavior seem to be closely regulated by the patterns of meaning associated with syntactical structures. Consider, for example, the use of clichés and proverbs as guides to conduct: "Don't count your chickens before they are hatched," "A stitch in time saves nine." In a similar way, self-description statements, such as "I want people to like me," or "I don't bother too much about other people's opinions," may express guides or rules of conduct. The self-concept as a whole is a map for, or a guide to, personal conduct, *except* that it is a compromise product between what people wish themselves to be and what they really are, so that individuals may make mistakes or fail to make full use of their opportunities for development. The development of a realistic self-concept is a lifelong process. It is associated with a continual revision by individuals of their self-descriptions (see Butler, 1968) and a continued attempt to establish compatibility between the different aspects of self that guide their conduct on different occasions.

Contrary to what is asserted by Ossorio and Davis (1968), the task of conceptualizing the "person" is *not* like the task of axiomatizing arithmetic. There is no question of our being able to exhibit the *necessary* relationships which underlie normal behavior, for the simple reason that our theoretical notions do not form a relatively closed, formal, normative, or axiomatic system, like geometry, but rather a relatively open, informal, positive, or approximate system, like biology or geography. The analogy drawn by Ossorio and Davis between the use of descriptive terms in chess and human behavior is misleading because it implies that we already know all the "pieces," "moves," and "rules" in chess (even if we do not know all the ways in which games can be played) and therefore know all the relevant determinants, processes, and laws in human behavior (even if we do not know all the games people play!). Unfortunately, our notions of how human behavior is to be conceptualized are nothing like as simple and as clear as our notions of how to play chess. The meaning of terms like "trait," "habit," "feeling," "motive," and "attitude" is by no means clear and fixed; we have no clear idea of the psychological processes with which they are associated, and even less understanding of how they are organized into a working system.

Where the term "structure" is used in relation to the self, it usually refers to an assemblage of characteristics which people attribute to themselves, e.g., abilities and attainments, habits and traits, social relationships, beliefs, and attitudes. These attributes form a loosely organized array which varies from time to time depending upon factors within the person and factors in the circumstances which surround the person; it is associated with feelings of various kinds, such as self-satisfaction and self-blame. The structure of this array can be thought of as a semantic structure (a structure or pattern of meaning) revealed either explicitly in the verbal description or account that individuals give of themselves or else implicitly in the self-attributions that can be assumed by an observer on the basis of the subjects' behavior (see Brandt, 1972, pp. 229–234). On this interpretation, the self-concept becomes simply one of many frames of reference used by individuals in coming to terms with their environment. It becomes psychologically interesting insofar as the individual may exhibit self-regulated behavior which is not entirely under social control, or insofar as it is an unrealistic or ineffective frame of reference which leads to maladjustment.

We cannot even begin to formulate and systematize our ideas about the self and personality until we have examined, in some detail, how we talk about human behavior, human experiences, and human psychological characteristics. This is what I have tried to do in my examination of personality description in ordinary language (Bromley, 1977). The end result of this inquiry is a complex system of concepts and procedures by means of which we can organize and summarize our understanding of ourselves and others as individual persons.

There is, however, nothing in the proposed system of concepts which resembles geometry, or algebra; nevertheless, like biology or geography, it attempts to categorize and to classify, to make important distinctions, to show the rules, relationships, and processes by means of which human behavior and experience are organized. These features of the system are to a large extent implicit in common sense and tacitly accepted in the ordinary language of everyday life—e.g., the classification of attributes as abilities, beliefs, or motives, the distinction between expressive and deliberate behavior, the demonstration that behavior is a joint function of dispositional and situational factors. The accounts we give, in the ordinary language of common sense, of our own behavior and that of others, contain terms referring to overt behavior as well as terms referring to covert states of mind and dispositional characteristics of a psychological sort. The words and phrases of ordinary language enable us to *fuse* these terms into complex sentences which convey "psychobehavioral" meanings. However, our use of language is acquired so early in life, and with so little question, that we find it difficult to move beyond a commonsense level of analysis—hence, perhaps, the familiar puzzle of not knowing how we know another person's state of mind.

CONCLUSIONS

I have not considered the history of the concept of self: Gergen (1971) includes a brief outline and some references; Lukes (1973) gives an extended account of the rise of "individualism" in politics, religion, economics, and so on, but with little reference to psychological studies of personality and the self. I have also excluded from consideration a great deal of experimental work on the self, for example that reviewed by Wylie (1961, 1974), and that dealing with self-awareness (e.g., Duval & Wicklund, 1972), self-evaluation, (e.g., Diggory, 1966; Webster & Sobieszek, 1974), and self-disclosure (e.g., Jourard, 1971).

My own preference, in a psychological account of individuality and the self, has been to trace their origins from infancy through childhood to their mature status in adult life and their subsequent fate in old age. We can understand mature adult forms of the self better if we know its juvenile psychological development, and we can understand its development better if we know the mature adult forms which it normally reaches.

Unfortunately, our scientific thinking about the self is embedded in a cultural view of human nature in which value judgments and presuppositions are important. Hence we tend to assume, without too much questioning, that a psychology of the self must be concerned with the dignity of the individual (self-esteem), with the individual as an autonomous being (an active, independent agent), and with the individual as a separate person (identity, privacy, self-development). We should try to separate these questions about values and presuppositions, which belong properly to ethics and politics, from questions about how we describe and analyze the psychological (and behavioral) aspects of the self. In particular, we should adopt a skeptical and searching attitude towards those psychological theories and explanations which guide our interests and interpretations in the study of individuality and the self.

It is clear, for example, that one's view (or account) of oneself changes substantially during the juvenile period, and varies even from one occasion to another. This raises the question of continuities and discontinuities in the self as a historical sequence; it raises questions about how people retain their identity following substantial changes in their physical and mental health or their circumstances, how they rearrange basic strategies of adjustment, and how they cope with momentary fluctuations in self-awareness associated with tactical adjustments to temporary situations. A further question is how the many components of the self are brought into relationship with one another, especially when some of these components are explicit, open to self-awareness, whereas others are implicit (or perhaps even denied). Further problems arise because consciousness is not well understood, and it is very likely that we have not fully appreciated the different forms that human awareness can take. Consider, for example, the awareness associated with driving a car as compared with the awareness associated with the realization that one is driving the wrong way. Thus, perhaps the "realization" that one is behaving in the "wrong" way—in a way that is not consistent with one's own interests, beliefs, principles, abilities, attitudes, and so on—is not always a realization that one's self-system is inconsistent, but rather that the plan or program of action is not appropriate to the particular situation (having been terminated too soon or too late, or having been put into operation by mistake). Such errors and confusions in routine conduct may be acknowledged and corrected, or excused, or covered up, or otherwise dealt with by the individual concerned. Genuine inconsistencies and omissions in the organization of the self cannot be so easily rectified, but call for self-examination and reorganization of the central organizing processes, although this may be partial and defensive rather than impartial and accepting. Some of the mechanisms by means of which individuals seem to organize their self-concept (form an impression of themselves as a person) and regulate their conduct have been described in the literature of psychodynamics and social psychology.

I have argued that the self-concept can be understood in part as a frame of reference for self-understanding, self/other comparisons, and for the self-regulation of individual behavior. This frame of reference is a fairly straightforward commonsense system expressed in the ordinary language of everyday life. It provides people with a common, or shared, social construction of human nature, society, and the individual. Some aspects of human nature find a central place in self-awareness, other aspects are more peripheral. This depends to some extent on cultural and historical factors, such as sexual inclinations, religious beliefs, family relationships, and physical appearance. At the same time, in addition to being influenced by cultural norms, individuals may differ in the way they organize their "self," some attaching greater importance to social dominance, some to academic achievement or to self-denial.

The way in which we arrive at a given conception of ourselves can be studied only in terms of a psychological biography or autobiography. Our self-conception is not a single idea, but rather a complex system of ideas, feelings, and desires, not necessarily well-articulated or coherent. A self-concept has a history which can be thought of in terms of being adaptive in an evolutionary sense, that is, in relation to our capacity to vary our self-regulated behavior in response to the constraints and opportunities presented by the changing situations in which we find ourselves (and which we help to engender). This is not to say that we tend to develop a better-adapted self-concept (in the sense of being able to improve and extend the range of our individual self-regulated behavior), but rather that we tend to establish an individualized behavioral niche in which some kind of equilibrium is reached between situational constraints and opportunities on the one hand and our capacity for self-regulation (and variation) on the other. Thus, for example, we may "choose" to stay within the confines of a safe social milieu and resist attempts by others to persuade us to diversify our behavior and to adopt a more adventurous conception of ourselves. It is probably unwise to regard self-conception as causally prior to self-regulated actions, or vice versa; it seems more than likely that the individuals' understanding of the relationships between their actions on the one hand and their psychological aspirations and states of mind on the other is the product of reflection on *both* external behavior and internal states. We are talking about *one* system: a *psychobehavioral* system.

The self-concept and the self-regulation of behavior are, of course, influenced by a range of factors outside our personal control. For example, we are subject to other people's opinions, to physiological influences of which we are not aware; we are subject to the peculiarities of the language and commonsense notions characteristic of the culture to which we belong; we are subject to important formative experiences long before we achieve any substantial degree of self-awareness and self-regulation.

REFERENCE NOTES

1. Stein, M. I., & Neulinger, J. A typology of self-descriptions. In M. R. Katz, J. O. Cole, & W. E. Barton (Eds.), *The role and methodology of classification in psychiatry and psychopathology*. Washington: U.S. Department of Health, Education and Welfare, Public Health Service, 1968.
2. Stein, M. I. *Ecology of typology*. Paper presented at the Association of American Medical Colleges Conference on Personality Measurement in Medical Education, Des Plaines, Illinois, June 1971. (Available from Research Center for Human Relations, Department of Psychology, New York University.)
3. Meehl, P. E. *Minnesota-Ford pool of phenotypic personality items*. Unpublished manuscript, University of Minnesota, 1962.
4. Gordon, C. *The person-conceptions system for computer-aided content analysis*. Unpublished manuscript, Rice University (Sociology Dept.), 1975.
5. Richardson, S. A., Dornbusch, S. R., & Hastorf, A.H. *Children's categories of interpersonal perception*. Washington: National Institute of Mental Health, Research Grant M–2480, 1961.
6. Bilsbury, C. *Person perception in educationally subnormal children*. Unpublished manuscript, University of Liverpool, 1977.

REFERENCES

Allport, G. W. *Becoming: Basic considerations for a science of personality*. New Haven, Conn.: Yale University Press, 1955.
Aronfreed, J. *Conduct and conscience: The socialization of internalized control over behavior*. New York: Academic Press, 1968.
Baldwin, J. M. *Social and ethical interpretations in mental development* (1897). Quoted in "The self-conscious person" in C. Gordon and K.J. Gergen (Eds.), *The self in social interaction. Vol. 1: Classic and contemporary perspectives*. New York: Wiley, 1968.
Bannister, D. (Ed.). *Perspectives in personal construct theory*. London: Academic Press, 1970.
Bem, D. J. Self-perception theory. In L. Berkowitz (Ed.), *Advances in experimental social psychology* (Vol. 6). New York: Academic Press, 1972.
Brandt, R. M. *Studying behavior in natural settings*. New York: Holt, Rinehart & Winston, 1972.
Bromley, D. B. The social psychology of reputation. *Bulletin of the British Psychological Society*, 1966, **19**, 73. (Abstract)
Bromley, D. B. An approach to theory construction in the psychology of development and aging. In L. R. Goulet & P. B. Baltes (Eds.), *Life-span developmental psychology*. New York: Academic Press, 1970.

Bromley, D. B. Informal systems in psychology. *Bulletin of the British Psychological Society*, 1973, **26**, 135. (Abstract)

Bromley, D. B. *Personality description in ordinary language*. London: Wiley, 1977.

Bugenthal, J. F. T., & Zelen, S. L. Investigations into the "self-concept": I. The W.A.Y. technique. *Journal of Personality*, 1950, **18**, 483–498.

Butler, R. N. The life review: An interpretation of reminiscence in the aged. In B. L. Neugarten (Ed.), *Middle age and aging*. Chicago: University of Chicago Press, 1968.

Cooley, C. H. *Human nature and the social order*. New York: Charles Scribner's Sons, 1902.

Diggory, J. C. *Self-evaluation: Concepts and studies*. New York: Wiley, 1966.

Duval, S., & Wicklund, R. A. *A theory of objective self awareness*. New York: Academic Press, 1972.

Erickson, E. H. The problem of ego identity. *Psychological Issues*, 1959, **1**, 101–166.

Feffer, M. Developmental analysis of interpersonal behavior. *Psychological Review*, 1970, **77**, 197–214.

Feldman, C. F., & Toulmin, S. Logic and the theory of mind. In W. J. Arnold and J. C. Cole (Eds.), *Nebraska Symposium on Motivation, 1975* (Vol. 23), Lincoln: University of Nebraska Press, 1976.

Fiske, D. W., & Maddi, S. R. (Eds.). *Functions of varied experience*. Homewood, Ill.: Dorsey Press, 1961.

Flapan, D. *Children's understanding of social interaction*. New York: Teachers College Press, Columbia University, 1968.

Flavell, J. H. *The development of role-taking and communication skills in children*. New York: Wiley, 1968.

Gergen, K. J. *The concept of self*. New York: Holt, Rinehart & Winston, 1971.

Goffman, E. *The presentation of self in everyday life*. New York: Doubleday, 1959.

Gordon, C. Self-conceptions: Configurations of content. In C. Gordon & K. J. Gergen (Eds.), *The self in social interaction. Vol. 1: Classic and contemporary perspectives*. New York: Wiley, 1968.

Gordon, C. Self-conceptions methodologies. *Journal of Nervous and Mental Disease*, 1969, **148**, 328–364.

Gordon, C. Development of evaluated role identities. *Annual Review of Sociology*, 1976, **2**, 405–433.

Gordon, C., & Gergen, K. J. (Eds.). *The self in social interaction. Vol. 1. Classic and contemporary perspectives*. New York: Wiley, 1968.

James, W. *Psychology: The briefer course*. New York: Holt, 1910.

Jones, E. E., Kanouse, D. E.., Kelley, H. H., Nisbett, R. E., Valins, S., & Weiner, B. *Attribution: Perceiving the causes of behavior*. Morristown, N.J.: General Learning Press, 1972.

Jourard, S. M. *Self-disclosure: An experimental analysis of the transparent self*. New York: Wiley, 1971.

Kuhn, M. H., & McPartland, T. S. An empirical investigation of self-attitudes. *American Sociological Review,* 1954, **19,** 68–76.

Lewis, M., & Cherry, L. Social behavior and language acquisition. In M. Lewis & L. Rosenblum (Eds.), *Origins of behavior. Vol. 5: Communication and language: Interaction, conversation, and the development of language.* New York: Wiley, 1977.

Livesley, W. J., & Bromley, D.B. *Person perception in childhood and adolescence.* London: Wiley, 1973.

Lukes, S. *Individualism.* Oxford: Basil Blackwell, 1973.

Maddi, S. R. *Personality theories: A comparative analysis* (Rev. ed.) Homewood, Ill.: Dorsey Press, 1972.

McLaughlin, B. The WAI dictionary and self perceived identity in college students. In P. J. Stone, D. C. Dunphy, M. S. Smith, & D. R. Ogilvie (Eds.), *The general inquirer: A computer approach to content analysis.* Cambridge, Mass.: MIT Press 1966.

Mead, G. H. *Mind, self and society* (C. W. Morris, Ed.). Chicago: University of Chicago Press, 1934.

Mischel, W. *Personality and assessment.* New York: Wiley, 1968.

Ossorio, P. G., & Davis, K. E. The self, intentionality, and reactions to evaluations of the self. In C. Gordon & K. J. Gergen (Eds.), *The self in social interaction. Vol. 1: Classic and contemporary perspectives.* New York: Wiley, 1968.

Piaget, J. *The child's conception of the world.* London: Routledge & Kegan Paul, 1929.

Rheingold, H. L. The effect of environmental stimulation upon social and exploratory behavior in the human infant. In B. M. Foss (Ed.), *Determinants of infant behavior.* London: Methuen, 1961.

Richards, M. P. M. (Ed.). *The integration of a child into the social world.* London: Cambridge University Press, 1974.

Rogers, C. *On becoming a person.* Boston: Houghton Mifflin, 1961.

Schaffer, H. R. *The growth of sociability.* Harmondsworth: Penguin Books, 1971.

Selman, R. L. Taking another's perspective: Role-taking development in early childhood. *Child Development,* 1971, **42,** 1721–1734.

Shantz, C. U. The development of social cognition. In E. M. Hetherington (Ed.), *Review of child development research* (Vol. 5). Chicago: University of Chicago Press, 1975.

Vygotsky, L. S. *Thought and language.* Cambridge, Mass.: MIT Press, 1962.

Webster, M., & Sobieszek, B. *Sources of self-evaluation: A formal theory of significant others and social influence.* New York: Wiley, 1974.

Wylie, R. C. *The self-concept.* Lincoln: University of Nebraska Press, 1961.

Wylie, R. C. The present status of self theory. In E. F. Borgatta & W. W. Lambert (Eds.), *Handbook of personality theory and research.* Chicago: Rand McNally, 1968.

Wylie, R. C. *The self-concept* (Rev. ed.). Lincoln, University of Nebraska Press, 1974.

Empathy, Its Development and Prosocial Implications

Martin L. Hoffman

University of Michigan

*E*mpathy has long interested social philosophers and social scientists who see it as one of the basic human attributes supportive of social life. The term has over the years been defined in many ways, most of which fit into two broad rubrics. One pertains to the awareness of another person's feelings, thoughts, intentions, self-evaluations, and the like. This cognitive conception of empathy has inspired considerable research—under such headings as "person perception", role-taking, recognition of affect in others, and social cognition—which has been reviewed by Deutsch and Madle (1975), Shantz (1975), and others.

My concern is with the second conception, empathy as a vicarious affective response to others. The two conceptions undoubtedly interact, since the ability to respond vicariously may depend on the extent to which one can cognitively infer another's affective state. And, conversely, vicariously aroused affect supplies inner cues to the observer that may add meaning to the affect that he or she infers in another. Thus cognitive considerations cannot be ignored and they will be discussed in detail, but the main focus of attention will be on the affective dimension of empathy which has until recently been neglected by researchers. My purpose is to review and provide a critical synthesis of the amorphous and scattered literature on empathy and, by pointing up important theoretical and methodological issues and suggesting future lines of investigation, to stimulate further research on the topic.

It should first be noted that despite the paucity of empirical research the interest in empathy as vicarious affective arousal does have a long history, going back at least two centuries. Writers like Hume, Rousseau, Shelley, and Adam Smith, for example, wrote extensively about this aspect of experience and its significance for human interaction and organized social life. Early psychological theorists like Stern, Scheler, and McDougall advanced the view that empathy provided the motivational base for specific prosocial acts like helping and comforting others, taking turns, cooperating, and sharing. Some of these writers thought empathy was the basic prosocial bond making civilized life possible, though most simply considered it part of human nature, assuming that if people respond empathically to someone they are more likely to behave in a benevolent manner towards that person. These writers all seemed to share the conception of empathy as the basis for a prosocial motive, rather than a skill that might serve egoistic and prosocial motives alike.

This paper has two parts. The first is theoretical, including a discussion of the biological underpinnings of empathy and presenting a comprehensive theoretical model of its psychological functioning and development. The second part is a systematic review of the research literature.

BIOLOGICAL CONSIDERATIONS

Neural mechanisms. A possible neural basis for empathy has been suggested by MacLean (1958, 1962, 1967, 1973). According to MacLean, the limbic system—an ancient part of the brain which humans share with all mammals—has two parts; one is primarily concerned with the feelings, emotions, and behavior that insure self-preservation, while the other is primarily involved in expressive and feeling states, including empathy, that are conducive to sociability and preservation of the species. There are connections between the limbic system and the hypothalamus which help integrate emotions and viscerosomatic behavior. There are also connections between the limbic system and the prefrontal cortex, a newer formation of the brain, one of the functions of which is "helping us to gain insight into the feelings of others . . . [The pre-frontal cortex derives] part of this 'insight'—the capacity to see with feeling—from its connection with the limbic brain" (MacLean, 1973, p. 58). According to this theory, therefore, the brain structures required for a primitive affective involvement with others were present early in human evolution, and the addition of newer brain structures, mainly the prefrontal cortex, together with the connective neural circuits that have also been acquired, made it possible for the earlier primitive affect to be experienced in conjunction with a cognitively more advanced social awareness or insight into others. Empathy could thus have contributed to human social existence and continued to evolve into increasingly complex forms as the human brain developed and grew.

Not all writers share MacLean's views in their entirety. Some, for example, see the limbic system as encompassing a larger portion of the brain and playing an important role in long-term memory. Others have raised questions about whether it plays such a direct role in prosocial emotion. There is general agreement, however, that the limbic system is much older than the neocortex, that it mediates the emotions, and that it is intricately connected with the neocortex and other parts of the brain. It thus seems reasonable to conclude that the limbic system may provide a neural basis for empathic arousal, and that we may indeed be prewired in such a way that our own feelings of distress or joy are contingent not only on the direct impact of events on ourselves but also on the affective experiences of others.

Empathy and evolution. The argument for a biologically based empathic response in humans can also be made on grounds of natural selection. The theoretical issues bearing on human evolution are too complex to be fully treated here (see Alexander, 1971; Campbell, 1972; Hoffman, Note 1) but I will argue briefly that (a) some type of altruistic disposition was adaptive and (b) empathy may have provided the base for that disposition. There is, first of all, general agreement among evolutionary theorists, based on evidence from fossil remains (bones, tools, weapons), that during most of human evolutionary history people lived in a highly adverse environment under constant threat from starvation and predators. They coped with these conditions not alone but by banding together with others in small nomadic hunting and gathering groups. The obviously greater survival value of cooperative and social life over solitary life has led some writers to take the view that natural selection must have favored characteristics that benefit the group or species as a whole rather than a crude, unbridled egoism (e.g., Wynne-Edwards, 1962). Others, however, have pointed out that this is impossible: Since the unit of reproduction is the individual, natural selection must have favored egoistic traits that maximize the fitness of the individual (e.g., Williams, 1966). Both points of view have merit. So does Campbell's (1965) notion that the joint presence of egoistic and altruistic tendencies would have had the greatest survival value: Because of the varied and multiply contingent nature of the environment, egoistic behavior must have been adaptive at certain times and altruistic behavior at other times.

One solution is to find evidence for prosocial mechanisms that also contribute to individual fitness. Two such mechanisms have gained currency among evolutionary theorists: "kin selection" and "reciprocal altruism." Kin selection is the most influential, probably because it appears to provide the most parsimonious explanation of altruism that is also consistent with the traditional view that each organism functions to maximize its own survival. The central concept is "inclusive fitness" (Hamilton, 1964, 1971), which states simply that an individual's genetic fitness is measured not only by the survival and reproduction of the individual and his or her offspring, but also by the enhancement of the fitness of other relatives who share his or her genes. This allows for the evolution of acts that may be beneficial to others and detrimental to the individual's own survival or reproduction, and are therefore by definition altruistic. Since organisms function to maximize inclusive fitness, the genes inducing an individual to perform an altruistic act will be positively selected if the recipient of the act is related to the individual sufficiently closely so that a net increase in the latter's genes results. Degree of altruism is thus positively related to closeness of the relationship.

An important extension of kin selection has been made by Eberhard (1975), who shows mathematically that any small degree of relatedness between donor and beneficiary can serve as the basis for kin selection, as long as the degree of relatedness is even slightly above average for the population. Furthermore, the probability of altruism is increased if the beneficiary stands to gain a great deal (e.g., in emergencies); if the cost to the donor is low (e.g., if the donor is excluded from reproducing on his or her own or is in control of an abundant resource); if the donor is particularly efficient at giving aid; or if the beneficiary is particularly efficient at using it. It is thus possible for kin selection to operate among quite distant relatives.

Trivers' (1971) model of reciprocal altruism, like kin selection, also focuses on direct benefit to the reproductive unit, the individual, rather than the group. Here the altruist and recipient may be totally unrelated, however. Trivers uses a rescue model to show that natural selection had to favor altruism because of the long-run benefit to the organism that behaves altruistically. In the model, individual A encounters another person, B, whose life is in danger (e.g., from drowning). It is assumed that (1) the probable cost to A of rescueing B is far less than the gain to B, and (2) there is a high likelihood of a role reversal in the future. Trivers shows mathematically that if the entire population is sooner or later exposed to the same danger, the two who make the attempt to save the other will be more apt to survive than two who face these dangers on their own. It is therefore in the individual's long-run selfish interest to take the relatively low risk associated with helping others in danger. Trivers notes certain limitations of the model; for example, the possible selection for "cheating." Nevertheless, the model does provide a possible biological basis for altruism toward others who are members of one's social unit though unrelated through kinship.

The issue is by no means resolved, but it does seem reasonable to conclude that the tendency to help others in distress may be a part of human biological inheritance, despite the fact that our contemporary social and physical environment differs markedly from that of our remote ancestors and may, for example, no longer support the one-to-one reciprocity assumed by Trivers. This of course is not to deny that human beings are also by nature selfish and aggressive in the individual sense (e.g., Tinbergen, 1968) or even that helping others may often be selfishly motivated or fostered by such essentially irrelevant personality characteristics as courage and independence (London, 1970). Indeed, as already noted, the acquisition of both egoistic and altruistic structures would appear to have been most adaptive in human evolution. The argument does suggest, however, that a built-in mechanism for mediating helping behavior is a tenable hypothesis, however fragile it may at times appear in individualistic societies such as our own.[1]

What might this mechanism be? It is probably not an automatic helping response ("fixed action pattern") because this would ignore egoistic needs and thus not allow the flexibility needed for survival. As Campbell (1972) notes, fixed altruistic action patterns can exist in certain insect societies because the individuals who are genetically programmed to sacrifice themselves for the group are not those programmed to carry out the reproductive functions. This genetic separation of the altruistic and reproductive functions does not exist

---

1. There are other arguments, aside from evolutionary considerations, for the existence of an altruistic motive system (Hoffman, 1975, Note 1).

in humans. What therefore must have survived through natural selection is not a fixed action pattern but a predisposition or motive to act altruistically. Furthermore, this predisposition must be amenable to influence by perceptual and cognitive processes. Kin selection, for example, implies that it was adaptive for people to evolve mechanisms for perceptually discriminating the extent to which others are related to—perhaps the extent to which they resemble—the self. And, following Trivers' model of reciprocal altruism, though an individual may be disposed to help another in distress, a judgmental process must intervene wherein one weighs the risk to oneself and the gain to the other. In other words, natural selection requires that a motive to help others in need is reliably aroused but also subject to some degree of perceptual and cognitive control.

Empathy appears to fulfill all these criteria. First, as we shall see, it is a prevalent human response and appears to be accompanied by a predisposition to help, though not necessarily by actual helping behavior. Second, MacLean's work suggests there is a neural basis both for empathic affect arousal and the necessary cognitive intervention between arousal and action. Third, there is evidence that cognition may be an inherent part of empathic arousal: (a) Empathy, like other emotions, is tied to visceral arousal, and visceral arousal apparently does not occur until 1–2 seconds after the person attends to the precipitating stimulus, a lag which allows time for cognitive appraisal to occur; (b) Observing someone in pain results in the usual increase in skin conductance but also in a deceleration of the heart rate, which often signifies attention and cognitive functioning; the direct experience of pain, by contrast, produces a skin conductance rise and heart rate acceleration, which is often a sign of stress (Lacey, 1959; Craig & Lowery, 1969). It thus appears that empathy is reliably aroused, predisposes one to help, and is subject to cognitive control.

TOWARD A THEORY OF EMPATHY AND ITS DEVELOPMENT

As for the ontogenetic development of empathy, the only theoretical account in the literature thus far is my own initial attempt and its most recent revision (Hoffman, 1975, in press–a), which I will summarize after a brief discussion of two definitional issues. The first issue pertains to the veridicality of the observer's response. Most writers agree that there must be some match between the affective experience of the observer and that of the model, but some (e.g., Feshbach & Roe, 1968) apply rather strict criteria and insist on an exact match, while others (e.g., Stotland, 1969) require only that there be general agreement as to positive or negative tone. My view is that a certain amount of veridicality should be expected because all humans have the same basic nervous system, and they also share a number of affect-producing experiences, especially during the long period of socialization. Insisting on a high degree of veridicality as part of the definition, however, may only add to the confusion between the cognitive and affective processes involved in empathic arousal and may obscure certain fundamental issues in the development of empathy. The degree of veridicality, for example, as well as the range of emotions with which people can empathize, should increase with age because of their perceptual and cognitive development and the increasing variety of affects they experience directly.

A second issue pertains to the nature of the cues or stimuli that evoke an empathic response. For a response to be labeled empathetic, must the observer respond to direct (e.g., facial) cues reflecting the model's affective experience, or is it still empathy if the response is to situational cues alone? Most writers ignore this issue although some (e.g., Iannotti & Meacham, Note 2) suggest we use the facial cue as the essential criterion. I think this is an unwise restriction because it rules out many instances in which we respond vicariously to people's verbal or written communication about their feelings, or to information we may receive about them in their absence.

I suggest that empathy be defined simply in terms of the arousal of affect in the observer that is not a reaction to his or her own situation but a vicarious response to another person. The focus of the definition then is on the *process* of vicarious affect arousal. Veridicality and type of eliciting cue are variables to be studied, for example developmentally, rather than part of the definition.

In the theoretical model proposed here empathy has three components: an affective, a cognitive, and a motivational component. The focus is on empathic distress, which is pertinent to prosocial motivation, although I assume the model may bear on other empathically aroused affects as well.

Modes of Empathic Arousal

There appear to be at least five distinct modes of empathic arousal which vary in degree of perceptual and cognitive involvement, type of eliciting stimulus (e.g., facial, situational, symbolic), and amount and kind of past experience required. They are here presented roughly in order of their appearance developmentally.

1. There is evidence that 1- and 2-day-old infants will cry in response to the sound of another infant's cry (Sagi & Hoffman, 1976; Simner, 1971). Furthermore, this reactive cry is not merely a response to a noxious stimulus, since the infants do not cry as much to equally loud nonhuman sounds, including computer-simulated infant cries. Nor is it a simple imitative vocal response lacking an affective component. Rather, it is vigorous, intense, and in all observable respects resembles a spontaneous cry (Sagi & Hoffman, 1976). In other words, exposure to a cue of distress in another infant produces distress in the newborn. The newborn's reflexive cry must therefore be considered as a possible early precursor of empathic arousal, though obviously not a full empathic response since it lacks a cognitive component.

Whether this cry is learned or a biologically based isomorphic response to another's cry is problematic. Conditioning of the heart rate is apparently possible in 2-day-olds (Crowell, Blurton, Kobayashi, McFarland, & Yang, 1976), and it seems likely that a response so natural and frequent in newborns as crying can also be conditioned. If so, this lends credence to a classical conditioning explanation of the newborn's reflexive cry; that is, it may be a conditioned distress response to a cue (sound of the other's cry) that resembles cues associated with the infant's own past cries of distress. Both hypotheses—that the cry is innate and that it is learned—would then remain tenable. The final test may require further research, preferably in the delivery room before the infants have had their own distress experiences. Even then, of course, the birth cry and the pain of the birth process might provide the necessary conditions for explanations based on conditioning principles to apply. Should the birth cry be needed for an explanation, however, this would indicate that the reflexive cry is for all practical purposes constitutionally based.

2. The second mode, which requires some perceptual discrimination capability and therefore appears a bit later than the reflexive newborn cry, is a type of classical conditioning of empathy that results from the bodily transfer of the caretaker's affective state to

the infant through physical handling (Hoffman, 1976). For example, when the mother experiences distress, her body may stiffen, with the result that the child (if he or she is being handled at that time) also experiences distress. Subsequently, the mother's facial and verbal expressions that initially accompanied her distress can serve as conditioned stimuli that evoke the distress response in the child. Furthermore, through stimulus generalization, similar expressions by other persons become capable of evoking distress in the child. This mechanism has been advanced to explain the behaviors fitting Sullivan's (1940) definition of empathy as a form of "nonverbal contagion and communion" between mother and infant (e.g., the infant is viewed as automatically empathizing with the mother, feeling euphoric when she does and anxious when she is.)[2]

3. The third mode is a more general variant of the classical conditioning paradigm. It holds that cues of pain or pleasure from another person or from that person's situation evoke associations with the observer's own past pain or pleasure, resulting in an empathic affective reaction (Humphrey, 1922). A simple example is the boy who cuts himself, feels the pain, and cries. Later, on seeing another boy cut himself and cry, the sight of blood, the sound of the cry, or any other distress cue or aspect of the situation having elements in common with his own prior pain experience can now elicit the unpleasant affect initially associated with that experience. This mode is not limited to distress originating in physically communicated tensions or confined to early infancy. It may therefore provide the basis for a multiplicity of distress experiences with which the child can empathize.

4. The fourth mode was advanced some time ago by Lipps (1906), who viewed empathy as the result of an isomorphic, presumably unlearned "motor mimicry" response to another person's expression of affect. This conception is reminiscent of McDougall's (1908) "primitive passive sympathy", wherein the expression of emotion in one individual is viewed as the innate adequate stimulus for the same emotion in the observer. Lipps was more explicit than McDougall, however, about the actual mechanism involved. According to Lipps, the observers automatically imitate the other person with slight movements in posture and facial expression

---

2. It can also account for Escalona's finding (1945), in a women's reformatory in which infants were cared for by their own mothers, that the infants were more upset on the days when their mothers were anxiously waiting to appear before a parole board.

("objective motor mimicry"), thus creating in themselves inner cues that contribute, through afferent feedback, to their understanding and experiencing of the other person's affect. Lipps appears to share with James (1890) and Tomkins (1962) the view that the experience of an emotion is the result of situationally induced bodily processes, mainly the activity of visceral and facial muscles respectively.[3] According to James, for example, if a situation calls for running, we run, and the running, together with the resulting skeletal and especially visceral responses, causes the conscious experience of fear. And in Tomkins' view, feedback from the activity of the facial musculature, when transformed to conscious form, constitutes the experience or awareness of emotion. All three writers make the assumption that the inner cues are different for each emotion and that by perceiving these cues the person becomes aware of just what emotion he or she is experiencing. The unique feature of Lipps's theory is of course that the inner bodily processes are produced not by the person's own situation but by cues indicating the affective state of someone else.

Although this conception has been ignored over the years, there is recent, modest support for it. First, we know from recent infancy research that the human face is salient and has considerable drawing power (e.g., Haaf & Bell, 1967). And, in a study by M. L. Hamilton (1973), children were found to display appropriate facial expressions and presumably respond emotionally when viewing films depicting people in various affective situations. It thus seems reasonable to expect, although the hypothesis is yet to be tested directly, that children will attend to facial expressions and respond emotionally, possibly even in the absence of situational cues.

With adults there is direct evidence for motor mimicry, in studies showing that people engage in increased lip activity and increased frequency of eyeblink responses when observing models who stutter or blink their eyes (Berger & Hadley, 1975; Bernal & Berger, 1976). There is also evidence for afferent feedback: Though visceral activity has long been known to lack specificity, the different emotions appear to be accompanied by different degrees of tone in the skeletal muscles (e.g., the loss in muscle tone which accompanies sadness is associated with characteristic postures which are diametrically opposed to those seen in a happy mood) and by different

3. James's earlier views, preceding Lange's influence, were closer to those advanced by Tomkins in stressing the importance of feedback from facial and voluntary muscles as opposed to visceral muscles.

patterns of facial muscle activity (e.g., Gelhorn, 1964; Izard, 1971). Finally, it appears that cues from one's facial musculature may contribute to the actual experience of an emotion. In a series of remarkable experiments by Laird (1974), subjects were instructed to arrange their facial muscles, one at a time, into positions that corresponded to "smiles" or "frowns," without knowing that their faces were set in smile or frown positions. This was done by asking the subject to contract various muscles (e.g., experimenter touched the subject lightly between the eyebrows with an electrode and said, "Pull your brows down and together . . . good, now hold it like that"). The subjects reported feeling more angry when their faces were set in the frown position and more happy when their faces were set in the smile position even though they were unaware of frowning or smiling. They also reported that cartoons viewed when "smiling" were more humorous than cartoons viewed when "frowning." Though further research is needed to see if motor mimicry occurs not only for eyeblinks and stuttering but also for the facial muscle patternings associated with different emotions, the findings thus far justify considering motor mimicry as at least a possible mechanism of empathic arousal.

5. The previous two modes have certain things in common that make it difficult to predict which one appears first developmentally. They are both involuntary and minimally cognitive, requiring only enough perceptual discrimination to detect the relevant cues from the other person (mimicry) or from his or her situation (conditioning). The fifth mode, imagining how it would feel if the stimuli impinging on the other person were impinging on the self, is clearly the most advanced developmentally. The pertinent research has been done by Stotland and his associates. In one study (Mathews & Stotland, Note 3) nursing students watched a training film in which a severely ill patient, followed from the time of entry into the hospital, finally dies. Those who indicated previously that they often imagine themselves in the other person's place (in the movies, for example) showed more palmar sweat if they imagined themselves in the place of the dying woman. In a second study (Stotland, Sherman & Shaver, 1971), subjects who were first led to believe that they would undergo a painful heat treatment, and then told later that they would not, showed an enhanced palmar sweat response when observing someone else undergo the treatment. It seems likely that while waiting for the treatment themselves the subjects were imagining what it would be like, and that this anticipation

resulted in an increased tendency to imagine themselves in the victim's place while he or she received the treatment.

In a third study (Stotland, 1969), subjects instructed to imagine how they would feel and what sensations they would have in their hands if exposed to the same painful heat treatment being applied to another person gave more evidence of empathic distress, both physiologically and verbally, than (a) subjects instructed to attend closely to the other person's physical movements and (b) subjects instructed to imagine how the *other* person felt when he or she was undergoing the treatment. The last finding in particular suggests that imagining oneself in the other's place may produce an empathic response because it reflects processes generated from within the observer, rather than from the observer's orientation to the model. These may be processes in which connections are made between the stimuli impinging on the other person and similar stimulus events in the observer's own past. That is, imagining oneself in the other's place may produce an empathic response because it has the power to evoke associations with real events in one's own past in which one actually experienced the affect in question. The process, then, may have much in common with the third mode, discussed earlier, the conditioned stimulus in this case being the mental representation of oneself in the other's situation. The important difference is of course that here the arousal is triggered by a cognitive restructuring of events (what is happening to the other is viewed as happening to the self) and is thus more subject to conscious control.

The dominance of cognitive and probably voluntary processes is also indicated by Stotland's (1969) finding that the palmar sweat response of subjects instructed to imagine themselves in the other's place did not begin to increase until as much as 30 seconds after the experimenter announced that the painful heat was being applied to the victim—a far longer latency than occurs in the absence of such instruction. This finding also is consistent with the view that the empathic affect may be linked to the imagined stimuli impinging on the self rather than to the stimuli directly perceived as impinging on the other. It suggests, too, that this mode of arousal may provide the primary basis for empathizing with someone who is not present.

I do not regard these five modes of empathic arousal as forming a stage sequence in the sense of each mode superseding the previous ones. The first two operate in infancy and are superseded by the others. The remaining three, however, once operative, may con tinue to function throughout life and, indeed, they may all operate in the same situation. It is problematic, however, whether they facilitate or hinder each other. The set to imagine oneself in the other's place, for example, may intensify the effects of conditioning or mimicry because it directs one's attention to the other's facial expression or his or her situation. It may, on the other hand, interfere with these modes, as suggested by Stotland's finding of a delay in physiological arousal.

Cognitive Transformation of Empathy

Before discussing the cognitive component of empathy I should note that cognitive processes did enter into the discussion of the affective component, in two ways. First, imagining oneself in the other's place is a cognitive process that may trigger empathic arousal. Second, whatever the mode of arousal, cognition must often mediate between the facial and situational cues of the model and the affect aroused in observers. The role of cognitive mediation is especially apparent when the observers respond to the meaning of stimuli rather than their physical attributes, for example, when they are empathically aroused by the model's verbal or written communication about his or her feeling or situation, or by information supplied about the model by a third person in the model's absence. What I mean by the cognitive component, however is something more fundamental and unique to empathy. That is, since empathy is a response to another person's feeling or situation, mature empathizers know that the source of their own affect is something happening to another person and that person's affective response to these events, and they have a sense of what the other is feeling. Young children who lack a self-other distinction may be empathically aroused without these cognitions. Thus how people experience empathy depends on the level at which they cognize others; and that process undergoes dramatic changes developmentally (Hoffman, 1975). Briefly, for most of the first year children appear to experience a fusion of self and other. By about 12 months, they attain "person permanence" and become aware of others as physical entities distinct from the self. By 2 or 3 years, they acquire a rudimentary sense of others as having inner states (thoughts, perceptions, feelings) independent of their own; this is the initial step in role-taking which continues to develop into increasingly complex forms. Finally, by late childhood or perhaps sooner (the research is unclear here), they become aware of others as having personal identities and life experiences beyond the immediate situation.

As children pass through these four stages the experience of empathy may be expected to include, in addition to a purely affective component, an increasing awareness of the source of the affect as lying in someone else's situation and a more veridical awareness of the other's feelings. I will now describe the four hypothetical levels of empathic response that result from this coalescence of empathic affect and the cognitive sense of the other, as exemplified by one type of empathy—that resulting from observing another person in distress.

1. For most of the first year, before the child has acquired "person permanence," distress cues from others may elicit a global empathic distress response—presumably a fusion of unpleasant feelings and of stimuli that come from the infant's own body (through conditioning or mimicry), from the dimly perceived "other", and from the situation. Since infants cannot yet differentiate themselves from the other, they must often be unclear as to who is experiencing any distress that they witness, and they may at times behave as though what is happening to the other is happening to them. Consider a colleague's 11-month-old daughter who, on seeing another child fall and cry, first stared at the victim, appearing as though she were about to cry herself, and then put her thumb in her mouth and buried her head in her mother's lap—her typical response when she has hurt herself and seeks comfort. This first stage of empathic distress may be described as a primitive, involuntary response based mainly on the "pull" of surface cues and minimally on higher cognitive processes.

2. With the emergence of a sense of the other as distinct from the self, the affective portion of the children's empathic distress is extended to the separate "self" and "other" that emerge. At first children may be only vaguely and momentarily aware of the other as distinct from the self, and the image of the other, being transitory, may often slip in and out of focus. Consequently, children at this stage probably react to another's distress as though their dimly perceived self-and-other were somehow simultaneously, or alternately, in distress. I know a child whose typical response to his own distress, beginning late in the first year, was to suck his thumb with one hand and pull his ear with the other. At 12 months, on seeing a sad look on his father's face, he proceeded to look sad and suck his

thumb, while pulling his father's ear. The co-occurrence of distress in the emerging self, and in the emerging "other," may be an important factor in the transition from the first to the second stage.

The second stage is the one in which children first become capable of empathic distress while also being aware of the fact that another person, and not the self, is the victim. They cannot yet distinguish between their own and the other's inner states, however, and are apt to assume they are the same, as evidenced in their efforts to help, which consist chiefly of giving the other what they themselves find most comforting. Examples are a 13-month-old child who responded with a distressed look to an adult who looked sad, and then offered the adult his beloved doll; and a child who ran to fetch his own mother to comfort a crying friend even though the friend's mother was equally available.

3. By 2–3 years of age children begin to be aware that other people's feelings and thoughts may sometimes differ from their own, that others' perspectives may be based on their own needs and interpretations of events. (Such children may still at times project their own feelings to others, especially in the absence of objective data about others' feelings, as even adults often do. Such projective attributions often are correct, since people share the same basic nervous system and thus respond similarly to the same situation, e.g., despite the errors in the anecdotal examples cited earlier, the children's assumptions about how the other person felt were basically correct). More importantly, because children now know that the real world and their perception of it are not the same, and that the inner states of the other are independent of their own, they become more cautious and tentative in their inferences and more alert and responsive to cues (other than their own responses) about the feelings of others. Thus their sense of what the other is feeling is based on more veridical processes. By about 4 years most children respond with appropriate affect and can recognize signs of happiness or sadness in others in simple situations (e.g., Borke, 1971; Feshbach & Roe, 1968). And we may assume that with further role-taking ability they can detect the cues of complex and mixed emotions, as well as become capable of being empathically aroused by imagining themselves in the other's place.

4. Sometime during late childhood, owing to the emerging conception of self and other as continuous persons each with his or her own history and identity, children become aware that the other feels pleasure and pain not only in particular situations but also in the

context of a larger pattern of life experiences. Consequently, though they may continue to react to the immediate situational distress of others, their concern is intensified when they know it reflects a chronic condition. That is, they can now respond empathically not only to others' transitory, situation-specific distress but also to what they imagine to be others' general condition. This fourth stage, then, consists of empathically aroused affect together with a mental representation of the general plight of others—their typical day-to-day level of distress or deprivation, the opportunities available or denied to them, their future prospects, and the like. If this representation falls short of what the observer conceives to be a minimally acceptable standard of well-being, an empathic distress response may result even if contradicted by the other's apparent momentary state. That is, the observer's mental representation may at times override contradictory situational or facial cues.

To summarize, individuals who progress through these four stages become capable of a high level of empathic distress. They can process various types of information—that gained from their own vicarious affective reaction, from the immediate situational cues, and from their general knowledge about the other's life. They can act out in their minds the emotions and experiences suggested by this information, and introspect on all of this. They may thus gain an understanding and respond affectively in terms of the circumstances, feelings, and wishes of the other, while maintaining the sense that this is a separate person from themselves.

It also seems likely that with further cognitive development people may be able to comprehend the plight not only of an individual but also of an entire group or class of people, such as those who are economically impoverished, politically oppressed, socially outcast, victims of war, or mentally retarded. Because of people's different backgrounds, their own specific distress experiences may differ from that of others. All distress experiences probably have a common affective core, however, and that, together with the individual's high cognitive level at this age, provides the requisites for a generalized empathic distress capability. The combination of empathic affect and the perceived plight of an unfortunate group would seem to be the most advanced form developmentally of empathic distress.

Sympathetic distress. Thus far, I have suggested that empathic distress includes both an affective component and a cognitive component that is derived from the observers' cognitive sense of the other and their awareness that the other's state is the source of the affect. Many affect theorists, notably Schachter and Singer (1962) and Mandler (1975), suggest that how a person labels or experiences an affect is heavily influenced by certain pertinent cognitions ("One labels, interprets, and identifies this stirred-up state in terms of the characteristics of the situation and one's apperceptive mass. . .," Schachter & Singer, 1962, p. 380). These writers are explaining how we distinguish among different affects (e.g., anger, joy, fear) aroused directly. Quite apart from this issue,[4] the cognitive sense of others appears to be so intrinsic to *empathically* aroused affect as to alter the very quality of the observer's affective experience. More specifically, once people are aware of the other as distinct from the self, their own empathic distress, which is a parallel response—that is, a more or less exact replication of the victim's actual feelings of distress—may be transformed at least in part into a more reciprocal feeling of concern for the victim. This transformation is in keeping with how people report they feel when observing someone in distress. That is, they continue to respond in a purely empathic, quasi-egoistic manner—to feel uncomfortable and highly distressed themselves—but they also experience a feeling of compassion or what I call sympathetic distress for the victim, along with a conscious desire to help because they feel sorry for him or her and not just to relieve their own empathic distress.

In young children, only a part of the empathic distress may be transformed into sympathetic distress, as perhaps illustrated by the child described earlier who sucked his thumb and pulled his father's ear. With further advances in social cognition and a sharpened sense of the other, the transformation of empathic distress into sympathetic distress should become more complete, although there is evidence that an element of pure empathic distress may remain even in adulthood. This is suggested by the observation that nurses often experience conflict between feelings of sympathy, which include an intense desire to help their severely ill patients, and their own empathic distress which makes it difficult at times even to stay in the same room with them (Stotland, Mathews, Sherman, Hansson, & Richardson, in press). This finding also highlights the distinction between empathic and sympathetic distress.

In any case, the last three stages of empathic distress may also be

---

4. Izard, Tomkins and others argue that the differentiation of affects has a neural rather than a cognitive basis.

viewed as stages of sympathetic distress. Insofar as the transformation of empathic into sympathetic distress takes place, the description of the stages should be modified to stress the interaction between affective and cognitive components and the important qualitative change in feeling tone that results.

Guilt and other transformations of empathic distress. The burgeoning literature on causal attribution suggests that young children as well as adults have a natural tendency to make inferences about the causes of behavior and events. Since empathic distress is a response to someone else's plight, any cues about what led to that plight, if salient enough, may serve as cognitive inputs, in addition to those deriving from the observer's sense of the other, that help shape the observer's affective experience. Furthermore, once children have the capacity to recognize the consequences of their actions for others and to be aware that they have choice and control over their own behavior, they have the necessary requisites for a self-critical or self-blaming response to their own actions. If the cues in a situation in which they respond empathically to someone in distress indicate that they are the cause of that distress, their response may then have both the affectively unpleasant and cognitive self-blaming component of the guilt experience, and their empathic distress may be transformed by the attribution of self-blame into a feeling of guilt, as I have discussed at length elsewhere (Hoffman, 1976, in press–b).

It also seems reasonable to suppose that if the cues in the situation point to the victim's being responsible for his or her own plight, the observer's empathic distress might be transformed into some sort of derogatory feeling toward the victim. Finally, a cultural molding of empathic responsiveness may take place whereby certain people are classified as less than human (e.g., the Untouchables in India). Empathic responses to these people may also be transformed into derogatory feelings, or otherwise neutralized.

Empathy and Prosocial Motivation

Although it has long been assumed that empathy provides a motivational base for prosocial action, a comprehensive explanation of how it does so has not yet been offered. As a beginning attempt at such an explanation, I refer first to my earlier argument, based on natural selection, which suggests a biological basis for prosocial motivation. Second, in considering the psychological processes involved, it seems clear that the pure empathic distress which, as I have suggested, may continue through life as part of a person's response to another's misfortune, may result in prosocial action because it is an aversive state which can often best be alleviated by giving help to the victim. Since the act of helping another may thus contribute to a reduction of the actor's own aversive state, it might appear that empathic distress is just another egoistic motive. This view has been advanced by several writers (e.g., Piliavin, Rodin, & Piliavin, 1969; Gaertner & Dovidio, 1977). My argument against it is that all motives may prompt action that is potentially gratifying to the actor, but this must not obscure certain fundamental differences among them. Empathic distress, even if experienced primarily as aversive to the self, differs from the usual egoistic motives (e.g., sensual pleasure, material gain, social approval, economic success) in three significant ways: It is aroused by another person's misfortune, not by one's own; a major goal of the ensuing behavior is to help the other, not just oneself; and the potential for gratification in the observer is contingent on his acting to reduce the other's distress. For these reasons alone it seems appropriate to designate empathic distress as a prosocial motive and distinguish it from more directly self-serving, egoistic motives.

In addition, as noted earlier, with the partial transformation of empathic distress into sympathetic distress (stage 2) the conscious aim of people's actions is gradually changed at least in part from relieving their "own" empathic discomfort to relieving the distress perceived in the other. Their motive to help is now more genuinely prosocial, although their efforts may continue to be misguided due to their limited understanding of the precise nature of the other's distress and the type of action needed to relieve it. With further development of the self-other distinction, more veridical reality-testing procedures may be employed, including trial and error, response to corrective feedback and, eventually, utilization of information about the other's general life condition. Efforts to help should then become more appropriate. The entire previous discussion of the modes of empathic distress arousal and its transformation into sympathetic distress may thus be viewed as a theory of prosocial motivation and its development.

Empathic overarousal. There is evidence that altruistic action may require a certain amount of need fulfillment in observers, so as to reduce their self-preoccupation and leave them open and responsive to cues signifying the other's affect and need for help. For example, the arousal of deprived need states such as concerns about failure, social approval, and even physical discomfort due to noise has been found to interfere with altruistic action (e.g., Murphy, 1937; Staub & Sherk, 1970; Moore, Underwood & Rosenhan, 1973; Wine, 1975; Mathews & Canon, 1975). Since empathic distress may itself be extremely aversive under certain conditions, it may at times direct the attention of observers to themselves and thus actually decrease the likelihood of an altruistic act. Consider one of the experimental groups in a study of kindergartners by Kameya (1976) who were presented with several stories involving children who were ill, deprived, in pain, or combinations of these. The subjects took turns playing each of the roles and then discussed the feelings of the story children. In this group empathy was found to relate *negatively* to one of several helping behaviors. Kameya suggests that the experimental treatment, though designed to improve role-taking skills, may have instead evoked extreme empathic distress, especially in the high-empathy subjects, thus accounting for the negative relation. Perhaps there is an optimal range of empathic arousal—determined by individuals' levels of distress tolerance—within which they are most responsive to others. Beyond this range, they may be too preoccupied with their own aversive state to help anyone else.

Another possibility is that once over their threshhold of distress tolerance, observers may employ certain mechanisms to reduce the level of arousal itself. They might, for example, avoid interacting with people in pain, like the empathic nursing students in the Stotland et al. study mentioned earlier. (Stotland, Mathews, Sherman, Hansson, & Richardson, in press). Or they might employ certain empathy-inhibiting perceptual and cognitive strategies. Here is an illustrative quotation from a study by Bandura and Rosenthal (1966) in which adult subjects were given a strong dose of epinephrine before observing someone who was receiving electric shocks.

"After the first three or four shocks, I thought about the amount of pain for the other guy. Then I began to think, to minimize my own discomfort. I recall looking at my watch, looking out the window, and checking things about the room. I recall that the victim received a shock when I was thinking about the seminar, and that I didn't seem to notice the discomfort as much in this instance." (p. 60)

This quotation illustrates at once the involuntary tendency

to empathize with someone in distress, the aversive quality of empathic distress, and the use of defensive strategies to eliminate the aversive state or reduce it to a more tolerable level.

Empathic overarousal and its disruptive effects on prosocial behavior may at first appear to contradict our earlier discussion of altruism and natural selection. On further reflection, however, it appears that the phenomenon may well have been adaptive. Thus empathic overarousal may be assumed to have occurred when the distress cues from the victim were extremely intense. In the natural state this must often have occurred when the victim's situation was hopeless. For the observer to try to help under these conditions would have served no useful purpose and might at times have been suicidal. Empathic overarousal, then, might be a self-preserving mechanism that, alone with cognitive appraisal, as discussed earlier, contributed to the survival of the species. I might also note that by surviving, the observer remains available to help others when help is more appropriate, that is, when the probable gain to the victim is greater than the loss to the observer. Analogously, the nurses who minimized contact with terminally ill patients (Stotland, Mathews, Sherman, Hansson, & Richardson, in press) may have been thus enabled to continue to give help to patients who could derive greater benefit from it.[5] Apart from the validity of this evolutionary interpretation, the findings on empathic overarousal do suggest that empathic distress may trigger prosocial action increasingly, up to the point of the observer's level of distress tolerance. Beyond that point, it may trigger egoistic, self-protective action.

RESEARCH REVIEW

Thus far I have used some anecdotes and scattered research findings to illustrate certain theoretical concepts. I shall now review the major substantive findings on empathy, after some comments on the different measures used, their advantages, and limitations.

5. This is not to deny that people who are dying want human contact. They do, and they presumably derive emotional benefit from it. Yet, though it may be unpleasant to contemplate, natural selection would seem to have required that providing help to prolong someone's life would take precedence over providing emotional support to the terminally ill.

The Measurement of Empathy

An ideal empathy index would include evidence that (a) affect has been aroused in the observer and (b) the quality and direction of the affect correspond sufficiently to that experienced by the model to warrant calling it a vicarious response.

Physiological indices. Physiological indices, which have been used with adults and at first appear ideal, may fall down somewhat on the second criterion. An increase in skin conductance, for example, when observing someone being exposed to a highly noxious stimulus may usually signify an empathic reaction. It has been suggested by Berger (1962) and others, however, that some subjects may be enjoying the other person's pain (e.g., "I was rather embarrassed to see that I was grinning when my partner got shocked" [Bandura & Rosenthal, 1966])." The response may also reflect a startle reaction to the victim's bodily movements, a direct response to the noxious stimulus or to the sound of the victim's scream, or even the fear that what happened to the victim might happen to the self. In the latter case the victim's response serves merely as a source of information about the observer's own probable fate. Examples of these "pseudo-vicarious affects" are the young boy who responds with fear to the sound of someone's cry or to the sight of a sibling being spanked for no apparent reason; or who feels sad when his mother is sad because past experience tells him that when she is sad she is not likely to satisfy his needs. Finally, a physiological response when observing someone engaged in a pleasurable activity may reflect annoyance that someone else, and not the self, is experiencing pleasure (Stotland, 1969).

Thus, although physiological measures may indicate degree of emotional arousal, to measure empathy with confidence requires taking certain precautions and supplementing the physiological with other sources of data indicating the nature and direction of the affect aroused in the observer. This may be done in different ways. Craig & Weinstein (1965), for example, simply told their subjects that the model was being shocked; and the model, a confederate, made no sudden movement that might produce a startle response in the observer. Also, to avoid a fear response, the subjects were told that they would serve only as observers and not as models. Stotland (1969) and Krebs (1975) included verbal reports, to make sure that physiological arousal reflected an empathic response. The limitation here of course is that verbal reports may be vulnerable to "social desirability." Krebs also used an interesting procedure to rule out startle effects. In one experimental condition it was necessary for the model to jerk his arm in response to an apparent shock; to offset this a control group was included in which the model jerked his arm as part of a "reaction-time experiment" which did not include a shock.

Another, perhaps more fundamental difficulty with physiological indices of empathy is suggested in a study by Buck, Savin, Miller, and Caul (1972). Subjects who were called "senders" watched a series of slides designed to elicit various affects. Other subjects watched the senders' faces over closed-circuit television and made judgments about the nature and intensity of their affect. Skin conductance and heart rate data were recorded for the senders. The main finding of interest here was a *negative* relationship between the senders' skin conductance and the accuracy with which their facial expressions communicated affect to the observer. In other words, people who expressed affect through changes in skin conductance tended not to express affect through their facial expressions; those who expressed affect through facial expressions tended not to do so physiologically. Buck et al. cite other research, some of it with children, showing the same thing. None of these studies dealt with empathy but the findings suggest there may be a fundamental problem in relying exclusively on physiological indices of any emotion, whether directly or empathically aroused.

With all the problems, we may ask whether there is any evidence for the validity of physiological indices of empathy. Intuitively, and on evolutionary grounds, a physiological response to another's distress should more likely reflect an empathic than a sadistic or other negative reaction, and there is some evidence for this. First, the investigators report that sadistic responses are infrequent. Second, there is evidence that watching someone being shocked not only raises one's skin conductance but also makes one feel distressed (Craig & Lowery, 1969). Third, as will be seen later, most people who respond physiologically to another's distress are also predisposed to help. Fourth, in an experiment by Krebs (1975) subjects in the condition designed to produce the most empathy did respond physiologically and also stated that they identified with the victim, to a greater degreee than subjects in other conditions. And fifth, the physiological responses appear to be associated with a general tendency to put oneself in the other person's place: Subjects who obtained high scores on a questionnaire measure of the tendency to put oneself in the place of characters in plays, novels, and movies showed greater skin conductance increases when observing someone in physical pain (though not when observing someone in a neutral situation) than people who obtained low scores (Stotland, 1969).

The evidence, then, is that a physiological response to another's distress is typically associated with empathic feelings, at least in adults. Physiological measures of empathy have not yet been used with children perhaps because of concerns about hooking them up to electrodes and preventing freedom of movement. The technique of obtaining telemetered heart rate data would seem to handle these problems, and since it has already been used successfully in other work with children (e.g., Cheyne, Goyeche, & Walters, 1969), it may be recommended for research on empathy. This technique may also be one of the few methods appropriate for different ages, hence uniquely well suited for developmental studies of empathy.

Verbal and behavioral indices. Whereas the physiological measures of empathy may tap more effectively the degree of affect aroused than its direction, most of the measures used with children seem more attuned to direction than to degree of arousal. The most frequently employed measure, devised by Feshbach and Roe (1968), consists of a series of slide sequences in which children the same age and sex as the subject are shown in different affect-eliciting situations (e.g., the child has lost a pet dog). Accompanying each sequence is a short narration, which includes no affective labels, describing the events depicted in the slides. After presenting a slide sequence, the child is asked "How do you feel?" The responses are recorded verbatim and later assigned empathy scores based on their accuracy, that is, the extent to which they approximate the investigators' judgment of the affect conveyed in the story.

There is modest evidence for the construct validity of this measure, which will be presented later. The measure seems fraught with problems, nevertheless. First, it provides no information on arousal intensity. Second, it seems unlikely that a subject's emotions can be so easily manipulated as to shift rapidly from story to story. Third, relying on verbal responses makes the measure vulnerable to "social desirability" effects. Fourth, some of the stories represent more than the one designated emotion. In an "anger" story, for example, a child is playing with a friend who breaks a window and then, when the principal comes out, blames it on the first child. To receive full credit for an empathic response subjects must say they feel angry, although fear would also seem appropriate for this story. Finally, as I noted earlier, there is a question of just how accurate the response should be in order to receive full credit for an empathic response. Are young children who say they feel "sad," in response to slides depicting another's fear, any less empathic than children who say they feel afraid? I think that under most conditions the answer is no, because the children are just as highly aroused emotionally, though they may lack the cognitive and linguistic discrimination skills needed to differentiate between fear and sadness. Giving credit for accuracy may thus confound empathy with the child's level of cognitive development. If we are interested in empathy as an affective response, all that may be necessary is a rough correspondence between the subject's and the model's affect.

A related issue is raised by Iannotti and Meacham's (Note 2) modification of the Feshbach and Roe technique. Illustrated stories are presented in which the facial response of the child in the story is inappropriate to the situation, e.g., a boy is frowning at his birthday party. High empathy scores are assigned responses that fit the emotion indicated by the story child's facial expression but not the emotion appropriate to his situation. This approach has several problems. First, previous research shows that children under five years are often confused cognitively when personal and situational cues are contradictory (F. Deutsch, 1974; Burns & Cavey, 1957). Iannotti and Meacham's method like Feshbach and Roe's, may therefore confound subjects' empathic affect with their cognitive level. Second, the method may not be ecologically valid since in real life both personal and situational cues are generally congruent, and situational cues are often necessary to give meaning to personal cues. Third, there is no reason to assume that a response is more empathic if it derives from personal rather than situational cues. It appears, then, that although Iannotti and Meacham's measure may (as it was designed to do) prevent the subject from obtaining a high empathy score by projecting his or her own probable feelings in the situation, it may also serve to mask the young child's empathic responsiveness in everyday life.

Another method that has been used with chidren is to rate their facial expressions while they watch a movie. The possibility of judging emotional states from facial expression alone was largely abandoned some years ago because of doubts about the accuracy of this method. More recently, however, writers like Tomkins (1962) and Izard (1971) have argued persuasively that accurate judgments of emotions can be made from analyses of facial behavior. And, in a recent study by M.L. Hamilton (1973), this technique was used successfully to tap empathic responsiveness in young children. The subjects watched a film depicting people in happy, sad, and other types of emotional situations. Empathy scores were based on the subjects' facial expressions as they watched the film, and a high degree of accuracy was obtained. A high degree of accuracy has also been reported in adults (Zuckerman, DeFrank, Hall, & Rosenthal, 1976). This type of measure, then, does seem promising, and it has the advantage of being spontaneous, nonverbal, and less subject to "social desirability" than the Feshbach and Roe measure.

To sum up, different measures have been used with different age groups. Each measure taps one aspect of empathy (physiological, verbal, facial expression) reasonably well and reveals something about either the intensity or direction of the affect aroused, but not both.[6] If all measures were tapping the same thing we might expect them to interrelate positively. As noted earlier, there is evidence with adults that physiological and verbal indices may do so, but the findings reported by Buck et al. suggest an inverse relation between physiological and facial indices. Until the research needed to resolve this issue is done, investigators should where possible consider using more than one index.

Despite the methodological shortcomings there appears to be emerging a small but cumulative body of empirical research that bears on some of the theoretical issues raised earlier—those pertaining to the prevalence of empathy in humans, its possible contribution to prosocial behavior, and the effect of similarity between observer and model. This research will now be examined critically. The findings on sex differences will also be discussed.

Prevalence of Empathy as a Human Response

There is considerable evidence that people have a tendency to respond empathically. Thus most 4- to 8-year-old children give em-

6. The Mehrabian and Epstein (1972) inventory index of empathy was not included in this review because of its highly questionable validity. Though some items clearly pertain to empathy (e.g., seeing people cry upsets me), others do not (e.g., sometimes the words of a song can move me deeply; I would rather be a social worker than work in a job training center).

pathic responses to the Feshbach and Roe slide sequences (e.g., Fay, 1970; Feshbach & Feshbach, 1969; Levine & Hoffman, 1975). Most 4- to 10-year-olds give empathic facial responses while watching films of people in different situations (M. L. Hamilton, 1973). And adults typically give the physiological signs of empathy when witnessing another person in a physically painful situation or failing in a task (e.g., Berger, 1962; Craig & Weinstein, 1965; Gaertner & Dovidio, 1977; Geer & Jarmecky, 1973; Stotland, 1971; Tomes, 1964). Finally, there is evidence for an involuntary element in empathic arousal. Stotland, Sherman & Shaver (1971) found that instructing adult subjects to "avoid experiencing the same type of emotion as the person experiencing the heat treatment" did not result in a reduction in their level of physiological arousal. Since each of these studies deals with only one modality—physiological, verbal, facial—and there is evidence, discussed earlier, that people may express affect primarily through a single modality, these findings may actually underestimate the human proclivity to empathize.

An apparent exception to the generalization that people respond empathically is the study by Lerner and Simmons (1966). Adult subjects who watched a model being given electric shocks in the course of learning a task were found to view the model afterwards as less attractive. There is evidence, however, that the finding may have been due to an empathy-inhibiting set created by the intructions. As noted by Aderman, Brehm, and Katz (1974), Lerner and Simmons instructed their subjects "to observe closely the emotional state of the model and watch for cues indicating her state of arousal" (p. 206). Using these instructions, Aderman et al. replicated Lerner and Simmons's results. However, when the subjects were told to observe the model and imagine as vividly as possible how it would feel to be in her place, they actually rated the model as more attractive than themselves. These findings parallel those obtained by Stotland (1969), whose subjects observed someone undergoing a painful, pleasurable, or affectively neutral heat treatment. The subjects instructed to attend very carefully to the model's leg, arm, foot, hand, head movements, bearing, and posture were apparently unaffected (as indicated by palmar sweat) by the nature of the treatment given the model, whereas those instructed to imagine how they would feel if in the model's place were affected. In an earlier study by Speisman, Lazarus, Mordkoff, and Davison (1964), subjects instructed to take the view of an anthropologist while watching a film of a painful circumcision rite were less aroused physiologically than those for whom the traumatic aspects of the operation were emphasized. These findings all suggest that an observational set that fragments other people, or makes them an object of intellectual scrutiny or a source of data, may put distance between them and the observer and reduce the latter's empathic response.

The issue still remains as to which of these observational sets are ecologically valid. Are people typically open to cues of another's affective state or do they usually distance themselves from others who are experienceing emotions? Do people have a set to imagine themselves in the place of other people, or to examine their behavior in minute detail? Research is needed to answer these important questions, as well as that of the cultural molding of the set to respond empathically, mentioned earlier. Meanwhile, we may assume that the research in which subjects were given no particular observational set—the bulk of that done so far—provides the best approximation of what usually happens in natural settings. This research, as summarized earlier, indicates that empathy rather than derogation of the victim or some other defense is the usual response to another in distress.

Age as a variable. Whether empathy increases or decreases with age is a question about which we have little data, owing to the different measures used at different ages. The results of three studies suggest that empathy may increase each year between 5 and 8 (Fay, 1970; Feshbach & Feshbach, 1969; Kuchenbecker, Feshbach, & Pletcher, Note 4). All three used the Feshbach and Roe measure, however, and the combination of a verbal response and a scoring system in which accuracy is weighed heavily may have virtually guaranteed an increase in empathy scores with age. In any case, the study by M. L. Hamilton (1973), in which empathy was measured by the subject's spontaneous facial expressions to happy and sad films, produced very different results. The facial expressions of most preschoolers, second- and fifth-graders corresponded quite well to the emotions depicted in the films, and there were no differences between the age groups. It is possible of course that empathic arousal does increase with age but the increase is canceled out due to the acquisition of "display rules," whose function is to reduce the intensity of, mask, or neutralize an emotion (Ekman, Friesen, & Ellsworth, 1972). We might then expect fewer facial manifestations of empathy among adults, but this is counterindicated by the Zuckerman et al. study mentioned earlier. To fully understand the developmental changes in empathic responsiveness may require supplementing facial expression with physiological indices of arousal.

We may also ask whether there are developmental shifts in the pattern of empathic sensitivity to different emotions. It is obvious that people can respond empathically to more complex and subtle emotions as they grow older but, degree of complexity aside, do they become more empathically responsive to certain emotions than others? The evidence thus far is suggestive, though crude. Pre-schoolers are more apt to give verbal empathic responses to stories depicting children in happy situations than in situations depicting sadness, fear, or anger (Feshbach & Feshbach, 1969; Levine & Hoffman, 1975). By 6 or 7 years this difference appears to disappear. Adults, on the other hand, seem to show a somewhat less reliable physiological reaction when observing someone experiencing plea-sure than when observing someone experiencing pain (Stotland, Sherman, & Shaver, 1971). These findings suggest there may be a developmental shift in the direction of a greater empathic sensitivity to negative affective states.

The research done thus far suggests that people of all ages tend to empathize. The subjects were all North American, however, and cross-cultural research is obviously needed as a test of the argument that the tendency to empathize is universal.

Empathy and Prosocial Behavior

As indicated earlier, many writers assume that empathy provides a motive base for prosocial behavior, but the relevant empirical evi-dence has not yet been examined systematically. Until recently the relation between empathy and prosocial behavior was studied only indirectly. Aronfreed (1970) experimentally tested the hypothesis that prior association between positive affect in the child and posi-tive affect in another person results in an empathic response in the child, which leads him to behave altruistically toward the other person. The hypothesis was confirmed but no evidence was pre-sented that empathy actually occurred. Similarly, the frequent finding of a positive relation between inductive discipline techniques (which point up the effects of the child's behavior on others) and both consideration for others and moral internalization (Hoffman, 1970a) has been explained as being due in part to the empathic response often elicited by inductions (Hoffman, 1963,

1977a). There is no evidence as yet that empathy is actually aroused by inductions. We now turn to the research in which independent measures of empathy and prosocial behavior have been obtained.

Correlational research. In the earliest study of empathy and prosocial behavior, Murphy (1937) found a positive correlation between empathic behaviors such as "responding to another child's distress by staring with an anxious expression," and behaving in a comforting manner. Empathy also related positively to aggression, however. Murphy suggested that the pattern may simply have reflected the child's social activity level: highly active children were more empathic, helpful, and aggressive. The relation between empathy and both prosocial and aggressive behavior has since been investigated in a more controlled manner. Feshbach and Feshbach (1969) replicated Murphy's aggression findings for boys: 4- to 5-year-old boys who obtained high empathy scores were rated as more aggressive by nursery school teachers than boys with low empathy scores. For 6- to 7-year-old boys there was a negative relation between empathy and teacher ratings of aggressiveness, which suggests that by this age empathy may have begun to take hold as an inhibitor of aggression. There was no relation between empathy and aggression for girls at either age level.

Levine and Hoffman (1975) examined the relation in 4-year-olds between the Feshbach and Roe measure of empathy and a modified version of Kagan and Madsen's (1971) measure of cooperation. No correlation was found between empathy and cooperation, for either sex. In this study the cooperative subjects were asked why they cooperated. Only a few answered in empathic terms (e.g., "Because he wanted me to help him," or "Because he would cry if I didn't"); most referred to the requirements of the game, or to reciprocity. Thus, the emotional state of the other child was not salient during the game, even to the cooperating child, whose empathic capabilities may thus not have been engaged. This suggests a possible explanation for the weak findings obtained in the studies of very young children: Their empathic capability may not often be engaged because their attention is easily captured by other more or less irrelevant social demands such as the experimenter's instructions.

In an elaborate study of kindergarten boys, Kameya (1976) examined the relation between the Feshbach and Roe measure and several indices of helping behavior which included helping an experimenter who dropped a pile of paper clips and expressed pain after bumping his knee, donating candy to poor children, and volunteering to color pictures for hospitalized children. Empathy did not correlate with any of these behaviors, perhaps for the reasons advanced by Levine and Hoffman. However, among subjects who did volunteer to color pictures for hospitalized children, those who actually took the pictures with them and showed signs of following through on their promise had higher empathy scores than those who showed no signs of following through. This "follow through" behavior is the only altruism index involving considerable self-sacrifice over a prolonged period (the subjects were told they would have to do the coloring during two successive recess periods while the other children were playing). A possible limitation is that since the actions involved in following through were not anonymous, they might have been engaged in by children in need of social approval. The evidence against this interpretation is the large body of research indicating that children who lack social approval and thus may be highly motivated to attain it are *less* likely to help others (e.g., Murphy, 1937; Staub & Sherk, 1970). We may therefore tentatively interpret Kameya's finding as suggesting that although empathy may not often be engaged in young children, when it is engaged it may serve as a rather effective prosocial motivation.

To summarize, the correlational research is inconclusive, providing at best slight support for the proposition that empathy may sometimes contribute to prosocial behavior. It also raises questions about the way in which empathic arousal operates that can probably best be answered by experimental research, to which we now turn.

Experimental research. The experimental research, all with adults, provides consistent support for the relation between empathic arousal and prosocial action. It may be useful first to state the kind of evidence needed. If empathic or sympathetic distress does motivate prosocial action, (1) it should be associated with a tendency to help, (2) it should precede and contribute to the helpful act, and (3) it should diminish in intensity following a helpful act but continue at a high level in the absence of action. The evidence is supportive on all three counts.

1. There are many studies showing that when people are exposed to another in distress they either respond empathically or with an overt helping act, whichever is being investigated (e.g., Berger, 1962; Clark & Word, 1972; Craig & Weinstein, 1965; Lazarus, Speisman, Mordkoff, & Davison, 1962; Piliavin, Rodin, & Piliavin 1969; Severy & Davis, 1971; Staub, 1970; Stotland, 1969; Tannenbaum & Gaer, 1965; Tomes, 1964). This suggests that if data were collected

on both empathy and helping in the same study, subjects would typically show both, which has indeed been found (Darley & Latané, 1968; Gaertner & Dovidio, 1977; Geer & Jarmecky, 1973; Krebs, 1975; Murphy, 1937; Weiss, Boyer, Lombardo, & Stich, 1973). There is also evidence that as the magnitude of the pain cues from the victim increases, the latency of the helping act decreases, that is, the subject acts more quickly (Geer & Jarmecky, 1973; Weiss et al., 1973). Furthermore, the intensity of empathic arousal has been found to relate positively to the speed of helping (Gaertner & Dovidio, 1977). Clearly, there is a relation between empathic or sympathetic distress and helpful action.

2. The question remains as to whether the empathic distress merely accompanies or actually precedes and motivates the act of helping. The studies by Krebs (1975) and by Gaertner and Dovidio (1977) are important here. Krebs employed physiological indices of empathy, introspective reports about the extent to which the subjects identified with a model undergoing shock, and an altruistic index that required subjects to choose between helping the other at a cost to themselves or helping themselves at a cost to the other. The opportunity for altruism followed the empathy trials. There were two experimental conditions and the one in which the subjects showed more empathy, both physiologically and verbally, was the same one in which they showed more altruistic behavior. In that experimental condition, then, empathic arousal preceded an altruistic act. Gaertner and Dovidio's design was quite different and the findings are perhaps more convincing. The subjects, female undergraduate students, observed (through earphones) a situation in which a confederate left an experimental task in order to straighten out a stack of chairs that she thought was about to topple over on her. A moment later the confederate screamed that the chairs were falling on her, and then was silent. The main finding was that the greater the subject's cardiac responsiveness (as indexed by heart-rate acceleration), the more quickly she intervened. Furthermore, the physiological arousal was not merely the artifactual result of the subject rising from her chair, since the arousal preceded the rising. The heart-rate acceleration score was based on data obtained during the 10-second period immediately following the confederate's scream, whereas the median latency for rising was 40 seconds. Thus the speed of intervention was systematically related to the magnitude of the heart-rate acceleration just prior to the intervention.

Several experiments by Weiss are also pertinent (Weiss, Buchanan, Alstatt, & Lombardo, 1971; Weiss et al., 1973). The subjects viewed a model who evidenced overt signs of stress (e.g., sweating, reflex kicking) while performing a motor task and apparently receiving continously painful shocks. The subject's task was to make evaluations of the model's performance and record them by pressing certain buttons. Pressing the buttons also terminated the shock, as indicated by visible signs of relief from the model. There were 15 training trials. The main finding was that the subjects acquired the button-pushing response without any reinforcement other than the victim's expressions of relief. Furthermore, the learning curves closely resemble those obtained in more conventional escape conditioning studies. For example, the speed of the button-pushing response increased at an increasing rate over the 15 trials; it also increased when the distress cues from the model were more intense; and variables like partial reinforcement and delay of reinforcement operated just as they do in conventional studies. It therefore appears that the consequences to the observer of helping someone in distress correspond closely to the consequences of conventional reinforcement. This suggests that an aversive state such as empathic distress might have been induced in the observer, and the termination of that state functioned as a reinforcer in acquiring the helping response.

Weiss et al. unfortunately did not collect systematic data on the affect aroused in the subjects. They did note anecdotally, however, that the subjects "sweat visibly and show other signs of strain" (Weiss et al., 1973, p. 397). From this, as well as from the evidence for empathic arousal in similar experiments cited earlier, we may conclude that the subjects probably did experience empathic distress. Weiss et al. also note that the subjects often said they wished they could do something to help the confederate. We are not told when these statements were made but they must have been made in the early training trials before the subjects learned that there was something they could do, namely, push the buttons. This is important because the speed of the button-pushing response was accelerated in the later trials. The study thus appears to provide suggestive evidence that the subjects did experience empathic distress, which was accompanied by a felt desire to help, and followed by helping behavior. It is difficult to explain the pattern of results without assuming that the empathic distress was causally related to the helping act.

3. There is evidence that observers' empathically aroused affect diminishes in intensity after they engage in a helpful act. Darley and Latané (1968) report this pattern in adults who heard sounds indicating that someone was having an epileptic fit. Those who did not respond overtly continued to be aroused and upset, as indicated by trembling hands and sweaty palms; those who did respond showed fewer signs of continued upset. A similar finding was obtained in Murphy's (1937) nursery school study: When children overtly helped others, their affective response appeared to diminish; when they did not help, the affect was prolonged. (This was true of the older children; the younger children rarely helped.)

Developmental evidence. A developmental line of argument is also applicable. The acquisition of a motive often precedes the development of cognitive and coping skills necessary for appropriate action. It follows that when a motive is aroused early in life it may be followed by inappropriate action or no action, but as the child grows older it should increasingly be accompanied by appropriate action. This developmental pattern appears to characterize the relation between empathy and prosocial behavior. In several anecdotes cited earlier I described young children who reacted to another's distress with a worried, anxious look but did nothing or acted inappropriately. This was also true of the younger nursery school children observed by Bridges (1931) and Murphy (1937); the older children, on the other hand, typically appeared upset but nevertheless did engage in an overt helpful act. And in adulthood, as we have seen, empathic distress is associated with appropriate altruistic action. This developmental pattern of empathic arousal being followed, as the person grows older, with increasingly more appropriate action clearly fits the view that empathy is developmentally antecedent to and possibly causally related to altruism.

To summarize all the findings and arrange them developmentally: (a) very young children typically respond empathically to another's distress but often do nothing or act inappropriately, probably because of their cognitive limitations; (b) older children and adults also respond empathically but this is usually followed by appropriate helping behavior; (c) with children as well as adults there appears to be a drop in empathic arousal following an act of helping, and a continuation of the arousal if there is no overt attempt to help; and (d) there is good evidence that empathic arousal often precedes helping behavior and functions in other ways like a motive, at least in adults. These findings as a group fit exactly the pattern that we would expect if empathic or sympathetic distress did serve as a prosocial motive, though not necessarily the only prosocial motive.

Empathic arousal does not guarantee altruistic action any more than other motives can guarantee action. I have already noted the phenomenon of empathic overarousal and its possible negative contribution to altruistic action. Other factors, too, may operate— for example, the extent to which the situation points up the observer's responsibility to act rather than indicating that responsibility is diffused among many people (Geer & Jarmecky, 1973; Latané & Darley, 1970; Schwartz, 1970; Tilker, 1970). Furthermore, in individualistic societies the motive to help will often be overridden by more powerful egoistic motives, as evidenced by the negative relationship obtained between helping others and competitiveness (Rutherford & Mussen, 1968). As noted by Hoffman (1970b) and Staub (1970), American middle-class children are often socialized both to help others and to respect authority and follow the rules, but in some situations one cannot do both. Perhaps the best known instance of the way authority may serve as a deterrent to prosocial behavior is Milgram's (1963) finding that adult males will administer high levels of shock on instruction from the experimenter, despite strong feelings of compassion for the victim. It should be noted, however, that in a partial replication Tilker (1970) found that when subjects were assigned the role of observer they not only showed increasing empathic distress as the shock levels to the victims were increased but often intervened to stop the experiment, despite specific instructions to the contrary and continuing opposition from the person administering the shock.

Thus, although distress cues from another may trigger empathic distress in observers and an initial tendency to act, they may or may not help, depending on the circumstances.

Effect of Similarity Between Observer and Model

The research on empathy and similarity between observer and model, though sparse, is in keeping with the evolutionary perspective discussed earlier which predicts more empathic and prosocial responses to models perceived as similar to the self. Feshbach and Roe (1968) found that 6- to 7-year-old girls verbalized more empathy in response to slide sequences depicting girls, and the boys gave more empathic responses to sequences depicting boys. Klein (1971) constructed new slide sequences depicting either black or white girls in comparable affective states, using situations relevant to both black and white cultures. The subjects, all girls, verbalized more empathy in response to slides depicting children of the same race. Klein's study also included a more abstract, cognitively mediated type of similarity: In one condition the attempt was made to induce a perception of similarity between observer and model by stressing their common preferences, attitudes, and interests. The empathy scores were not increased by this manipulation in either white or black subjects.

A similar attempt to induce a perception of similarity in adults, however, was found by Krebs (1975) to increase physiological empathic responses. The subjects were given personality tests and told that they were paired with another person on the basis of a computer analysis of the test responses. Half the subjects were told that the other person was similar to them and half were told that he or she was different. As expected, subjects who believed they were similar to the other gave more pronounced physiological responses when that person appeared to be experiencing pleasure or pain, reported that they identified more with the person, and felt worse while he or she waited to receive an electric shock. Krebs suggests that the human capacity to make judgments of similarity on the basis of abstract dimensions such as values and personality may both extend and limit the ability of humans to act in a prosocial manner. It may on the one hand make it possible for people to "adopt a universal role-taking perspective and see the essential similarities that exist among all humanity" . . . or "it may give rise to highly selective we-they (similar-dissimilar) discriminations that may mediate bigotry, scapegoating, ethnocentrism . . . and other acts of selfishness and aggression that further the lot of the ingroup" (p. 1145).

Sex Differences in Empathy

According to prevailing sex-role stereotypes, females are more empathic than males. Interestingly, the relevant theorizing is in essential agreement with this stereotype. This includes theorists as diverse as Freud and Parsons, one heavily biological and the other social structural in emphasis. According to Parsons and Bales (1955) and Johnson (1963) the family, like any other social unit, requires someone to perform (a) the "expressive" role—being responsive to the needs and feelings of others, so as to maintain the family as an intact, harmonious entity and (b) the "instrumental" role—acting as liaison between the family and other social institutions, especially those related to the occupational sphere. Females have traditionally been socialized to acquire expressive traits such as empathy, compassion, and giving and receiving affect. Males are initially socialized expressively but with age are increasingly encouraged to acquire instrumental traits such as mastery and problem solving. Freud's view (1925/1961) was that, owing to anatomical differences, girls are not compelled to resolve the Oedipus complex quickly and dramatically and therefore do not identify with the parent as completely as boys do. Consequently, females acquire weaker egos and superegos and their social interactions are guided more by affect than by reality considerations. Other psychoanalytic writers see females as more "intuitive" (H. Deutsch, 1944), "allocentric" (Gutmann, 1965), and open to the subjective states of others because of a relative lack of distinction between self and other (Bakan, 1966; Wyatt, 1967). There appear to be no major theorists who contradict the stereotype.

I have gone over the research literature and pulled out all the sex differences involving the various empathy indices (e.g., newborn reflex cry, verbal response to slide sequences, facial response while watching films, verbal and physiological response to another's pain.) The results, presented elsewhere (Hoffman, 1977b), will be summarized here with an attempt to relate them to some of the issues presented earlier.

The most striking thing about the findings is that, except for the slight tendency for males to obtain higher galvanic skin response (GSR) scores than females, which will be discussed later, in every case, regardless of the subject's age and the measure used, the females obtained higher scores than the males. Though few of the differences are statistically significant, and in some instances the magnitude of the difference is slight, the females did obtain higher scores in 16 out of 16 independent samples. The probability of this occurring by chance is only 1 out of 64,000. Analysis of the findings within age groups is also revealing. Newborn females were found to cry more in response to the sound of another infant's cry, in five independent samples, which is statistically significant. The combined results of two studies of preschool children, employing the Feshbach and Roe measure and done by different investigators, are significant. And the one finding obtained with adults is significant. Thus the findings overall provide a stronger case for the proposition that females are more empathic, through the life cycle, than that no sex difference exists.

I have also reviewed the research on recognition of affect in others, and, cognitive role-taking. There were no sex differences (Hoffman, 1977b), which highlights the distinction between the affective and cognitive conceptions of empathy noted earlier. When encountering someone in an emotional situation both sexes can apparently assess the other's feelings equally well but in females this awareness is more apt to be accompanied by a vicarious affective response. Why is this? One possibility is that females are more prone to motor mimicry, which could explain how they can be more empathic without being more cognitively aware of another's feelings. Females do tend to blink their eyes more than males when observing a model whose eyes blink (Bernal & Berger, 1976), but of course this does not bear directly on empathy. Another way to test the hypothesis of greater motor mimicry in females is to see if they respond more empathically to another's facial expression without any situational cues. Unfortunately, none of the empathy studies involve facial cues alone. Several affect recognition studies do, however, and the results suggest no sex difference (Hoffman, 1977b). Furthermore, in a study using incongruous facial and situational cues (e.g., a person frowns in response to someone's friendly gesture) preschool girls discriminated situational cues more accurately than facial cues (F. Deutsch, 1974); and in another such study elementary school girls were more likely than boys to rely on situational and ignore facial cues (Kurdeck & Rodgon, 1975). Should these findings be replicated in studies of empathic arousal, this would argue against the motor mimicry explanation.

Another hypothesis is that while females may be no more competent than males at assessing another's feelings when instructed to do so, they may have a more natural set to imagine themselves in the other's place, which may trigger an empathic response. This view is consistent with the suggestive evidence just mentioned that females may be more responsive to situational than facial cues. It also fits with the conception of an inner duality in females suggested by writers like Bakan (1966) and Wyatt (1967). It does not, however, imply the simple diffusion of self-other boundaries that these writers see as underlying the duality, since females can cognitively assess another's inner state, even when it differs from their own, as well as males. A brief, temporary suspension of the boundaries (regression in the service of empathy?), however, would enable females to alternate more freely between their own and the other's perspective, as well as fit in well with the entire pattern of the findings.

Males, on the other hand, may have a different set, as suggested by several theories characterizing them as more instrumental or "agentic" (Bakan, 1966; Parsons & Bales, 1955; Johnson, 1963). This view is supported more directly by a recent finding with preschool subjects obtained with the Feshbach and Roe measure (Hoffman & Levine, 1976). Though the subjects were asked how they felt in response to slide sequences depicting children in problem situations, the boys gave more active, coping responses (e.g., "I'd just follow his tracks" in response to a story about a lost pet dog; "I'd call the police" in response to one about a child unjustly accused of breaking a window), as well as fewer empathic responses. Giving an instrumental response to a request for feeling suggests a preexisting orientation toward instrumental, ameliorative action. The boys' responses may thus reflect a tendency to consider action alternatives rather than empathize—to act rather than feel—in interpersonal situations. Whether this is merely a different set or also reflects a difficulty in responding affectively—perhaps a type of resistance or defensive misinterpretation of the experimenter's request for feeling—is a question for further research.

Antecedent factors. That females appear to be more empathic than males may reflect their socialization for "expressiveness." That males may have a set to act even in situations that call for feeling may reflect their socialization for instrumentality, active mastery, and inhibition of feeling (L. W. Hoffman, 1972). There is evidence that children who cry when distressed are more empathic than those who try to be brave and avoid crying (Lenrow, 1965). Thus the socialization of boys not to cry may play a role in making them less empathic.

It is of course possible that socialization may not provide a full explanation. Consider the earlier argument for an innate empathic disposition in humans, together with the finding that newborn females are more likely to cry in response to another infant's cry. This cry may be a constitutional precursor of empathy which, together with differences in socialization, may contribute to later sex differences in the mature empathic response. It should be noted, however, that a female infant cry was used as the stimulus, and while it may seem unlikely that newborns respond differently to male and female cries, the test must be made with a male cry before we can theorize with confidence about constitutional precursors of greater empathic sensitivity in females.

An alternative interpretation. I have discounted the GSR findings (Berger, 1962; Craig & Lowery, 1969; Craig & Weinstein, 1965), in which a slight trend appears for males to obtain higher scores than females, for three reasons. First, in none of these studies was the sex of the experimenter matched to the sex of the subject. This match appears to be necessary in testing for sex differences in physiological arousal, as indicated in a study of direct aversive stimulation by Fisher and Kotses (1974): Male GSR's were only slightly higher than female GSR's when this match existed, but two to three times higher than female GSR's when one experimenter, no matter which sex, was used for both male and female subjects. Though the subjects were directly exposed to aversive stimulation, the effect is probably the same when observing a model exposed to aversive stimulation, since the experimenter performs the same functions in both conditions. Second, in the studies by Craig and associates the model was always a male, and as noted earlier, the magnitude of empathic arousal is enhanced by similarity between observer and model. Third, in the only study that included both physiological arousal and introspective reports, the females reported more intense feelings of empathic distress, even though their level of physiological arousal was lower than that of the males (Craig & Lowery, 1969).

Despite these problems the trend toward higher GSR scores in males may still reflect a real difference that will hold up under controlled study. In that event, a different interpretation of the overall pattern of sex differences may be necessary and I will present one briefly. First, I mentioned earlier the inverse correlation between expressing emotions facially and physiologically, obtained by Buck et al. (1972). Sex differences were also reported in that study: Men obtained higher GSR scores and women were higher on facial expressiveness. The investigators suggest these findings may be due to the fact that girls are socialized to express affect openly and males are discouraged from doing so. The same reasoning could account for the sex differences in empathy obtained with children, since facial expressions and verbal responses were used to tap empathic responsiveness in children. The overall results might then be viewed as demonstrating not that females are more empathic than males but that the two sexes express empathy through different modalities. Females express it overtly in words and facial expressions, whereas males tend to keep empathic feelings to themselves and express them internally through action of the autonomic nervous system. When the opportunity to act instrumentally presents itself, however, males may also express empathy through overt action. Such action may contribute to reducing their empathic discomfort, as suggested in our earlier discussion of empathy and prosocial behavior.

CONCLUDING REMARKS

A rudimentary theoretical model of empathic arousal, its developmental course, the cognitive transformations it undergoes, and its motivational implications has been presented. The model is as yet loose and tentative. Though consistent with the research to date, which was also reviewed, it cannot be properly assessed until hypotheses derived specifically from it are tested. An example is the hypothesis that empathic distress is transformed into sympathetic distress as the child begins to acquire a sense of the other. Another is the hypothesis that the use of childrearing practices that direct the child's attention to other people's inner states (e.g., inductive discipline) may foster sympathetic distress and prosocial tendencies, although their excessive use may contribute to a tendency toward empathic overarousal and the use of strategies designed to reduce the resulting aversive state. The model would also predict that the arousal of empathic distress will increase the feeling of guilt one may have after harming another person.

Aside from specific hypotheses, the model suggests the need for research on the different modes of empathic arousal, when and how they originate, and their interrelationships. I find motor mimicry particularly interesting. Does motor mimicry actually occur and is it often a mechanism of empathic arousal? If so, how does it progress developmentally? It should of course increase with age because of the necessary neural requisites. At some point, however, it may begin to drop off, as individuals begin to use "display rules" which reduce their own facial responsiveness and thus deprive themselves of some of the cues of what the other person is feeling. This drop may be more likely to occur in males than females. Another important research question pertains to the age at which the motivational component of empathy is engaged. The evidence for a positive relation between empathic distress and prosocial action is so far impressive only for adults, but the experimental study of this relation has thus far been done mainly with adults. To find out when, developmentally, empathic arousal becomes a reliable force in motivating prosocial action will probably require devising experimental techniques for use with children, at different ages. Finally, there are some basic methodological issues that need investigating, such as the interrelationships among different levels of empathic arousal (physiological, facial, verbal).

Relevance of the model to directly experienced affect. Should our three-component model survive the empirical test, it might be worthwhile to try to extend it to other empathically aroused affects besides distress. Indeed, the model may be applicable in a general way to directly experienced affect as well as empathic affect. The arousal modes would of course be different in this case because people would be responding to events impinging on themselves rather than on someone else. The cognitive component would probably be linked to the cognitive awareness of self rather than the cognitive awareness of others, but these two types of awareness probably develop together and interactively. The motivational component of directly experienced affect may operate much the same as that of empathic affect, with the possible exception of overarousal because here the distinction between a vicarious response to another and a direct response to stimuli impinging on the self becomes blurred.

The role of cognition. Though I have stressed empathy as an affective response, cognition has loomed large. It may be useful to review the different ways in which cognitive processes operate. First, in some arousal modes (e.g., conditioning), cognitive processes play an important role in mediating between the cues of affect in the model and the affective response of the observer. That is, cognition makes sense out of the physical and especially the symbolic cues from the model and thus communicates the model's feelings to the observer. Second, in one arousal mode, the use of imagination actually generates the empathic affect. Third, the cognitive processes of distinguishing between self and other, and making causal attributions, produce a transformation of the quality of the observer's experience, for example, from empathic distress to sympathetic distress or guilt. Finally, cognitive processes serve the motivational component of empathy since they are obviously involved in assessing what, if anything, should be done to help the other person. Thus, while the vicarious arousal of affect may ordinarily occur regardless of cognition, cognitive processes do appear to be involved in all aspects of the empathic experience.

Practical implications. It is perhaps obvious that research on empathy may have practical implications. The research on the effects of similarity, summarized earlier, provides one example. A reasonable inference from the findings is that it may be possible to bring about an increase in empathy and prosocial behavior by simply educating people to be more aware of the similarity between themselves and others, both in their own and other cultural groups. However, the fact that simple, visually-based similarity (sex, race) can enhance empathic responsiveness in children, and that the more abstract perception of similarity in personality appears only to affect adults, suggests that any attempt to educate people to see the essential similarities among humans and to respond empathically on the basis of a universal role-taking perspective may not succeed until they acquire the capacity for abstract thought.

REFERENCE NOTES

1. Hoffman, M. L. Is altruism part of human nature? Unpublished manuscript, University of Michigan, 1977.
2. Iannotti, R. J., & Meacham, J. A. *The nature, measurement and development of empathy.* Paper presented at the meeting of the Eastern Psychological Association, Philadelphia, April 1974.
3. Mathews, K., & Stotland, E. *Empathy and nursing students' contact with patients.* Unpublished manuscript, 1973, Spokane, Washington, 1973. (Mimeo)
4. Kuchenbecker, S., Feshbach, N., & Pletcher, G. *The effects of age, sex and morality upon social comprehension and empathy.* Paper presented at the Western Psychological Association Annual Meeting, San Francisco, April 1974.

REFERENCES

Aderman, D., Brehm, S. S., & Katz, L. B. Empathic observation of an innocent victim: The just world revisited. *Journal of Personality and Social Psychology*, 1974, **29**, 342–347.

Alexander, R. D. The search for an evolutionary philosophy of man. *Proceedings of the Royal Society of Melbourne*, 1971, **84**, 99–120.

Aronfreed, J. The socialization of altruistic and sympathic behavior: Some theoretical and experimental analyses. In J. Macaulay & L. Berkowitz (Eds.), *Altruism and helping behavior*. New York: Academic Press, 1970.

Bakan, D. *The quality of human existence*. Boston: Beacon Press, 1966.

Bandura, H., & Rosenthal, L. Vicarious classical conditioning as a function of arousal level. *Journal of Personality and Social Psychology*, 1966, **3**, 54–62.

Berger, S. M. Conditioning through vicarious instigation. *Psychological Review*, 1962, **69**, 450–466.

Berger, S. M., & Hadley, S. W. Some effects of a model's performance on observer electromyographic activity. *American Journal of Psychology*, 1975, **88**, 263–276.

Bernal, G., & Berger, S. M. Vicarious eyelid conditioning. *Journal of Personality and Social Psychology*, 1976, **34**, 62–68.

Borke, H. Interpersonal perception of young children: Egocentrism or empathy. *Developmental Psychology*, 1971, **5**, 263–269.

Bridges, K. M. B. *The social and emotional development of the preschool child*. London: Kegan Paul, 1931.

Buck, R. W., Savin, V. J., Miller, R. E., & Caul, W. F. Communication of affect through facial expressions in humans. *Journal of Personality and Social Psychology*, 1972, **23**, 362–371.

Burns, N., & Cavey, L. Age differences in empathic ability among children. *Candian Journal of Psychology*, 1957, **11**, 227–230.

Campbell, D. T. Ethnocentric and other altruistic motives. In D. Levine (Ed.), *Nebraska Symposium on Motivation*, 1965 (Vol. 13). Lincoln: University of Nebraska Press, 1965.

Campbell, D. T. On the genetics of altruism and the counter-hedonic components in human culture. *Journal of Social Issues*, 1972, **28**, 21–38.

Cheyne, J. A., Goyeche, J. R., & Walters, R. H. Attention, anxiety, and rules in resistance-to-deviation in children. *Journal of Experimental Child Psychology*, 1969, **8**, 127–139.

Clark, R. D., & Word, L. E. Why don't bystanders help? Because of ambiguity? *Journal of Personality and Social Psychology*, 1972, **24**, 392–400.

Craig, K. D., & Lowery, J. H. Heart rate components of conditioned vicarious autonomic responses. *Journal of Personality and Social Psychology*, 1969, **11**, 381–387.

Craig, K.D., & Weinstein, M. S. Conditioning vicarious affective arousal. *Psychological Reports*, 1965, **17**, 955–963.

Crowell, D. H., Blurton, L. B., Kobayashi, L. R., McFarland, J. L., & Yang, R. K. Studies in early infant learning: Classical conditioning of the neonatal heart rate. *Developmental Psychology*, 1976, **12**, 373–397.

Darley, J. M., & Latané, B. Bystander intervention in emergencies: Diffusion of responsibility. *Journal of Personality and Social Psychology*, 1968, **8**, 377–383.

Deutsch, F. Female preschoolers' perceptions of affective responses and interpersonal behavior in videotaped episodes. *Developmental Psychology*, 1974, **10**, 733–740.

Deutsch,F., & Madle, R. A. Empathy: Historic and current conceptualizations, measurement, and a cognitive theoretical perspective. *Human Development*, 1975, **18**, 267–287.

Deutsch, H. *The psychology of women: A psychoanalytic interpretation*. New York: Grune & Stratton, 1944.

Eberhard, M. J. The evolution of social behavior by kin selection. *Quarterly Review of Biology*, 1975, **50**, 1–33.

Ekman, P., Friesen, W. V., & Ellsworth, P. *Emotion in the human face: Guidelines for research and an integration of findings*. New York: Pergamon Press, 1972.

Escalona, S. K. Feeding disturbances in very young children. *American Journal of Orthopsychiatry*, 1945, **15**, 76–80.

Fay, B. *The relationships of cognitive moral judgment, generosity and empathic behavior in six and eight year old children*. Unpublished doctoral dissertation, University of California, Los Angeles, School of Education, 1970.

Feshbach, N. D., & Feshbach, S. The relationship between empathy and aggression in two age groups. *Developmental Psychology*, 1969, **1**, 102–107.

Feshbach, N. D., & Roe, K. Empathy in six- and seven-year-olds. *Child Development*, 1968, **39**, 133–145.

Fisher, L. E., & Kotses, H. Experimenter and subject sex effects in the skin conductance response. *Psychophysiology*, 1974, **11**, 191–196.

Freud, S. [Some psychical consequences of the anatomical distinction between the sexes.] In J. Strachey (Ed. and trans.), *The complete psychological works of Sigmund Freud* (The Standard Edition, Vol. 19). London: Hogarth Press, 1961. (Originally published, 1925.)

Gaertner, S. L., & Dovidio, J. F. The subtlety of white racism, arousal, and helping behavior. *Journal of Personality and Social Psychology*, 1977, **35**, 691–707.

Geer, J. H., & Jarmecky, L. The effect of being responsible for reducing another's pain on subject's response and arousal. *Journal of Personality and Social Psychology*, 1973, **26**, 232–237.

Gelhorn, E. Motion and emotion: The role of proprioception in the physiology and pathology of the emotions. *Psychological Review*, 1964, **71**, 457–472.

Gutmann, D. L. Women and the conception of ego strength. *Merrill-Palmer Quarterly*, 1965, **11**, 229–240.

Haaf, R. A., & Bell, R. Q. A facial dimension in visual discrimination by human infants. *Child Development*, 1967, **38**, 893–899.

Hamilton, M. L. Imitative behavior and expressive ability in facial expression of emotion. *Developmental Psychology*, 1973, **8**, 138.

Hamilton, W. D. The genetic evolution of social behavior. *Journal of Theoretical Biology*, 1964, **7**, 1–52.

Hamilton, W. D. Selection of selfish and altruistic behavior in some extreme models. In J. F. Eisenberg & W. S. Sillon (Eds.), *Man and beast: Comparative social behavior*. Washington, D. C.: Smithsonian Institution Press, 1971.

Hoffman, L. W. Early childhood experiences and women's achievement motives. *Journal of Social Issues*, 1972, **28**,129–156.

Hoffman, M. L. Parent discipline and the child's consideration for others. *Child Development*, 1963, **34**, 573–588.

Hoffman, M. L. Moral development. In P. H. Mussen (Ed.), *Carmichael's manual of child psychology* (3rd ed.; Vol. 2). New York: Wiley, 1970. (a)

Hoffman, M. L. Conscience, personality, and socialization techniques. *Human Development*, 1970, **13**, 90–126. (b)

Hoffman, M. L. Developmental synthesis of affect and cognition and its implications for altruistic motivation. *Developmental Psychology*, 1975, **11**, 607–622.

Hoffman, M. L. Empathy, role-taking, guilt, and development of altruistic motives. In T. Lickona (Ed.), *Moral development and behavior: Theory, research and social issues*. New York: Holt, Rinehart & Winston, 1976.

Hoffman, M. L. Moral internalization: Current theory and research. In L. Berkowitz (Ed.), *Advances in experimental social psychology* (Vol. 10). New York: Academic Press, 1977. (a)

Hoffman, M. L. Sex differences in empathy and related behaviors. *Psychological Bulletin*, 1977, **84**, 712–722. (b)

Hoffman, M. L. Toward a theory of empathic arousal and its development. In M. Lewis & L. Rosenblum (Eds.), *Affect development*. New York: Plenum, in press. (a)

Hoffman, M. L. Adolescent morality in developmental perspective. In J. Adelson (Ed.), *Handbook of adolescent psychology*. New York: Wiley Interscience, in press. (b)

Hoffman, M. L., & Levine, L. E. Early sex differences in empathy. *Developmental Psychology*, 1976, **12**, 557–558.

Humphrey, G. The conditioned reflex and the elementary social reaction. *Journal of Abnormal and Social Psychology*, 1922, **17**, 113–119.

Izard, C. E. *The face of emotion*. New York: Appleton-Century Crofts, 1971.

James, W. *The principles of psychology*. New York: Holt, 1890.

Johnson, M. J. Sex role learning in the nuclear family. *Child Development*, 1963, **34**, 319–333.

Kagan, S., & Madsen, M. C. Cooperation and competition of Mexican, Mexican-American and Anglo-American children of two ages under four instructional sets. *Developmental Psychology*, 1971, **5**, 32–39.

Kameya, L. I. *The effect of empathy level and role-taking training upon prosocial behavior*. Unpublished doctoral dissertation, University of Michigan, 1976.

Klein, R. *Some factors influencing empathy in six and seven year old children varying in ethnic background*. (Doctoral dissertation, University of California, Los Angeles, School of Education, 1970.) *Dissertation Abstracts,* 1971, **31**, 3960A. (University Microfilms No. 71–3862).

Krebs, D. Empathy and altruism. *Journal of Personality and Social Psychology,* **32**, 1124–1146.

Kurdek, L. A., and Rodgo, M. M. Perceptual, cognitive, and affective perspective-taking in kindergarten through sixth-grade children. *Developmental Psychology,* 1975, **11**, 643–650.

Lacey, J. I. Psychophysiological approaches to the evaluation of psychotherapeutic process and outcome. In E. A. Rubenstein & M. B. Parloff (Eds.), *Research in psychotherapy.* Washington, D. C.: National Publishing Co., 1959.

Laird, J. D. Self-attribution of emotion: The effects of expressive behavior on the quality of emotional experience. *Journal of Personality and Social Psychology,* 1974, **29**, 475–486.

Latané, B., & Darley, J. Bystander intervention in emergencies. In J. Macaulay and L. Berkowitz (Eds.), *Altruism and helping behavior.* New York: Academic Press, 1970.

Lazarus, R. S., Speisman, J. C., Mordkoff, A. M., and Davison, L. A. A laboratory study of emotional stress produced by a motion picture film. *Psychological Monographs,* 1962, **76** (34, Whole No. 553).

Lenrow, P. B. Studies in sympathy. In S. S. Tomkins and C. E. Izard (Eds.), *Affect, cognition, and personality.* New York: Springer, 1965.

Lerner, M. J., & Simmons, C. Observer's reaction to the innocent victim: Compassion or rejection? *Journal of Personality and Social Psychology,* 1966, **4**, 203–210.

Levine, L. E., & Hoffman, M. L. Empathy and cooperation in 4-year-olds. *Developmental Psychology,* 1975, **11**, 533–534.

Lipps, T. Das Wissen von fremden Ichen. *Psychologische Untersuchungen,* 1906, **1**, 694–722.

London, P. The rescuers: Motivational hypothesis about Christians who saved Jews from the Nazis. In J. Macaulay & L. Berkowitz (Eds.), *Altruism and helping behavior.* New York: Academic Press, 1970.

MacLean, P. D. The limbic system with respect to self-preservation and the preservation of the species. *Journal of Nervous Mental Disease,* 1958, **127**, 1–11.

MacLean, P. D. New findings relevant to the evolution of psychosexual functions of the brain. *Journal of Nervous Mental Disease,* 1962, **135**, 289–301.

MacLean, P. D. The brain in relation to empathy and medical education. *Journal of Nervous Mental Disease,* 1967, **144**, 374–382.

MacLean, P. D. *A triune concept of the brain and behavior.* Toronto, University of Toronto Press, 1973.

Mandler, G. *Mind and emotion.* New York: Wiley, 1975.

Mathews, K. E., & Canon, L. K. Environmental noise level as a determinant of helping behavior. *Journal of Personality and Social Psychology*, 1975, **32**, 571–577.

McDougall, W. *An introduction to social psychology*. London: Methuen, 1908.

Mehrabian, A., & Epstein, N. A measure of emotional empathy. *Journal of Personality*, 1972, **40**, 525–543.

Milgram, S. A behavioral study of obedience. *Journal of Abnormal and Social Psychology*, 1963, **67**, 371–378.

Moore, B. S., Underwood, B., & Rosenhan, D. L. Affect and altruism, *Developmental Psychology*, 1973, **8**, 99–104.

Murphy, L. B. *Social behavior and child personality*. New York: Columbia University Press, 1937.

Parsons, T., & Bales, R. F. *Family, socialization, and interaction process*. Glencoe, Ill.: Free Press, 1955.

Piliavin, I.M., Rodin, J., & Piliavin, J. A. Good samaritanism: An underground phenomenon. *Journal of Personality and Social Psychology*, 1969, **13**, 289–299.

Rutherford, E., & Mussen, P. Generosity in nursery school boys. *Child Development*, 1968, **39**, 755–765.

Sagi, A., & Hoffman, M. L. Empathic distress in newborns. *Developmental Psychology*, 1976, **12**, 175–176.

Schachter, S., & Singer, J. E. Cognitive, social and physiological determinants of emotional state. *Psychological Review*, 1962, **69**, 379–399.

Schwartz, S. Moral decision making and behavior. In J. Macaulay & L. Berkowitz (Eds.), *Altruism and helping behavior*. New York: Academic Press, 1970.

Severy, L. J., & Davis K. E. Helping behavior among normal and retarded children. *Child Development*, 1971, **42**, 1017–1031.

Shantz, C. U. The development of social cognition. In E. M. Hetherington (Ed.), *Review of child development research* (Vol. 5). Chicago: University of Chicago Press, 1975.

Shure, M. B., Spivack, G., & Jaeger, M. Problem-solving thinking and adjustment among disadvantaged preschool children. *Child Development*, 1971, **42**, 1791–1803.

Simner, M. L. Newborn's response to the cry of another infant. *Developmental Psychology*, 1971, **5**, 136–150.

Speisman, J. C., Lazarus, R. C., Mordkoff, A., & Davison, L. Experimental reduction of stress based on ego-defense theory. *Journal of Personality and Social Psychology*, 1964, **68**, 367–380.

Staub, E. A child in distress: The influence of age and number of witnesses on children's attempts to help. *Journal of Personality and Social Psychology*, 1970, **14**, 130–140.

Staub, E., & Sherk, L. Need for approval, children's sharing behavior, and reciprocity in sharing. *Child Development*, 1970, **41**, 243–253.

Stotland, E. Exploratory investigations of empathy. In L. Berkowitz (Ed.), *Advances in experimental social psychology* (Vol. 4). New York: Academic Press, 1969.

Stotland, E., Mathews, K. E., Sherman, S. E., Hansson, R., and Richardson, B. Z. Empathy, Fantasy and Helping. Beverly Hills, California: Sage, in press.

Stotland, E., Sherman, S. E., and Shaver, K. G. *Empathy and birth order.* Lincoln: University of Nebraska Press, 1971.

Sullivan, H. S. *Conceptions of modern psychiatry.* London: Tavistock Press, 1940.

Tagiuri, R. Person perception. In G. S. Lindsey & E. Aronson (Eds.), *The handbook of social psychology* (Vol. 3) New York: Addison-Wesley, 1969.

Tannenbaum, P. H., & Gaer, E. P. Mood changes as a function of stress of protagonist and degree of identification in a film-viewing situation. *Journal of Personality and Social Psychology,* 1965, **2**, 612–616.

Tilker, H. A. Socially responsible behavior as a function of observer responsibility and victim feedback. *Journal of Personality and Social Psychology,* 1970, **14**, 95–100.

Tinbergen, N. On war and peace in animals and man: An ethologist's approach to the biology of aggression. *Science,* 1968, **160**, 1411–1418.

Tomes, H. The adaptation, acquisition, and extinction of empathically mediated emotional responses (Doctoral dissertation, Pennsylvania State University, 1963.) *Dissertation Abstracts,* 1964, **24**, 3442–3443. (University Microfilms No. 64–1423).

Tomkins, S. S. *Affect, imagery, consciousness.* New York: Springer, 1962.

Trivers, R. L. The evolution of reciprocal altruism. *Quarterly Review of Biology,* 1971, **46**, 35–57.

Weiss, R. F., Boyer, J. L., Lombardo, J. P., & Stich, M. H. Altruistic drive and altruistic reinforcement. *Journal of Personality and Social Psychology,* 1973, **25**, 390–400.

Weiss, R. F., Buchanan, W., Alstatt, L., & Lombardo, J. P. Altruism is rewarding. *Science,* 1971, **171**, 1262–1263.

Williams, G. C. *Adaptation and natural selection.* Princeton, N. J.: Princeton University Press, 1966.

Wine, J. D. Test anxiety and helping behavior. *Canadian Journal of Behavioral Science,* 1975, 216–222.

Wyatt, F. Clinical notes on the motives of reproduction. *Journal of Social Issues,* 1967, **23**, 29–56.

Wynne-Edwards, V. C. *Animal dispersion in relation to social behavior.* Edinburgh, Oliver & Boyd, 1962.

Zuckerman, M., DeFrank, R., Hall, J., & Rosenthal, R. Encoding and decoding of spontaneous and posed facial expressions. *Journal of Personality and Social Psychology,* 1976, **34**, 966–977.

Children's Developing Awareness and Usage of Intentionality and Motives[1]

Charles Blake Keasey
University of Nebraska–Lincoln

*I*t is important to recognize that the concepts of intentionality and motive are not equivalent. The concept of intentionality does not deal with what the particular motive might have been but rather with whether the action was motivated or accidental; if the action is judged as accidental, then there is no need to consider the concept of motive. Consequently, the concept of motive should come into consideration only after an act has been judged as intentional. However, it is quite possible that the actor's motive may be perceived by the observer as being so obvious that there is no need to consider whether the action was accidental or intentional. Thus, although it might be conceptually convenient to argue that the intentionality of an act is assessed before the search for a motive is undertaken, this temporal sequence may not actually reflect reality.

There is a substantial quantity of data strongly suggesting that a sophisticated understanding of the concepts of intentionality and motive requires many years to develop. In reviewing this developmental literature, it comes as something of a surprise to discover that the need for the intentionality/motive distinction has been recognized only recently (Berndt & Berndt, 1975; Shantz, 1975). Despite its recency, it is a very useful distinction, and will serve as a central component in the following review of theoretical and empirical work on the development of the two concepts.

1. A substantial portion of this chapter was written while the author was on a Senior Faculty Summer Research Fellowship awarded by the University of Nebraska Research Council.

PIAGET'S PIONEERING OBSERVATIONS

Virtually all of the more than 50 studies on the development of the concepts of intentionality and/or motive not only cite Piaget's classic work *The Moral Judgment of the Child* (1932) but also have employed some variant of an assessment procedure introduced by Piaget in that book. First of all, it needs to be recalled that Piaget described two general stages of moral reasoning in children (see Hoffman, 1970, for a review). Embedded within these two broad stages were perhaps as many as 11 different aspects of moral reasoning. Piaget described how children's conceptions along each of these aspects changed as the child matured. Only the aspect which Piaget termed objective/subjective responsibility has direct relevance to the concepts of intentionality and motive.

Piaget included both concepts under his broader concept of subjective responsibility, without an attempt to distinguish between them; in fact, at times he seems to use intentionality and motive interchangeably. The term subjective responsibility denotes a child's attention to internal and hence subjective processes in other people, the child's judgment about the intentional or accidental nature of an individual's overt behavior, and the child's assumptions about the underlying motive for that behavior. In contrast, objective responsibility refers to a focus on the external, visible features of an action, such as its appearance or consequences. It was the relative influence of these two types of responsibility on children's judgments of others' actions that was of prime interest to Piaget.

Piaget was well aware of the methodological difficulties involved in assessing their relative influence. He noted that "pure observation is the only sure method, but it allows for the acquisition of no more than a small number of fragmentary facts" (1932, p. 107). Thus instead of examining a child's actual behavioral decisions or even his memory of his actions, Piaget chose to study how children evaluated actions attributed to other children in stories. But because of the indirectness of this procedure, Piaget recognized that he might be unable to make the child concretely realize the types of behavior that he was being asked to judge. Piaget also believed that hypothetical stories might lead to different judgments:

> In real life the child is in the presence, not of isolated facts, but of personalities that attract, or repel him as a global whole. He grasps people's intentions by direct tuition and cannot there-

fore abstract them. He allows, more or less justly, for aggravating and attenuating circumstances. This is why the stories told by children themselves often give rise to different evaluations from those suggested by the experimenter's stories. (p. 116)

Piaget went on to note that "it may simply be the case that the evaluations obtained from the stories that were told by them lag in time behind the direct evaluations of daily life" (p. 116). The reason for a time lag follows from an important general distinction that Piaget makes within his more encompassing theory of children's cognitive development. He states:

The child's verbal thinking consists of a progressive coming into consciousness, or conscious realization of schemas that have been built up by action. In such cases verbal thought simply lags behind concrete thought, since the former has to reconstruct symbolically and on a new plane operations that have already taken place on the preceding level. (pp. 112–113)

Piaget suggested that perhaps in a similar fashion there is a time lag in the moral sphere between the child's concrete everyday moral decisions and his verbal judgments of the behavior of others. He asserted that the conscious realization reflected in verbal moral judgments represents a reconstruction and consequently a new and original construction superimposed on the constructions already formed by concrete actions.

If Piaget's distinction is justified, it has far-reaching methodological implications. Clearly, verbal morality will be elicited whenever a child is requested either to judge the actions of other people that do not directly interest him or to give voice to general principles regarding his own conduct independently of his actual behavior. Only through direct observation could one witness a child's active moral thought in operation. Because of the paradigm Piaget used to assess children's relative preference for objective versus subjective responsibility, he was clearly measuring their verbal rather than their practical moral reasoning. To the extent that subsequent investigators of intentionality and/or motives have used story presentations, they too will have data on verbal rather than active moral thinking.

At this point we need to consider Piaget's original paradigm for assessing the relative influence of objective and subjective responsibility. He presented children with pairs of stories, in one of which the actions resulted in a low amount of damage, in the other in a high amount of damage. The act which resulted in the greater amount of damage was "entirely fortuitous, or even the result of a well-intended act" (p. 118). In contrast, the smaller amount of damage resulted from an ill-intended act. After each pair of stories Piaget interviewed the child as to which story character he thought was naughtier and why. Although Piaget employed story-pairs about clumsiness, stealing, and lying, most subsequent research has focused on clumsiness. The following is an example of clumsiness and perhaps the best known story-pair:

A little boy, who is called John, is in his room. He is called to dinner. He goes into the dining room. But behind the door there was a chair, and on the chair there was a tray with 15 cups on it. John couldn't have known that there was all this behind the door. He goes in, the door knocks against the tray, bang go the 15 cups and they all get broken.

Once there was a little boy whose name was Henry. One day when his mother was out he tried to get some jam out of the cupboard. He climbed up on to a chair and stretched out his arm. But the jam was too high up and he couldn't reach it and have any. But while he was trying to get it he knocked over a cup. The cup fell down and broke.

Having outlined Piaget's method and some of its limitations that he recognized, it would seem appropriate to go on to the data he collected. However, before doing so it must be made perfectly clear that Piaget's interest was in the gradual replacement of objective responsibility with subjective responsibility as the basis for judging naughtiness, and *not* in the young child's growing awareness and usage of the concepts of intentionality and motive. That fact is indicated by his system of scoring objective and subjective responsibility. First and foremost it was based on the child's choice of who was naughtier and not upon the means by which the child justified his choice: Responses including both the actor's motives and explicit reference to the intentional/accidental distinction (e.g., "on purpose," "didn't know") were still scored as objective if the child judged the story character producing the greater damage as naughtier. Although most of the representative responses that Piaget scored as subjective included both motives and intentionality, some contained only one of the two components. That responses need not include any reference to the intentional/accidental distinction in order to be scored as subjective is indicated by the following example. (These responses deal with a plate having been broken by the children being questioned.) "I wanted to wipe it" was interpreted as reflecting helpfulness by Piaget and scored as subjective, while "I wanted to play with it" was scored as objective.

Piaget's data are based on interview responses to his story-pairs by approximately 100 children between the ages of 6 and 10. He observed that the influence of objective responsibility gradually gave way to that of subjective responsibility; though some children continued to give responses reflecting objective responsibility up to age 10, he did not find a definite instance of objective responsibility after that age. He also pointed out that often the very same child judged one situation according to objective responsibility and another according to subjective responsibility. (That some of this mixture was attributable to the particular stories is indicated by Piaget's observation that "some stories point more definitely to objective responsibility than others," p. 120.)

The pattern of findings led him to conclude that objective and subjective responsibility are two distinct processes of thinking, but that they do not represent clearcut stages of development. Piaget did not provide detailed normative data, but rather stated that if responses of children under age 10 were classified as objective or subjective, then seven was the average age for objective responsibility.

However, the meaning of this last statement must be carefully interpreted in light of another of Piaget's conclusions—namely that many of these younger children who gave predominantly objective responses were actually well aware of the actor's intentionality and/or motives, but failed to consider them more important than damage when judging the relative naughtiness of the two actors. Thus even though their verbal responses contained references to motive and/or intentionality, they still judged the child causing the greater damage as naughtier.

For our purposes it is neither the shift from objective to subjective responsibility nor the precise age at which this occurs that is important, but rather the fact that Piaget found children as young as 6 years of age using the concepts of intentionality and motive in their verbal moral reasoning. Having that evidence, our next question should concern the age at which these same concepts are reflected in the *active* moral thinking of children.

It turns out that Piaget made observations concerning the

emergence of both these concepts in active moral thinking. The fact that these data are in the very same chapter as his interview data comes as a bit of a surprise, since they have been ignored until quite recently (Berndt & Berndt, 1975; Keasey, 1977; Keasey & Sales, 1977a, 1977b). Piaget's observations on the development of intentionality were based largely on his own children. These observations led him to conclude that before the age of about 2½ children lack any clear consciousness of moral intention, in the sense that they cannot "distinguish between what is 'done on purpose' (an action carried out knowingly and in voluntary defiance of the command) and what is 'not done on purpose'" (p. 176). Piaget suggested that much of the physical damage produced by young children is merely the result of "experiments in physics." He gave the example of his daughter at 2½ pulling the threads out of a bath towel. I have observed my own daughter at a comparable age unravel her sock from the top to the heel while it was still on her foot.

However, observations of his own children at slightly older ages led Piaget to conclude that by about three or four years of age a child was able to differentiate

> . . . intentional faults from voluntary breaches of the moral code. And soon after that he learns to excuse himself by the plea of "not on purpose." But when it comes to the deeds of those around him, things appear in a very different light. Generally speaking, it is not going too far to say that the child—like ourselves—is more severe with others than with himself. The reason for this is quite simple. The conduct of other people appears in its outward shape long before we can understand the intentions behind it; so that we are apt immediately to compare this outward shape with the established rule and to judge the action by this essentially objective criterion. (p. 180)

Interestingly enough, it was in children of about the same age that Piaget observed the emergence of the concept of motive. In *The Language and Thought of the Child* (1926), Piaget reported that children began asking why-type questions between the ages of 3 and 4. One of the many different types of questions asked by them dealt with the psychological motives of others.

In summarizing Piaget's observations, it appears that he collected data dealing with two very different issues. One concerned the emergence of the concepts of intentionality and motive while the other concerned the increasing influence of these two concepts (termed subjective responsibilty) upon children's moral judgments. And the data reflect two different kinds of thinking: That associated with motive and intention reflects what Piaget would term active thinking, while the interview data reflect verbal thinking. It is this last set of data which indicates that it is not until after age 7 that children's moral judgments of the actions of others are more influenced by subjective than by objective responsibility.

The greater reliance on subjective responsibility when judging the behavior of others seems to require at least two capacities beyond the child's early awareness of the concept of intentionality. First of all, the child must generalize the application of the accidental/ intentional distinction from the judgment of his own everyday behavior to that of others with whom he directly interacts. Secondly, the child must transform this new distinction from the level of practical action used in direct interaction with others to the more abstract verbal level required when asked to judge imagined individuals in hypothetical situations. Although Piaget's work on the development of the concept of motive is much less well developed, presumably a similar sequence occurs.

There would seem to be little sense in continuing unless we had some assurance that Piaget's original observations on the shift from objective to subjective responsibility had received substantial confirmation from other investigators. For this reason we will examine the results of a number of replication studies.

Replication Studies

Piaget's theory of moral development did not initially meet with as much skepticism as his more encompassing theory of cognitive development. Nonetheless, several replication studies were undertaken to check on the existence of the multitude of phenomena he observed and reported. None of the early replication studies (Abel, 1941; Harrower, 1934; Lerner, 1937) dealt with objective and subjective responsibility; instead they focused on other aspects within Piaget's system, such as punishment and immanent justice. It was not until after the rediscovery of Piaget in the mid-1950s that investigators attempted to replicate his observations on the shift from objective to subjective responsibility (Boehm, 1962; Boehm & Nass, 1962; Grinder, 1964; Johnson, 1962; MacRae, 1954; Whiteman &

Kosier, 1964). In addition to replicating Piaget, the studies examined a number of possible correlates—IQ, sex, social class, child-rearing attitudes and practices, personality characteristics, moral behavior, attendance at Sunday School, and membership in scouting organizations. They had better luck in replicating Piaget's original findings than in discovering any significant correlates. All six of the studies found empirical support for an increasing preference for subjective responsibility in children from 6 through 17 years of age: Significant positive correlations between age and preference for subjective responsibility were reported by Johnson (1962) and MacRae (1954)—.35 and .53, respectively—and significant age group differences were found in the other four studies. Of all the other possible correlates, only IQ was consistently found to be positively related to preference for subjective responsibility. Johnson (1962) obtained correlations in the low .30s for children in grades 5, 7, and 9, but one of only .20 for 11th graders. Boehm (1962) and Whiteman and Kosier (1964) compared groups of children of normal, subnormal, and above normal IQs and found that the higher IQ groups evidenced significantly more advanced moral reasoning, though neither study reported correlations.

Only one study (Johnson, 1962) looked at important measurement issues such as reliability and construct validity. On a short scale of only four stories, Johnson obtained test-retest reliabilities ranging from .30 to .58 with an average of .44. The intercorrelation of performance among these four stories ranged from .30 to .42 with an average of .36. These correlations were higher than those obtained between the four responsibility stories and stories concerning five other aspects of morality within Piaget's system (X = .22, range = .09–.29). Thus, Johnson obtained evidence of low to moderate reliability for stories assessing objective/subjective responsibility and some evidence for both convergent and discriminant construct validity. But since Johnson used an older sample (11–17) than most of the other studies used, it is unclear whether his correlations over- or underestimate those that would be found in a younger sample.

Since no other research has addressed these important psychometric questions, one can do nothing more than project the age trends in Johnson's sample onto a younger age range. Although his various validity estimates were fairly stable with age, the reliability estimates for objective/subjective responsibility fell with increasing age from .58 to .38. That his highest reliabilities were obtained with the youngest children is perhaps a hopeful indication of what would be found among children under 10 years of age. Of course, without psychometric data on younger children, the above reasoning is nothing more than guided speculation which awaits empirical testing.

In addition to providing confirmation of the shift from objective to subjective responsibility, the data from some of the replication studies are presented in sufficient detail as to provide useful age norms. Since both of Boehm's studies (Boehm, 1962; Boehm & Nass, 1962) employed the same two stories to assess objective/subjective responsibility in comparable samples of children (N's = 237 and 160), her findings can be combined. The following percentages represent the proportion of all responses given at each age that reflected subjective responsibility: six (35%), seven (49%), eight (54%), nine (84%), ten (77%), and eleven (71%). Whiteman and Kosier (1964) administered three stories to 126 children and obtained the following percentages of responses reflecting subjective responsibility: seven (45%), nine (60%), and eleven (89%).

When we examine specific age norms coming from the replication studies, it appears that it is not until age 8 that the majority of responses reflect subjective responsibility; at the age of 7, slightly less than half of the responses reflect it. Even as late as age 11, a sizable minority of responses were still being based on objective consequences. It should be noted that the norms reported by the replication studies are slightly more advanced than those reported by Piaget some 25 to 35 years earlier. Perhaps these slight changes represent cultural changes occurring over a quarter of a century (Tomlinson-Keasey & Keasey, 1972); indeed this type of explanation has been suggested in a personal communication from Inhelder to Boehm (1962) stating that Piaget's staff was finding that Swiss children were developing more rapidly in moral reasoning.

Since a fairly consistent picture emerges from this set of replication studies, some reasonable generalizations are possible. First, it seems clear that children's preferences for subjective responsibility do increase with age. Secondly, objective and subjective responsibility do not appear to represent distinct stages, but rather two distinct ways of thinking. This is suggested by the frequent finding in replication studies that both are evidenced by children of the same age and often by the very same child. Both these sets of findings confirm Piaget's original observations and conclusions.

HEIDER'S LEVELS OF RESPONSIBILITY

The concepts of intentionality and motive can be found in the levels of responsibility described by Heider (1958). His perspective, quite different from Piaget's, represents an extension of Gestaltist conceptions of perception to the realm of interpersonal perception. Although Heider took little interest in the development of the numerous processes about which he theorized, one exception was his conception of responsibility. In this instance he delineates five levels of responsibility representing a changing balance of personal and environmental forces. Heider describes them as "successive stages in which attribution to the person decreases and attribution to the environment increases" (p. 113). Descriptions of each of Heider's five levels follows.

1. *Global Association*. At this most primitive level, responsibility represents a global concept in which the person is not differentiated from all things associated with him. Consequently he is held responsible for any effect that is in any way associated with him. For example, if it is his baseball that breaks a window, he is held responsible even though he wasn't playing there, but had lent his baseball to the neighborhood children.

2. *Causality*. At this level anything caused by the individual is ascribed to him. Here the individual is viewed as a necessary condition for the occurrence of the event. Although ability to produce the event is attributed to the individual, neither intention nor motivation is inferred. Heider notes that this level is what Piaget (1932) referred to as objective responsibility.

3. *Foreseeability*. Here the individual is considered responsible for any effect that he might have foreseen. As in Level 2, the individual is seen as a necessary condition, but neither intention nor motivation is inferred. The production of such events is often described as resulting from carelessness.

4. *Intentionality*. At this level responsibility is attributed only if the individual was trying to accomplish the action and thus had the intention to accomplish the action. Heider points out that this corresponds to what Piaget (1932) called subjective responsibility.

5. *Environmental Coercion*. Here intention and ability are attributed to the individual, but he is viewed as operating under a certain amount of environmental coercion. Thus his motives are not ascribed entirely to him, but are seen as having their source in the environment. Heider emphasizes that he is referring to cir-

cumstances in which most people would feel and behave in a similar fashion—as, for example, when a normally well-behaved child blatantly disobeys his favorite teacher under threat from several male classmates.

Heider's system offers several refinements over Piaget's in regard to both responsibility and the accidental/intentional distinction. First of all, he offers three additional levels of responsibility. His level of global association is not reducible to either of Piaget's two levels but rather represents a downward extension to a level even more primitive than objective responsibility. As such it resembles the kind of pseudocausal reasoning that Piaget (1926) referred to as syncretistic, in which the child fails to make appropriate differentiations between causes, effects, and unrelated phenomena. In similar fashion, Heider's fifth level, environmental coercion, appears to represent an upward extension beyond Piaget's subjective responsibility. Heider suggests that his third level, foreseeability, falls between Piaget's objective and subjective levels of responsibility. Although Piaget did not conceive of foreseeability as a separate level, the concept was incorporated in some of his stories about clumsiness. A good example is his story about the cups, cited above, which states that John couldn't have known that a tray with 15 cups was on a chair right behind the door he was about to push open.

There is little need to differentiate between motive and intentionality in Heider's first three levels of responsibility; as Heider points out, "neither intention nor motivation is inferred" at levels two or three. The distinction begins to emerge in the fourth level and is even more clearly drawn in the fifth level, where the intentionality of an act is seen as internal, but at least part of the motive is perceived as external to the actor. Thus it appears that Heider treats motive and intentionality as separate concepts, in a manner quite similar to that suggested at the beginning of this chapter.

Since Heider assumed that his levels reflect underlying cognitive processes which determine the attribution of responsibility, they may be thought of as a developmental sequence. But surprisingly few studies have examined the developmental significance of the five levels. Of the studies that employ Heider's levels and include children, several are concerned with the influence of culture (Shaw, 1969; Shaw, Briscoe, & Garcia-Esteve, 1968) or IQ (Shaw & Schneider, 1969) on the various levels, and do not report tests of age differences for the different levels. Of the three studies which do report such tests, one (Shaw & Iwawaki, 1972) found no difference in levels between two age groups (9–10 vs. 11–13) and another (Shaw & Sulzer, 1964) found only minimal differences between second graders and college students.

Since Shaw and Sulzer did not report results of statistical tests between age groups or between levels within age groups, conclusions must be inferred from their graphs. The greater differentiation within levels by college students seems to be due primarily to their greater attribution of responsibility for intentionality (Level 4) for both positive and negative outcomes, and for environmental coercion (level 5) for negative outcomes. Unfortunately this last finding runs counter to expectations. There do not appear to be any significant differences in the extent to which second graders and college students attribute responsibility at any of Heider's first three levels. Therefore, the central assumption that children's attribution of responsibility would be less well differentiated within Heider's five levels than that of college students was only minimally supported.

In the third study (Hardy & Keasey, Note 1), 6-, 8-, and 10-year olds were presented with 20 stories similar to those developed by Shaw and Sulzer (1964). The four stories at each of Heider's five levels represent the four possible combinations of high and low damage outcomes and positive and negative outcomes. The attribution patterns within Heider's five levels were very similar for the three age groups. There was a steady rise through the first four levels and a sharp decline at the fifth. Almost no responsibility was attributed on the basis of global association (Level 1)—only six of twenty 6-year-olds did so. Consequently all three age groups attributed significantly less responsibility at Level 1 than at any other level. However with regard to the other four levels, there was evidence that the 6-year-olds' pattern of attribution was less well differentiated than that of either the 8- or 10-year-olds. The two older groups had identical attribution patterns, with significantly more responsibility being attributed to intentionality (Level 4) than to foreseeability (Level 3) and to foreseeability than to causality (Level 2). Equal responsibility was attributed to causality (Level 2) and environmental coercion (Level 5). In contrast, 6-year-olds attributed comparable amounts of responsibility to causality (Level 2), foreseeability (Level 3), and environmental coercion (Level 5). However, significantly more responsibility was attributed to intentionality (Level 4) than to either causality (Level 2) or environmental coercion (Level 5).

The two outcome variables interacted in an interesting way.

Whereas for all three age groups the amount of responsibility attributed to high or low outcomes was not differentiated for negative outcomes, it became more sharply differentiated with increasing age for positive outcome situations. Thus in general it appears that children's willingness to blame and/or punish declines somewhat with age but remains little affected by the magnitude of negative outcomes. In contrast, as children grow older, their willingness to praise and/or reward seems to become more affected by the magnitude of positive outcomes. It is difficult to say exactly what happens to this pattern with increasing age. Although Shaw and his colleagues, in their studies with children, almost always obtain significant main effects for each variable, they find an interaction between the two only about half of the time, and they find the same pattern with adults (Shaw, Floyd, & Gwin, 1971; Shaw & Reitan, 1969).

In concluding this section, it appears that children's attribution of responsibility within Heider's levels continues to differentiate with age. However, these age changes are not dramatic and the basic attribution pattern does not seem to change after age 8.

PARADIGM CHANGES SINCE 1970

In the research conducted since 1970, there are several interesting commonalities among the relevant studies. Perhaps the most important one is reflected in their titles. With very few exceptions (Armsby, 1971; Buchanan & Thompson, 1973), neither objective/ subjective responsibility nor moral judgment represent the emphasis of the title. Instead almost all have incorporated terms such as intentionality (Berg-Cross, 1975; Berndt & Berndt, 1975; Chandler, Greenspan & Barenboim, 1973; Gutkin, 1972), intention (Hewitt, 1974, 1975; Imamoglu, 1975; King, 1971; Rule & Duker, 1973; Rule, Nesdale & McAra, 1974), intent (Costanzo, Coie, Grumet & Farnill, 1973; Farnill, 1974; Hebble, 1971), or motive (Collins, Berndt & Hess, 1974) into their titles.

That this is much more than a superficial change is indicated by the nature of the criticism of Piaget's original paradigm commonly expressed by these investigators. Several of them (Berg-Cross, 1975; Buchanan & Thompson, 1973; Chandler et al., 1973; Costanzo et al., 1973; Hebble, 1971; Imamoglu, 1975) have pointed out that with results obtained using Piaget's original paradigm it is not possible to determine whether children are aware of or capable of using intentionality because it is confounded with consequences. Because most of Piaget's story-pairs contrast a high damage/good intent story with a low damage/bad intent story, the relative contribution of intentionality and consequence in the children's moral judgments is uncertain. Imamoglu (1975) argues that this methodological problem prevents one from selecting from among at least three alternative explanations for the objective responsibility evidenced by young children: Perhaps they (a) are unable to discriminate between intentional and accidental occurrences, or (b) are unaware of the significance of intentionality for moral judgments, or (c) simply find consequence to be the more salient cue within Piaget's paradigm.

It is not surprising that Piaget's paradigm is criticized by recent researchers: It is bound to be insufficient for their purposes because Piaget designed it to answer a different question from that which they are asking. As indicated above, his concern was with objective/subjective responsibility, not with the developing awareness of motive and intentionality. For new questions, new paradigms are needed. And the general focus of the new question appears to be the age at which children first begin to use intentionality in making moral judgments.

So far there have been at least eight different modifications of the original paradigm. Two rather different ones represent attempts to avoid the problem of confounding. In one paradigm, children evaluate each of the four basic story types (good intent/high damage, good intent/low damage, bad intent/high damage, bad intent/low damage) separately (Buchanan & Thompson, 1973; Costanzo et al., 1973; Hebble, 1971; Imamoglu, 1975). The other paradigm uses story-pairs and requires children to identify the naughtier central story character in each of the six possible pairings of the four basic story types (Gutkin, 1972). Several investigators (Gutkin, 1972; Irwin & Moore, 1971; Keasey, 1977; Keasey & Sales, 1977b) have modified this second paradigm to include only some of the six possible pairings; the use of a reduced number of pairings is based on Gutkin's findings that some of the pairings receive almost identical ratings.

Berg-Cross (1975) attempted to assess the relative effectiveness of these two new paradigms in detecting use of intentionality in young children. Both single stories and story-pairs were administered to a large sample (N = 153) of first graders (mean age = 6–7). The stories presented in the single-story format differed from those in the story-pair format in that the accidental or intentional nature of the actions was made quite explicit: "'Accident' stories clearly stated that the act was an accident" and "'Intentional' stories clearly stated that the child did the act on purpose" (p. 971). After each story, children rated the story character along a 5-point punishment scale and gave reasons for their ratings. Berg-Cross found that 60% of the reasoning responses given in the single-story format were mature (i.e., reflected subjective responsibility), whereas only 35% of those given in the story-pair format were mature.

However, the presence of several design features prevents one from using these data to conclude that the single-story format is the more effective paradigm. First, since Berg-Cross's two conditions involved different sets of stories as well as different formats, it is unclear whether her results reflect story format differences, story content differences, or both. Secondly, the percentage of subjective responsibility responses may have been significantly inflated in the single-story format because of the explicitness of the language used to convey the accidental or intentional nature of stories. Lastly, it is unclear whether any counterbalancing was used to avoid a possible order effect. Consequently the question of relative effectiveness remains open until the same story content is presented within each paradigm and appropriate counterbalancing is employed.

Other modifications deal with different issues. Armsby (1971) and Berg-Cross (1975) have both pointed to the limited range through which Piaget varied the severity of the consequences in his stories. Both suggest that greater variation in the range might demonstrate that severity of consequences is an important variable. In order to test this notion, Armsby (1971) employed four levels of severity ranging, for example, from the breakage of one cup to that of a brand-new television set. As expected, the frequency of subjective responses declined systematically among both 6- and 8-year-olds as the severity of the consequences increased; the decline was more pronounced among the 6-year-olds. Since the proportion of 10-year-olds giving subjective responses remained at or above 92% across all four conditions, it appears that by age 10 children are minimally influenced by the severity of the consequences. Since Berg-Cross (1975) employed only one age level (6-year-olds) and only two damage levels, no more can be concluded from her study than from all the others which have employed only two damage levels—that children view greater damage as naughtier.

It also appears that more subjective responses are given by young children when the negative consequences are directed toward a human being rather than toward a physical object (Berg-Cross, 1975; Imamoglu, 1975). Berg-Cross found that the three stories involving damage or potential damage to humans all received higher punishment scores from 6-year-olds than the three involving nonhuman objects. Keasey, Sales, Morris, and Bragg (Note 2) investigated children's naughtiness ratings of crimes such as homicide, battery, larceny, and burglary. They found that children from kindergarten through fifth grade rated crimes against humans as the naughtiest and those against inanimate objects as the least naughty. Imamoglu (1975) found a number of differences concerning the human/nonhuman distinction. First, he found that all children (5-, 7-, 9-, and 11-year-olds), but especially the younger ones, evaluated accidental acts damaging physical objects more quickly than those injuring humans. Children showed greater ability to differentiate between accidental and intentional acts when humans rather than physical objects were affected. In fact, children's evaluations of intentional and accidental acts affecting physical objects did not seem to reflect any clear difference until about age 11. In contrast, when human beings were affected, children's evaluations clearly differentiated intentional from accidental acts at age 7. Buchanan and Thompson (1973) used stories involving both personal and property injury, but do not report any analyses relevant to the distinction.

Another modification of the paradigm has been in the mode of presentation. Although Piaget and most subsequent investigators have read stories to children, some have used media such as films (King, 1971) and videotape (Berndt & Berndt, 1975; Chandler et al., 1973; Collins et al., 1974; Dorr & Fey, 1974; Farnill, 1974) which better approximate real-life encounters. Two of these studies compared the relative effectiveness of reading stories aloud versus videotape presentation in eliciting subjective responses. Chandler et al. (1973) found that first graders (average age = 6–9) gave significantly more subjective responses to videotape, but Berndt and Berndt (1975) found no difference among 4-, 8-, and 11-year-olds.

Even though Farnill (1974) did not directly compare the two media, he noted that kindergartners in his study were able to differentiate their judgments by intention even when the consequences were negative, whereas those in the Costanzo et al. (1973) study were unable to do so when presented with stories through the verbal media. On the basis of this comparison, Farnill suggests that the videotape media seems able to elicit more advanced intentionality consideration. However, there are enough methodological dissimilarities between the two studies to question the appropriateness of Farnill's conclusion. Interestingly enough, a fourth set of investigators who use videotapes (Collins et al., 1974) are of the opinion that consequences have a greater salience than motives in that medium. They suggest that most dramatic TV fare for children typically depicts motives more subtly and inexplicitly than consequences.

At the present time it is impossible to resolve the contradictory data and opinions as to the relative effectiveness of verbal versus videotape presentation in eliciting subjective responses from young children. However, the issue would seem to hinge upon the relative salience of the two components in the different media. It is quite possible that within either media one component could operationally have been given greater salience than the other. This possibility seems more likely than some intrinsically greater salience for either component in a particular media.

Salience also seems to be influenced by the order in which intention and consequence components are presented in the stories. Nummedal and Bass (1976) argue that the usual order, intention-consequence, "may serve to draw the young child's attention to the most recent and thus most salient consequence cue, thereby masking the child's competence vis a vis intent" (p. 475). Half of their 96 children (6-, 8-, and 10-year-olds) were presented 16 stories representing either order and asked to rate the story character's naughtiness on an 11-point scale. Order clearly influenced ratings, but in a complex manner which varied with age. In general, the ratings of the 6-year-olds were based almost totally on the second component. For the two older age groups, ratings by children in the intention-consequence order reflected an increasing integration of the two components, whereas ratings by children in the consequence-intention order continued to be based almost totally on the second component, intention.

Another modification was designed to test Piaget's assertion (1932, 1968) that children develop concepts first in relation to themselves and then later apply them to others. Nummedal and Bass (1976) failed to find any differences in the naughtiness ratings by 6-, 8- and 10-year-olds of stories in which they themselves or someone else was the central story character. Keasey (1977) also found no difference among 7-year-olds, but his 6-year-olds used significantly more intentionality concepts in their reasoning when exposed to the self-oriented stories.

Because of some important differences between the two studies, it is possible to integrate their findings without ignoring real contradictions. First, Keasey's 6-year-olds were, on the average, 7 months younger than Nummedal and Bass's and in kindergarten rather than first grade. Secondly, Keasey used story-pairs and reasoning, rather than single stories and ratings. Obviously the first difference is the more important and suggests that young children, when asked to respond to hypothetical situations, consider intentionality first in relation to their own actions and later (between 6.0 and 6.7) apply this concept to the behavior of others. This pattern is quite consistent with Piaget's original notion of a self/other lag in young children's abstract moral thinking.

The final paradigm arises from the claim by Armsby (1971) and Berg-Cross (1975) that Piaget's story-pairs often failed to clearly differentiate accidental from intentional actions. In order to correct for this problem, Armsby (1971) designed four story-pairs which clearly contrasted an accidental act with an intentional one. These revised story-pairs were administered to 120 6-, 8- and 10-year-olds. Three of Piaget's original story-pairs were administered to a comparable set of children from Armsby's larger sample. Armsby found significantly more children at each level giving intentionality responses to the revised story-pairs (6-year-olds, 75% vs. 28%; 8-year-olds, 95% vs. 52%; 10-year-olds 95% vs. 82%). Although clear conclusions can be drawn from Armsby's procedure and findings, the same is not true for Berg-Cross's (1975). As discussed earlier (see p. 233), her revised stories were not in a story-pair format and the language she used to clearly contrast accidental and intentional behavior was probably too explicit.

It appears from this review of paradigm modifications that the salience of intentionality can be heightened in many different ways. However, the extent to which one can continue to increase the incidence of intentionality found in young children's verbal moral reasoning by incorporating more and more of these modifications into a single paradigm is unclear. This uncertainty arises from the fact that most investigators have incorporated only two or three of these eight possible modifications into their own assessment paradigms. In spite of this, it does seem clear that the normative data obtained by any study will be very much affected by the salience of the intentionality information presented in the particular assessment paradigm employed. Certainly if the current question of interest is the age at which children's verbal moral reasoning first begins to reflect intentionality, then it would seem essential that the salience of intentionality be maximized in the assessment paradigm. To fail to do so would leave one open to doubts and perhaps to some variant of the criticism that the absence of intentionality in one's subjects was merely an artifact of some feature of the assessment paradigm.

Unfortunately we currently lack the empirical data needed to determine just what combination of modifications would constitute the optimal assessment paradigm. However, even without this data, it might be possible to decide which modifications would be most crucial to the paradigm.

Some further ideas in this direction have recently been advanced by Karniol (in press) in a review of children's use of intention cues. Karniol concludes that the assessment of children's understanding of the accidental/intentional distinction requires that stories be employed which clearly differentiate between accidental and intentional actions. Since the stories used by Piaget and most subsequent investigators failed to do so, Karniol argues that the usefulness of their paradigms in assessing intentionality is questionable.

A careful examination of Piaget's original story-pairs indicates that Karniol's claim is quite justified. In fact, often both the high- and low-damage consequences result from accidents, because consequences are not systematically connected to the actor's motives. For example, in Piaget's story about the broken cups, one child's motive was to get some jam but he accidentally broke a cup while in the process; the motive of the other child was to go into the dining room for dinner but on his way he accidentally broke 15 cups. It turns out that the contrast between motives is even greater in most of Piaget's other story-pairs in that story characters are attempting to help someone rather than merely responding to a call to dinner. Interestingly enough then, it appears as if Piaget's original story-pairs provided much greater differentiation with regard to motives or consequences than in terms of the accidental/intentional distinction.

Although Piaget and most subsequent investigators have failed to employ stories which clearly differentiate between accidental and intentional actions, a few have. After reviewing the three studies (Armsby, 1971; Buchanan & Thompson, 1973; Farnill, 1974) which seemed to meet this requirement, Karniol concludes that young children judge story characters engaging in intentional negative acts as naughtier than those whose accidents produced greater damage. All three studies found substantial numbers of 6-year-olds evidencing an awareness of the accidental/intentional distinction in their verbal moral reasoning. Similar findings were obtained in a fourth study (Berg-Cross, 1975) involving 6-year-olds.

The Influence of Consequences on Intentionality

Although the above four studies employed stories which clearly differentiated between accidental and intentional actions, they also contained consequence information and sometimes motive information. To what extent did this surplus information make it more difficult for young children to demonstrate their understanding of the accidental/intentional distinction? In order to answer this question we need to look at the influence of both consequences and motives upon intentionality.

We will begin with the influence of consequences because this source of influence is much better documented. Recall that virtually all investigators, including Piaget, have assumed that consequences mask young children's ability to differentiate accidental from intentional actions. This assumption led investigators to develop two different paradigms designed to unconfound the operation of intentionality and consequences. Data resulting from studies using these two paradigms found substantial numbers of children as young as age 6 who could distinguish accidents from intended actions.

However, if we are interested only in children's ability to distinguish accidents from intended actions, it might make better sense to eliminate consequence information altogether rather than holding it constant across story pairs or having children rate single stories. If children's awareness of intentionality is indeed masked by consequence information, then its very absence should increase their ability to differentiate accidents from intended actions. This is exactly the pattern found in a recent study by Morrison and Keasey (Note 3). When 5-year-olds were presented with story-pairs without consequences that contrasted an accident with an intended action, over half of the 5-year-olds correctly answered the question of which story character was trying to bring about the resulting act. However, when identical positive consequences were added to each story, the proportion of correct responses dropped to only 10%. A similar pattern of findings emerged with both 7- and 9-year-olds. Thus it appears that the mere presence of consequence information reduces young children's ability to demonstrate their understanding of the accidental/intentional distinction. It is important to note that this reduction occurred even when the consequences of the accidental and intentional actions were identical. Several other studies (Buchanan & Thompson, 1973; Gutkin, 1972; Keasey, 1977; Keasey & Sales, 1977b) have demonstrated that an even greater reduction occurs when consequences are varied across story-pairs rather than held constant.

Some evidence for a developmental sequence into which this pattern of findings can be placed has been presented by Gutkin (1972). He presented 6-, 8-, and 10-year-olds with Piaget-type story-pairs in which consequences either varied or were held constant. Since Gutkin's story-pairs did not clearly differentiate between accidental and intentional actions, Karniol's caution must be kept in mind. Gutkin interpreted his data as providing evidence for a four-stage progressive refinement in children's usage of intentionality. At the least mature stage, children judged the two story characters as equally naughty when they produced equal amounts of damage regardless of differences in motives and intentionality. Children at the second stage took motives and/or intentionality into account when consequences were identical, but judged only on the basis of damage when damage, motive, and intentionality all varied. Children at the third stage considered intentionality and/or motives more important than consequences when all three components varied. When only consequences varied, they judged on the basis of consequences alone. However, children at the last stage considered intentionality and/or motives more important than damage under all possible combinations.

Once the pattern of findings reviewed earlier in this section is viewed in terms of Gutkin's four-stage progression, a possible developmental sequence of the influence of consequences upon the usage of intentionality comes into focus. It appears that young children first evidence an understanding of the accidental/intentional sequence when consequence information is not present. Next they can make the distinction if the consequences are identical but not when they vary. Finally they can make it even when consequences vary.

In attempting to explain this descriptive sequence, it might be helpful to reconsider each of the three alternative explanations of objective responsibility offered by Imamoglu (1975). His first explanation—of objective responsibility as a manifestation of young children's inability to discriminate between accidental and intentional actions—may account for some children's responses but not all. Both Piaget (1932) and more recently Morrison and Keasey (Note 3) observed that young children who are aware of the accidental/ intentional distinction nevertheless give objective responses. Imamoglu's two remaining explanations were that young children either found consequences to be the more salient cue within Piaget's paradigm or were simply unaware of the significance of intentionality for moral judgments. Evidence relevant to the saliency explanation will be reviewed here while that concerning the remaining explanation will be postponed to a later section on instructional sets.

Piaget (1932) dealt with the issue of salience in terms of his concept of centration. Many subsequent investigators (Armsby, 1971; Berg-Cross, 1975; Chandler et al., 1973; Costanzo et al., 1973; Crowley, 1968; Glassco, Milgram, & Youniss, 1970; Sternlieb & Youniss, 1975) have referred to that concept. In essence, centration describes the young child's inability to attend to more than one feature of an event or object at a time. Instead young children center their attention on what to them is the single most salient feature and thus are unable to decenter their attention and attend to other features. The centration argument clearly implies that the young child is aware of intentionality, but fails to attend to it when making moral judgments because his attention is centered on the more salient feature—consequences.

Although these several investigators have considered centration to be a major factor in objective responsibility, only one study Sternlieb & Youniss, 1975) has examined the relationship between the two. Forty 7-, 8-, and 9-year-olds were presented with six Piaget-type story-pairs and a test for conservation of weight. Only those children giving all correct responses were classified as intentional or conserving. Sternlieb and Youniss conclude that "subjects who were successful on a conservation task were more likely to be consistently intentional (n = 18) than not (n = 4)" (p. 895). However, they do not comment on the fact that their 18 nonconservers were equally likely to be consistently (n = 10) or inconsistently (n = 8) intentional.

What can be said about these 10 consistently intentional nonconservers? It could be argued that using conservation of weight as the index of decentration might have underestimated the number of subjects who could actually decenter. This argument is based on the typical finding that conservation of weight is preceded by conservation of mass. It is possible that many more of the intentional as opposed to nonintentional nonconservers might have evidenced decentration had conservation of mass rather than weight served as the index of decentration. It is also possible that many more of the intentional nonconservers would have been classified as able to decenter had the criteria not been so high—no errors.

Two other features of the study may have contributed to the somewhat confusing pattern of results. Since the criteria for passing the two tests were so high, perhaps a more sensitive test of the strength of the relationship between conservation of weight and intentionality would involve correlating children's scores on the two tasks. That the correlation might not have been very substantial is suggested by Sternlieb and Youniss's statement that "intentional judgments were correlated, although not decisively, with the general developmental indicator of conservation" (p. 897). It is also possible that the correlations may have varied as a function of age (Keasey, 1975). However, this data is not available since the investigators lumped together the responses of the 7-, 8-, and 9-year-olds. It might have been the case that the four nonintentional conservers were among the youngest conservers and had only most recently begun to conserve. Due to these many unanswered issues, the findings of Sternlieb and Youniss can be taken as only very tentative evidence for the decentration explanation. Consequently neither of Imamoglu's explanations of objective responsibility discussed here appear to have much empirical support.

THE INFLUENCE OF MOTIVES
UPON INTENTIONALITY

Before considering the influence of motives upon intentionality, it is essential to determine if the distinction is empirically justified. In their review of the distinction, Peterson and Keasey (Note 4) conclude that it had not been explicitly made either conceptually or methodologically by investigators prior to the Berndt and Berndt study in 1975. Furthermore, they suggest that because of various limitations of previously used paradigms, the resulting data cannot be used to evaluate the need for the distinction. These limitations arise largely from the unsystematic covariation of intentionality and motive information in most assessment stories. Several of the investigators who intentionally avoided this confounding nevertheless employed scoring systems which appear insensitive to the intentionality/motive distinction. Berg-Cross (1975) used Piaget's original scoring criteria which were designed to distinguish between objective and subjective responsibility, not intentionality and motive. Other investigators have talked about scoring intentional responses (Chandler et al., 1973; Gutkin, 1972) or explanations based on motives (Collins et al., 1974), but not in sufficient detail as to indicate whether motives, intentionality, or some combination of the two concepts served as the basis for scoring children's reasoning responses.

Only three studies (Keasey, 1977; Keasey & Sales, 1977b; King, 1971) have employed scoring systems which explicitly code children's responses in terms of intentionality. For example, Keasey (1977) scored responses as evidencing an awareness of the accidental/intentional distinction only if they contained phrases such as "on purpose," "meant to," or "accident." Keasey (1977) found explicit reference to intentionality in 40% of the reasoning responses of kindergartners (mean age = 6:0) and in 68% of the first graders' (mean age = 7:0) responses. A comparable proportion of intentionality responses was found in slightly younger kindergartners (mean age = 5:9) by Keasey and Sales (1977b). However, all three of these studies fail to clearly differentiate between intentionality and motive, probably because of their emphasis on intentionality; motive information was generally neglected by their scoring systems.

We are left then with only two studies (Berndt & Berndt, 1975; Peterson & Keasey, Note 4) which appear to have adequate methodologies for providing data bearing directly on the intentionality/motive distinction. The Peterson and Keasey study will be reviewed second as it represents an extension of the earlier Berndt and Berndt study.

Berndt and Berndt worked with a sample of 72 children from three age groups (mean ages = 4:11, 8:2, 11:2). Each child was presented with a set of four videotapes and a set of four stories. Four types of motive/intentionality combinations (instrumental aggression, displaced aggression, altruism, and accidental) were depicted in each media, but within different contexts. Unlike most previous investigators, Berndt and Berndt did not use children's reasoning responses to assess their understanding of the concepts of intentionality and motive.

They assessed children's understanding of motives from their descriptions of what happened in the different stories and videotapes. If the information was not given initially, then more specific questions were asked. With increasing age, the group averages of correct understanding of the immediate causes (near motives) were 58%, 80%, and 91%. As expected, the group averages for the more distant causes (far motives) were somewhat lower—47%, 72%, and 84%. Children's descriptions of what happened in the stories were not used to assess their understanding of intentionality. Instead they were asked a very direct question after each story: Was the action done "on purpose"? With increasing age, the group averages of correct answers for the "on purpose" question were 69%, 78%, and 89%.

On the basis of these two sets of findings, Berndt and Berndt conclude that even their 5-year-olds "understood both the concept of motive as a reason for acting and the accidental-intentional distinction" (p. 910). However, it must be recognized that their motive assessment procedure was by far the more difficult task. Whereas it required children to make inferences and then communicate them verbally, the intentionality task required only a yes or no answer to a question on which the chance probability of being correct was 50%. In order to take this into account, the percentages reported by Berndt and Berndt were tested by myself to see if they were significantly greater than those that would be expected by chance alone. It turns out that the percentages for two of the motive/intentionality combinations (instrumental and displaced aggression) were significantly greater than chance, the altruism combination approached significance ($p = .068$), and the accidental one did not.

In addition to assessing children's understanding of intentionality and motive, Berndt and Berndt also had children rate the story characters. They found that motives affected evaluative ratings at all ages, but that differences in intentionality affected the evaluative ratings of grade school children but not preschoolers. On the basis of their data on children's understanding and ratings, Berndt and

Berndt conclude that where 5-year-olds understand both the concepts of motive and intentionality, their evaluative ratings of others are influenced only by motive. They suggest, therefore, that the development of the two concepts follows different sequences and hence requires different explanations.

However, as pointed out above, because of the experimenters' noncomparable assessment procedures it is questionable whether their preschoolers really understood both concepts. It could be argued that their 5-year-olds did not really understand the concept of intentionality. Even if this were the case it would not challenge their suggestion that these two concepts follow different developmental sequences and thus require different explanations. Unfortunately most other studies which have included preschoolers (Irwin & Moore, 1971; Peterson, Peterson, & Finley, 1974; Schleifer & Douglas, 1973) have failed to differentiate between motive and intentionality and thus provide no greater clarity as to their understanding and usage by preschoolers.

The other study of preschoolers which differentiates between motive and intentionality, that of Peterson and Keasey (Note 4), involved 36 children from three age groups (mean ages = 3:8, 4:4, 4:11). Each child was presented with three stories that all ended with identical positive outcomes. However, in one the outcome was an accident, whereas in the other two it resulted from either a good or a bad motive. In order to avoid problems arising from noncomparable assessment procedures, Peterson and Keasey used the same set of four measures for assessing both motive and intentionality. This set included reaction times, evaluative ratings, comprehension, and reasoning.

Although there was no systematic pattern of findings obtained from the reaction-time data there were for the other three measures. Ratings by children at all three age levels clearly differentiated between actors with good versus those with bad motives, regardless of the fact that their actions led to identical positive outcomes. For all three age groups, the mean rating of the accidental story fell between those of the two opposing motives stories. However, inspection of the individual data clearly indicated that the ratings of the accidental stories were not in the middle of a seven-point good/bad scale but were randomly distributed. Thus the impression that accidents were consistently rated as more naughty than acts resulting from good motives but less naughty than acts resulting from bad motives is totally without grounds. Instead children at all three age levels seemed unable to systematically differentiate accidents from either good or bad motives.

This difference in children's usage of the concepts of intentionality and motive is further illustrated by the reasons they gave for their evaluations. Slightly over a quarter of the reasons given for their evaluations of story characters with either good or bad motives reflected a correct understanding of the actor's motive. In sharp contrast, only one child out of 36 gave a reason for his evaluation of the accident which came close to identifying its unintentional nature. In other words, none of the children in any of the three age groups gave reasons explicitly dealing with the accidental/intentional distinction.

An integration of the findings from these two studies suggests that children as early as age three understand and use the concept of motive to evaluate others. These findings correspond rather nicely with Piaget's (1926) observation that children between three and four years of age begin to ask questions about psychological motives. Both studies also demonstrate that children under five do not systematically use intentionality in their evaluations of others. Peterson and Keasey found no evidence for a verbalized usage of the concept of intentionality in children under age five. Because of the possible problems with Berndt and Berndt's measure of children's understanding of intentionality, it is unclear whether the majority of their 5-year-olds evidenced even a nonverbal usage of the concept.

In conclusion, data from both these studies strongly suggest that the development of the concepts of intentionality and motive follows very different sequences, at least during the preschool years. This further suggests the continued need for using terminology which will distinguish between these two different usages of the term intentionality.

Certainly, as has been the case in many other areas, it is quite possible that future studies, employing more ingeniously designed assessment procedures, may be able to demonstrate greater understanding and usage of intentionality in children under five years of age. Until that time, it appears that it is not much before their sixth birthday that substantial numbers of children evidence a verbalized usage of the concept of intentionality (Keasey, 1977; Keasey & Sales, 1977b).

Since the intentionality/motive distinction seems to be well grounded empirically, we will consider the influence of motives on intentionality. However, before turning to this issue, we will focus on children's developing conceptions of motives. Recall that Piaget (1926) observed children asking questions about psychological motives as early as ages 3 and 4. Since Piaget's early observations, several studies (Berndt & Berndt, 1975; Hewitt, 1974, 1975; Rule & Duker, 1973; Rule et al., 1974; Weiner & Peter, 1973; Peterson & Keasey, Note 4) have examined the influence of good and bad motives upon children's evaluative ratings of others. With only one exception (Hewitt, 1975) these investigators have found that children rate bad motives as naughtier than good ones.

The youngest children to demonstrate this differentiation in their ratings were 3-year-olds. Peterson and Keasey found that seven of 12 3-year-olds had no trouble differentiating in their ratings of story characters with good and bad motives. Good and bad motives were easily differentiated by 4- and 5-year-olds. These findings were not confounded by either intentionality or consequences, as these two components were held constant.

The robustness of the influence of motives on children's ratings is reflected in at least two ways. First, all studies but two (Rule et al., 1974; Peterson & Keasey, Note 4) have manipulated variables in addition to motive valence. These other variables have included intentionality (Berndt & Berndt, 1975), outcome valence (Weiner & Peter, 1973), outcome intensity (Hewitt, 1974, 1975; Rule & Duker, 1973), and provocation (Hewitt, 1975). In spite of the presence of these other variables, all of these studies still obtained significant main effects for the good/bad motive manipulation. The robustness is also indicated by the diversity of ways in which good and bad motives have been operationalized in different studies. Good motives have included showing the aggressor something interesting (Hewitt, 1974), teaching the aggressor something about football, roller skating, etc. (Hewitt, 1974), teaching the aggressor not to aggress again (Rule & Duker, 1973), aggression in the service of some prosocial norm (Rule et al., 1974), helping another child (Weiner & Peter, 1973; Peterson & Keasey, Note 4), and wanting to make another child happy (Berndt & Berndt, 1975). Bad motives have included wanting to hurt another child (Hewitt, 1974, 1975; Rule & Duker, 1973; Rule et al., 1974; Peterson & Keasey, Note 4), aggression in the service of hedonism (Berndt & Berndt, 1975; Rule & Duker, 1973; Rule et al., 1974; Peterson & Keasey, Note 4), not helping another child in need (Weiner & Peter, 1973), displaced aggression (Berndt & Berndt, 1975), and wanting to make another child feel bad (Rule et al., 1974).

From this set of studies it can be concluded that young children's evaluative ratings of others are strongly influenced by the goodness or badness of others' motives. This ability to differentiate seems to begin as early as age 3 (Peterson & Keasey, Note 4), continues to improve up to age 8 or 9, and then remains relatively stable until at least age 18 (Weiner & Peter, 1973).

Although preschoolers seem able to readily discriminate good from bad motives, they do not mention them with equal frequency when asked to justify their ratings. Peterson and Keasey (Note 4) found that 10 of 12 5-year-olds gave reasoning responses dealing explicitly with the actor's motive for bad-motive stories, but none for good-motive stories. Although explicit responses were less common among 3- and 4-year-olds, bad motives were still reported more often (6 vs. 1). Overall, then, of the 17 reasoning responses dealing explicitly with the actor's motives, only one concerned a positive motive and the remaining 16 were for bad motives. Similar findings come from the only other study (Berndt & Berndt, 1975) which obtained more than rating data. Berndt and Berndt found that their story involving a good motive (altruism) was less well understood than their aggression story by 5-, 8-, and even 11-year-olds.

This difference may arise because children acquire the concept of bad before the concept of good. Evidence for this explanation was reported by Rhine, Hill, and Wandruff (1967). They asked preschoolers to point to the child engaging in good or bad behavior displayed in sets of pictures. The correct identification of bad behaviors was near chance among their youngest preschoolers (24–29 months) but reached 100% by age 5. In contrast, the identification of good behaviors was significantly lower than that of bad behaviors for all but their youngest preschoolers. Rhine et al. conclude that "the verbal concept bad appears to come into cognitive focus around the age of 2, or possibly earlier, and to be well acquired by 6. The concept good is understood during the ages of 3 and 4 years and is well acquired by 6" (p. 1040).

Rhine et al. suggest that the differential acquisition rates for the two concepts may reflect differing socialization pressures experienced by young children. More frequent and affectively laden adult feedback is likely to follow bad as opposed to good behavior. Whereas adults would attend to most bad behavior, it "would drive an adult to distraction if he tried to tell the child everything that was not bad" (p. 1041). Piaget (1932) advanced essentially the same line of reasoning to explain why children would learn the concept of good after the concept of bad.

Possibly a further understanding of this good/bad discrepancy can be gained by an idea recently advanced by Hill and Enzle (Note 5). They suggest that the results of previous studies (Costanzo et al., 1973; Jensen & Hughston, 1973; McKechnie, 1971) indicate that children learn to evaluate bad behavior independent of consequences earlier than they do good behavior. They point out that McKechnie (1971) found that children judged two story characters producing unequal consequences as equally naughty when the motives of both of them were bad rather than good. Similarly they note that Jensen and Hughston (1973) found preschoolers' judgments of good acts to be much more influenced by whether the act was rewarded or punished than were their judgments of bad acts. Hill and Enzle reinterpret findings by Costanzo et al. (1973) as actually showing that children learn to consider intentionality in judgments of bad behaviors before they do for good behaviors. Findings by Imamoglu (1975) are also consistent with Hill and Enzle's point of view. Imamoglu found that 5-year-olds attributed considerably more importance to intentions when asked to indicate their degree of liking or disliking for story characters causing bad as opposed to good outcomes. In contrast, when the story outcomes were good, 5- and 7-year-olds liked the story characters equally well irrespective of intentionality.

How can the evidence for differential levels of understanding of the concepts of good and bad by preschoolers be integrated with their demonstrated ability to differentially rate good and bad motives? Perhaps the key lies in McKechnie's (1971) finding of much less differentiation by children between good and neutral acts than between bad and neutral ones. This suggests that once preschoolers come to know what is bad, they can readily discriminate bad from all else. When asked to justify their ratings, they are somewhat limited to speaking about bad as opposed to good motives. However, at a later age when they have divided the not-bad class into neutral and bad, then they would be more able to include good as well as bad motives in their reasoning.

Karniol (in press) carries Hill and Enzle's line of reasoning one step further and suggests that young children not only evaluate good motives in terms of consequences but that they do the same for accidental ones. Consequently when presented with stories varying consequences, intentionality, and/or motives, the young child's evaluation of the story character with a good motive who accidently produces a high damage outcome is not independent of that high damage outcome. Instead the magnitude of the damage becomes the major component in determining the child's evaluation.

Perhaps an appropriate methodology for investigating Karniol's line of reasoning would be that developed by Morrison and Keasey (Note 3): Initially simple stories are presented in which only intentionality or motives are manipulated; at the next level of complexity stories present various combinations of intentionality and motive; and lastly, and most importantly from Karniol's perspective, negative consequences of varying magnitudes are added to the simpler stories.

Karniol points out that the later independence of good motives and accidents from consequences is quite consistent with Piaget's (1932) notions of the relationship between moral reasoning and socialization. Piaget suggested that parents have two fairly strong tendencies; they tend to punish in terms of the negative consequences produced by the child's act, and the punishment given out tends to vary systematically with the magnitude of the damage. So it should be of little surprise that young children come to evaluate their behavior and that of others in terms of the magnitude of the damage done. Thus for young children magnitude of damage, more than anything else, comes to define right and wrong.

I would like to suggest that motives influence intentionality in much the same way that consequences influence both intentionality and motives. My reasoning goes as follows: Since young children's understanding and usage of the concept of motive seem to develop in advance of intentionality (Berndt & Berndt, 1975; Peterson & Keasey, Note 4), then it is likely that they would evaluate situations in terms of motives before intentionality. Consequently, subjective responsibility may initially reflect a discrimination along the lines of motives and not intentionality. This would occur because young children should select the story character with the good motive who accidentally produces substantial damage as less naughty than the one whose bad motive results in minimal damage, because of their difference in motives and not intentionality. That this was indeed the case in most previous studies is strongly suggested by the fact that, as noted frequently above, a clear differentiation between accidental and intentional events was rarely contained in the stories presented to children (Karniol, in press). Here again the methodology developed by Morrison and Keasey (Note 3) would seem most appropriate for investigating the merits of my suggestion.

Before leaving this section, it might be useful to consider some of Piaget's observations as they might relate to the later development of intentionality relative to motives. In some of his earliest work (Piaget, 1929), Piaget noted that young children attributed purpose indiscriminately to almost everything. Lacking any conception of chance or probability, the young child will always look for the cause. When these notions are moved to the realm of human behavior, they suggest that young children will initially find psychological motives behind all behaviors. Thus, their discovery of the accidental/intentional distinction must await their developing some notions of chance and probability.

WHAT SHOULD THE CHILD BE ASKED?

Now that the relative merits of the numerous paradigm modifications have been evaluated and a few guidelines offered, there still remains the question of what response will be required of the subject. Before attempting to debate the advantages of various options, some notion of their diversity is needed. In his original work, Piaget (1932) obtained moral opinions as to which of two story characters was naughtier and the reasoning behind each opinion. Although most of the replication studies use both opinions and reasoning, MacRae (1954) used only opinion data. Grinder (1964) introduced a multiple choice format "in order to facilitate data collection" (p. 885). Asking children for the reasoning behind their moral opinions has become less common among the studies that have come after the replication. Among the training studies, six (Cowan, Langer, Heavenrich, & Nathanson, 1969; Dorr & Fey, 1974; Jensen & Larm, 1970; Lickona, in press; Schleifer & Douglas, 1973; Sternlieb & Youniss, 1975) examined both opinions and reasoning, while three (Bandura & McDonald, 1963; Crowley, 1968; Glassco et al., 1970) analyzed only opinion data.

Most of the paradigm-modification studies have employed a new type of response differing from either moral opinions or reasoning. In order to better quantify the child's use of intentionality many investigators (Buchanan & Thompson, 1973; Costanzo et al., 1973; Farnill, 1974; Hebble, 1971; Hewitt, 1974, 1975; Imamoglu, 1975;

Irwin & Moore, 1971; Nummedal & Bass, 1976; Rule & Duker, 1973; Rule et al., 1974; Shantz & Voydanoff, 1973) have instructed their subjects to rate the story character's degree of naughtiness along 5- to 11-point scales. Recently even the child's latency in giving a moral opinion has been used (Imamoglu, 1975; Peterson & Keasey, Note 4).

Of course a reasonable and important question to ask is whether or not the use of different indices leads to comparable findings. Although several studies have employed at least two of the above four indices (most commonly moral opinions and ratings) only two have conducted comparative analyses of the results obtained. Imamoglu (1975) found that accidental acts were evaluated more slowly than intentional ones by four age groups (5-, 7-, 9- and 11-year-olds). However, only the ratings of the three older age groups differentiated accidental from intentional acts. Thus, through the use of a latency measure, evidence of an awareness of intentionality was found at a younger age than with a rating procedure. Unfortunately the only other study to employ latencies (Peterson & Keasy, Note 4) failed to find any differences among 3-, 4-, and 5-year-olds. Because of the minimal overlap in the ages employed in the two studies, it could be argued that reaction-time differences may not appear until around five years of age. Even so, Peterson and Keasey's findings undermine Imamoglu's interpretation. For if, as Imamoglu suggests, reaction times are a more sensitive index of intentionality than ratings, one would expect latency differences among children five and under. But Peterson and Keasey found none.

So far the most thorough comparison of various indices of intentionality has been conducted by Keasey and Sales (1977b). In addition to obtaining moral opinions, underlying reasoning, and ratings from 5-, 6-, and 7-year-olds, they also asked these children what was meant by the word "accident." Thus they used three of the four indices used by previous investigators and introduced a new one. Comparison among three of their indices was greatly facilitated by representing the data in percentages. The percentage of situations in which the child intentionally damaging less was judged as naughtier than the child accidentally damaging more were as follows: 5-year-olds, 67%; 6-year-olds, 83%; and 7-year-olds, 90%. The percentages of underlying reasons explicitly dealing with the accidental/intentional distinction were: 5-year-olds, 40%; 6-year-olds, 56%; and 7-year-olds, 64%. The percentages of children at each age who could adequately define the word "accident" were: 5-year-olds, 20%; 6-year-olds, 40%; and 7-year-olds, 55%. Thus not only do these three indices reflect an expected improvement with age, but they also show an identical pattern of relative difficulty across all three age groups. Keasey and Sales point out that since the rating data could not be readily transformed to a percentage format, its difficulty level could not be easily compared to that of the other three indices. However, they note that since the 5-year-olds gave differential ratings similar to those of the two older groups and the task required no verbal production, its difficulty level was probably comparable to that of the moral opinion task, and easier than either the reasoning or definition tasks.

The pattern of difficulty levels reported by Keasey and Sales is consistent with the stages suggested by Breznitz and Kugelmass (1967) and Kugelmass and Breznitz (1968). The rating and moral opinions tasks both fit Breznitz and Kugelmass's first stage of a preverbalized usage of the principle of intentionality. The reasoning and definition tasks both fit their second stage of a verbalized usage of the principle of intentionality.

In response to the question of which index is best, one would have to counter with "For what?" Keasey and Sales (1977a) argue the merits of the reasoning index because they wish to minimize the number of false positives identified within the legal process. Peterson and Keasey (Note 4) also favor moral reasoning over the other indices; they argue that because of all the confounds in most of the paradigms used thus far, it is very difficult to infer the basis for childrens' reaction times, moral opinions, or ratings. They also point out the shortcomings of several systems (Berg-Cross, 1975; Chandler et al., 1973; Gutkin, 1972) employed to score reasoning responses for intentionality. It is their opinion that the most compelling evidence for intentionality has come from studies (Keasey, 1977; Keasey & Sales, 1977b; King, 1971) employing very explicit scoring systems.

If, however, one is interested in the age when children first begin to differentially respond to the accidental/intentional distinction, as most psychological researchers seem to be, then either the moral opinion or rating task would seem more appropriate. The former requires a story-pair format, whereas the latter can fit either a story-pair or single-story format.

In concluding this section, it seems clear that different indices will produce different results. However, their order of increasing difficulty is fairly consistent across several different age groups. In most cases the question under investigation will probably dictate which index would be most appropriate.

Perhaps the most important question to ask a child is whether or not he really understood the story, videotape, etc. Although some statement about comprehension is typically included in the method section of most studies, little is said about how it was assessed. Furthermore, surprisingly few studies have done anything with the comprehension data after collecting it.

Presumably comprehension is important because a child's performance should be substantially affected by the degree to which he comprehends the assessment paradigm. Some evidence for this presumption comes from the Peterson and Keasey (Note 4) study. They found that the extent to which preschoolers differentially rated good and bad motives correlated significantly, $r(36) = +.43$, with the degree to which they comprehended the good- and bad-motive stories. More evidence comes from two studies (Shantz & Voydanoff, 1973; Fitzhenry-Coor, Note 6) using somewhat older children. Shantz and Voydanoff required half of their 7-, 9-, and 12-year-old subjects to recall all story elements prior to indicating how aggressively they would respond to different provoking situations. Children in the recall condition, from all three age groups, differentiated more between accidental and intentional provocation than those not in the recall condition.

Clearly the most sophisticated techniques used to assess comprehension have been employed by Fitzhenry-Coor. (Note 6). She used story recall and information-probing questions to assess comprehension. Both techniques are currently being used in the field of comprehension research (Brown, 1975). Story recall was analyzed by means of linguistic units (Mandler & Johnson, 1977). In addition to these two measures of comprehension, three intentionality stories were presented to 36 first, third, and fifth graders. Performance on the comprehension and intentionality tasks were found to be significantly related. In fact, intentionality was predicted equally well by the comprehension data and the age and grade information. Fitzhenry-Coor suggests that story recall is a better predictor of intentionality than information-probing questions, the reason being that probing questions involve much more cueing than either of the other two tasks. Results from these three studies clearly indicate that comprehension is an important element which should be included in any paradigm designed to study intentionality.

ON BEYOND MORALITY: THE INFLUENCE
OF INSTRUCTIONAL SETS

Findings by Farnill (1974) suggest that young children's usage of intentionality may be seriously constrained within the context of moral judgments. Farnill contrasted the typical moral judgment task with a value-maintenance task. The instructional set of the latter disposes the subject to consider others in terms of his own personal goals. Children from three age groups (mean age = 6:1, 7:0, 9:4) were presented with six videotapes, which represented combinations of two levels of damage and three mixtures of intentionality and motive. These three mixtures were: malicious motive/ intentional, positive motive/accidental, and positive motive/inept. In the moral-judgment task, children were instructed to rate the film characters positively or negatively; in the value-maintenance task, they were instructed to rate the film characters in terms of potential helpfulness to themselves.

Farnill found that children's ratings were more differentiated with respect to intentionality in the value-maintenance task. Furthermore, ineptness was equated with maliciousness within the value-maintenance set, but with the accident in the moral-judgment task. In summarizing his various age effects, Farnill concludes that if they "are considered developmental, then the effects of the value-maintenance set may be thought of as evoking more developmentally advanced ratings than the moral-judgment set" (p. 282). Farnill interprets his obtained differences between instructional sets as reflecting the greater freedom of children in the value-maintenance set to select among several bases for making judgments. In contrast, the moral-judgment set seemed to inhibit consideration of intentionality.

The influence of instructional sets has also been examined by Morrison and Keasey (Note 3). They presented story pairs at different levels of complexity to 5-, 7-, and 9-year-olds. The simplest story pairs contrasted either intentional and accidental acts or good and bad motives. Those of intermediate complexity involved the above two contrasts plus consequences. Story pairs at the most complex levels involved various combinations of all three components— intentionality, motives and consequences. After each story pair, children were asked three different sets of questions: Which story character was nicer? Which would you want as a friend? and Which was trying?

Morrison and Keasey suggest that a young child's understanding of the accidental/intentional distinction can be better assessed by asking him which story character was trying rather than which was naughtier. The other two questions, focusing on niceness and potential friendship, were designed to assess children's ability to differentiate good from bad motives. In almost all instances, Morrison and Keasey found that the highest percentage of correct answers for the accidental/intentional story pairings was given in response to the trying question rather than to the niceness or friendship questions. In contrast, the highest percentage of correct answers for the motive contrasts were given in response to the niceness question.

Both of these studies demonstrate the greater sensitivity of instructional sets other than the pervasive naughtiness question in detecting children's understanding of the accidental/intentional distinction. It seems more appropriate to use the naughtiness question to assess children's ability to differentiate good from bad motives. Perhaps the trying question is the most appropriate instructional set for assessing a child's understanding of the accidental/intentional distinction.

Another way in which instructional sets undergo change is through shifting from moral situations to some other realm. For example, Baldwin and Baldwin (1970) found that children's judgments of kindness demonstrated a differentiation between intended and unintended outcomes at an earlier age than has generally been found in moral judgment research. Of course, a more direct test would require a comparative study in which children make judgments of both kindness and naughtiness.

It should be clear from the above studies that young children's use of the accidental/intentional distinction is substantially influenced by the instructional set they are given. Furthermore, it appears that the set traditionally used in moral judgment studies tends to reduce childrens' use of intentionality more than several other sets. One possiblity for this reduction is that young chidren have not learned of the importance of intentionality for moral judgments (Imamoglu, 1975). Certainly there are other possiblities.

SUMMARY AND CONCLUSIONS

If, as it appears, investigators since 1970 have been searching for the age at which the accidental/intentional distinction first begins to manifest itself in the thinking of young children, then it is most

Piaget never intended it for that purpose; instead he was seeking to determine the relative influence of objective and subjective factors (including intentionality) on children's moral judgments. Almost all of the modifications of Piaget's original paradigm attempt to unconfound the operation of intentionality and consequences or heighten the salience of intentionality relative to consequences. As such they employ paradigms which do not clearly differentiate between accidental and intentional events and they fail to distinguish between intentionality and motives.

There is now evidence that the concepts of intentionality and motive need to be differentiated from each other. In fact, the two concepts seem to follow different developmental sequences, with the concept of motive emerging earlier. Children as young as three years of age seem able to differentiate between good and bad motives, and the concept of bad is learned before the concept of good. In contrast, it is not much before their sixth birthday that children seem able to clearly differentiate between accidental and intentional events.

A number of methodological issues need to be considered in the design of assessment paradigms. First, all three components—consequences, intentionality, and motives—must be considered when constructing any assessment paradigm. If any one of the components is not purposefully excluded, then it must be held constant or manipulated systematically; to do otherwise will lead to confounding. Secondly, different indices such as reaction times, ratings, reasoning, etc., produce different normative data. In general, any index which requires children to verbalize the accidental/ intentional distinction or discuss the concept of motive is more demanding than ones which only require children to rate good and bad motives or accidental and intentional actions. Thirdly, children's comprehension of the assessment paradigms relates to their performance on them and needs to be systematically assessed. Fourthly, children's understanding of the accidental/intentional distinction seems to be better assessed by questions which focus on "trying" rather than by those which focus on "naughtiness"; questions which focus on "naughtiness" or "niceness" are more appropriate for assessing children's understanding of the concept of motive. Lastly, evidence suggests that it might be better to study children's developing understanding of the concepts of intentionality and motive outside the sphere of morality.

REFERENCE NOTES

1. Hardy, D., & Keasey, C. B. *Children's usage of Heider's levels of responsibility.* Unpublished manuscript, University of Nebraska–Lincoln, 1977.
2. Keasey, C. B., Sales, B. D., Morris, R., & Bragg, R. *When a wrong becomes criminal: Children's concepts of crimes.* Unpublished manuscript, University of Nebraska–Lincoln, 1977.
3. Morrison, L., & Keasey, C. B. *Children's use of intentionality and consequences under different instructional sets.* Unpublished manuscript, University of Nebraska–Lincoln, 1977.
4. Peterson, W. C., & Keasey, C. B. *Preschoolers' conceptions of intentionality and motives.* Unpublished manuscript, University of Nebraska–Lincoln, 1976.
5. Hill, K. A., & Enzle, M. E. *Interactive effects of training modality and age on children's moral judgments.* Unpublished manuscript, University of Alberta, 1976.
6. Fitzhenry-Coor, I. *Children's comprehension and inference in stories of intentionality.* Paper presented at the Biennial Meeting of the Society for Research in Child Development, New Orleans, March 1977.

REFERENCES

Abel, T. M. Moral judgments among subnormals. *Journal of Abnormal and Social Psychology*, 1941, **36**, 378–392.
Armsby, R. E. A reexamination of the development of moral judgments in children. *Child Development*, 1971, **42**, 1241–1248.
Baldwin, C. P., & Baldwin, A. L. Children's judgments of kindness. *Child Development*, 1970, **41**, 29–47.
Bandura, A., & McDonald, F. J. Influence of social reinforcement and the behavior of models in shaping children's moral judgments. *Journal of Abnormal and Social Psychology*, 1963, **67**, 274–281.
Berg-Cross, L. G. Intentionality, degree of damage, and moral judgments. *Child Development*, 1975, **46**, 970–974.
Berndt, T. J., & Berndt, E. G. Children's use of motives and intentionality in person perception and moral judgment. *Child Development*, 1975, **46**, 904–912.
Boehm, L. The development of conscience: A comparison of American children of different mental and socioeconomic levels. *Child Development*, 1962, **33**, 575–590.
Boehm, L., & Nass, M. L. Social class differences in conscience development. *Child Development*, 1962, **33**, 565–574.
Breznitz, S., & Kugelmass, S. Intentionality in moral judgment: Developmental stages. *Child Development*, 1967, **38**, 469–479.
Brown, A. L. Recognition, reconstruction and recall of narrative sequences by preoperational children. *Child Development*, 1975, **46**, 156–166.

Buchanan, J. P., & Thompson, S. K. A quantitative methodology to examine the development of moral judgment. *Child Development*, 1973, **44**, 186–189.

Chandler, M. J., Greenspan, M., & Barenboim, C. Judgments of intentionality in response to videotaped and verbally presented moral dilemmas: The medium is the message. *Child Development*, 1973, **44**, 315–320.

Collins, W. A., Berndt, T. J., & Hess, V. L. Observational learning of motives and consequences for television aggression: A developmental study. *Child Development*, 1974, **45**, 799–802.

Costanzo, P. R., Coie, J. D., Grumet, J. F., & Farnill, D. A reexamination of the effects of intent and consequence on children's moral judgments. *Child Development*, 1973, **44**, 154–161.

Cowan, P. A., Langer, J., Heavenrich, J., & Nathanson, M. Social learning and Piaget's cognitive theory of moral development. *Journal of Personality and Social Psychology*, 1969, **11**, 261–274.

Crowley, P. M. Effect of training upon objectivity of moral judgment in grade-school children. *Journal of Personality and Social Psychology*, 1968, **8**, 228–232.

Dorr, D., & Fey, S. Relative power of symbolic adult and peer models in the modification of children's moral choice behaviour. *Journal of Personality and Social Psychology*, 1974, **29**, 335–341.

Farnill, D. The effects of social-judgment set on children's use of intent information. *Journal of Personality*, 1974, **42**, 276–289.

Glassco, J. A., Milgram, N. A., & Youniss, J. Stability of training effects on intentionality in moral judgments in children. *Journal of Personality and Social Psychology*, 1970, **14**, 360–365.

Grinder, R. E. Relations between behavioral and cognitive dimensions of conscience in middle childhood. *Child Development*, 1964, **35**, 881–891.

Gutkin, D. C. The effects of systematic story changes on intentionality in children's moral judgments. *Child Development*, 1972, **43**, 187–195.

Harrower, M. R. Social status and the moral development of the child. *British Journal of Educational Psychology*, 1934, **4**, 75–95.

Hebble, P. W. The development of elementary school children's judgment of intent. *Child Development*, 1971, **42**, 1203–1215.

Heider, F. *The psychology of interpersonal relations*. New York: Wiley, 1958.

Hewitt, L. S. Children's evaluations of harmdoers as a function of intentions and consequences. *Psychological Reports*, 1974, **35**, 755–762.

Hewitt, L. S. The effects of provocation, intentions and consequences on children's moral judgments. *Child Development*, 1975, **46**, 540–544.

Hoffman, M. L. Moral development. In P. H. Mussen (Ed.), *Carmichael's manual of child psychology* (3rd ed.; Vol. 2). New York: Wiley, 1970.

Imamoglu, E. O. Children's awareness and usage of intention cues. *Child Development*, 1975, **46**, 39–45.

Irwin, D. M., & Moore, S. G. The young child's understanding of social justice. *Developmental Psychology*, 1971, **5**, 406–410.

Jensen, L. C., & Hughston, K. The relationship between type of sanction, story content, and children's judgments which are independent of sanction. *Journal of Genetic Psychology,* 1973, **122,** 49–54.

Jensen, L. C., & Larm, C. Effects of two training procedures on intentionality in moral judgment among children. *Developmental Psychology,* 1970, **2,** 310.

Johnson, R. C. A study of children's moral judgments. *Child Development,* 1962, **33,** 327–354.

Karniol, R. Children's use of intention cues in evaluating behaviour. *Psychological Bulletin,* in press.

Keasey, C. B. Implication of cognitive development for moral reasoning. In D. J. DePalma and J. M. Foley (Eds.), *Moral development: Current theory and research.* Hillsdale, NJ: Lawrence Erlbaum Associates, 1975.

Keasey, C. B. Young children's attribution of intentionality to themselves and others. *Child Development,* 1977, **48,** 261–264.

Keasey, C. B., & Sales, B. D. Children's conception of intentionality and the criminal law. In B. D. Sales (Ed.), *Psychology in the legal process.* New York: Spectrum Publications, 1977. (a)

Keasey, C. B., & Sales, B. D. An empirical investigation of young children's awareness and usage of intentionality in criminal situations. *Law and Human Behavior,* 1977, **1,** 45–61. (b)

King, M. The development of some intention concepts in young children. *Child Development,* 1971, **42,** 1145–1152.

Kugelmass, S., & Breznitz, S. Intentionality in moral judgment: Adolescent development. *Child Development,* 1968, **39,** 249–256.

Lerner, E. The problem of perspective in moral reasoning. *American Journal of Sociology,* 1937, **43,** 249–269.

Lickona, T. An empirical test of Piaget's theory of moral development. *Merrill-Palmer Quarterly,* in press.

MacRae, D. A test of Piaget's theories of moral development. *Journal of Abnormal and Social Psychology,* 1954, **49,** 14–18.

Mandler, J., & Johnson, N. Remembrance of things passed: Story structure and recall. *Cognitive Psychology,* 1977, **9,** 111–151.

McKechnie, R. J. Between Piaget's stages: A study of moral development. *British Journal of Educational Psychology,* 1971, **41,** 213–217.

Nummedal, S. G., & Bass, S. C. Effects of the salience of intention and consequence on children's moral judgments. *Developmental Psychology,* 1976, **12,** 475–476.

Peterson, C., Peterson, J., & Finley, N. Conflict and moral judgment. *Developmental Psychology,* 1974, **10,** 65–69.

Piaget, J. *The language and thought of the child.* London: Routledge & Kegan Paul, 1926.

Piaget, J. *The moral judgment of the child.* New York: Harcourt, Brace, 1932.

Piaget, J. *On the development of memory and identity.* Barre, Mass.: Clark University Press, 1968.

Rhine, R. J., Hill, S. J., & Wandruff, S. E. Evaluative responses of preschool children. *Child Development,* 1967, **38,** 1035–1042.

Rule, B. G., & Duker, P. Effects of intentions and consequences on children's evaluations of aggressors. *Journal of Personality and Social Psychology*, 1973, **27**, 184–189.

Rule, B. G., Nesdale, A. R., & McAra, M. J. Children's reactions to information about the intentions underlying an aggressive act. *Child Development*, 1974, **45**, 794–798.

Schleifer, M., & Douglas, V. I. Effects of training on the moral judgment of young children. *Journal of Personality and Social Psychology*, 1973, **28**, 62–68.

Shantz, C. U. The development of social cognition. In E. M. Hetherington (Ed.), *Review of child development research* (Vol. 5). Chicago: University of Chicago Press, 1975.

Shantz, D. W., & Voydanoff, D. A. Situational effects of retaliatory aggression at three age levels. *Child Development*, 1973, **44**, 149–153.

Shaw, M. E. Negro-white differences in attribution of responsibility as a function of age. *Psychonomic Science*, 1969, **16**, 289–291.

Shaw, M. E., Briscoe, M. E., & Garcia-Esteve, J. A cross-cultural study of attribution of responsibility. *International Journal of Psychology*, 1968, **3**, 51–60.

Shaw, M. E., Floyd, F. A., & Gwin, N. E. Perceived locus of motivation as a determinant of attribution of responsibility. *Representative Research in Social Psychology*, 1971, **2**, 43–51.

Shaw, M.E., & Iwawaki, S. Attribution of responsibility by Japanese and Americans as a function of age. *Journal of Cross-Cultural Psychology*, 1972, **3**, 71–81.

Shaw, M. E., & Reitan, H. T. Attribution of responsibility as a basis for sanctioning behavior. *British Journal of Social and Clinical Psychology*, 1969, **8**, 217–226.

Shaw, M. E., & Schneider, F. W. Intellectual competence as a variable in attribution of responsibility and assignment of sanctions. *Journal of Social Psychology*, 1969, **78**, 31–39.

Shaw, M. E., & Sulzer, J. L. An empirical test of Heider's levels in attribution of responsibility. *Journal of Abnormal and Social Psychology*, 1964, **69**, 39–46.

Sternlieb, J. L., & Youniss, J. Moral judgments one year after intentional or consequence modeling. *Journal of Personality and Social Psychology*. 1975, **31**, 895–897.

Tomlinson-Keasey, C., & Keasey, C. B. Long-term cultural change in cognitive development. *Perceptual and Motor Skills*, 1972, **35**, 135–139.

Weiner, B., & Peter, N. A cognitive-developmental analysis of achievement and moral judgments. *Developmental Psychology*, 1973, **9**, 290–309.

Whiteman, M. Children's conceptions of psychological causality, *Child Development*, 1967, **38**, 143–155.

Whiteman, P. H., & Kosier, K. P. Development of children's moralistic judgments: Age, sex, IQ, and certain personal-experimental variables. *Child Development*, 1964, **35**, 843–850.

Stability and Oscillation in Interpersonal Awareness: A Clinical-Developmental Analysis[1]

Robert L. Selman and Dan Jaquette

Judge Baker Guidance Center and
Laboratory of Human Development
Harvard Graduate School of Education

I. INTRODUCTION: INTEGRATING A DEVELOPMENTAL APPROACH WITH SOCIAL AND CLINICAL PSYCHOLOGY: THE STUDY OF INTERPERSONAL RELATIONSHIPS

Kurt Lewin is often quoted as saying: "There is nothing so practical as a good theory." Lewin might well have added that there is no better validation of a theory than its real-life application. The purpose of this chapter is to spell out how the methods and theoretical approaches of developmental psychology can be integrated to yield information relevant to the practical concerns of clinical and social psychological child and adolescent psychology. Its further purpose is to demonstrate how research undertaken in the natural settings of practitioners, clinicians, and educators can help developmental theorists and researchers realistically examine some of the more thorny conceptual and methodological issues their approaches generate.

1. Dan Jaquette is a doctoral student in the Human Development Program at the Harvard Graduate School of Education, and a trainee in the clinical-developmental research training program at the Judge Baker Guidance Center.

The research reported in this chapter was supported by a grant from the Spencer Foundation. The authors wish to express particular appreciation to Ms. Debra Lavin, who participated in many aspects of the research, to Ms. Carolyn Newberger for clinical suggestions, to Dr. Marc Lieberman for help in statistical analysis, to Anne Selman for editorial assistance, and to Nancy Jacobs for immeasurable secretarial support. The authors also express their thanks to the staff of the Manville School of the Judge Baker Guidance Center who have facilitated this research and to Dr. Julius Richmond, Director of the Center, for his continued support of child development research.

In attempting to achieve these aims, the following route is taken. First, in Section II, a model is described which integrates a cognitive-developmental approach to interpersonal development with issues of relevance to child clinical and social psychology. The relationship of this particular model to the more general cognitive or stage-developmental approach (Piaget, 1970; Kohlberg, 1969) to social development is also clarified. Following this, Section III summarizes evidence from a longitudinal interview study of interpersonal awareness which speaks to the validity of the developmental principles which underlie this research. Also, in Section III, some conceptual and methodological concerns common to cognitive-developmental research are discussed in conjunction with a description of some ongoing naturalistic studies. Thus the hope is to clarify both the strengths and weaknesses of the social-cognitive/stage approach while pointing to some new directions this approach can and must take to become a "practical theory."

A. Clinical/Developmental Concerns

The "developmental" analysis of interpersonal awareness represents a blending of developmental with clinical and social psychological concerns. In the attempt to integrate clinical and developmental approaches, the task is to assess the congruence of the clinical emphasis on adaptation/maladaptation of behavior (Hartmann, 1958) and the cognitive-developmental emphasis on maturity/immaturity of reasoning. Child clinicians have traditionally defined healthy social development as the ability to cope with social reality as it exists independent of the individual. They have looked for sources of pathology either inside the subject (e.g., personality traits, intrapsychic dynamics, ego strength) or in the environment (e.g., deprivation theory). Developmental researchers, on the other hand, have focused on the growing maturity of social awareness (Kohlberg, 1969; Turiel, 1975; Selman, 1976b) as children construct their own model of social reality. This construction over time is a function of the reciprocal interaction of internal (self, cognitive) structures and external (experiential, societal) structures. By describing the progressive and sequential development of the way children naturally construct social relationships as they grow up, the developmentalist identifies developmental milestones or benchmarks for clinicians trying to understand social orientations of children with poor social relations. Reciprocally, by comparing the reasoning and behavior of children with clinically diagnosed difficulties to that of their better-adjusted peers (the clinical-comparative method), the developmentalist may gain some insight into the relation between maturity of thought and socially adaptive behavior.

B. Social Psychological/Developmental Concerns

The integration of social psychological and developmental approaches requires a renewed look at the relation of social situational variables (e.g., principles of group dynamics), and individual social-cognitive capabilities as they interact to influence social behavior and utilization of social or moral insight. Generally speaking, both cognitive-developmental and social psychological researchers have paid little real attention to each other's concerns. The primary task of the cognitive-developmental approach, the description of developing sequences of social and moral conceptualization theoretically applicable to all children's development, has often been accomplished at the expense of a basic understanding of how variations in social and psychological factors might influence the functional level of awareness under specific conditions or at given times. On the other hand social psychologists' investigation of social or group processes have often been carried out with little or no regard to age- or stage-related variations in the social awareness capabilities of the subjects being observed.

For example, in their otherwise classic and fascinating research, White and Lippitt (1960) used 10-year-old children to demonstrate the value of democratic leadership without noting Piaget's (1932) work on consistent and characteristic differences in preferred leadership qualities of children at different ages. In *The Moral Judgment of the Child* (1932), two developmental phases in social awareness are described. From ages 5 to 8, children reason at what Piaget calls the *heteronomous* or constraint stage, where social relations are thought to be governed by absolute deference to authorities with greater physical power. At the *autonomous* or cooperative stage, developed in the years 8 to 12, group relations are seen as based on bilateral interests and respect for others as equals. A developmental replication of the White and Lippitt study would include younger children, who conceive of leadership as based on constraint, or, as one 7-year-old told the authors, "doing what the captain wants you to do." It might well show that 7-year-olds most strongly value authoritarian group leadership. What White and Lippitt may in part have empirically documented is a developmental trend whereby older children prefer a democratic form of leadership and younger children an authoritarian form, in both words and actions.

C. Toward an Integration

Given this convergence of interests among and around the developing interpersonal world of the child and the adolescent, in both research and practice, it is somewhat surprising to find so few attempts to integrate knowledge of the child's developing social and interpersonal conceptualizations with clinical or social psychological variables.

How can such diverse approaches be used collaboratively to generate a more robust model of social development than each alone can provide? The authors' integrative concerns have been greatly influenced by interpersonal theorists such as Harry Stack Sullivan, who emphasized the importance of peer-oriented experiences among the young as both a therapeutic and educational necessity:

> Because of the real society which emerges . . . the preadolescent begins to have useful experience in social assessment and social organization . . . Within the gang, experience in social organization is reflected in how closely integrated the gang is, how stable its leadership is and how many leaders for different things there are . . . which is pretty refined social organization in miniature . . . (And) the fact that one looks out for oneself and is regarded as incredibly individual begins very strikingly to fade from the center of things; and that is an exceedingly fortunate experience to have had.(1953, p. 257)

Sullivan's observations underscore the interdisciplinary approach required for the meaningful study of interpersonal relations and interactions among developing children. He mentions a developmental concern with shifts within the socially maturing child—in this case from a juvenile orientation (limited to a naive self-interest and instrumental cooperation with others) to a developmentally more mature collaborative orientation emerging in preadolescence. Sullivan also expresses a basic social psychological concern with the effects of social organization on interpersonal interactions (Sherif, 1966).

The psychologist must attend to both individual and social determinants of behavior. He must be cognizant of the developmental stability that the child brings to the situation at the same time as he is aware of the oscillation in interpersonal orientation due to the fluid dynamics of external and internal forces. The examination of the factors of stability and oscillation is the major focus of this paper.

II. THE DEVELOPMENT OF INTERPERSONAL AWARENESS: DEFINING ISSUES AND DOMAINS

A. Domains and Issues

A structural developmental approach begins by describing what eventually may prove to be a developing sequence of stages in the individual's understanding of some category of experience, beginning in early childhood and continuing through to maturity. The analysis is structural in that it makes use of a posited developmental sequence of basic patterns of social-cognitive organization which underlie the more overt, conscious, or surface social conceptions used by the individual in his day-to-day relating. Ideally, the emphasis is placed equally on a *formal* analysis of the way concepts are developmentally organized and a *functional* analysis of how these concepts are used (Flavell & Wohlwill, 1969).

Our particular work has been describing the child's developing interpersonal awareness in certain role relationships and the ways these descriptions can help to clarify broad trends in the means by which children relate to others. The specific focus has been on conceptions in three *domains* which are felt to be both critical to healthy development and intrinsically related to one another: (1) awareness of the individual (e.g., developing conceptions of self-esteem, self-awareness, and personality, etc.), (2) awareness of close friendship relations, and (3) awareness of group processes and organization. (See Table 1 for a brief developmental description of stages in each domain.)

Within each domain, a set of *issues* has also been specified. These

Table 1

Sequence of Stages Across Domains of Interpersonal (Individual, Friendship, Peer Group) and Perspective-taking Awareness

		Interpersonal			Perspective-taking
Stage	Individual	Friendship	Peer Group	Level	
0	Physical entity	Momentary physical playmate	Physical connections	0	Undifferentiated/ egocentric
1	Intentional subject	One-way assistance	Unilateral relations	1	Subjective/ differentiated
2	Introspective self	Fairweather cooperation	Bilateral partnerships	2	Reciprocal/ self-reflective
3	Stable personality	Intimate-mutual sharing	Homogeneous community	3	Mutual/ third person
4	Complex self-systems	Autonomous in- terdependence	Pluralistic organization	4	In-depth/societal

Table 2

Issues of Interpersonal Awareness Related to Conceptions of the Individual, Close Friendships, and Peer Group Organization

Individual	Friendship	Peer Group
1. SUBJECTIVITY: covert properties of persons (thoughts, feelings, motives); conflicts between thoughts or feelings within the person 2. SELF-REFLECTION: awareness of the self's ability to observe its own thoughts and actions 3. PERSONALITY: stable or predictive character traits (a shy person, etc.) 4. PERSONALITY CHANGE: how and why people change (growing up, etc.)	1. FORMATION: why (motives) and how (mechanisms) friendships are made; the ideal friend 2. CLOSENESS: types of friendship, ideal friendship, intimacy 3. TRUST, doing things for friends; reciprocity 4. JEALOUSY: feelings about intrusions into new or established friendships 5. CONFLICTS: how friends resolve problems 6. TERMINATION, how friendships break up	1. FORMATION: why (motives)and how (mechanisms) groups are formed; the ideal member 2. COHESION/ LOYALTY: group unity 3. CONFORMITY: range and rationale 4. RULES/NORMS: types of rules, and reasons for them 5. DECISION-MAKING: setting goals, resolving problems working to- gether 6. LEADERSHIP, qualities, and function of the group 7. TERMINATION: why groups break up or members are excluded

issues represent the basic and common concerns that subjects discuss when asked questions about their understanding of each of the domains. The identification of the most relevant issues within a domain is, then, the second step in the construction of a developmental/social-cognitive map (Redl & Wineman, 1956), a map which can allow the specification in some detail of normal growth in the way children think about their interpersonal world. (See Table 2.)

These interpersonal domains and issues were chosen for several reasons. First, as already mentioned, there is a particular concern among clinical and social psychologists with how children relate to and organize their interactions within themselves and with their friends and peers. Second, among the children in our pool of interviewees, an intense and often untapped interest in these issues has been demonstrated, e.g., in what it means to be a good friend or in how one best wends one's way into a clique or group. These are ideas about the social sphere which develop as guides to one's social interaction (Hartup, 1975). Third, there is an interest in comparing the interpersonal awareness of children in general with that of children who have difficulty in their social relationships and self-perceptions. Such a comparison will generate an understanding of how individual, friendship, and group concepts help to determine both specific social behaviors and the more general ways that children relate to the social world.

The following steps were taken to arrive at the domains and issues. Initially, following a recommendation made by Flavell (1974), issues were defined around concerns of social and clinical adult psychology, such as Group Cohesion, as "potential developmental targets." It is the developmentalist's task to chart progression in understanding of each of those interpersonal processes as it goes through an ontogenetic sequence of cognitive stages. Whereas the issues or processes obviously are "adult" categories, the assumption is that children have experiences with the kinds of processes which the issues and domains reflect and therefore construct their own increasingly differentiated and integrated conceptions of these categories. Although at lower levels these categories may not be differentiated in the children's minds, nevertheless the categories are applicable to their interactions.

Such target categories should be kept loosely defined and flexible initially, but maintained as rough guidelines to devise a first approximation of the kinds of interview questions which might best be asked of subjects. While it would be foolish to assume that one can begin to interview subjects across wide age ranges with no framework at all, the other extreme, a too rigidly defined, preformed, and prefabricated system, would cut off researchers from many issues and trains of thought that might emerge as critical to the subjects themselves.

This conceptual starting point then had to be reshaped by its trial application to the real-world substance of children's and adolescents' thoughts and ideas. This second and reciprocal source of developmental mappings or issues was pilot interviewing and observation of a wide range of subjects. Through open interviews and conversations with children and adults, through naturalistic eavesdropping on the peer conversations of children and adolescents in school lunchrooms and at recess, and through conversations with parents of often defensive, hard-to-interview teenagers and preteens, a common or "culturally universal" core of concerns across ages began to emerge–the issues which comprise the final list. (See Table 2.)

To be sure, seldom was a fifth grader heard to claim that his street gang "lacked cohesiveness" (Peer Group Issue II) or a third grader to ask his friends for better ways to "resolve conflicts" (Friendship Issue IV). These are researchers' terms for ideas the subjects in the pilot work spontaneously expressed in their own rich and often colloquial language, concerns about how to "get team spirit" going in a faltering group or ways close friends could "get it back together," "make up," or "stop hassling each other." The developmentalist's issues really are generated, then, from the ongoing and reciprocal interaction between "academic" conceptual analysis and the common "everyday" parlance and naive psychology (Heider, 1958) of the subjects themselves.

Reflecting the developmentalists's methodological and theoretical bias, the final criterion for the selection of issues and interview questions was that they should provide responses which are easily categorized according to some cognitive or structural developmental system, i.e., these issues and questions should yield responses which are capable of being reliably ordered in a hierarchical sequence of stages (Selman & Jaquette, Note 1).

Several procedures were used in the descriptive identification and analysis of development in these interpersonal issue areas: discussions of both real and hypothetical interpersonal problems, drawings and their interpretation, and responses to projective measures.

The result of this extensive interviewing has been the definition of developmentally distinct stages of interpersonal awareness which cut across the three major domains and the 17 more specific issues (See Tables 1 and 2). The working hypothesis was that at each stage there would be a certain common structure crossing both the domains and the interpersonal issues but that at the same time each issue represented a sufficiently distinct aspect of social experience to merit its description separately from the others. The common developmental structure or logic assumed to underlie an individual's interpersonal awareness is that individual's basic understanding of relations between self and others, a form of developing awareness termed social perspective-taking (Selman, 1976a). The process of defining interpersonal stages represents a constant interchange between the underlying logic of perspective-taking levels and the rich social concepts expressed by the child.

As an example of the result of this process, excerpts from one of the 17 issues, leadership, here follow; they are taken from a manual we constructed for research purposes. Five stages are described for the issue of leadership. Following the description of these levels is an explanation of how each perspective-taking level provides an underlying logic for each interpersonal stage.

B. Leadership—An Example

Included in the issue of leadership (Issue III.6; see Table 2) are the functions of leadership in the group, the qualities of a good leader, and the possible negative consequences of having a leader.

Stage 0. General Leadership Structure–Physicalistic Connections. At Stage 0, leadership is seen as undifferentiated physical power over others. The child knows that the leader is supposed to tell followers what to do ("I could boss everyone around") and the followers are supposed to do it ("and they do what you say"). There is, however, no awareness of group functions of leadership nor is there any conscious moderation of the leader's actions on the basis of whether the followers want that kind of leader.

WHAT KIND OF LEADER SHOULD A GROUP HAVE?
. . . There should be more than one leader like two leaders.
WHY TWO?
Because if there is a whole bunch of people and one person for a leader, that's no good, but a whole bunch of people and two

leaders then that's better. Because if one person wouldn't have a loud enough voice, but if both persons said the same thing at the same time, they would all hear. (age 6:2)

Here being a leader means being physically capable of controlling others ("having a loud enough voice").

Stage 1. General Leadership Structure—Unilateral Relations. There are two aspects which appear to characterize leadership concepts at Stage 1. First the leader is seen to have a specific function as the one who is best skilled and knows the most. Second, leadership is seen as a series of unilateral authoritarian relationships.

Focusing on the former aspect, the child realizes that leaders perform a definite function for the group in helping them to perform collaborative activities successfully ("tell them what to do and tell them not to do things that will make them lose"). The leader is seen to be at the top of a pyramid of specific knowledge about group activities which is transmitted downward. The resulting conception of group leadership is the firm belief that the leader must be the best, know the most about the group's activities, and transmit the knowledge in a *one-way* fashion downward.

SUPPOSE YOU WERE MIKE AND WERE ELECTED LEADER OF THE JETS. WHAT WOULD YOU DO TO MAKE THE CLUB BETTER?
I would teach them to do tricks with the ball, like teach them to hit the ball way up in the air and then when it had landed it could land right in the net. I would teach them a lot of tricks.
WHAT KIND OF THINGS SHOULD A LEADER FIRST DO FOR HIS CLUB?
Give them time and make sure they do the right thing and help them.
WHY IS HELPING THEM IMPORTANT?
If they don't get help, they could fall down and hurt themselves. (age 6:0)

On the positive side, the child believes the leader helps other members improve their individual skills ("teach them to do tricks"). However, the child has no understanding of the possibilities for cooperative interchange of information. The leader knows best. Significantly, the leader does not yet act as an organizer or coordinator for the various interests present in the group.

The latter aspect is similar to that described in Piaget's heteronomous stage of unilateral respect, where there is absolute deference to authorities. However, the present findings show that what appears to be an unchanging power structure is actually a series of absolute authorities. The problem is that the child capable only of Stage 1 awareness can conceive of the disposing of one unilateral leader but does not have the social-cognitive capabilities to conceive of changing the structure of leadership from its basic unilateral nature.

Stage 2. General Leadership Structure–Bilateral Partnerships. At Stage 2 the subject looks at the leadership of the group from the reciprocal perspectives of both the leader and the followers. There is a concern that leadership be based on equal treatment as pragmatically benefiting both parties (e.g., "if everybody is equal, then nobody bosses anybody," age 8:11). Leadership is based on a bilateral equality and reciprocity of interests. A good leader is believed to be an "arbitrator," not a "dictator" as in Stage 1. The leader should attempt to organize the different claims made by members in order to produce some coordinated effort. This allows the group to move beyond the stalemate of conflicting interests of individual members.

IS IT GOOD TO HAVE A LEADER IN A GROUP?
Yah, you have to have a leader because you have to have someone to follow around. If you don't have a leader you have someone saying, I am going first in the house, I am, I am, I am but the leader keeps organizing it so everybody gets a chance to go in the house and everybody takes turns going in. (age 8:3)

Rather than directing primarily through individual decree, the leader is seen as using encouragement and attempting to "get along with everybody" and being "an understanding person" (age 10:3). However, leadership is unstructured in that the leader is not yet able to create a formal organization.

Stage 3. General Leadership Structure–Homogeneous Community. At Stage 3 the subject sees the group as a social system in which the function of leadership is to marshal group solidarity (e.g., "the leader helps to structure the group," age 15:3). The leader should reflect the concerns of the group itself, not impose his or her own will. The leader is seen as a catalyst in the creation of a formal structure of the group as a social system.

DO YOU THINK IT IS GOOD TO HAVE A LEADER IN A GROUP?
It depends on whether the rest of the group wants a leader or not.

WHY WOULD IT BE GOOD TO HAVE A LEADER?
You probably wouldn't be going every which way. He would probably take you someplace as a whole, do something as a whole together, instead of having everyone go his own way.
WHAT MIGHT BE SOME OF THE PROBLEMS?
That he might be the one to decide everything all the time and the group wouldn't be able to have a group decision. . . . (age 13:1)

Stage 4. General Leadership Structure—Pluralistic Organization. The subject reasoning at Stage 4 believes leadership to be one of many social role responsibilities which function for the collective good of the group. The individual holding the office is distinguished from the duties and expectations of the office ("authority figure"; "the office of the presidency"). The leader is seen to fill a position created by the organizational demands of a complex and pluralistic organization.

WHAT KIND OF PERSON MAKES A GROUP LEADER?
He should be somebody who symbolizes the finest in the group. I think they probably selected him as the embodiment of the group spirit, the group's existence. The president would be the light of the group, so that the outside world knows what the leadership is. (age 26)

In this sense the leader is "an embodiment." The power of leadership rests in the nature of the role itself ("to define the goals of what the group wants"), and a leader does not possess this power except as the "embodiment of the group spirit." Abuses are seen to occur when an "authority figure" personally assumes the power of the office ("they sort of let the power go to their head"). At this level, group leadership becomes differentiated into several functions or several roles. Each leadership role serves as a complementary function to the group as a complex system ("the task leader"; "the person who smooths the rough edges").

C. A Core Structure of Interpersonal Awareness— Social Perspective-taking

The form and substance of any developmental-descriptive analysis will be in part determined by the describer's assumptions of what the underlying structure of that domain is thought to be. (See Selman, 1976b, for a more detailed discussion of this point.) The present analysis was based upon the assumption that the child's developing awareness of the relation between self's and others' understanding of each other's point of view (social perspectivism) helps give form to developing interpersonal (and moral) concepts (Selman, 1976a; Selman & Damon, 1975). This construct does not represent simply the accretion of information about what others think, feel, or intend, but the qualitative development of a child's subjective awareness of basic social relations.[2] Table 3 gives a brief synopsis of these levels.

The construct of social perspective-taking, or social perspectivism, can be thought of in two ways. First, from the position of the subject, it is a fundamental developing awareness of the nature of how persons are aware of each other. Second, from the position of the analysis of social-role relation concepts, it is an analytic tool for clarifying the developmental structure of the various interpersonal domains and issues which involve relational processes among persons (e.g., leadership, conflict resolutions, etc.). The initial work on social perspective-taking began with its analysis as a developing process in its own right, i.e., as a developmental ability (Selman, 1976a). Our more recent developmental-descriptive work in social cognition has used perspective-taking in the second way (Selman, 1976b; Selman & Jaquette, Note 1): Perspective-taking levels are used to help characterize the structural and developmental characteristics of each domain and issue. For example, the procedure by which issues were categorized at a particular stage involved two reciprocal processes. First, using each of the perspective-taking levels "metaphorically" as a skeletal model, the interpersonal conceptions of issues such as leadership at each stage were built up around each perspective-taking level. Stage 2 conceptions of leadership, for example, based upon a reciprocity and coordination between leader and follower, logically relate to level 2 perspective-taking, at which point the child can coordinate reciprocal perspectives. Stage 3 conceptions of leadership, oriented to facilitating

2. Whereas we would tend to agree with Turiel's assertion (this volume) that the construct of "role-taking" popularly and prolifically found in recent child development literature has been vaguely defined as a catch-all term for the general developing ability to gather various social information about others' covert experiences, our own use of "social perspectivism" is basically a *relational* concept and not one that is focused only on gathering data about the content of another's mind.

Table 3
PERSPECTIVE-TAKING: *Relation Between Perspective of Self and Other(s)*

Stage 0—Egocentric or undifferentiated perspectives. Although children can recognize the reality of subjective perspectives (e.g., thoughts and feelings) within the self and within the other, because they do not clearly distinguish their own perspective from that of the other they do not recognize that another may interpret similarly perceived social experiences or courses of action differently from the way they do. Similarly, there is still some confusion between the subjective (or psychological) and objective (or physical) aspects of the social world, for example, between feelings and overt acts, or between intentional and unintentional acts.

Stage 1—Subjective or differentiated perspectives. Children understand that even under similarly perceived social circumstances the self and the other's perspective may be either the same or different. Similarly, children realize that the self and the other may view similarly perceived actions as reflections of disparate or distinct individual reasons or motives. Of particular importance, children at Stage 1 are newly concerned with the uniqueness of the covert, psychological life of each person.

Stage 2—Self-reflective or reciprocal perspectives. Children are able to reflect on their own thoughts and feelings from another's perspective—to put themselves in the other's shoes and to see the self as a subject to other. This new awareness of the relation between self and other's perspective also allows children to consider their own conceptions and evaluations of other's thoughts and actions. In other words, children are able to take a second-person perspective which leads to an awareness of a new form of reciprocity, a reciprocity of thoughts and feelings ("I know that he likes me; he knows that I like him") rather than a reciprocity of action ("he does for me; I do for him").

Stage 3—Third person or mutual perspectives. The subject at Stage 3, aware of the infinite regress potential of the chaining of reciprocal perspectives, moves to a qualitatively new level of awareness, the awareness of a person's ability to abstractly step outside of an interpersonal interaction and coordinate simultaneously the perspectives of each party in the interaction. This ability to take the third-person perspective leads to the awareness of the mutuality of human perspectives and hence of the self-other relationship.

Stage 4—Societal or in-depth perspectives. The subject conceptualizes subjective perspectives of persons toward one another (mutuality) to exist not only on the plane of common expectations or awareness, but also simultaneously at multi-dimensional or deeper levels of communication. For example, perspectives between two persons can be shared at the level of superficial information, at the level of common interests, or at the level of deeper and unverbalized feelings. Also, perspectives among persons are seen as forming a network or system. These perspectives become generalized—e.g., into the concept of society's perspective, or the legal or moral point of view.

"team spirit," correspond to the level 3 perspective-taking awareness of a mutual system network in interpersonal relations.

Second, using this skeleton, the empirical search continued for the different aspects of thinking about leadership that seemed to hang together for each child at a given stage. Once this second network is in place, it is, figuratively speaking, possible to remove the perspective-taking core, and the interpersonal reasoning stages should be structured so that they stand on their own structural soundness. While perspective-taking levels may represent a core or logical structure for these stages of interpersonal awareness, the intention is not to argue that interpersonal awareness can simply be reduced to these levels, i.e., it is not assumed that subjects capable of a given level of social perspectivism will function at the structurally parallel stage of interpersonal awareness across all of the 17 issues.

In sum, these (social) cognitive-developmental analyses are attempts to sample as wide a range of (interpersonal) conceptions as possible for the purpose of forming a fairly logical and integrated systematization of social thinking. The approach has been to move from a core social-cognitive structure, perspective-taking levels, to conceptions more relevant to the child's own social world. Although its analytical importance to social cognition in general is stressed, perspective-taking as here defined is difficult to observe in the child's social discourse because it is abstracted from a social context. Whether a developmental analysis of social cognition uses perspective-taking or some other construct as a core, the analyses maintain certain similarities: a moving back and forth from the deeper or more theoretical model to the more surface data in an attempt to postulate a theoretically and empirically valid, stable, and sequential, developmental-descriptive system.

D. Developmental Properties of Interpersonal Awareness Stages

The cognitive-developmental approach entails assumptions of qualitative differences between stages, invariance of sequence through stages, structured wholeness within stages, and hierarchical integration among stages. Stage analyses are applicable to varying degrees to two sets of phenomena, the concepts themselves and the way that children, adolescents, and adults actually use or apply these concepts. Simply applying developmental principles to interpersonal concepts, divorced from the subject's usage of them, may be interesting from the point of view of the philosophical implications of conceptual development, i.e., developmental forms (Werner, 1948), but this aspect of the analysis has much less bearing on the robustness of the psychology of development, i.e., on developmental functioning. To understand developmental functioning, the psychology of social-cognitive development must be determined within the context of empirical research, not by logical analyses alone. The authors' working interpretations of these developmental principles as applied to interpersonal awareness are as follows:

1. Stages of interpersonal awareness imply *qualitative* differences in the way social reality is organized. These differences are qualitative because they represent a fundamental restructuring of the way in which an individual views issues within individuals, close friendships, or peer groups, not a *quantitative* or linear increase in knowledge.

2. Different modes of interpersonal awareness form an invariant sequence of stages in social-cognitive development. While environmental or physiological factors may alter the *rate* of progression, they do not alter the *sequence*. For example, recent research (Selman, Jaquette, & Lavin, 1977) demonstrates that whereas emotionally disturbed children function at a lower level than matched peers, the sequential development of their reasoning appears to be the same. Most of the disturbed children appear to conceptualize peer interaction at a level characteristic of normal children three or four years younger. What seems to be occuring are developmental lags rather than abnormalities.

3. Each stage of interpersonal awareness represents a *structured whole*. A given stage response does not merely represent factors specific to that task, but an underlying cognitive logic which characterizes thought at that stage for a variety of interpersonal processes. For example, Stage 2 responses concerning group *leadership* will have an underlying structure of coordinating interests (e.g., "If you don't have a leader, you have some saying 'I am going first, I am, I am' . . . but the leader keeps organizing it") which parallels Stage 2 group *cohesion* as cooperative "partnerships" of "teamwork" (e.g. "If you don't pass to your teammates, then they won't pass to you . . ."). These parallel conceptions of peer group processes such

as cohesion and leadership at Stage 2 are, in turn, parallel to Stage 2 conceptions of all interpersonal domains/issues: personality change in individuals, conflict resolution in friends, and so on. The structured wholeness refers primarily to the underlying logic of parallel concepts. This does not mean that a particular child in all situations will use the same level in organizing his or her interpersonal world views. In fact, little direct knowledge yet exists about variation in stage usage when an individual is faced with varying real-life social experiences. Structured wholeness implies only that there is a *logical* correspondence between types of thinking at a given stage. Once these logically parallel stages are defined, the question is why and/or whether an individual may apply different stages of awareness under different circumstances.

4. Stages of interpersonal awareness are *hierarchical integrations.* They form an order of increasingly comprehensive structures which are used to answer common problems about social life. The hierarchical properties which develop as one progresses through the stages are: (1) an increasing awareness of the degree of *psychological interdependence* between persons, (2) the development of a *systems approach* to persons, friendships, or group dynamics, and (3) movement from a concern only with *overt behaviors* to a concern for thoughts and *generalized expectations*. As individuals attain higher stages of interpersonal awareness, they are able to make more adequate use of these dimensions in resolving problems in social interaction. Lower stages are not discarded but built upon. Subjects capable of higher stages will occasionally answer problems using conceptions available from lower stages. However, children capable of only lower stage thought will be unable to generate higher stage solutions. For example, in one of the hypothetical peer-group interview measures, children are asked to figure out what has gone wrong with a street hockey team. Children at Stage 1 see the problem as one of individual skill or material problems, such as "lousy players," "not enough practice," or "not enough people." At Stage 2 children point out problems of bilateral cooperation, such as "not enough teamwork" or "they argue when they should be friendly." At Stage 3 children's concern is with achieving a sense of solidarity, such as "the team has to work together as a unit." The stages are hierarchical in that persons reasoning at Stage 3 may also list such problems as "lousy plays" or "not enough teamwork" in addition to "working together as a unit." However, regardless of how much "teamwork" or "togetherness" is needed, children who have at-

tained only stage 1 will be unaware of these methods for solving the group's problems.

It is the interpretation here of the last two principles which may represent the greatest controversy within the ranks of those using the cognitive-developmental approach. The issue at hand is which of the two interpretations of the nature of stages is the more powerful and useful as a psychological construct, the more behaviorally robust: the transformational view of stages (Kohlberg, 1969; Turiel, 1974)[3] or the hierarchical view (Werner & Kaplan, 1963). If individuals really reason across a wide range of issues at one stage, and do not fluctuate in their reasoning level about the same issue or problem under different social psychological (e.g., heightened peer pressure) or clinical psychological (e.g., increased anxiety) conditions, then the transformational view is supported. If however, individuals who have achieved a given stage of reasoning still use a lower level under particular conditions, then the hierarchical view would appear to be more valid. (See Rest, Note 2, for a similar analysis.)

III. INTERPERSONAL AWARENESS RESEARCH: RECENT FINDINGS AND FUTURE RESEARCH

A. Stable Characteristics of Developing Interpersonal Awareness Under Interview Conditions

For the past four years, our major task has been the construction and validation of the developmental description of interpersonal awareness in the form of social-cognitive stages. Using the clinical interview technique (Piaget, 1929) and hypothetical dilemmas (Kohlberg, 1969), data have been gathered on children, adolescents, and adults of both sexes and across a wide range of socioeconomic strata. In addition, a sample of children and adolescents with severe

3. One important distinction between Kohlberg's work and that of others who have provided stage descriptive analysis is that Kohlberg claims to have described stages of moral judgment, not of social concept development (personal communication). Judgmental ability and its assessment may indeed, as Kohlberg claims, differ from social conceptualization in that it requires the "application of concepts," rather than the simple "understanding of concepts," and so may have different psychological properties, and may be more "structurally whole," in the sense that subjects who attain a particular stage reject lower stages rather than use them differentially.

emotional and interpersonal difficulties placed in special treatment schools has been interviewed. This section selectively draws upon research findings to demonstrate how the developmental principles discussed in the previous section guided the design and data analysis of this research (more complete data analysis can be found in Selman, Jaquette, & Lavin, Note 3). Results are directed toward four major areas of social-cognitive/stage theory. First, some demographic data is discussed concerning age trends and the effects of sex and socioeconomic status. Second, information is presented regarding the structured wholeness or stage variability across the issues and domains of interpersonal awareness under controlled interview conditions. Third, longitudinal evidence is offered supporting an understanding of the invariant sequence and hierarchical properties of interpersonal development. Fourth, clinical-comparative findings regarding children with interpersonal difficulties who have been matched with better adjusted peers are discussed. The discrepancy in interpersonal awareness between public school children and "disturbed" children speaks to the problem of performance versus capability and the implications of an interpersonal lag for clinical notions of social adjustment.

The analysis of the development of interpersonal awareness comes from three sample populations. The *normative sample* consisted of 225 interpersonal awareness interviews with subjects of both sexes and across the socioeconomic strata. The ages of these subjects ranged from 4:6 to 32 years. The *longitudinal sample* was composed of 48 boys interviewed in 1974 and again in 1976 as a two-year follow-up. In 1974 their ages ranged from 6:0 to 12:1 and in 1976 from 7:11 to 14:3. The *clinical-comparative* sample was made up of 21 boys who in 1974 attended day schools for children with emotional and interpersonally based learning problems. These 21 "disturbed" boys were matched with 21 of the normal longitudinal sample on the basis of age, sex, race, socioeconomic status, and IQ. Eleven of the 21 matched pairs came from middle-class families and ten from working-class backgrounds. Since 1974 and 1976 data exist for both the disturbed and matched member in each pair, the clinical-comparative sample is also longitudinal.

Each subject received one or more hypothetical dilemma questionnaires which used an interpersonal conflict as the jumping-off place for an interview on various interpersonal issues. For each of the three domains (i.e., individuals, close friendship, and peer group), one of two story forms was given, depending on the age of the subject. As an example of the method, the assessment of friendship concepts begins with a filmstrip or narrated story in which a girl has been asked by a new friend to a special event. The invitation conflicts with a previous date with a long-time close friend who already feels threatened by the new friendship. Following the story, a standard series of questions pertaining to the relevant interpersonal issues is asked (Selman & Jaquette, Note 1). For example, the issue of Trust and Reciprocity is explored through the following questions:

> Do you think it is important for the two old friends to trust each other in order to stay good friends? Why?
> What is trust, anyway?
> Is there a difference between the trust you have in a best friend and the trust you have in someone you just know from school or somewhere else?

Although the questions have become semi-standardized, there still exists a need to maintain a clinical flexibility in these assessment procedures, particularly with young children. Depending on the situation and the disposition of the child, questions can be directed toward the hypothetical story, the child's own experiences, or the child's general understanding of interpersonal relations. The fundamental interviewing process explores the child's own naive theory of interpersonal relations and probes the reasons underlying his or her surface beliefs and opinions about interpersonal issues. Interviewing requires both an appreciation of the child's ability to put together a coherent interpersonal philosophy and a sensitivity to specific stage-related responses which might require further follow-up probes.

Each interview is analyzed according to a previously developed manual which provides criteria to assess each of the 17 issues at each of five stages. An overall interpersonal awareness score is computed by averaging each subject's reasoning across all 17 interpersonal issue scores. This quantitative score can also be translated into a global interpersonal awareness score. The manual also reports test-retest, alternate form, and interrater reliability all above .71.

Despite these attempts to meet standards of reliable assessment, the primary aim has not been to develop another social-cognitive test but rather to devise a procedure useful both for an in-depth clinical understanding of the child's interpersonal insights and for a better theoretical understanding of social-cognitive development and assessment in general.

1. *Demographic Data.* In Figure 1, quantititative interpersonal awareness scores for all 225 assessments in the normative sample are used to plot a mean stage by age progression in interpersonal awareness. The outer lines represent two standard deviations from the mean stage for each age.

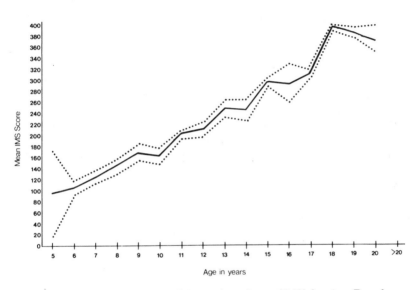

Figure 1. Mean Interpersonal Awareness Score (IMS)-by-Age Development (outer lines represent two standard deviations from mean).

Interestingly, when this age-by-stage progression of interpersonal development was examined separately in working class and middle class chidren of ages 7 through 14, it was found that working class children generally express lower levels of interpersonal awareness until age 11, at which time their development matches that of middle class peers. These data can be interpreted as evidence of the power of the preadolescent peer group across class boundaries for stimulating interpersonal awareness, as well as for the responsiveness of awareness levels to social influences.

To assess the possibility of sex differences in interpersonal development, 46 female subjects were matched with 46 males on the basis of age, race, and social class; the difference in level between the male and female sample was insignificant. However, when the 46 pairs were divided into age quartiles, an interesting trend in the age-by-sex data was the early spurt in social awareness among the young girls (ages 5:1 to 8:0) which appeared to be later matched by the boys at preadolescence. This age-related trend is consistent with developmental findings concerning the earlier social development of girls. This analysis of sex differences is reported more to indicate the appropriateness of the interview for both sexes than to uncover meaningful trends in sex-related social development. Further sex-related interpersonal research must more carefully select a sample from across a wide range of ages and social experiences.

2. *Structured Wholeness and Variability.* A primary concern from a cognitive-developmental perspective is the claim of structured wholeness, the claim that an individual's level of insight is internally consistent. When attempting to explore the logical consistency of a developmental system, variations in the type of tasks used need to be held to a minimum in order to maximize the possibility of intraindividual consistency. In other words, the attempt is to hold task constant and look at relations among concepts. Therefore, the data from our samples cannot speak to the coherence and stability of interpersonal insight beyond this reflective interview context.

Three kinds of analyses are applicable here: full and partial correlations, factor analyses, and cross-domain level of reasoning comparisons within subjects. Full and partial correlations can help to provide information about the degree of coherence across domains, for example when variations in chronological age, logical reasoning ability (measured by Piagetian tasks), and psychometric intelligence are controlled.

The full correlations, which initially were between .73 and .87 among the domains, remained significantly high even when each external variable was controlled. Predictably, controlling for IQ had the least effect on the correlations (.73–.87). The cognitive abilities involved in a psychometric test are not generally developmental; IQ holds relatively constant across age while cognitive stage varies with age. Controlling for logical ability (.52–.78), and to a greater extent age (.37–.75), decreased the correlations among the three domains. However, they remained relatively high, indicating considerable independent, internal coherence across domains.

Factor analysis provides a summary statistic for characterizing the variation in level of interpersonal awareness across all 17 interpersonal issues. A first factor of issue correlations accounted for between 61% and 65% of the variance, depending on sample. The second factor was far smaller, accounting for at the most 14.2%. While correlational and factor analyses lend support to the unity of interpersonal awareness, they do not demonstrate structural synchrony across issues or domains within subjects. Interpersonal domains or issues could correlate highly across subjects but reasoning in a particular domain or issue could still develop at an earlier or later period than in other domains. For example, one possible hypothesis is that Group Relations concepts, because of their greater organizational complexity, might emerge at a slower rate than conceptions within the Individual or Friendship domains. Figure II represents a cross-sectional representation of Individuals, Friendship, and Peer Group awareness development from ages 6 through 15. It shows that Individual concepts generally emerge at a slightly earlier

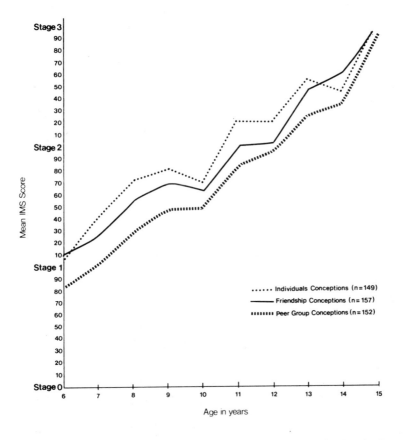

Figure 2. Mean Stage-by-Age Trends in the Development of Individuals, Friendship, and Peer Group Conceptions.

period, followed by Friendship and finally by Group Relations concepts. Although these results could be an artifact of the task difficulty of the various dilemmas, this explanation is made less likely by the fact that the dilemma was only one part of the interview process.

3. *Longitudinal Data.* One of the crucial questions in social-cognitive/stage theory is the degree to which individual cases conform to invariant and hierarchical sequence properties in their development over time. Although a two-year follow-up assessment does not constitute a sufficient test of longitudinal sequence, it would seem that few if any subjects should regress in their interpersonal awareness interview over that time period. The results support a tentative conclusion of longitudinal growth: Of the 48 boys included in the longitudinal sample, eight remained at the same global level, 20 advanced roughly one-third of a stage, 17 advanced two-thirds of a stage, and three moved up a full stage.

4. *Clinical-Comparative Results.* In addition to the defining levels of interpersonal development, an extensive part of this research has been development of the clinical-comparative approach. If "disturbed" children are found to lag in their development of interpersonal awareness, three conclusions can be drawn. First, the measure of interpersonal awareness gains a certain construct validity by accurately assessing a clinical lag among a sample of emotionally disturbed children. Second, a notion of a developmental lag among emotionally disturbed children adds to the understanding of what is meant by healthy versus maladaptive social development. Third, a developmental lag in social reasoning points toward directions for clinical intervention to stimulate interpersonal maturity in children with interpersonal difficulties.

At both times of measurement the difference between the 21 public school–clinic pairs (the clinical-comparative sample) on their level of interpersonal awareness was highly significant. At time 1 the mean level of interpersonal awareness was 1.36 (stage 1[2]) among the 21 "disturbed" cases and 1.83 (stage 2[1]) among the 21 public school matches ($t = 6.23$, $df = 20$, $p < 0.0005$). At time 2 average interpersonal awareness was 1.69 (stage 2[1]) for the disturbed group and 2.25 (stage 2[3]) for the public school matches ($t = 5.73$, $df = 20$, $p < 0.0005$).

A second question deals with the longitudinal nature of interpersonal development in emotionally disturbed children. We propose an interpretation of interpersonal dysfunction in children as a lag in interpersonal development. If this is true, emotionally disturbed children should progress in interpersonal awareness, but lag behind their peers, and the hierarchical and invariant characteristics of social-cognitive stages should still hold true. Therefore, there should be no greater incidence of stage regression under interview conditions among disturbed children than among normal children.

Overall the average quantitative change in interpersonal awareness for the clinical sample is slightly less than that of their public school matched counterparts (.32 of a stage versus .42 of a stage), but in all of the clinic cases, interpersonal global stage either remained the same (8/21) or increased by one (5/21), two (6/21), or three (2/21) transitional steps. The fact that interpersonal development proceeds, but at a slightly slower rate, among emotionally disturbed children is support for both the invariant and hierarchical properties of interpersonal development and the interpersonal lag theory for emotionally disturbed children.

However, Redl (1956) has described the child with interpersonal difficulties as not so much lagging in social acuity as being inconsistent in the utilization of interpersonal insights. The child may occasionally demonstrate high level abilities but more often than a normal child will regress to use of less adequate interpersonal conceptions. Redl's distinction calls to mind differences between performance and capability. Because the interpersonal awareness measure covers one's level of awareness across seventeen interpersonal issues, it might be said to measure *performance* under interview conditions. *Capability* can be measured by looking at the child's *highest* issue score, without averaging it with other lower scores. For the 21 disturbed and matched boys, the highest single stage score found across all issues was recorded. In comparing the resulting *highest* capability scores for both the normal and disturbed boy in each pair we find that in only six cases does the public school boy demonstrate a higher interpersonal *capability*, as compared to 17 pairs in which the public school boy's *overall* interpersonal global score is higher than that of the disturbed boy. In other words, in only six out of 17 cases in which there is a clinical lag in *performance* is the difference due to differences in maximum *capability*. The other 11 cases of a clinical lag appear to be due to how the disturbed child performs across a series of interpersonal questions.

The qualities of interpersonal awareness among disturbed children might, therefore, be marked by an inconsistency in awareness, whereby higher capabilities are offset by lower stage oscillations, a hypothesis which will be explored in greater detail in the next section.

B. Oscillation in Interpersonal Reasoning and Relating Under Natural Conditions

This chapter has stressed the distinction which needs to be made between (a) research and theorizing whose major purpose is the *description* of the formal characteristics of a developmental sequence of social conceptions and (b) research which takes the next step, a step toward understanding the functional *applications* of a developmental model. By distinguishing between formal and functional analyses, the intention is to emphasize the need to understand the subjects' application of developmental levels of awareness in actual or natural social settings and interactions. Formal or structural developmental descriptions are not seen as incorrect, but as insufficient to the task of understanding how each individual uses his concepts and reasoning abilities in his everyday behavior (Flavell & Wohlwill, 1969).

In this final section of the paper, the task is to outline several critical and recurring methodological and conceptual concerns which require both further conceptualization and fresh empirical approaches. To accomplish this task, a naturalistic setting and a research strategy which may be of some use in the clarification of these concepts is described. The section closes with several preliminary observations which may provide some direction for future research as well as give the reader a feeling for the strengths and weaknesses of naturalistic methods as they are applied to the study of both theoretical and practical problems in social-cognitive development.

1. The concerns

a. *Fluctuations in awareness level*. Although many developmental psychologists recognize that formal analyses can be applied to social concepts, many of the most thoughtful are hesitant to accept the claim that stage models capture the complexity of social development in a psychologically realistic way (Flavell, 1977). Research reviews appear to indicate too much variability when either context or content are manipulated (Shantz, 1975). Therefore, the first and most obvious concern of those using stage models as working hypotheses is to gain a better understanding of how to characterize whether or to what extent fluctuations occur in an individual's level of reasoning under variations in natural conditions. Do people fluctuate in reasoning under variations in natural conditions? Do some people fluctuate in reasoning level more than others? What are the interactive processes involved here? Can research generate information which will help to characterize either typical or abnormal degrees of fluctuation, consequently providing information as to the validity of the stage model?

b. *Hypothetical versus natural reasoning.* A correlated but more methodologically focused concern is that of better understanding the relationship between the level of interpersonal awareness expressed in a reflective, clinical, and/or hypothetical interview and the level of awareness expressed in more naturalistic conditions, i.e., during the course of the child's daily social interactions. Can one expect the two levels so obtained to be the same, or would one predict that the level expressed in a reflective interview would always be a higher level (Damon & Gerson, Note 4)?

Both these questions are critical to a better understanding of cognitive-developmental systems. If in naturalistic observations it can be seen that children vigorously and stubbornly use a predominant level of reasoning time and time again, then it may be very appropriate to talk about "the child who is reasoning at stage x." If, on the other hand, greater variation of reasoning level across contents and context is found, it may be necessary to invoke greater distinctions between capability level and performance level. Evidence in this latter direction does not lead to abandonment of the formal developmental stage model, but does necessitate its integration with a more interactional and functional social-cognitive model.

c. *Action versus reflective awareness.* In addition to shedding light on the validity of the "structured wholeness" question in social-cognitive development, naturalistic approaches allow researchers to more fully and richly investigate the dynamics of long-term social interactional patterns of children at varying levels of interpersonal awareness capability. This in turn can generate a better conceptualization of the relationship between interpersonal stages as tapped through verbal-reflective or conceptual structures and the structure of interpersonal awareness as observed through interactions. In response to questions about reasoning and behavior, Furth (1977) has asserted that from a developmental perspective, the gap between a theory of action and a theory of knowledge is a pseudo-problem, often created by an inadequate theory of knowledge. From Furth's developmental perspective, a child's reflective knowledge of interpersonal relations would be derived developmentally from interpersonal interactions as the organizers of experience. In other words, an adequate social developmental theory should show parallels between the development of social interactional practices and of reflective social awareness. Theoretically, actions should parallel words (i. e., reasons), although not necessarily in the same child at the same time. This concern is of particular importance with regard to the present findings of a developmental lag in the interpersonal awareness interviews of children with disturbed interpersonal relations. To be psychologically meaningful, the characterization of the interactional relations of such children needs to be in terms which make sense in relation to their immature reasoning. The construction of a developmental model of interpersonal interaction might provide construct validity for the interpersonal awareness model as well as point toward remedial social interventions which might serve to reduce the lag in both interpersonal awareness and behavior.

2. The clinical-exploratory research context

To explore more systematically the three concerns just discussed, we have made use of a clinical setting which provides educational and socio-emotional support to troubled children, children who have great difficulties in relating to peers, parents, and authorities. Such clinical research, designed to feed back to theoretical concerns in developmental psychology, requires a great range and flexibility of methods. In this context, the term "clinical approach" or "clinical research" has several meanings. Psychiatrically, it can refer to the descriptive study of pathological or maladaptive behaviors or functioning. Methodologically, it can refer to a flexible and relatively open-ended method of inquiry or to a case study or field study approach to data collection. In clinical research designs, investigators usually gather a greater range of information on a more limited sample than is the case in experimental research designs. Often a characteristic of the clinical approach is the use of naturalistic settings as laboratories for observing human behavior.

Researchers in developmental psychology studying the social and cognitive develpment of the child have a long-standing tradition of using clinical-comparative approaches. Heinz Werner, for example (1948), has demonstrated how the study of pathological processes in individuals can give fresh illumination and insight to the understanding of developmental principles. Piaget's early observations of his own children in his home provide an example and a role model from developmental psychology to demonstrate how intensive clinical observations can be the descriptive starting point for generating potentially testable hypotheses about universal patterns of development (Piaget, 1952).

The present clinical or exploratory research effort uses observational methods in a clinical intervention setting to look at the several concerns (which were identified previously) of investigators studying social cognition and its development. Some early and tentative findings of this project are presented, and suggestions for the extension of this model beyond psychiatric populations to normative populations are made.

As previously pointed out, critics of the methods used by social-cognitive/developmental researchers (such as Bigelow, 1977; Chandler, Paget, & Koch, in press; Damon, 1976; Furth, 1977; Selman, 1976b; Turiel, 1975; Broughton, Note 5) have expressed an appropriate concern about whether people do really reason at one level across various situations, experiences, and interactions. They question whether the level of reasoning obtained in hypothetical or reflective interviews corresponds to the level of functioning that the individual uses in the real world. These criticisms acquire weight in the face of the seeming reluctance of most cognitive developmentalists to go beyond verbal/clinical interviews to other means of data collection, assessment, or diagnosis. Kuhn and Brannock (1977) express a similar concern about research in physical cognition. The present work began with the construction of a developmental system of levels of interpersonal conceptions using a reflective interview approach; to test certain developmental concerns it has proven useful to go beyond the interview procedure to examine concepts as they are applied in real-life circumstances. In this way, one begins to see if the developmental descriptive levels derived from reflective interviews can be used to analyze social reasoning-in-action— children's negotiation of decisions and resolution of conflicts which have real-life consequences.

To study this problem, the relatively detailed developmental descriptions of interpersonal awareness issues have been augmented by the incorporation of issues studied by other developmentalists. This group of issues is now in use as an observational social-cognitive/developmental coding scheme for the analysis of peer-group discussion in natural psychoeducational and social group settings. The hope is that through the use of this coding scheme, a better understanding will be gained of the range and consistency of levels of expressed social reasoning that both "normal" and "disturbed" children use in natural group situations.

3. The clinical setting: A structured social developmental environment

The application of this naturalistic coding scheme is taking place in the Manville School at the Judge Baker Guidance Center. The Manville School provides an educational and psychological treatment program for learning disabled and emotionally disabled children from ages 7 to 15. A major difficulty for these children, and a common referral complaint, is disturbance in interpersonal relationships, particularly peer relationships. In order to help these children develop more adequate social skills, as well as to permit the study of social reasoning in action, new and previously developed psychological and educational programs are being used which stress the importance of interpersonal awareness and of peer relations in class and group activities, in sports, and at recess. The staff encourages the children to provide support and feedback to each other within the immediate context of the peer group (peer sociotherapy). Structured programs are designed to help children help each other with such issues as cooperation, trust, conflict resolution, leadership, and conformity—the same issues on which developmental citings (refer to Table 1) have been taken.

An integral part of this program is a strong basic research effort. The primary research concern is not simply an outcome evaluation of the program, but rather a formative process observation of the social interactions and social reasoning children use during the various structured, social-educational aspects of the program.

Five school programs are currently used to encourage the children to reason about interpersonal issues of importance to them. The first is the weekly class meeting. Lasting from thirty minutes to one hour, class meetings use the existing interpersonal conflicts, goals, personalities, and relationships within the classroom as the basis for group discussion of interpersonal issues. Over time, class meetings have acquired a relatively formal and autonomous organization with student leaders, weekly leadership seminars, regular evaluations, of class relations, crisis mini-meetings, a student-initiated agenda, voting on proposals, and debate and petition procedures. Class meetings stress small group interactions with eight to ten students, action resolutions of real-life interpersonal problems, and cooperative goals.

Second, as a more purely educational adjunct to class meetings, there are various forms of interpersonal awareness curricula. Using discussions of fictional interpersonal dilemmas and perspective-taking exercises, the interpersonal curricula are designed to develop fundamental social concepts in a less stressful and more objective atmosphere than is possible in class meetings. For example, children may discuss a hypothetical dilemma which utilizes the concept of "peer pressure," and then apply that concept to their real-life inter-personal problems.

Weekly activity groups provide a third chance to improve social skills outside the classroom milieu. Students plan with counselors a series of weekly field trips and activities, such as a cross-country ski trip, which emphasizes development in self-concept and group cooperation. After each activity the members discuss how well things went and what could be done to improve the planning and social interactions of the members.

A fourth opportunity for observation and analysis, which does not include the entire group, occurs during what Redl and Wineman (1956) have called Life Space Crisis interviewing. At times during the course of the school day, children find their responses to a perceived frustration or injustice so overwhelming that even class discussion is not a powerful enough support system to help the participant(s) sort out the facts and feelings. At these times, the children are allowed to go to a private "time out" section of the school, where they can regain composure and control. Here they have the opportunity to discuss with a trusted school counselor, one who is, ideally, cognizant of developmental levels, their personal interpretation of the nature of the conflict, its cause, its course, and some alternative resolutions. An effort is made to engage the child's own awareness skills, not hand down ready-made adult beliefs.

Finally, observations are also made during a social studies and current events discussion period. Students are encouraged to examine broader interpersonal issues in world affairs, such as the death penalty, presidential elections, or intervention in other coun-tries. By comparing the social processes of the more immediate classroom with those of the larger world, children gain a better perspective on both. (The work of Furth, 1977, Turiel, 1975, and Kohlberg, 1969, is particularly relevant here.)

These activities allow the observation of social reasoning in action, the generation of hypotheses about how troubled children think about their actual interpersonal problems, and the observation of how they apply their interpersonal and socio-moral reasoning to resolve school and peer related issues and problems or to make plans which have foreseeable consequences for each child.

By tape-recording and transcribing these various meetings and experiences throughout the school year, recordings which are made with the children's knowledge and permission, a substantial data base is being compiled. The intention is to continue to tape-record and keep logs of the group discussions and social interactions in both classroom and activity groups of the same children over a two-year longitudinal period. For the sake of comparison, data are also being gathered on the level of interpersonal reasoning in reflective interviewing.

The type of issues the children focus on as well as the developmental maturity of their reasoning about the issues are of paramount interest. In addition, fluctuations in expressed reasoning levels over time and across recurring situations or unique incidents can be observed to develop testable hypotheses about the possible causes for such fluctuations, if they exist. These hypotheses can then be tested on larger and more representative groups under more controlled conditions, beginning a hypothesis-testing phase in the research.

4. The process observation approach

To summarize what has been said so far, examination of levels of social reasoning-in-action requires at least two tools. The first is a stage-by-interpersonal awareness issue chart broad enough and yet detailed enough to be used to locate the substance and structure of each group discussion. The second is an (educational) atmosphere which encourages children to express social reasoning under conditions which can be observed. These situations need to be structured such that the issues identified through clinical interviews will emerge and such that these issues can be addressed at the range of levels of social reasoning of which the participants are capable.

Using the example of leadership, the first tool is a developmental descriptive mapping of leadership concepts. The previously described five stages are being used. The second tool is a set of activities which both stimulate thinking about leadership and provide leadership opportunities. Each child has the opportunity to function as class leader during the class meetings. Extra skill training for the children is also provided through "leadership seminars" in which three children practice and discuss with an adult such leadership skills as communicating clearly, keeping order and keeping discussions on target.

The data upon which the following description is based come primarily from a year of observations and transcript analysis in one classroom composed of eight children, two girls and six boys, between the ages of about 12 and 14. The intent here is to share some hypotheses which are based on these initial and exploratory observations. The hypotheses are oriented toward the problem of oscillation of interpersonal awareness and the idea of developmental parallels between the structure of reflective interpersonal reasoning and interaction.

    a. *Observations of oscillation in interpersonal awareness.* There are two aspects to observing the functioning of interpersonal awareness. The first is the comparison of developmental level found in the clinical interview setting with that found in naturalistic discussions which have real-life consequences for the participants. Observations concerning the relationship of *affect and cognition* are discussed, particularly those relating to the impact on interpersonal awareness of severe stress and inability to cope with anxiety. The second aspect is the observation of real-life interpersonal awareness under variations in natural conditions. Two sorts of situational determinants of interpersonal oscillation are presented, (a) perceived status within the group and (b) interpersonal awareness used in judging others versus that employed in judging the self.

    As previously noted, some critics have argued that the fast pace of naturally occurring interpersonal relations may cause the level of natural reasoning to be lower than that of reflective reasoning (Brown, 1975). On the other hand, some have argued that the verbal skills and abilities necessary for participants in a reflective interview may place skewed limitations or penalties on children for whom verbal expression is difficult. The present clinical evidence supports both these intuitions in certain instances, but also shows evidence for some remarkable predictability from one circumstance to another—with certain children and under certain conditions. In the pilot class, three children reasoned at a relatively high level fairly consistently, one child reasoned at a consistently low level, and the other four showed more oscillation between high and low level reasoning. These individual differences appear to hold up whether comparing hypothetical and natural discussion or reasoning in various natural situations over time and across contexts.

    The four children who as a group are termed the interpersonal oscillators are the most clinically interesting group. In the normative sample (Figure 1) we find that at age 12–13, most subjects are capable of reasoning at levels 2 or 3; in the pilot class, level 3 reasoning was rarely observed. The "high level" students used level 2 predominantly; the "low level" reasoner consistently used level 1; the "oscillators" moved between these two levels.

One explanation of the interpersonal oscillation observed in these children is that they are "transitional" between two stages, e.g., stage 2 may be used less frequently because the children have not yet fully mastered these higher level concepts. Yet this does not really explain when and under what conditions children with the capability of a higher level will actually use that level or will use a lower level. In other words, clinical observations are needed to specify the conditions and factors which predict when a child will utilize his highest level and when he will resort to more familiar but less mature forms of social interaction and explanation. So far the interpersonal observations indicate that when compared to hypothetical reasoning, naturalistic reasoning can be either higher or lower depending on the occasion. These observations indicate that reflective interview reasoning is not always an optimal score, but probably should be viewed as simply another context in which some children do better and some do worse.

An example of oscillation between interview and real-life reasoning is the case of "Dwight," age 13.[4] Dwight is capable of expressing a level of thinking both in the interpersonal and intellectual domains that is typical of his age. However, under certain stresses, his real-life level of reasoning appears to be lower. In an interview, Dwight said that a good class leader should "ask the kids what they want to talk about," a statement indicative of the bilateral approach to leadership characteristic of stage 2. When it was Dwight's turn to be a class leader, he was terribly frightened people would laugh at him and refused to participate. In fact, during a life-space interview following some regressive behavior, he told a trusted counselor, "I'm not going to be the class leader. The kids will all laugh at me." When the meeting was finally held later that day, Dwight was still very anxious. As class leader he was extremely domineering over the interests of others ("You, you there! I'm giving you a warning"). In both his authoritarian leadership style and in his concern over others laughing at him, Dwight demonstrated an orientation toward unilateral relations and a physicalistic reciprocity. This level of awareness differs from what Dwight utilized during the clinical interview. Under the stress of the

4. All names are fictitious.

class meeting, Dwight lost sight of his stage 2 understanding of the facilitator role that class leader can play.

One of the advantages of a clinical setting for exploratory research is that additional information is available to help investigators understand how other aspects of children's functioning may facilitate or interfere with the expression of their most mature reasoning. For example, discussion with Dwight's psychotherapist revealed that Dwight does not have the usual psychological mechanisms for moderating and coping with anxiety. When he experiences stress, anxiety immediately escalates into overwhelming panic, and he feels vulnerable in a world where everyone can hurt him. The function of leadership then becomes to keep people from hurting him by making them do everything he says. Without the stressful situation of being class leader, or his anxiety reaction to that situation, Dwight might have oriented his real-life reasoning to the level 2 understanding of which he was capable. Dwight lacked not the social-cognitive capability but the emotional capability to function at level 2 when placed in this position. Children such as Dwight may not differ from their better-functioning peers in their capacity to understand social and moral issues, but in their ability to maintain their highest level of understanding in the face of stressful social experiences.

Observations of interpersonal functioning within a natural setting show that oscillation does occur on the basis of varying situational conditions in the class, particularly conditions such as perceived status and the specific content of issues being discussed. These situational factors interact with particular psychological or psychodynamic concerns of individual children. It would seem, then, that explanations of fluctuation must include a clinical orientation toward individual characteristics with an integrated social psychological analysis of group dynamics.

In Dwight's case, being class leader interacted with his particular anxieties to produce in interpersonal functioning an oscillation downward from his interview reasoning level. In the case of "Jerry," on the other hand, being class leader dramatically pushed his reasoning up from both his reflective interview level and his usual functional stage during class discussions. It appeared that his perceived status as class leader enabled Jerry to move beyond his usual nonverbal and physicalistic orientation to the world, i.e., his real-life reasoning oscillated across situations.

On several occasions during his tenure as class leader, Jerry utilized stage 2 reasoning. During a discussion about why being class leader is important, Jerry said that it "makes you feel good about yourself." On another occasion during a leadership seminar, Jerry helped the staff understand the difficulty one of his friends was having with group discussions:

"Yah, 'Daryl' feels bad 'cuz he is embarrassed about the way he acts, like in group. He doesn't like to act like a jerk. He doesn't want to come to school, but I think he is going to make it."

In both instances Jerry's awareness of reflective feelings ("feel good about yourself," "embarrassed about the way he acts") was indicative of stage 2 concepts of self-awareness (Issue 2, Self-awareness, Stage 2; see Table 1).

The analysis of Jerry's upward oscillation takes into consideration his desire for special attention and the way in which being class leader helped to fulfill that desire. At home and at school, Jerry is often looked down upon as "dumb" by other children and adults. However, when put in a position of respect and treated with respect, perhaps he felt the support necessary to overcome some of his frustrations. His upward fluctuation may have resulted from a feeling that others were listening to him and that his thoughts were appreciated despite his difficulty in verbalizing them.

A most intriguing example of interpersonal oscillation comes from observing the social reasoning of "Daryl" when he judges others and when others are judging him. Daryl is a bright child, but his ability is generally channeled toward exploitation of others. This perception of his behavior was changed by some recent moments when he demonstrated real interpersonal maturity and insight. Both occasions dealt with the behavior of others; Daryl himself was out of the limelight. In the first case, Daryl was pointing out the faults of another's leadership style:

"You are not supposed to tell us what to do. We are supposed to share our ideas, and you are supposed to share your ideas with us."

The notion of a leader's sharing ideas would be scored at least stage 2—psychological reciprocity. In another situation where a friend had left the group, Daryl made the following insightful and helpful remarks:

"He is mad because he couldn't get a big, big ice cream. He wanted his way. Everybody can't get their way. (*To his friend*) Just sit there and if you want to talk, talk, and if you sit there and listen, listen to what people say and as long as you are at the meeting, we don't care."

But Daryl's functioning is not always so mature or insightful, particularly when he is in a position of being judged by his peers. In such situations, Daryl fluctuates downward to the one-way, individualistic concerns of stage 1. His verbal expressions of interpersonal maturity were particularly low when he took over as class leader. When the class began to criticize him for goofing off, Daryl quit. The class then wanted to know his reasons.

CHUCK: Okay, Daryl. Why don't you want to be the class leader?
DARYL: Because I said I don't, and that is final.
CHUCK: There has to be a reason.
DARYL: I didn't want to. I knew I wasn't going to work, but I wanted to be leader. . . .
ADULT LEADER: Daryl, do you want to help your class members?
DARYL: Yah, I want to help them, but I don't want to be class leader.
ADULT: How are you going to help them?
DARYL: I'll help them, depends who's going to help me. If somebody smacks them, I'll smack the other kid for them.

Perhaps because of his sense of insecurity and strong need to be undisputed, the role of class leader as facilitator was more than Daryl could cope with. When he resigned, the class investigation of his reasoning backed Daryl against a wall. Under these conditions, his interpersonal reasoning stance was that of stage 1. Motives were based on individualistic concerns ("because I want to") and relations with others were based on physicalistic reciprocity ("If somebody smacks them, I'll smack the other kid for them").

The previous examples give an idea of the techniques that are being developed to assess reasoning in natural settings and of how the exploratory research model can be used to generate theoretically relevant hypotheses about social-cognitive development. These examples also show that it is possible, although difficult, to demonstrate that changes in interpersonal expression are not just different attitudes, but are in fact orderable along a developmental continuum in which certain naturalistic expressions of interpersonal awareness are developmentally more advanced than others.

b. *The structure of reflective interpersonal awareness and of interpersonal action.* Werner, in his developmental psychology (1948), tried to show that the concept of development was a tool by which underlying parallels could be seen in behavior which on the surface appeared to be disparate. Recently Piaget (1976) has applied this concept of "developmental parallelism" to his conception of practical and reflective knowledge. He has argued and attempted to demonstrate that in the domain of *physical* reality, though practical intelligence at the level of actions may develop prior to its reflective counterpart, the sequences of development in both processes are organizationally similar. However, few researchers who have studied the relation between *social* thought and social action have tried to use this concept of "developmental parallelism" to clarify understanding. More common has been the attempt to correlate specific levels of reasoning with specific classes of action in social situations (cf. Brown, 1975). But if conceptual knowledge is a reflection upon experience, then it may make more sense to investigate whether the same developmental model can be applied to both actions and reflections.

Obviously, difficulties arise. For example, because much social intercourse uses language as a medium, the behavioral observation of social action structures is more difficult; thought and action structures in social relations are more difficult to differentiate empirically than are physical interactions because interpersonal interactions are usually accompanied by verbal interchange.

Nevertheless, the stages of reasoning about interpersonal issues which have emerged in reflection have been of particular use because of their particular salience to interpersonal interactions and relations. Recently, there has been an informal attempt to use the clinical setting in conjunction with the stage descriptions to try to better understand stages of interpersonal interaction, behavior, or functioning. The expectation is not that the child would necessarily demonstrate the same level in reflection and in action, but that organization in each sphere should have similar sequential and hierarchical characteristics, e.g., subjects with higher level structures would be capable of lower level performance but not the reverse.

Some very preliminary naturalistic observations are now under way of relationship *behavior* in those areas which have already been described conceptually, e.g., leadership styles, trust relations, or conformity/cohesiveness behavior. During group recess activity children are asked to undertake social functions which require less inherent verbalization than do class discussions, for example, to act as leader in a sports competition. By observing children across a relatively wide age span, behavioral styles can be delineated that may parallel stages of reflective awareness.

Three different leadership styles, used by children ranging in age from 7 to 11 have been observed. The first can be called the *pushy* style. "Kenny" (age 8:1) was chosen to be leader of a group kickball game. His responsibilities were left unspecified by his counselor. During the game, Kenny's sole leadership style was to use physical force. He did not communicate specific commands or instructions, but, without much rationale, occasionally pushed or shoved another child into a particular function (e.g., being at bat). The second leadership style can be called the *bossy* style. "Bryan" (age 10:3) was selected as leader for a slightly older group. He postured himself to command children to move this way or that, but did not fill them in on the reasons. From the observer's perspective, the overall effect of his orders seemed arbitrary. He did not seem to have a social organization in mind, but merely the notion of telling others what to do so they might perfect their individual skills. A third group of slightly older boys (11–12) selected a leader named "Roger" (age 11:3), and he used what can be called the *organizing* style. Roger tried to position his men for a group game and organize their offense. He was bossy, but his bossiness included a coordination of several members of his team. It provided a means toward keeping the team in line, not as individual players, but as a group with interdependent roles.

The behaviors mentioned are a common assortment of interpersonal styles found in children of these ages. The question is whether a developmental analysis helps to organize them in some sequential, hierarchical, and coherent manner. It is possible that the *pushy* style is analogous to stage 0, where leadership is viewed purely as a matter of asserting personal needs with no function for the group itself. By only pushing people, Kenny seems to show that he does not have a concern for the coordination of personal actions. The *bossy* leadership style, demonstrated by Bryan, shows some improvement in interpersonal functioning, the boss now communicating directives to the group which appear to have the function of improving their playing skills ("hold the stick right"). But what is the boss doing for the group's organization? At best he helps individuals; at worst, he acts as a tyrant. This *bossy* stage of leadership style parallels what is associated with stage 1, an arbitrary ruling over individuals aimed at perfecting their individual skills. In Roger's case, the leader demonstrates the intention of *organizing* relations within the group. He coordinates positions, establishes a turn-taking order, or in some other manner coordinates the group and does not just work on individual behaviors. As with stage 2 awareness, there appears to be an awareness of a reciprocal relationship between leader and followers where communication about information is established.

The suggestion is not that Kenny *is* stage 0, or that Brian *is* stage 1. Nor is it that Roger *is* stage 2 in his behavioral awareness and perhaps stage 1 in his conceptual awareness, as if stages could be located solely inside the child. Rather, an example of three children, each faced with the same structured situation (social context) has been given, with a demonstration of how a descriptive model of social developmental stages derived from reflective interviews can be applied to the developmental analysis of the organization of each of the three children's social interactions with others. The particular recess activity is a good example because it lends itself to being spontaneously structured by each child in accordance with that child's social capabilities, i.e., it allows for a range of developmental levels of social organization.

But just as the structure of reflective awareness cannot be divorced from that which is being reflected upon, neither can the structure of interactive awareness be examined independent of the context of the interaction. For example, even 11-year-old Roger, who showed that he was capable of "level 2 leadership awareness behavior," may function on the plane of action at developmentally lower levels in other social contexts, contexts which are less conducive to higher level functioning. On the other hand, even if a situation or social context allows for higher level interactive awareness, it is extremely unlikely that Kenny, age 7, would be able to function at a level much higher than he has exhibited; he simply does not have higher level awareness of leadership either as action or reflection.[5]

The description of these three styles represents an initial and very speculative attempt to construct stages of actual interpersonal re-

5. One can also see developmental parallels between ontogenetic stages of interpersonal reasoning and the "microgenetic" phases one finds in the development of particular relationships. For example, forming a friendship relationship may be heuristically characterized as a process that begins with the actual physical meeting of the other person (stage 0) and which optimally develops through to autonomous interdependence (stage 4). But, as with ontogenesis, fluctuations can be expected back and forth in accordance with the nature of the social context. The developmental analysis here is just that, a means to understanding the relative maturity of the interaction, where it has come from, and where it may go developmentally.

lating behavior which parallel stages of conceptualizations about the issues of interpersonal awareness. Eventually, a developmental description of interpersonal behavior styles as related to each of the interpersonal issues might be assembled in which behavioral observations are graded along a developmental continuum similar to that of conceptual stages. Such a system would go a long way toward answering some of the complex questions of the relationship between thought and action, as well as possibly give indications of directions for potentially useful educational or clinical interventions. This analysis suggests that from a developmental perspective, the most useful way to think about this concern is to consider each a form of the same developing awareness, forms not located solely in the subject, but truly located in the interaction of self and other(s).

IV. SUMMARY

This paper has examined the research questions and strategies used by those who attempt to study social development from a cognitive-developmental orientation. It began by pointing to the need to integrate the descriptive work done by social-cognitive/ developmental researchers with some of the approaches taken by clinical and social psychologists in studying the same general phenomenon: interpersonal relations. An issue-by-stage social-cognitive map developed on the basis of both conceptual and empirical investigations was described, as were some of the properties which defined these stages. Following this, empirical evidence was cited from several ongoing studies which both supported the theoretical claims of logical coherence and pointed research in several new directions. One direction of particular importance is the naturalistic study of social and interpersonal reasoning and relating.

Taken together, the interview data and the naturalistic observations appear to present a paradox. Evidence from the descriptive research appears to support the principle of stage consistency across categories of experience. On the other hand, the impact of the naturalistic findings is to point out oscillations in reasoning across varying real-life conditions. It should be noted, however, that several of the children in the classroom study did reason fairly consistently across a wide range of contexts; these children, perhaps not coincidentally, were the ones who had shown the greatest improvement in their interpersonal functioning and were soon to return to a more traditional educational milieu. Such clinical evidence points to the strong need to study better-adjusted children under similar conditions to see if real-life oscillation is as pronounced as it is in more pathological groups (Inhelder, 1943/1968).

Our conclusion is that the cognitive-developmental approach, viewed in the proper perspective, can accommodate and make coherent data which suggest both variability and uniformity of reasoning, but that for such an accommodation to take place, greater attention must be paid to the critical social psychological and clinical variables which reciprocally interact with level of social-cognitive capability.

REFERENCE NOTES

1. Selman, R., & Jaquette, D. *The development of interpersonal awareness: A working draft manual*. Unpublished scoring manual, Harvard-Judge Baker Social Reasoning Project, Cambridge, Mass., 1977.
2. Rest, J. *The stage concept in moral judgment research*. Unpublished manuscript, University of Minnesota, 1977.
3. Selman, R. L., Jaquette, D., & Lavin, D. *Fourth annual report, Harvard–Judge Baker Social Reasoning Project*: Unpublished report, Harvard University.
4. Damon, W., & Gerson, R. *Hypothetical and "real-life" moral judgment*. Paper presented at the 1975 meeting of the Eastern Psychological Association, New York, April 1975.
5. Broughton, J. *Epistemology as ideology: The cognitive development of subject/object concepts*. Unpublished paper, Columbia University, 1976.

REFERENCES

Bigelow, B. J. Children's friendship expectations: A cognitive-developmental study. *Child Development* 1977, **48**, 246—253.
Brown, R. Moral reasoning and conduct. In R. Brown & R. Herrnstein, *Psychology*. New York: Harcourt, Brace, Jovanovich, 1975.
Chandler, M. J., Paget, K. F., & Koch, D. A. The child's demystification of psychological defense mechanisms: A structural-developmental analysis. *Developmental Psychology* in press.

Damon, W. Some thoughts on the nature of children's social development. In J. Meyer (Ed.), *Reflections on values education*. Waterloo, Canada: Laurier Press, 1976.

Flavell, J. H. The development of inferences about others. In T. Mischel (Ed.), *Understanding other persons*. Oxford: Blackwell, Basil & Mott, 1974.

Flavell, J. *Cognitive development*. Englewood Cliffs, N. J.: Prentice-Hall, 1977.

Flavell, J. H., & Wohlwill, J. F. Formal and functional aspects of cognitive development. In D. Elkind & J. H. Flavell (Eds.), *Studies in cognitive development: Essays in honor of Jean Piaget*. New York: Oxford University Press, 1969.

Furth, H. G. Young children's understanding of society. In H. McGurk (Ed.), *Social development*. Amsterdam: North-Holland Publishing Co., 1977.

Hartmann, H. *Ego psychology and the problem of adaptation*. New York: International Universities Press, 1958.

Hartup, W. W. The origins of friendships. In M. Lewis & L. Rosenblum (Eds.), *Friendship and peer relations*. New York: Wiley, 1975.

Heider, F. *The psychology of interpersonal relations*. New York: Wiley, 1958.

Inhelder, B. *The diagnosis of reasoning in the mentally retarded*. New York: John Day, 1968. (Originally published, 1943.)

Kohlberg, L. Stage and sequence: The cognitive-developmental approach to socialization. In D. A. Goslin (Ed.), *Handbook of socialization theory and research*. Chicago: Rand McNally, 1969.

Kuhn, D. & Brannock, J. Development of the isolation of variables schemes in experimental and "natural experiment" contexts. *Developmental Psychology*, 1977, **13**, 9–14.

Piaget, J. *The child's conception of the world*. London: Routledge & Kegan Paul, 1929.

Piaget, J. *The moral judgment of the child*. London: Kegan Paul, 1932.

Piaget, J. *The origins of intelligence in children*. New York: International Universities Press, 1952.

Piaget, J. Piaget's theory. In P. H. Mussen (Ed.), *Carmichael's manual of child psychology*. (3rd ed., Vol. 1) New York: Wiley, 1970.

Piaget, J. *The grasp of consciousness*. Cambridge, Mass.: Harvard University Press, 1976.

Redl, F. & Wineman, D. *Children who hate*. Hinsdale, Ill.: Free Press, 1956.

Selman, R. Social-cognitive understanding: A guide to educational and clinical practice. In T. Linkona (Ed.), *Moral development and behavior*. New York: Holt, Rinehart & Winston, 1976. (a)

Selman, R. Toward a structural analysis of developing interpersonal relations concepts: Research with normal and disturbed preadolescent boys. In A. Pick (Ed.), *X Annual Minnesota Symposium on Child Psychology*. Minneapolis: University of Minnesota Press, 1976. (b)

Selman, R., & Damon W. The necessity (but insufficiency) of social perspective taking for conceptions of justice at three early levels. In D. DePalma &

J. Foley (Eds.), *Moral development: Current theory and research*. Hillsdale, N.J.: Lawrence Erlbaum Associates, 1975.

Selman, R., Jaquette, D. & Lavin, D. Interpersonal awareness in children: Toward an integration of developmental and clinical child psychology. *American Journal of Orthopsychiatry*, 1977, **47**, 264–274.

Shantz, C. U. The development of social cognition. In E. M. Hetherington (Ed.), *Review of child development research* (Vol. 5). Chicago: University of Chicago Press, 1975.

Sherif, M. *In common predicament: Social psychology of intergroup conflict and cooperation*. Boston: Houghton Mifflin, 1966.

Sullivan, H. S. *The interpersonal theory of psychiatry*. New York: Norton, 1953.

Turiel, E. Conflict and transition in adolescent moral development. *Child Development*, 1974, **45**, 14–29.

Turiel, E. The development of social concepts: Mores, customs and conventions. In D. DePalma & J. Foley (Eds.), *Moral development: Current theory and research*. Hillsdale, N. J.: Lawrence Erlbaum Associates, 1975.

Werner, H. *Comparative psychology of mental development*. New York: Science Editions, 1948.

Werner, H., & Kaplan, B. *Symbol formation: An organismic developmental approach to language and the expression of thought*. New York: Wiley, 1963.

White, R., & Lippitt, R. *Autocracy and democracy*. New York: Harper & Row, 1960.

Children's Social Attributions: Development and Change

Marcia Guttentag and Cynthia Longfellow[1]

Harvard University

THE TWO STREAMS: COGNITIVE DEVELOPMENTAL THEORY AND SOCIAL PSYCHOLOGICAL THEORY

Social attribution refers to the process of explaining the behavior of self and others. Underlying social attribution theory is the assumption that all individuals seek to understand, explain, and predict their own behavior and the behavior of other human beings (Shaver, 1975). Who am I? Why do I do what I do? And why do others behave as they do?

The study of children's attribution processes is very much akin to the research on the development of social cognition in that both are concerned with how children come to know their social environment and how this knowledge affects their social behavior (Shantz, 1975). The two differ, though, in their emphases and orientations. Social cognition, growing out of work on the stages of cognitive development, vis-à-vis the objective world, has tended to emphasize the similarities between the child's constructions of his or her social and physical worlds. The emphasis has been primarily on the variations in the child's "intuitive or logical representation of others" (Shantz, 1975), i.e., variations in cognitive structuring at different ages or developmental levels.

In contrast, social attribution theory coming out of the discipline of social psychology has focused on how variation in the *object* of thought affects one's understanding of social behavior. Specifically, it is concerned with social psychological variables—those dimensions of the social stimulus that carry a "social meaning" to the observer. The sex, age, and race of the persons being observed, for example—their roles, the situations in which they are being perceived—all may be potent social psychological, situational variables which significantly influence how one thinks about or knows those persons.

1. Cynthia Longfellow is a doctoral student in the Graduate School of Education, Harvard University.

Both social psychological research and cognitive developmental research have been criticized for ignoring those dimensions which form the central concerns of the other. For example, Chandler (1976) has pointed out that implicit in too many studies of children's social cognitive development is the assumption "that all meaningful variation in the developing system lies within the child" (p. 235). Carroll and Payne (Note 1) similarly point out that social psychology is obsessed with "task" descriptions, i.e., variations in the social stimulus, often to the exclusion of "process" descriptions—changes in the cognitive processing of that information.

It is not simply variation in the social world that is of concern in the study of attribution processes; a realization of the interaction of the perceiver and the object is essential. In addition to the importance of the cognitive level of the perceiver, there are variables such as age, sex, race, and the affective relationship and relative status between the perceiver and the observed which will influence the perceiver's understanding of his or her social world. There are other situational effects, like peer influences, that determine which issues are salient to the perceiver.

Past understanding of social attribution processes has been based almost exclusively on work with adult subjects, and has thus ignored the dimension of central concern to the child psychologist—developmental differences in the structures of thought. Similarly, as cognitive developmental theory has turned its attention to the social domain, it has had to confront the fact that the development of social cognition does not conform so readily to the orderly progression and relative unity that seem to characterize children's thinking about their physical world. The study of the development of children's attribution processes occurs at an intersection of these two theoretical positions.

In this paper, we will present a review of research that has been done on children's developing attributional processes. The discussion begins with causal attributions—the choice between possible causes, and the self-other distinction in attribution. Then achievement attributions are dealt with, including the use of causal themes in achievement attributions, the effect of setting on achievement attributions, attributions of positive and negative outcomes, and actor and perceiver characteristics. Finally, we present our own research study of attributional processes in the development and change in the sex-role attributions of children ages 6, 11, and 15.

Causal Attributions: The Choice
Between Possible Causes

One of the central concerns of attribution theory is how people arrive at a causal explanation for behavior. All of the major attribution theorists have distinguished between person factors, i.e., something about the actor's personality or dispositional makeup, and situational factors, i.e., something about the particular circumstances or setting, as possible causes of behavior (Heider, 1958; Jones & Davis, 1965; Kelley, 1967, 1972).

Do children make a similar distinction between situational and psychological causes? The question hinges on whether children have a concept of psychological existence which motivates or causes behavior, and whether they can make accurate inferences about the actor's psychological states from his or her behavior. The term "psychological existence" includes a number of elements. Keasey (this volume) distinguishes between "motives"—the reasons behind an action—and "intentions"—the purposefulness of an action. Selman (Note 2) refers to the child's concept of subjectivity—an awareness that others have subjective thoughts, feelings, and motives—and the child's concept of personality—an understanding that the various attitudes, thoughts, and feelings of others are interrelated as traits or psychological dispositions. It might be better to ask *when* and not *whether* children make the psychological-situational distinction in their attributions of causality.

Little work has been done on the causal attributions of children under the age of 3, no doubt because of the verbal limitations of very young children. A notion of causality appears to be present even at the level of sensorimotor intelligence, according to Piaget (1954), who traced the origins of a schema of causality to infants' efforts to reproduce interesting effects. Once children acquire language, their queries and their explanations about various phenomena reveal that their notion of causality is a primitive, undifferentiated one. Piaget noted that up to the age of 4 or 5, the child invests *everything* with a kind of psychological purposefulness "which is at the same time both the efficient cause and the justification of the effect with which he is concerned" (Piaget, 1969, p. 232). In other words, every animate and inanimate object is endowed with an implicit consciousness which motivates it to "behave." It is only at the age of 5 or 6 that the child begins to sort out those things which have consciousness and those which do not, and to correctly apply the concept of psychological motivation to humans only (Piaget, 1969).

Consistent with Piaget's observations are the findings reported by Keasey that children as young as 3 make use of the concept of motive in their evaluations of others (Peterson & Keasey, as reported in Keasey, this volume). The concept of intentionality (the fact that an effect is produced "on purpose" rather than by chance) comes into use in the attribution process only around age 6 or 7 (Keasey, 1977, this volume). Piaget also noted that it is around this age that children begin to acquire a concept of chance or probability, relinquishing their preoperational notions of finality (Piaget & Inhelder, 1969). In Selman's words (Selman, Note 2), the child around the age of 6 or 7 recognizes that others have their own unique subjectivity and begins to distinguish between psychological elements (e.g., feelings, thoughts, intentions) and the person's actual actions. Prior to this "subjective level of perspective-taking" the child has a notion of psychological states, but the psychological and physical aspects of behavior are frequently undifferentiated. In sum, the work suggests that before the age of 6 or 7, children have a notion of a psychological motivational force, but the concept is global and undifferentiated, applied indiscriminantly to the animate and inanimate world. At the age of 6 or 7, they begin to distinguish between the possible causes for physical and social phenomena; with respect to the world of social behavior they are increasingly able to differentiate between inner subjective states and concrete behaviors, understanding that covert motives, thoughts, and feelings can underlie overt behavior (Selman, Note 2).

Although young children may have an understanding of psychological reasons as causes of behavior, this in no way implies that they make causal attributions in the same way that adults do. One attribution theory that has been put to the test with children is that of Harold Kelley (1971). The theory states that perceivers distinguish among multiple possible causes of an event by covarying the three dimensions of entities, time/modality, and persons. There are two types of causes: *inhibitory causes*, which reduce the probability of an event occuring, and *facilitative causes*, which increase the probability of an event occurring. The two types of causes may be either *internal* (within the person) or *external* (in the environment). Various combinations of causes can serve to produce the observed effect. For example, *multiple necessary causes* must all be present to produce the effect for which they are necessary. In this case, the perceiver who observes the effect can be sure that all causes were present. Or an effect may be observed if there are *multiple sufficient causes:* a particular cause or combination of causes is sufficient to produce the observed effect. In this case, the perceiver of an effect is not sure which particular causes combined to produce the effect. In order to make a causal attribution, one may apply the *discounting principle* which states that "the role of a given cause in producing a given effect is discounted if other plausible causes are also present" (Kelley, 1971, p. 8). Kelley suggests that an internal (inferred) cause of behavior may be discounted if there is an external (observed) cause for that same behavior, simply because an external cause is more unambiguous than the internal one (Kelley, 1972).

Shultz, Butkowsky, Pearce, and Shanfield (1975) tested children ages 5, 9, and 13 to see if they approached the search for causes as systematically as Kelley's theory predicts they should. Children were presented with a picture of an event and were provided information about the presence or absence of certain causes. They were then asked about the presence (or absence) of other causes (also represented pictorially). The investigators found that the 5-year-olds had no causal schemata. Both 9-year-olds and 13-year-olds had developed a scheme for multiple sufficient causes, i.e., they were able to identify when one of two causes was sufficient to produce the effect. Only the 13-year-old children had a scheme for combining information on inhibitory and facilitative causes. For example, if an inhibitory external cause were given (something that would reduce the likelihood of an event occurring), the oldest children inferred that there must be an internal facilitative cause present in order for the event to occur. And finally, only the 13-year-old children had developed a scheme of multiple necessary causes, whereby they inferred the presence of an additional cause when the effect they observed was extreme, and only a single cause was known.

Two other studies (Smith, 1975; Karniol & Ross, 1976) confirmed the same developmental trend in the use of the multiple sufficient cause schema, using a somewhat different paradigm than Shultz et al. (1975). Children in these studies were asked which of two story characters really wanted to play with a toy—the one whose mother either rewarded him for doing it or commanded him to do it, or the one who simply played on his own accord. If the children had a scheme of multiple sufficient causes, they would recognize that a mother's command or reward is a sufficient external cause for a child to play with a toy, and that therefore any internal cause, such as intrinsic interest in the activity, can be discounted. The child who simply plays with the toy has no reason to do so except for the fact that he wants to: The cause of his behavior is an internal one. Kindergartners in both studies did not use a scheme of multiple sufficient causes. Second graders used the scheme more than the kindergartners, but not as much as did fourth-grade children, whose use of the scheme was comparable to that of adults (Smith, 1975).

The schemes of multiple necessary causes and multiple sufficient causes require the coordination of various pieces of information: The presence or absence of an internal cause implies something about the presence or absence of an external cause; likewise, the presence or absence of an inhibitory cause implies something about the presence or absence of a facilitative cause. We might expect that the kindergartners in these studies, who were probably at the preoperational level of intelligence, would have a great deal of difficulty coordinating these two seemingly independent pieces of information. Recall that in Piagetian conservation tasks children at the preoperational level do not coordinate information about changes in both the length and width of a ball of clay as it is rolled into a sausage. At this stage they *center* their attention on one dimension of change, ignoring the other. Only when they begin to *decenter* their attention from one perceptually salient aspect of the task can they begin to shift their focus from one dimension to the other. Eventually they are able to attend simultaneously to the two dimensions, understanding the implication of the reciprocal changes—an ability that characterizes concrete operational thought (Inhelder & Piaget, 1958).

Although the scheme of multiple sufficient causes may require a degree of decentering of which the kindergarten child is simply not capable, it does appear that children at this age do make consistent causal attributions using a kind of partial scheme. Instead of discounting an internal cause when there was a known external cause which was sufficient to explain the behavior, the youngest children combined or added the two causes together (Karniol & Ross, 1976): They gave both an internal and an external reason to explain why the child receiving a reward or a command wanted to play with the toy more than the child who merely played with it of his own accord. The ability to combine the two possible causes in an additive way, even at the preoperational level, suggests that some decentering is taking place, enabling the young child to relate two pieces of causal information in a consistent way.

While the 9-year-olds demonstrated the use of the scheme for multiple sufficient causes (Shultz et al., 1975; Smith, 1975), they had neither the scheme for multiple sufficient causes with an inhibitory external cause nor the scheme for multiple necessary causes—both of which the 13-year-old had (Shultz et al., 1975). Shultz et al. suggest that these latter two schemes require more complicated information processing that may only be possible at the level of formal operations: In the first case, alternative possible causes must be coordinated on both the internal-external dimensions and on the facilitative-inhibitory dimension; in the other case (multiple necessary causes) alternative causes must be considered in coordination *and* the observed effect must be implicitly compared to other effects for its severity.

More recently, Weiner and Kun (in press) have argued that a more appropriate model of causal schemata would be a "graded-effects schemata" in which levels of strengths of causes are varied with levels of strengths of effects, rather than determining the presence or absence of any cause, given a certain effect. Given the choice, as in studies of achievement attributions, children and adults do vary the strength of possible causes along a continuum rather than making a presence-absence choice (Weiner & Kun, in press). Preliminary tests of this model suggest that children as young as first graders will attribute greater strength of a cause given greater strength of the effect—a finding that appears to contradict the development of multiple necessary causes as a formal operational phenomenon. The multiple necessary causal schemata, it will be recalled, states that given an extreme effect, an additional necessary cause must be inferred. However, tests of the two models ask subjects quite different questions, so they may be tapping quite distinct intellectual processes.

The studies reviewed here all suggest that the development of schemes for choosing among possible causes of behavior closely parallels the development of logical thought and appears to involve the same cognitive operations. The youngest children studied (5- and 6-year-olds) had only a partial scheme of causal attributions whereby they combined two possible causes additively rather than discounting one if they deemed the other sufficient. Thus, they evidenced some partial decentering. By the time children are 9 years old, they can clearly coordinate information on possible causes in an interrelated way because of their ability to decenter.

The Self-other Distinction

The studies testing Kelley's theory of causal schemata all asked children to make attributions about the behavior of *others* in hypothetical situations. A series of experiments investigating children's use of the discounting principle with respect to "explaining" their own behavior reveal a striking difference in the developmental timetable (Greene & Lepper, 1974; Lepper, Greene & Nisbett, 1973; Ross, 1975). In these experiments, children's intrinsic interest in a play activity is undermined or eroded by providing an extrinsic reason for engaging in the activity, in the form of a reward. In the typical experimental design, preschool children between the ages of 3 and 5 are invited to participate in an appealing (and thus presumably an intrinsically interesting) activity, for which they receive either an anticipated reward, or unexpected reward, or no reward at all. Subsequent observations are then made of the children in a free play situation to determine the amount of time they spend with the target activity when other (intrinsically interesting) activities are also available. These studies report that children who expected and received a reward subsequently engaged in the target activity for a significantly *less* amount of time than those children who did not *expect* a reward (even though they may or may not have received one).

The same principles of attribution theory that have been used to describe how individuals explain others' behavior can also apply to individuals' causal explanations of their own behavior (Nisbett & Valins, 1971; Bem, 1967). The principle states that if there exists a salient unambiguous external factor which is sufficient to explain another's behavior then intrinsic or internal causes of that behavior will be discounted. It is argued that offering children a *reward* to play an inherently interesting game is to "overjustify" any personal reason they may have for engaging in the activity. The result is a reattribution by the children: They are no longer engaging in the play for the sake of the play itself, but rather in order to receive some externally provided reward. Furthermore, since it is assumed that the type of attribution one makes will affect one's subsequent behavior, it is predicted and confirmed that children so rewarded show less intrinsic interest in the activity, as evidenced by a decreased amount of play with it in their subsequent exposures to it. It is predicted that the overjustification effect will occur any time that a situation results in an external causal attribution where previously only an intrinsic causal attribution was salient and sufficient to explain the observed effect.

It is important to point out that the studies of the overjustification hypothesis with young children (preschoolers) rely on observations of the children, often in naturalistic settings like their preschool classrooms, and not on their verbal reports of what *they* see as determining the underlying causes of their behavior. This represents both an advantage and a liability when compared to studies such as those by Shultz et al. (1975), Smith (1975), and Karniol and Ross (1976). The advantage is that findings are not susceptible to the limitations of a child's verbal ability. The liability is that it is the experimenter who is interpreting the meaning of the behavior in a way that is consistent with the theory he or she wishes to prove.

It is striking that children as young as 3 and 4 appear to undergo a process of attribution whereby they discount the previously sufficient cause for their behavior (their own personal interest in or enjoyment of the activity) and attribute their behavior to an external factor (the reward), which is now a sufficient cause for them to play with the toy. The change in their behavior represents a much earlier "application" of a scheme of multiple sufficient causes than the studies reviewed earlier would lead us to predict.

Piaget (1932/1965) noted a similar self-other distinction in children's moral reasoning. He found that children as young as 3 and 4 distinguished between intentional acts and accidental acts in their own real-life behavior, but did not apply this distinction when making judgments about the behavior of others in theoretical situations until much later (around age 7). Piaget suggests that the difference in active and theoretical moral thinking is a function of young children's egocentrism: their attention is arrested by the more perceptually salient external features of the other's behavior and they are unable to shift their focus to the possible underlying psychological motives or intentions. On the other hand, they directly experience their own psychological subjectivity, fully aware of what their own intentions and motives are. Even in hypothetical situations children show a use of psychological intention when making attributions about themselves before they use this type of information with regard to others (Keasey, 1977).

The self-other distinction has further implications for the content of causal attributions, at least for adults. Jones and Nisbett (1971) proposed that actors and observers make divergent causal attributions. The observer tends to attribute the behavior of the actor (other) to dispositional causes, whereas the actor (self) attributes this same behavior to situational causes. The theory suggests that the information is processed differently for selves and others. In observing another, it is the behavior—the action itself—that is the most salient aspect. It literally "engulfs" the field, and the locus of the cause tends to be attached to the person. On the other hand, the actor is likely to attend to the environmental cues that elicit his or her own behavior, considering actions in relation to situational factors rather than focusing on the physical behavior alone. In other words, actors attend to a variety of situational factors which may be sufficient causes to explain their own behavior, and therefore they are likely to discount any possible dispositional causes. Thus, one tends to view one's own behavior as a response to certain situational factors.

Studies with children have not directly tested the actor-observer divergence in causal attributions. At first glance, the theory seems inconsistent with what we have already noted about young children—that they consider their own psychological states in the attribution process long before they take into consideration the psychological processes of others. However, it should be noted that those experiments were designed to elicit children's understanding of and use of psychological factors in making attributions. What young children may be able to do with respect to themselves prior to being able to do it with others is to consider *both* situational and psychological factors in making an attribution of causality or responsibility. Whether this represents the origins of the self-other divergence described by Jones and Nisbett (1971) awaits empirical investigation.

Achievement Attributions: The Use of Causal Schemes

While studies on the development of causal schemes clearly demonstrate the relationship between the development of logico-physical and social cognition, the study of achievement attributions contributes to an understanding of the role of social-psychological variables in the social attribution process. In reviewing the work on children's achievement attributions we will attempt to consider both the developmental trends and the social-psychological factors affecting the attributional process.

The theoretical model that underlies most of the work in this area is based on Weiner, Frieze, Kukla, Reed, Rest, and Rosenbaum's (1971) classification of possible causes used to explain success or failure. Causes may be classified along two dimensions: internal-external (the psychological-situational distinction) and stable-unstable (see Figure 1).

	internal	external
stable	ability	task difficulty
unstable	effort	luck

FIGURE 1. Causes for Achievement Outcomes.

It should be noted that most studies provide the subject with these four possible causes, asking them to rate them for their explanatory value. The spontaneous explanations given by children and adults do include the use of ability, effort, and task difficulty in making attributions, but not luck (Frieze, 1976; Frieze & Snyder, Note 3). Other causes mentioned by adult subjects with some degree of frequency include mood, the incentive to do well, and the other person's role in affecting the outcome (Frieze, 1976). In addition to the spontaneous use of ability, effort, and task difficulty, children use intrinsic motivation (he wanted to do well) and an ability-task interaction (the task was too hard for him) (Frieze & Snyder, Note 3). Therefore, a word of caution is in order from the outset: The findings on achievement attributions may be somewhat distorted by the fact that subjects choose (or rate) from only a partial list of possible causes.

Certain information is considered relevant to the achievement attribution process. This information includes the history of the task outcome—whether it is consistent or inconsistent with past performance, the performance of others on the same task, the importance of the task, the incentive of the person to do well, and the type of task (Frieze, 1976; Frieze & Bar-Tal, Note 4). The schemes of causal attribution discussed previously apply equally well to the use of this information in arriving at a plausible causal explanation for achievement outcomes. Consider the following type of problem presented in a study by Frieze and Bar-Tal (Note 4). "You got a high grade on this test" (outcome—success or failure); "You have done very well on past tests in this class" (past performance—consistent or inconsistent); "Everyone else did poorly on this test" (others' performance—comparable or different). The subject is then asked to judge the relative explanatory power of each of the possible causes: luck, task difficulty, ability, and effort. In order to do this, one must be able to coordinate the various pieces of information available. Thus, in this example, one would discount task ease as a possible cause (it clearly was not easy for most of the class), and one would discount luck (the performance is consistent with the past—success on this test is not merely a random occurrence). In fact, because the observed effect is extreme—you were the *only one* who passed—the theory of multiple necessary causes predicts that you would probably attribute your success to a combination of ability and effort: Neither cause alone is sufficient to explain the outcome, given what you know about the situation. Based on the findings of children's development of causal schemes we might expect to find developmental differences in children's ability to integrate the information about an achievement outcome and select among possible sufficient (or necessary) causes.

In the study by Frieze and Bar-Tal (Note 4), children were presented with the achievement situation described above and other similar situations, and were provided with information about the outcome of the task, past performance, importance of the test (incentive to do well), and the performance of others. Children in grades four through twelve were asked to judge how much each of five possible causes helped to explain their hypothetical achievement outcome. Note that the children were asked to evaluate each possible cause independently as to its sufficiency in explaining the outcome; they were not being asked to choose among multiple possible causes. The fact that there were no significant age differences suggests that children at every grade level utilized the combined information in similar ways to evaluate the plausibility of the various causes. In other words, they all had a scheme for determining a sufficient cause—a scheme which appears to be characteristic of concrete operational thought (Shultz et al., 1975). Thus, outcomes consistent with past performance were attributed to stable factors (ability and task difficulty), while outcomes that contradicted past performance were more often attributed to unstable factors (luck or effort). Older children were more consistent in the use of information on past history than were younger children. Success on an important task was more often attributed to effort, while failure was attributed to task difficulty. Conversely, on an unimportant task, children attributed success to task ease and failure to lack of effort. Older children also made greater use of information about the performance of others. This may represent the continuation of a developmental trend observed with children even younger than fourth graders. Children as young as 5 have been observed to compare their performance to that of another child for the explicit purpose of seeing "how well" the other child is doing (Ruble, Feldman, & Boggiano, 1976). However, using the performance information in making attributions was characteristic only of older children, second grade and beyond (Ruble, Feldman, & Boggiano, 1976; Ruble, Parsons, & Ross, 1976).

Another study suggests that even younger children (age 6) are able to integrate information about ability and effort when asked to predict another's achievement outcome (Kun, Parsons, & Ruble, 1974). The study required children to perform a kind of reverse attributional process in which the causes are given and the child is asked to predict the effect. Younger children (age 6) combined the information additively while older children (8 to 10-year-olds and adults) combined it in a multiplicative manner. In other words, the older children realized that the level of effort and the level of ability interact with each other in producing an outcome. They use information about the two causes in an interrelated manner. The younger subjects simply failed to account for this interaction even though they did evidence some ability to decenter by including both pieces of information in making their judgments. Again, these findings are consistent with the shift from preoperational to concrete operational thought that seems to occur around this age.

An interesting finding is that in predicting others' achievement outcomes, children 8 years and older made increasingly greater use of effort information than they did of ability information (Kun et al., 1974). Weiner and Peter (1973) also noted the special role effort played in influencing children's evaluations of achievement outcomes. They found that between the ages of 4 and 12, children gave increasing weight to effort in determining whether to reward a successful outcome or to punish failure. Children between the ages of 12 and 18 decreased their emphasis on effort, though never to as low a level as the youngest children. It also appears that children at all ages gave greater rewards to successful outcomes resulting from effort than they did to those resulting from ability. The emphasis on effort may be the result of socialization patterns. Our society and certainly our school system places a high value on effort, assuring us—in the words of the old maxim, "try hard and you will succeed"—that our efforts will be justly rewarded. Attributing success or failure to effort rather than to ability also serves to preserve one's sense of competence and self-esteem since one has much more control over the effort one exerts than over ability—a relatively fixed attribute (Kun et al., 1974).

The Effect of Setting on Achievement Attributions

Certain causes may assume greater importance in achievement attributions depending on the setting in which the achievement outcome occurs. Most studies have provided children with real or hypothetical test situations of an *academic* nature. It may well be that the pattern of attributions associated with achievement outcomes depends at least in part on the meaning of the social setting in which they occur. Frieze and Snyder (Note 3) found that the reasons invoked by children (grades one, three, and five) to explain their success (or failure) on a school task were not the same ones used to explain their success (or failure) on a favorite leisure-time activity—catching frogs. Over 80% of the reasons spontaneously supplied by children for their academic outcomes were ability and effort. These reasons along with two other internal reasons—intrinsic motivation and ability-task interaction—accounted for 91% of children's achievement attributions for school-related tasks. In contrast, the reasons most often given for success or failure in catching frogs were task difficulty (easy or hard) (31%) and effort (28%). The reasons least often given were ability and intrinsic motivation. Thus, not only do children's causal attributions vary according to the setting in which they occur, but academic outcomes are clearly believed to be caused by internal factors. Because attribution of achievement outcomes to internal causes is known to be strongly related to feelings of pride and shame (Weiner et al., 1971), it appears that the academic setting has a powerful impact on the child's self-esteem.

Attributions of Positive and Negative Outcomes

Research on achievement attributions and responsibility attributions consistently finds that children provide different explanations for positive and negative outcomes. For example, Frieze and Bar-Tal (Note 4) found in their study of fourth through twelfth graders that the children, overall, were more likely to attribute their successes to ability, effort, and the teacher, and their failures to task difficulty. Studies on children's moral judgments find that if the outcome is negative in the sense that persons or material objects are harmed, younger children tend to hold the offender responsible even if he or she meant no harm. However, if the outcome is positive these same age children clearly differentiate their attributions of responsibility on the basis of whether or not the actor intended those benefits. More credit and more positive evaluations are given to those whose motives were good (Costanzo, Coie, Grumet, & Farnill, 1973; Imamoglu, 1975; Weiner & Peter, 1973). This effect has been observed in children as young as 5 years 8 months (Costanzo et al., 1973). Even adults attribute greater responsibility to a person for negative outcomes than for positive outcomes (Shaw & Sulzer, 1964).

Some authors have suggested that negative outcomes, because of their actual or implied threat to person or property, evoke greater affective arousal in parents than do positive outcomes. Parents are apt to scold or punish children on the basis of how much damage they have done in spite of any good intentions on the part of the children; therefore the child sees a model whose primary response to actions resulting in negative consequences appears to be based on the consequences alone (Farnill, 1974; Costanzo et al., 1973). Failure in an achievement situation threatens a person's self-esteem, just as success enhances it. Attributing failure to internal factors, especially ability, results in feelings of shame (Weiner et al., 1971), while attributing failure to an external cause such as task difficulty can help to reduce the loss of esteem by reducing one's feelings of responsibility for the outcome. Attributions of success to internal factors serves to bolster self-pride: The person then can claim full responsibility for the positive results.

A developmental study of the relationship between affect, outcome, and attributions suggests that children at the kindergarten level base their rating of another's affect on outcome only; second graders begin to consider the attributions the other has made, as well as the outcome, in rating affect; and the high school student clearly conceptualizes affective reactions to achievement outcomes as mediated by the attributions made (Ruble & Underkoffler, Note 5). The authors suggest that the shifts may be a function of developmental changes in information processing (i.e., the ability to coordinate various pieces of information), or increasing familiarity with the meaning of academic success and failure, or both.

Actor Characteristics

We have already pointed out the very important distinction between attributions to oneself and attributions to another. Are there additional characteristics of the "other" which affect children's attributions, such as sex, race, or age?

Shaw and Sulzer (1964) conducted two identical experiments except that one used a young male child as the central character, and the second used a college student as the central figure. Comparing the findings from the two studies, the authors noted that children tend to attribute greater responsibility to the adult than to the child in situations with positive or negative outcomes. The difference is especially pronounced for positive outcomes. Similarly, the adult subjects gave more credit to adult actors effecting positive outcomes than they gave to young children actors producing similarly favorable consequences. Could it be that both adult and child subjects are tacitly acknowledging the fact that adults in general are more capable of planning and executing beneficial actions consistent with their role as prosocializers and nurturers?

Studies of children's dispositional attributions—their descriptions of others in terms of personality traits—find that children ages 7 to 15 describe other children in greater detail and degree of differentiation than they do adults (Livesley & Bromley, 1973). Males are described in more detail and with a greater degree of differentiation than are females. Livesley and Bromley suggest that the emphasis on peers may reflect both the increased frequency of contact that children have with peers during this age period, and the greater similarity between oneself and one's peers. The sex difference may be a reflection of an already pervasive influence of sex-role typing: males are seen as having greater "value" and "interest" than females (Livesley & Bromley, 1973, p. 104). The male role also encompasses a broader range of activities and attributes than does the female role. The question of sex-role attributions will be more fully described in a later section.

In a similar study, Peevers and Secord (1973; Secord & Peevers, 1974) found that children (kindergarten, grades three, seven, and eleven, and college) used more "dispositional" items to describe *disliked* persons than to describe *liked* persons. The use of a dispositional item represents the most sophisticated or conceptually integrated attribute a child can use. These were used sparingly by all children, and were used least of all by the younger children.

Secord and Peevers (1974) suggest that increasing differentiation of concepts of other persons occurs as a result of striking or dramatic behavior, which may be positive or negative. Others are often *disliked* because of some particularly outstanding offensive quality which clearly strikes the perceiver as unlikeable.

Perceiver Characteristics

Thus far we have considered only the characteristics of the social situation—the act, its consequences, and the actor—as they affect attributions. Equally important are certain perceiver characteristics such as sex, race (Weiner & Peter, 1973), set (Jones & Thibaut, 1955; Farnill, 1974), personality, motivation (Shaver, 1975), and of course, level of cognitive development. This last characteristic has been considered extensively throughout our discussion of the attribution process. In this section we will look at what appears to be an equally powerful determinant of attributions: sex.

Reformulation of achievement motivation in terms of attribution theory (Weiner et al., 1971) has focused attention not only on the different types of attributions that men and women make for achievement outcomes but also on the relationship between achievement attributions and achievement expectations. There is evidence to suggest that women are more likely to attribute their success to luck and their failure to lack of ability, whereas men are more likely to attribute their success to ability (Frieze, 1975; McMahan, Note 6). Attributions to stable causes, like ability, tend to create expectations for consistent future performance (Valle & Frieze, 1976; Weiner et al., 1971). In fact, expectations for success and failure serve to reinforce certain attributional patterns (Valle & Frieze, 1976); thus women continue to expect to do poorly, and men continue to expect to do well.

It has been shown that altering one's attributions can change the level of one's expectations (Valle & Frieze, 1976). Studies of the development of sex differences in children's achievement attributions serve to highlight the issue of how individuals develop different attributional patterns.

There is some disagreement about when sex differences in achievement attributions are first observed. For example, several studies have found that girls as young as 6 or 7 (kindergarten and first grade) have lower estimates of their ability, lower estimates of their relative performance (when comparing themselves to other children of both sexes), and lower expectations for future success than do young boys, *even though* their actual performance is as good as or better than that of boys (Parsons, Ruble, Hodges, & Small, 1976; Pollis & Doyle, 1972; Parsons & Ruble, in press). Other studies report no sex differences in achievement expectations at this age (Lester, 1967), but do note differences by the time children are 9 or 10 (Hodges, Note 7). Lowered expectations for future success imply certain attribution patterns as described above. (It should be noted, though, that most of these studies with young children were not asking them directly to make causal attributions in the way typical of the adult studies.) It seems reasonable to assume that once children enter school, fairly consistent patterns of achievement expectations and achievement attributions are established which differentiate males from females.

One might well wonder why, in the face of academic performance equal to that of boys (Maccoby & Jacklin, 1974), girls persist in their lowered expectations for success. If, as the theory predicts, causal attributions mediate expectancies for success, then we can expect to find distinct attributional patterns even for young children that exert a powerful influence over their sense of academic competence.

Some have speculated that sex differences in achievement attributions may be a function of the development of sex-role identity (Parsons et al., 1976): The child differentiates the two sexes by identifying sex-role stereotypes; then in order to identify with one's own sex, the child adopts the sex-role stereotype he or she has identified (Kohlberg, 1966).

Others have looked for differences in the socialization processes of girls and boys and have produced some very provocative findings. For example, fourth and fifth grade girls are more likely to attribute their failures to lack of ability and to desist in further efforts at the task if they are being evaluated by an adult or a female. If their evaluator is a peer or a male, they attribute the failure to lack of effort and persist at the task. Exactly the opposite is found for grade-school boys. If feedback is supplied by an adult, young boys attribute their failures to not trying hard enough and redouble their efforts, but if they are evaluated by a peer, they attribute their failures to lack of ability and no longer persist at the task (Dweck & Bush, 1976). The implication for the typical American classroom is painfully clear: Feedback from a female teacher has a negative deteriorating effect on girls' academic performance, while it seems to spur boys onward.

An observation of elementary classrooms confirmed the researchers' suspicions (Dweck, Davidson, & Nelson, Note 8): Teachers (who were all women with a good deal of experience) provided girls and boys with different patterns of feedback. It was not the amount of positive or negative feedback received that varied, but the ratio of discriminate to indiscriminate evaluation. About half of the negative evaluations of the boys' work referred specifically to its intellectual quality; the rest was irrelevant or indiscriminate (e.g., "stop mumbling your answer"—even though the response was correct). By contrast, 88 % of the negative evaluations of girls' academic work referred to its intellectual quality.

Dweck et al. hypothesize that in forming future achievement expectations, one will use the information from past performances that is the most clearcut and least ambiguous about one's ability. For girls, the most unambiguous information comes from the teacher's negative evaluations of the intellectual caliber of their work. Hence girls emphasize their past failures (and their criticized abilities) in forming future expectations. For boys, the least ambiguous information comes in the form of positive evaluation of their intellectual abilities. Thus, they emphasize past *successes* (and their praised abilities) in forming future expectations. It has been found that simply by manipulating the reinforcement contingencies one can change children's achievement attributions and their expectations for success or failure regardless of sex (Dweck et al., Note 8).

A STUDY OF SEX-ROLE ATTRIBUTIONS

We have seen that boys and girls often differ in the attributions they make to others and to the self. Both the sex of the perceiver and the sex of the perceived exert an influence on the attributions which are made.

A recent study conducted by Marcia Guttentag and her colleagues[2] provided detailed information about children's sex-role

2. Jane Amsler, Ginna Donovan, Wendy Willson Legge, Ronnie Littenberg, Helen Bray, Gordon Legge, Sumru Erkut, Anne Selman, and many other students contributed to this study. We are indebted to the Public Education Division of the Ford Foundation, Dr. Terry Saario, Program Officer, which supported this study. The discussion of the complete intervention and all materials used for it can be found in M. Guttentag and H. Bray, *Undoing sex stereotypes* (New York: McGraw-Hill, 1976).

attributions across a number of domains. In the first phase, the study probed developmental differences in sex-role attributions. In the final phase, the study introduced a school intervention which was designed to change children's sex-role attributions. The intervention program was designed to facilitate attitudinal and behavioral changes in a nonsexist direction. This part-time curricular experiment lasted for six weeks. Procedures were as follows.

Sampling and Design

Subjects were drawn from three school systems in the greater Boston area. Two of the communities were primarily lower middle class, and one was upper middle and middle class. Schools with large minorities of black or Spanish-speaking students were excluded in order to avoid confounding by racial or language variables. Still, there was considerable ethnic diversity in the sample with children of Anglo-Saxon, Irish, Italian, Armenian, Greek, Portuguese, and Polish descent. It was therefore possible to test the extent to which differences in early socialization experiences might be reflected in differences in inital sex-role attributions among these ethnic groups.

Entire classrooms were selected at the kindergarten, fifth-grade, and ninth-grade levels in order to have three age groups representative of distinct levels of cognitive, social, and sex-role development. All totaled, 409 children participated in the study—104 kindergartners from six classrooms, 134 fifth graders from six classrooms, and 171 ninth graders from seven classrooms. Fourteen of the nineteen classrooms received the intervention; the other five were used as controls. Because classrooms and not individuals were the basis for selection, there was no control over the relative numbers of boys and girls in the study. However, their numbers were approximately equal. It was also not possible to include an equal number of male and female teachers; because of the scarcity of men in school teaching, only three of the nineteen were men.

The study used a Solomon four-group design in order to determine the effects of the post-testing aside from the interventions, the effects of the experimental intervention itself, and the interaction between the testing and experimental intervention. Unfortunately, it was not possible to represent each of the three grade levels in each school system in all four experimental groups. Withdrawal from the study, lack of cooperation on the part of some teachers, and staff time and personnel shortages accounted for the gaps in the design.

All classrooms were observed once during the preintervention period, twice during the curriculum intervention, once immediately after, and once two weeks after the curriculum had ended. With these five observational sessions, it was possible to determine any changes in male-female pupil interactions with the teacher before, during, and after the intervention.

Measures and Observations

Two sets of measures were selected or developed, one for the purpose of measuring children's sex-role attitudes, and the other for making classroom observations of teacher-children interactions.

MEASURING SEX-ROLE ATTITUDES. The task of selecting and developing measures which would accurately depict children's sex-role attributions proved to be a challenging one. Measures had to meet a number of criteria. First, because cross-age comparisons were of central concern in the study, it was essential that the measures be suitable and comparable across all three age groups. Second, the measures had to allow the expression of sex-role attributions in a variety of contexts. Many standardized sex-role measures were rejected because they require bipolar choices; only measures which permitted the child to make "masculine" *and* "feminine" choices were used. The measures were designed to reflect the richness and variety of children's sex-role attributions; both projective and objective devices were used.

Following are brief descriptions of the various measures:

Picture Test: Children were shown pictures of men and women in stereotypical and nonstereotypical occupational roles, and were asked to tell a story about each picture. Stereotyped occupations were male mechanic and female teacher; nonstereotyped ones were female mechanic and male nursery school teacher. Stories were coded for the following categories: full or part-time job, job status, how successful the worker was, how much trouble the worker encountered in getting the job, approval or disapproval of job, and whether the worker was involved in family or interpersonal relationships.

Opposite-Sex Story Test: Children were asked to name the jobs that women could have, and that men could have. Answers ranged from no jobs to twenty-five jobs. Children were asked to describe men and women—the way they are and the way they act. Then they were asked to use the items they had listed for men in describing a woman, and similarly, the women's list for describing a man. These tasks provided rich data for analyzing the amount of stereotyping by sex for occupations and for persons, and provided the children with an opportunity to demonstrate flexibility by giving nonstereotyped descriptions.

Typical Day Measure: Children were asked to describe what a typical day in their lives would be like when they grew up. In addition, they were asked to describe a day in the life of a hypothetical woman named Barbara Smith and a man named Robert Wilson. Data analysis revealed aspirations about occupations and future family life, and permitted comparisons between the children's own aspirations and what they believed the life of typical adults are comprised of.

Semantic Differential Measure: This measure permitted an objective comparison between children's perceptions of themselves and their perceptions of the way most girls and boys are or should be. This measure was designed by selecting appropriate word pairs and treating them by standard semantic differential techniques.

Sex-Role Preference Questionnnaire: This instrument is a standardized test developed by Aletha Stein (Note 9). It identifies activities and other items which children believe are traditionally characteristic of men and women, and also measures the extent to which the child enjoys these activities.

CLASSROOM OBSERVATIONS. An observational technique developed by Serbin (1973) was used for the kindergarten classrooms (Serbin, O'Leary, Kent, & Tonick, 1973). This system identifies behaviors on the part of boys and girls which bring about a response from the teacher, and those behaviors which a teacher pays attention to in a boy or girl. For the fifth and ninth grades, the Flanders system of observation was used (Flanders, 1967). It notes the teacher's direct and indirect attempts to influence students, and student talk that initiates contact with the teacher or that is in response to the teacher's directives.

Nature of the Intervention

The intervention program included the selection of curricular material, a curriculum notebook, and a workshop training program for the teachers. Several hundred trade books were reviewed and those suitable for the project grade levels identified. All known feminist resource or research centers were contacted for available nonsexist items. The materials finally provided for the teachers included books, pamphlets, photographs, records, and toys. The curriculum notebook included background information for the teacher on sex-role stereotyping, suggestions for use of the curriculum materials or for nonsexist activities, bibliographies of nonsexist literature, and curriculum evaluation forms.

Prior to the workshop, teachers were given ample opportunity to read through the curriculum notebooks, in order to prepare them for participating in discussion. The training program included: (1) a slide show and discussion of sexism in children's literature, (2) an orientation to the curriculum intervention, (3) a summary of research on sex-role development, and (4) a discussion of research on teacher-pupil interaction. Teachers were encouraged to ask questions about how to integrate the nonsexist materials with their standard curriculum. They were also rotated through discussion sections devoted specifically to use of the curricular materials, to teacher-pupil interactions, and to teacher goals. Concerns about evaluation that were raised by teachers were handled through reassurances that they would not be evaluated for implementation of the curriculum. The choice of which materials to use and how they should be integrated into the teaching program was left to their professional judgment.

Children's Sex-Role Attributions: Before and After the Intervention

Results are reported here in two parts. First we will describe developmental differences in sex-role attributions—how children at each grade level described men and women, male and female roles, before and after the intervention. The second part presents additional findings about certain social psychological situational variables which seemed to influence the effects of the intervention.

While the use of multiple measures permitted many ways of access to children's sex-role attributions, it also complicated the picture in significant respects. For example, not all responses related to the issue of sex roles. Social class issues apparently entered into the mechanic and teacher stories; personality differences complicated the data on sex-role preferences. The younger children especially strayed far beyond the questions *we* were interested in, as they embellished their stories with fantastical detail.

KINDERGARTEN. Before the intervention, both boys and girls portrayed male and female jobs largely in stereotypical terms. Male jobs were even more stereotyped than female jobs, perhaps because of the high visibility of jobs which are stereotypically masculine, e.g., firemen, window washers, and construction workers. The jobs listed for women were more likely to emphasize interpersonal skills. Furthermore, the proportion of jobs which appeared on *both* lists (i.e., either a man or a woman could have them) was extremely low. More jobs were listed for men than for women. Other studies have also found that children as young as 5 or 6 are well acquainted with traditional sex-role stereotypes. They can accurately sex-type toys, play interests, and the ordinary activities of both children and adults (Fauls & Smith, 1956; Hartley, 1960; Williams, Bennett, & Best, 1975).

Following the intervention, the number of jobs on both male and female lists increased and the overlap between the two lists dramatically increased. Job stereotyping was reduced for female occupations only. Girls were almost as likely to list an interpersonal job for a male as for a female. Boys, however, maintained the initial attributions. Even on the kindergarten level, girls were much more interested in and affected by the intervention than were boys.

An interesting aspect of the kindergarten Job List Data concerns the status of the jobs. At first, girls recorded fewer male jobs as high status, undoubtedly because publicly visible jobs with which the children were familiar were relatively low in status. Yet other research reports that children (both sexes) at this age attribute greater power, prestige and competence to the male roles (Williams et. al., 1975). It may be that attributions of power and prestige are made solely on the basis of sex rather than on the basis of more subtle differences such as type of occupation or level of education. We know that children at this age are very concrete and tend to rely on the perceptually salient features of the environment when structuring the physical and social world (Selman, Note 2). Thus, they may simply associate psychological differences with physical size differences between the two sexes and make their attributions of competence and intelligence accordingly (Ullian, 1976).

Following the intervention, girls listed more high-status jobs for both men and women. This probably occurred because the intervention program provided the kindergartners with information about professional jobs like lawyer, doctor, and architect which are more open to women than many of the blue-collar jobs.

FIFTH GRADE. Fifth graders showed less agreement on attributes for men and women. Of the three groups, children at this age appeared to be the least sexist from the outset. Boys and girls differed little in the extent to which they stereotyped men and women, at least on the level of societal roles. This is contrary to what we would have expected from our review of the literature. Ullian (1976) found that children at this age were conforming and conventional, and firmly believed that social roles reflect social duties. However, activities which were not directly related to public equality of roles did show stereotyping by the children in our study; leisure-time activities for males, male time-spending, the male's amount and type of problems were highly stereotyped. Moreover, fifth-grade boys were more likely to stereotype the activities of the typical female by emphasizing activities like coffee klatches, baking cakes, and talking on the telephone. Both sexes described the typical female in stereotypical terms appropriate to the conventional socioemotional role of the sensitive, socially active, and nurturant female, despite the children's considerable awareness of issues of fairness and equality for the sexes.

Attitudes toward obstacles revealed differences on the Male and Female Typical Day stories. Fifth-grade boys more often said that men have no problems being or doing what they want. Similarly, they reported significantly fewer obstacles for themselves in their future typical days. Girls were much quicker to recognize the existence of obstacles in stories they told about both males and females. Thus, the 10-year-old girls acknowledged all types of problems in the outside world, while boys denied any external difficulties. This corresponds to the findings on achievement attributions which agree that by the age of 9 or 10 girls have lower expectations of future success than do boys (Parsons et. al., 1976; Parsons & Ruble, in press; Pollis & Doyle, 1972; Hodges, Note 7). Girls' expectations of future failure may alert them to obstacles which will prevent success.

There was a clear tendency (which occurred across all grades) for each sex to assign role-typical attributes to the opposite sex to a greater degree than they did to themselves. At the fifth-grade level, boys thought girls were neat, sensitive, gentle, cautious, good-looking, obedient, quiet, apt to cry a lot, and weak. Fifth-grade girls' scores on these attributes hovered much more closely around the neutral (neither masculine nor feminine). Likewise, fifth-grade girls' opinions of "Most Boys" tended toward the masculine attribution in eight out of twelve word pairs. In fact, both boys and girls expressed the belief that "Most Boys" are very close to the masculine stereotype. The stereotype for males may be stronger than that for females; it is certainly the one that children, both boys and girls, learn first (Williams et. al., 1975). Livesley and Bromley (1973) also reported that children of both sexes describe male peers in greater detail than they do female peers, suggesting that children have a greater familiarity with attributes that can be used to characterize boys.

Interestingly, in characterizing "Ideal Boys" and "Ideal Girls" on the Semantic Differential, girls but not boys modified their attributions and indicated characteristics which are considered to be desirable regardless of sex. It appears that prior to the intervention, fifth-grade girls were already more attuned than boys to the artificiality of sex-role stereotyping.

For self-attributions, boys described themselves as occupationally satisfied and respected, with few problems of any kind, and involved in typically masculine activities. Girls saw themselves as expressive, socially adept, and nurturant. One noteworthy difference was found in attributions of self as good-looking or ugly on the Semantic Differential: Boys rated themselves as attractive as "Most Boys," while girls rated themselves less attractive than "Most Girls." These reponses are consistent with self-image research which suggests that females have a more negative self-attribution than males.

In general we found that prior to the intervention, fifth graders believed that men and women should be treated equally in society, yet they maintained the more subtle masculine-feminine distinctions about obstacles, time-spending, and interpersonal concerns. Boys were more rigid about proper personality characteristics for the two sexes, especially for girls.

Most of the intervention effects of fifth graders occurred with the girls. Occupational roles that girls had previously stereotyped changed sharply toward a nonstereotyped stance. Girls also showed changes in the socioemotional measures, producing more varied lists of attributes for women, including intelligence and strength, and they also saw boys as having interpersonal qualities not attributed to them before the intervention.

NINTH GRADE. Prior to the intervention, on every measure males in occupations were consistently stereotyped as occupationally secure and satisfied by both ninth-grade boys and girls. Boys saw themselves as having no problems, while girls were less optimistic about themselves, acknowledging that women have social, internal, and societal problems. These findings conform to the studies reviewed earlier in this paper on sex differences in achievement attributions and expectations. In describing a Typical Day in their own future, both boys and girls made predictable sex-role attributions. Boys projected their future leisure time as filled with sports, all-male groups, or dating. Girls believed they would spend more of their daily time absorbed in homemaking duties and child care. Ullian (1976) found that children at this age reasoned that individuals should conform to stereotyped sex roles in order to maintain harmony between the sexes.

Boys and girls made similar self-attributions, perceiving themselves as friendly, sensitive, and adventurous. Boys were especially concerned about two additional qualities: being strong and never crying. This apparent discrepancy in stereotyping others but not oneself is supported by research on children's understanding of subjectivity of self and personality of others (Selman, Note 2). Children at this age are able to see themselves as having conflicting thoughts, feelings, and dispositions. Their conceptions of others are formed by abstracting from their specific behavior to arrive at generalizations about personality traits. However, at this level of reasoning, children tend to be somewhat rigid and oversimplified in their characterizations; in other words, they tend to stereotype others.

Of particular interest is the ninth-graders' report of their own physical attractiveness. Boys, as anticipated, claimed that they were about average in their appearance, while girls, who placed a high value on being good-looking, rated themselves as slightly below average in appearance,—an underevaluation which reflects the negative ratings which fifth-grade girls gave themselves.

Prior to the intervention the crucial sex difference at the ninth grade was that girls, in their stories about women, attempted to integrate occupational roles and socioemotional abilities; they positively valued both aspects of life. Boys did not integrate the two roles for women; they thought of women either with jobs or in the home. Males were stereotyped by everyone, although there was some tolerance (especially by the girls) of nurturant qualities in males.

The ninth graders were the most sensitive to the intervention. When changes in the direction of nonsexism occurred, these took place among the girls. Generally, the ninth-grade boys appeared to react against the intervention, showing *stronger* sex stereotypes afterwards. Boys and girls also changed in opposite directions on the measure which required them to describe socioemotional characteristics of men and women. After the intervention, girls showed greater flexibility and expansion of categories: They applied many more desirable adjectives to women, and increased the overlap in the characteristics attributed to both men and women. Boys more rigidly enforced sex-typed limitations, reemphasizing stereotyped interpersonal roles for women, while deemphasizing even more any interpersonal role requirements for men.

Although ninth-grade boys did make some nonsystematic changes in the direction of nonstereotyping, they generally did hold on more firmly to many stereotypes. Perhaps the boys were unconsciously more hesitant to support the equalization of roles because they felt themselves currently in the position of power and may have believed they had more to lose in prestige and occupational advantages. Men, the boys believed, are tightly geared toward vocations and monetary success, a context in which competition rather than cooperation is highly valued.

The generalizations about ninth graders must be qualified in view of classroom differences in the effects of the intervention. There were especially powerful changes following the intervention in one classroom, which had the most active and enthusiastic teacher in the study. Situational effects, e.g., teachers' enthusiasm and effective use of the curricula, were powerful in greatly modifying even the ninth-grade boys' attributional views.

Another situational effect was peer pressure. Observational data from ninth-grade classrooms, as well as data from projective and objective measures, clearly showed the power of peer-group pressures in the shaping of same-sex concepts and behaviors. The ninth graders banded together to decide, in the context of their peer group, whether the tasks were bothersome, and/or whether they need cooperate. Boys' peer groups devalued the intervention in some classrooms. This finding is in line with Selman and Jaquette's findings, reported in this volume, of the power of peer groups and conformity at this age level.

The ninth graders, therefore, responded to the intervention in ways which were different depending on the characteristics of the different ninth-grade classrooms. There was a strong interaction between the social structural character of the classroom, the teacher's role, and the effects of peer groups in each classroom.

Additional Findings: Social Psychological Situational Variables

Classroom Interactions. Classroom observations revealed that prior to the intervention, in both the fifth and ninth grades, boys talked more than girls in class, and talked longer. The boys also offered their ideas, discussions, and answers, when unsolicited, more often than did girls in the same class—a classroom verbal bias favoring the verbal expressions of boys.

In spite of some marked changes in the attitudes and attributions of fifth graders following the intervention, there were no noticeable alterations in their classroom interaction patterns. For the ninth graders, classroom interactions varied markedly in different classrooms, depending on their structure and the role of the teacher.

Traditional vs. Nontraditional Classrooms. The type of classroom structure interacted with the intervention to produce particular effects. It seems reasonable to assume that the traditional teacher, operating within a question-answer, I-lecture-you-listen format, might attempt to reverse sexist trends by evening up the amount of time spent in asking questions of and explaining matters to the girls and boys. A teacher in an open classroom, encouraging individual exploration and effort, might help the girls to participate more actively in the class by supporting their initiations and creative efforts. Examination of the Flanders teacher-pupil interaction data indicated that changes in classroom interactions after the intervention varied according to whether the classroom was traditional or nontraditional in structure. In a traditional classroom girls increased their responses to teachers' queries, while girls in a nontraditional classroom increased the number of initiations they made during a class session. Changes in the girls' behavior were particularly dramatic in the nontraditional ninth-grade classrooms.

Social Class Influences. Social class has traditionally been considered a major predictor of attitudes of all types, including sex-role concepts. To test its influence, the school systems were selected to represent three different social class populations—lower middle, middle, and upper middle. Information was gathered on father's job, mother's job, number and ages of siblings, ethnic background, and special circumstances, and categorized using an adaptation of the Hollingshead-Redlich Occupational Scale.

Attributions of sex roles occurred regardless of the predominant socio-economic status of the school system and of the children. On every analysis which compared the scores in each school system, the scores between school systems were not significantly different. Children who had working mothers, whether in low-status or very high-status jobs, were as prone to attributional contents of sex roles as children who did not have working mothers. Nor did children's sex-role attributions vary according to their cultural background. Social class and family differences were not sufficiently powerful sources of influence when compared with the influence of society.

Conclusions and Theoretical Implications

In this section, the theoretical implications of the study's findings for development and change in sex-role attributions of children are discussed. The study provides some further evidence for a social psychological understanding of the development of sex-role attributions. Within the limits of the child's cognitive capacities, sex-role contents are absorbed primarily from the child's social psychological surroundings. The values and stereotypes which create the child's social psychological situation are mediated by family, peers, classroom structures, teachers, and the mass media. Because these influences are external to the child, by changing some of them it was possible to have a profound impact on the content of the child's sex-role attributions.

Children in all grades were most stereotyped about male occupations. The occupational stories told about males portrayed them as competent, happy with their tasks, and as reaping the benefits from their jobs. Kindergartners had the lowest overlap in the content of their attributions about males and females. They saw the sexes in an "all or none" manner. Overlap in attributions to males and females was moderate for fifth graders and still greater for ninth graders. At fifth and ninth grade, both boys and girls showed considerable stereotyping of the socioemotional contents of sex-role attributions before the intervention. Girls' self-attributions gave socioemotional abilities and qualities a high priority. Yet boys were more stereotyped about the "Typical Woman" than were girls.

Ninth graders showed more diverse attributions. They tolerated interpersonal and nurturant concerns in males, although they emphasized those contents for females. Ninth-grade girls described women as capable. They attempted to integrate occupational competency and socioemotional values for women. In contrast, fifth graders often made internally contradictory statements about the female role, e,g., the woman mechanic wanted to go home in the afternoon to pick up her children at school. Ninth graders were better able than fifth graders to coordinate and integrate multiple roles. In accordance with other research on dispositional attributions, interpersonal conceptions were also better developed at this age.

The sex-role intervention permits a change-oriented view of development and change in sex-role attributions. The children in the study represented three distinct levels of cognitive development—preoperational (5-year-olds), operational (10-year-olds), and formal operational (14-year-olds). It is important to emphasize that the orientation of the study was more towards the *content* of the children's attributions than towards their reasoning about them. Even so, both the literature on children's social attributions and the findings from this study suggest the importance of a number of social psychological variables in the development of social attributions.

For one thing, we were surprised by some of the differences in the content of the children's sex-role attributions at the different ages. Other research has reported that on a descriptive level, children show a general consistency in their sex-typing across ages (Ullian, 1976). We found the fifth graders to be concerned with issues of justice and equality in sex-role differences and in general much less sexist prior to the intervention than were the ninth graders. Although ninth graders probably were cognitively at a formal operational level, the stereotyped content of their sex-role attributions is best explained by the strong peer influences on them. The 14-year-old boy, who actually has a better developed concept of justice and equality than does the 10-year-old, rigidly maintained stereotyped sex-role attributions—even more so after the intervention. Classroom characteristics—especially peer group influences—were the best predictors of change following the intervention.

We also found that children were much more likely to use sex-typed attributions for others than they use for themselves. Children at all levels had a fairly androgynous concept of themselves. None of them used the extreme categories of masculinity and femininity in self-descriptions; rather they blended the two types of personality characteristics together and chose socially desirable feminine characteristics balanced by socially desirable masculine characteristics. This androgynous attitude for self-concept did not, however, extend to views of their own family roles or even into subtle aspects of occupational roles. The self was seen as androgynous before others were so viewed. The self-other distinction was clearly evident in the children's development of sex-role attributions.

Across ages there was also a consistent over-attributionalizing of the opposite sex. This may be a part of the same phenomenon as the self-other divergence of causal attributions, i.e., the tendency to make dispositional attributions to others. Or it may be a part of Piaget's self-other distinction: What we develop exists first in relation to ourselves and then in relation to others (see Keasey in this volume). Perhaps it can be considered part of Shaver's (1975) "defensive" attribution—that there are different patterns of attribution for similar vs. dissimilar others. This, then, would be a motivational reason for the over-attributionalizing of the opposite sex found at every age.

After the intervention, girl's attitudes changed more than boys' at all ages. This seems to be a motivational factor related to self-esteem. Kohlberg (1966) postulated that this need for self-esteem is a mechanism in the development of sex-role attributions. Shaver's "defensive" attribution theory similarly supplies a plausible rationale for this finding. It suggests that there is a need to reduce the threat to one's self-esteem. Clearly, girls can reduce this threat by changing their attributions for females to more valuable and generally valued ones. Is this a true sex difference, or is it instead an indication of a stronger social impact on the more powerless individuals' attributions? It should be kept in mind that in the intervention the material emphasized a more positive and less powerless role for women in many spheres of action. Thus the greater changes in girls' attributions might have come about because they were grasping an opportunity to have more positive and less negative and restrictive role attributions.

The sex-role intervention study illustrates the importance of a number of social psychological variables in the development of social attributions. In many cases, these variables were the same as those identified in studies of achievement attributions, causal attributions, responsibility attributions, and dispositional attributions. These include sex of the perceiver, sex of the perceived, the self-other divergence, and possible motivational factors that seem to influence different attributions for negative and positive outcomes. In addition, peer group influences and classroom characteristics emerged as important modifiers in the attributional process. Yet not all social psychological variables are important: Culture, class, and occupation of parent(s) had no effect on children's attributions. In sum, levels of cognitive development provide one dimension in understanding development and change in children's social attributions. That understanding can be augmented by a knowledge of the social psychological influences on the attributional process.

REFERENCE NOTES

1. Carroll, J. A., & Payne, J. W. *Attribution theory: An information processing approach.* Unpublished paper. Pittsburgh: Carnegie-Mellon, 1976.
2. Selman, R. L. *The development of conceptions of interpersonal relations.* Harvard: Judge Baker Social Reasoning Project, 1974.
3. Frieze, I. H., & Snyder, H. N. *Children's beliefs about the causes of success and failure in school settings.* University of Pittsburgh: Learning Research and Development Center, 1977.
4. Frieze, I. H., & Bar-Tal, D. *Developmental trends in information utilization for making causal attributions.* Paper presented at the meeting of the Eastern Psychological Association, New York, 1976.
5. Ruble, D. N. & Underkoffler, D. *Attributional processes mediating affective responses to success and failure: A developmental study.* Paper presented at the meeting of the Eastern Psychological Association, New York, 1976.
6. McMahan, I. D. *Sex differences in causal attribution following success and failure.* Paper presented at the meeting of the Eastern Psychological Association, New York, 1971.
7. Hodges, K. *Sex differences in achievement: The role of expectancies for success.* Unpublished senior thesis, Princeton University, 1974, as reported in Parsons, Ruble, Hodges, & Small, Cognitive-developmental factors in emerging sex differences in achievement-related expectancies, *Journal of Social Issues,* 1976, 32, 47–61.

8. Dweck, C. S., Davidson, W., & Nelson, S. *Sex differences in learned helplessness: II. The contingencies of evaluative feedback in the classroom.* Paper presented at the meeting of the Society for Research in Child Development, Denver, April 1975.
9. Stein, A. *Sex role preference questionnaire.* Mimeographed paper. Pennsylvania State University, 1973.

REFERENCES

Bem, D. J. Self perception: An alternative interpretation of cognitive dissonance phenomena. *Psychological Review*, 1967, **74**, 183–200.

Chandler, M. Social cognition and life-span approaches to the study of child development. In H. W. Reese (Ed.), *Advances in child development and behavior* (Vol. II). New York: Academic Press, 1976.

Costanzo, P. R., Coie, J. D., Grumet, S. F. & Farnill, D. A reexamination of intent and consequence on children's moral judgments. *Child Development*, 1973, **44**, 154–161.

Dweck, C. S., & Bush, E. S. Sex differences in learned helplessness: I. Differential debilitation with peer and adult evaluators. *Developmental Psychology*, 1976, **12**, 147–156.

Farnill, D. The effects of social-judgment set on children's use of intent information. *Journal of Personality*, 1974, **42**, 276–289.

Fauls, L., & Smith, W. Sex-role learning of five-year-olds. *Journal of Genetic Psychology*, 1956, **89**, 105–117.

Flanders, N. Interaction analysis in the classroom: A manual for observers. In A. Simon, and E. G. Boyer, *Mirrors for Behavior*, (Vol 2). Philadelphia: Research for Better Schools, 1967.

Frieze, I. Women's expectations for and causal attributions of success and failure. In M. Mednick, S. Tangri, & L. Hoffman (Eds.), *Women and achievement: Social and motivational analyses.* Washington, D.C.; Hemisphere Publishing Corporation, 1975.

Frieze, I. Causal attributions and information seeking to explain success and failure. *Journal of Research in Personality*, 1976, **10**, 293–305.

Greene, D., & Lepper, M. R. Effects of extrinsic rewards on children's subsequent intrinsic interest. *Child Development*, 1974, **45**, 1141–1145.

Guttentag, M., & Bray, H. *Undoing sex stereotypes.* New York: McGraw-Hill Book Company, 1976.

Hartley, R. Children's concepts of male and female roles. *Merrill-Palmer Quarterly*, 1960, **6**, 83, 91.

Heider, F. *The psychology of interpersonal relations.* New York: Wiley, 1958.

Imamoglu, E. Children's awareness and usage of intention cues. *Child Development*, 1975, **46**, 39–45.

Inhelder, B., & Piaget, J. *The growth of logical thinking from childhood to adolescence.* New York: Basic Books, 1958.

Jones, E. E. & Davis, K. E. From acts to dispositions: The attribution process in person perception. In L. Berkowitz (Ed.), *Advances in experimental social psychology* (Vol. 2). New York: Academic Press, 1965.

Jones, E. E. & Nisbett, R. E. *The actor and the observer: Divergent perceptions of the causes of behavior.* Morristown, N.J.: General Learning Press, 1971.

Jones, E. E., & Thibaut, J. W. Interaction goals as bases of inference in person perception. In R. Tagiuri and L. Petrullo (Eds.), *Person perception and interpersonal behavior.* Stanford, Calif.: Stanford University Press, 1955.

Karniol, R., & Ross, M. The development of causal attributions in social perception. *Journal of Personality and Social Psychology,* 1976, **34,** 455–464.

Keasey, C. B. Young children's attribution of intentionality to themselves and others. *Child Development,* 1977, **48,** 261–264.

Kelley, H. H. Attribution theory in social psychology. In D. Levine (Ed.), *Nebraska Symposium on Motivation, 1967* (Vol 15). Lincoln: University of Nebraska Press, 1967.

Kelley, H. H. *Attribution in social interaction.* Morristown, N.J.: General Learning Press, 1971.

Kelley, H. H. *Causal schemata and the attribution process.* Morristown N.J.: General Learning Press, 1972.

Kohlberg, L. A cognitive-developmental analysis of children's sex-role concepts and attitudes. In E. Maccoby (Ed.), *The development of sex differences.* Stanford, Calif.: Stanford University Press, 1966.

Kun, A., Parsons, J. E., & Ruble, D. N. Development of integration processes using ability and effort information to predict outcome. *Developmental Psychology,* 1974, **10,** 721–732.

Lepper, M. R., Greene, D., & Nisbett, R. E. Undermining children's intrinsic interest with extrinsic rewards: A test of the "overjustification" hypothesis. *Journal of Personality and Social Psychology,* 1973, **28,** 129–137.

Lester, D. Determinants of resistance to extinction after three training trials: II. The child's expectations. *Psychological Reports,* 1976, **20,** 421–422.

Livesley, W. J., & Bromley, D. B. *Person perception in childhood and adolescence.* London: Wiley, 1973.

Maccoby, E. E., & Jacklin, C. N. *The psychology of sex differences.* Stanford, Calif.: Stanford University Press, 1974.

Nisbett, R. E., & Valins, S. *Perceiving the causes of one's own behavior.* Morristown, N.J.: General Learning Press, 1971.

Parsons, J. E., & Ruble, D. N. The development of achievement-related expectancies. *Journal of Social Issues,* 1976, **32,** 47–61.

Peevers, B. H., & Secord, P. F. Developmental changes in attribution of descriptive concepts to persons. *Journal of Personality and Social Psychology,* 1973, **27,** 120–128.

Piaget, J. *The construction of reality in the child.* New York: Basic Books, 1954.

Piaget, J. *The moral judgment of the child.* New York: Free Press, 1965. (Originally published, 1932.)

Piaget, J. *The child's conception of the world.* Totowa, N.J.: Littlefield, Adams, 1969.

Piaget, J., & Inhelder, B. *The psychology of the child.* New York: Basic Books, 1969.

Pollis, N. P., & Doyle, D. C. Sex-role status and perceived competence among first graders. *Perceptual and Motor Skills,* 1972, **34**, 235–238.

Ross, M. Salience of reward and intrinsic motivation. *Journal of Personality and Social Psychology,* 1975, **32**, 245–254.

Ruble, D. N., Feldman, N. S., & Boggiano, A. K. Social comparison between young children in achievement situations. *Developmental Psychology,* 1976, **12**, 192–197.

Ruble, D. N., Loebl, J., Parsons, J., & Ross, J. Self-evaluative responses of children in an achievement setting. *Child Development,* 1976, **47**, 990–997.

Secord, P., & Peevers, B. The development and attribution of person concepts. In T. Mischel (Ed.), *Understanding other persons.* Oxford: Blackwell, Basil & Mott, 1974.

Serbin, L., O'Leary, K., Kent, R., & Tonick, I. A comparison of teacher response to the preacademic and problem behavior of boys and girls. *Child Development,* 1973, **44**, 769–804.

Shantz, C. U. The development of social cognition. In E. M. Hetherington (Ed.), *Review of child development research* (Vol. 5) Chicago: University of Chicago Press, 1975.

Shaver, K. G. *An introduction to attribution processes.* Cambridge, Mass.: Winthrop Publishers, 1975.

Shaw, M. E., & Sulzer, J. L. An empirical test of Heider's levels of attribution of responsibility. *Journal of Abnormal Social Psychology,* 1964, **69**, 39–46.

Shultz, T. R., Butkowsky, I., Pearce, J. W., & Shanfield, H. Development of schemes for the attribution of multiple psychological causes. *Developmental Psychology,* 1975, **11**, 502–510.

Smith, M. C. Children's use of the multiple sufficient scheme in social perception. *Journal of Personality and Social Psychology,* 1975, **32**, 737–747.

Ullian, D. Z. The development of conceptions of masculinity and femininity. Unpublished doctoral dissertation, Harvard University, 1976.

Valle, V. A., & Frieze, I. H. The stability of causal attributions as a mediator in changing expectations for success. *Journal of Personality and Social Psychology,* 1976, **33**, 579–587.

Weiner, B., Frieze, I., Kukla, A., Reed, L., Rest, S., & Rosenbaum, R. M. *Perceiving the causes of success and failure.* Morristown, N.J.: General Learning Press, 1971.

Weiner, B., & Kun, A. The development of causal attributions and the growth of achievement and social motivation. In S. Feldman & D. Bush (Eds.) *Cognitive development and social development: Relationships and implications*. Hillsdale, N.J.: Lawrence Erlbaum Associates, in press.

Weiner, B., & Peter, N. A cognitive-developmental analysis of achievement and moral judgments. *Developmental Psychology*, 1973, 9, 290–309.

Williams, J., Bennett, S., & Best, D. Awareness and expression of sex stereotypes in young children. *Developmental Psychology*, 1975, 11, 635–642.

Subject Index

Author Index